Ethical Decision Making
in the Hospitality Industry

Ethical Decision Making in the Hospitality Industry

Christine Jaszay, Ph.D.

Paul Dunk

PEARSON

Prentice Hall

Upper Saddle River, New Jersey 07458

Library of Congress Cataloging-in-Publication Data

Jaszay, Christine.
  Ethical decision making in the hospitality industry / Christine Jaszay and Paul Dunk.-- 1st ed.
      p. cm.
  Includes bibliographical references.
  ISBN 0-13-113680-1
  1. Hospitality industry--Moral and ethical aspects. 2. Hospitality industry--Management. I. Dunk, Paul.
II. Title.
  TX911.3.E84J37 2005
  174'.964794--dc22

                              2004028218

Executive Editor: Vernon R. Anthony
Editorial Assistant: Beth Dyke
Senior Marketing Manager: Ryan DeGrote
Senior Marketing Coordinator: Elizabeth Farrell
Marketing Assistant: Les Roberts
Director of Manufacturing and Production: Bruce Johnson
Managing Editor: Mary Carnis
Production Liaison: Jane Bonnell
Production Editor: Mike Remillard, Pine Tree Composition, Inc.
Manufacturing Manager: Ilene Sanford
Manufacturing Buyer: Cathleen Petersen
Creative Director: Cheryl Asherman
Senior Design Coordinator: Miguel Ortiz
Cover Designer: Linda Punskovsky
Cover Image: Simon Watson, Getty Images/The Image Bank
Composition: Pine Tree Composition, Inc.
Printer/Binder: Courier Stoughton
Cover Printer: Courier Stoughton

Pearson Education LTD.   Pearson Education Canada, Ltd.
Pearson Education Australia PTY, Limited   Pearson Educación de Mexico, S.A. de C.V.
Pearson Education Singapore, Pte. Ltd.   Pearson Education—Japan
Pearson Education North Asia Ltd.   Pearson Education Malaysia, Pte. Ltd.

10 9 8 7 6 5 4 3 2 1
ISBN: 0-13-113680-1

This textbook is dedicated to
Betty Irene Dunk
and in loving memory of
Edward Francis Dunk

Contents

Preface

Ethics is a branch of philosophy, but this is not a philosophy textbook. Instead, *Ethical Decision Making in the Hospitality Industry* is a practical guide showing students how to behave and manage in an ethical manner. It is not about *ethics,* but, rather, about *how to be ethical.*

There is much discussion in the media lamenting the breakdown of ethics in our society. We need only glance at the headlines of a daily newspaper to see the ramifications of this malaise: scandal upon scandal after scandal. We can easily become overwhelmed by the futility of it all and just go about our business, looking out for No. 1, in an increasingly less civilized world. We must be reminded that if we are not part of the solution, we are part of the problem. However, it might be that the state of affairs is not so bleak after all. The hospitality industry is one of the largest industries in the world. Each year thousands of students graduate from hospitality management programs in the United States, most taking entry-level positions in the industry. Over time the industry will evolve to being managed, in large part, by these very graduates. Ergo, it is logical to assume that if all these individuals are grounded in ethics, they will subsequently have a profound influence on their employees, their companies, and the industry overall. Because of its sheer size, these influences can affect the ethical health of our entire society. In the decades to come, graduates of hospitality management programs will increasingly be the men and women who set the ethical standards. This textbook gives students a sound footing in ethical decision making that will in turn touch all those who work for them in the future. In this trickle-down manner, we can and will change the world.

To that end we focus on the ten **Ethical Principles for Hospitality Managers.** They are comprised of *honesty, integrity, trustworthiness, loyalty, fairness, concern and respect for others, commitment to excellence, leadership, reputation and morale, and accountability.* To make the text's subject matter more accessible, included is an ongoing case study of a fictional establishment called the *Freshwater Oasis Inn.* It is staffed by a cast of characters who encounter many of the ethical dilemmas our students will have to deal with in the future. By making the study of ethics more tangible, and perhaps even entertaining, we are providing an instructional tool that is more likely to succeed.

Students will be presented with situations in the case study where they are required to analyze the actions of specific individuals at the inn. By applying the above-mentioned ten principles to the decision-making process, students will discover that they can arrive at the proper decision every time. For instance, we (as managers) cannot be *honest* yet rude and still be considered ethical. That would violate the ethical principle of *concern and respect for others.* We cannot demonstrate *commitment to excellence* if we do not know how to present ourselves appropriately. Ethics, or the lack of ethics, pervade our every thought and action. Ethics encompass our whole lives.

In this text we also address the less obvious behavioral areas that have a direct influence on our ability to be ethical. We address topics such as civility, courtesy, problem solving, diversity, communication, stress management, delegation, time management, and humility—because to be ethical requires that we have the life skills and people skills necessary to provide the foundation for making ethical decisions and life choices. We cannot manage others successfully if we cannot manage ourselves, nor does it do much good to make proper decisions if we are unable to get anyone to go along with them. How we behave in our personal and professional lives are connected. If we cheat or lie at home, we are more likely to behave similarly at work. To be ethical requires more than just following a set of ethical rules. It requires that we understand other individuals as well as ourselves, and that we also possess the social skills necessary to ensure successful interaction with them.

There is an erroneous belief that it is impossible to teach college students ethics, the thinking being that if they have not learned ethics by now, it is too late. To the contrary, research has shown that college students may be guided into higher stages of moral reasoning through class discussions and "real-life" case studies. Critical thinking skills can be developed by listening to students and challenging and coaching them rather than by merely telling them what to think and how to go about doing so.

The Ethical Principles for Hospitality Managers are rules that have been determined through years of practice in the hospitality industry that, if adhered to in the decision-making process, should result in the best possible consequences for all parties involved. Hospitality students can be taught these rules, but they might not necessarily believe that honesty is truly the best policy or that loyalty to one's employer is always warranted. In this text, however, students are required to make hypothetical managerial decisions for a fictional establishment called the Freshwater Oasis Inn. They are guided into comparing consequences for each possible decision with regard to stakeholders (manager, employees, company, customers, etc.), and then into selecting decisions that lead to the most favorable outcomes. A pattern ultimately becomes apparent, and students are likely to adopt an automatic acceptance and application of the rules.

Ethical Decision Making in the Hospitality Industry is designed to teach college-level hospitality management students how to recognize and analyze ethical dilemmas and respond appropriately. While most hospitality educators address ethics in their individual courses, this text allows for an integrated approach that can be far more effective. There are two parts to the text. The first is a traditional chapter format wherein the body of instruction is put forth, and the second is comprised of case studies arranged chronologically. Students will be required to read specific case studies for chapters dealing with such positions as "housekeeping," or "front desk," or any of the various other jobs available at hotels and restaurants. While the text may be used for a stand-alone course on hospitality ethics, it is designed to be utilized throughout the curriculum, integrating a unit on ethics into each of the courses. Consistent ethics instruction, presented by faculty in all their courses (over a number of years), will powerfully reinforce the material.

The text is applications-based with the objective of increased ethical awareness, analysis skill, and ethical socialization. The first three chapters are introductory, the middle seven deal with operations, and the final five concern management issues and the design and implementation of ethics programs. It breaks down in the following manner:

- Chapter 1 introduces the ten Ethical Principles for Hospitality Managers.
- Chapter 2 summarizes the history of ethical thought.
- Chapter 3 discusses how to make good employment selections and introduces the Freshwater Oasis Inn (FOI) case study.
- Chapters 4–10 are operations chapters and concentrate on specific departments in the ongoing case study of the small hotel (FOI). Students are familiarized with situations that are likely to occur once they are in management, and are provided analysis tools that enable them to understand and deal with the potential ramifications of their decisions.
- Chapters 11–13 are management chapters that focus on ethical dilemmas involving human resource management, technology, and cost control.
- Chapters 14 and 15 describe how to design and implement ethics programs.

Ethical Decision Making in the Hospitality Industry takes into consideration the learning needs of young adults. Most students in hospitality programs have already worked in the industry as servers, front desk agents, housekeepers, or any of the other various positions available in hotels and restaurants. Many of our students have already encountered ethical dilemmas or the consequences of unethical decision making by their managers. Our students need a practical way of recognizing and dealing with ethical dilemmas, and not some stuffy philosophical tome.

The case study is designed to be entertaining and quite realistic. Students will get to know the fictional characters, be interested in the situations they confront in their day-to-day duties at FOI, and care about the outcomes. By text's end, students will have analyzed ethical dilemmas in each department within the case study hotel—ethical dilemmas they may have already encountered in their own jobs. They will be well acquainted with the Ethical Principles for Hospitality Managers, understanding how the principles apply in a multitude of situations. Overall, our goal is to make students adept at ethical analysis through "hands-on" exercises.

This text is designed for use as a stand-alone course on hospitality ethics, or, better yet, to be incorporated into all courses across the hospitality curriculum. The integrated case study approach is by far the most effective method for teaching ethics, and this text offers hospitality educators a comprehensive and student-friendly method. Again, this textbook is not about philosophy's great thinkers, but has been designed for students in the real world.

REVIEWERS

Carl Braunlich—Purdue University
Dr. Ronald J. Cereola—James Madison University
Candice Clemenz—University of West Florida
Peter Ricci—University of Central Florida
Dr. Wanda Costen—University of Nevada Las Vegas
Linda K. Enghagen, J.D.—University of Massachusetts–Amherst

About the Authors

Christine Jaszay, SFO, Ph.D., is Director of Isbell Hospitality Ethics and Associate Professor at the School of Hotel and Restaurant Management at Northern Arizona University. Dr. Jaszay has two graduate degrees in instructional design, studies philosophy and ethics, and has 15 years of hospitality industry experience and 18 years of university teaching experience. Dr. Jaszay shares ethics research on the Isbell Hospitality Ethics web page (www2.nau.edu/~clj5/Ethics/) and writes and lectures extensively on ethics.

Paul Dunk is a freelance writer from Chicago who previously worked for over 17 years in the hospitality industry. He is the author of many works of fiction including two novels, three novellas, and over eighty short stories. His books can be found online or through the help desk at any major bookstore.

Jaszay and Dunk also collaborated on *Training Design for the Hospitality Industry,* an instructional design text for hospitality students. Their work is a unique blend of academia and fiction.

Ethical Decision Making in the Hospitality Industry

Chapter 1

Ethical Principles for Hospitality Managers

Ethics are the rules of conduct we *decide* to live by. They are moral rules, though not necessarily laws. They make it possible for us to trust one another, to feel safe, and they enable us to leave our homes without fear of the consequences. Without these rules, we must constantly be on guard. Like it or not, it is our adherence to these unspoken rules that make us civilized. Conversely, it is a lack of ethics that make some of us barbarians.

Business ethics are the same as personal ethics. They are the rules we choose to live by in business so we can trust those we do business with. It is our responsibility—we who are educated and in positions of leadership—to foster ethical relationships with our customers and employees. It is up to us to foster an ethical business climate and ethical decision making, and to initiate ethical policies, thinking, and behavior.

Unfortunately, over the past 40 years, our **shared ethical values** have deteriorated. Our communal sense of right and wrong has become less clear. Exactly *why* is up to debate, but perhaps the breakup of the American family is partly to blame. With divorce rates exceeding 50%, many single parents find themselves raising children. Our society is also very mobile, and, because we have moved around so much, extended families are often not available to help these single parents in child rearing and nurturing.

Most jobs today are in the service industries and are low paying. It has become very difficult for one person to make enough money to support a family. Working parents need childcare, which is expensive and sometimes inadequate. Tired, frustrated, stressed, unhappy parents oftentimes do not have the energy to instill values in their children. Life has become more difficult and expensive, and ethical shortcuts have become the norm. Sadly, if this is all we see, we may even feel that we are foolish to be ethical.

Some of us may have been taught the rules as children, but life in the modern world has a way of diminishing our sensitivity to these rules. As managers, in order to meet our responsibility in fostering ethics, we may have to be taught or retaught how to recognize ethical dilemmas and, ultimately, learn how to avoid them. Many of us do not have the sense of shared ethics to serve as a basis for determining right and wrong. As a result, most of us need instruction in ethical decision making, or at least periodic brush-ups.

The following **Ethical Principles for Hospitality Managers** were adapted from Josephson Institute of Ethics' "Core Ethical Principles." They have served as the basis of ethics research coming out of Isbell Hospitality Ethics for the past 15 years. Analysis of numerous ethical dilemmas presented throughout this textbook provides persuasive evidence that adherence to the Ethical Principles for Hospitality Managers during the decision-making process will result in the best consequences for all parties involved.

1. **Honesty:** Hospitality managers are honest and truthful. They do not mislead or deceive others by misrepresentations.

2. **Integrity:** Hospitality managers demonstrate the courage of their convictions by doing what they know is right even when there is pressure to do otherwise.

3. **Trustworthiness:** Hospitality managers are trustworthy and candid in supplying information and in correcting misapprehensions of fact. They do not create justifications for escaping their promises and commitments.

4. **Loyalty:** Hospitality managers demonstrate loyalty to their companies in devotion to duty, and loyalty to colleagues by friendship in adversity. They avoid conflicts of interest; do not use or disclose confidential information; and, should they accept other employment, they respect the proprietary information of their former employer.

5. **Fairness:** Hospitality managers are fair and equitable in all dealings; they do not arbitrarily abuse power, nor take undue advantage of another's mistakes or difficulties. They treat all individuals with equality, with tolerance and acceptance of diversity, and with an open mind.

6. **Concern and Respect for Others:** Hospitality managers are concerned, respectful, compassionate, and kind. They are sensitive to the personal concerns of their colleagues and live the "Golden Rule." They respect the rights and interests of all those who have a stake in their decisions.

7. **Commitment to Excellence:** Hospitality managers pursue excellence in performing their duties and are willing to put more into their job than they can get out of it.

8. **Leadership:** Hospitality managers are conscious of the responsibility and opportunities of their position of leadership. They realize that the best way to instill ethical principles and ethical awareness in their organizations is by example. They walk their talk!

9. **Reputation and Morale:** Hospitality managers seek to protect and build the company's reputation, and the morale of its employees, by engaging in conduct that builds respect. They also take whatever actions are necessary to correct or prevent inappropriate conduct of others.

10. **Accountability:** Hospitality managers are personally accountable for the ethical quality of their decisions, as well as those of their subordinates.

When we read through the Ethical Principles for Hospitality Managers, most of us would agree that they are worthwhile. We think honesty is good, dishonesty is bad, that it is a good thing to have integrity, to be trustworthy, and so forth. We may have heard people say, or even thought ourselves, that rules are fine but sometimes in business we cannot afford to be ethical. The truth is, however, that we cannot afford to *not* be ethical.

The hospitality industry has become so competitive that if customers and employees are dissatisfied they will go elsewhere. We want to be able to trust the people we do business with. For example, as customers of a hotel, we do not want to feel like we were not sharp or sophisticated enough to get a good room rate. As diners, we do not want to have to send food back that was not prepared as the menu led us to expect. We do not want to have to worry about being hurt financially, emotionally, or physically as a result of doing business or being involved with a company.

Ethics are not relative. We do not decide for ourselves what is ethical. We have established rules—rules that have been found to hold true through countless analyses of situations. We can save time by accepting these rules and skipping the analysis. For instance, we may wonder whether or not we should bother taking a raincoat if it looks like rain. If we do not, and it rains, we get soaked. The next time it looks like rain, we do not have to go through the whole thought process. We can just put on our raincoats and trust that it is the right thing to do.

It is the same with the ethical rules. We can analyze every situation to see whether honesty is a good policy, and find each time that the consequences of dishonesty are far more painful. So, we, eventually, do not have to waste time doing the analysis. We can just accept that honesty and the nine other ethical principles are the right things to do, and then live by the principles!

The idea is to avoid ethical dilemmas. We will have to think through our decisions in advance and determine if any of the ethical principles will be violated by what we propose to do. We are going to ask ourselves whom our decisions will affect. We will think about the positive and negative consequences in advance, and then make our final decision based on the best possible outcomes for the greatest number of people.

In forthcoming chapters, an analysis tool will be provided and we will consider decision options in situations that arise within the various departments of a fictitious full-service inn. The analysis tool allows us to systematically identify all parties who might be affected by a decision, and in what ways. We will begin with a short discussion of each of the ten Ethical Principles for Hospitality Managers.

HONESTY

We all know that to "be honest" means that we do not lie, cheat, or steal. Though we might consider ourselves to be honest people, how many of us have ever padded our resume, failed to claim all of our tips, or neglected to tell a cashier we were given too much change back? These examples might seem like relatively minor infractions, but they are common examples of lying, cheating, and stealing. The fact most people have committed at least one or all of those acts is an indictment on just how far our society has lapsed—into a state of acceptable, yet still unethical, behavior.

To be honest means that we behave honorably—that is, according to the principles of honesty and integrity. To have integrity is to be morally sound, and to be morally sound requires honesty in all situations whether anyone knows about it or not. When we are honest, we are worthy of people's trust. We do not betray trust, and thus we are loyal. We treat people fairly and are concerned for them and respect them. We do our best work always and lead by our good example. Both our personal reputation and the reputation of our business are enhanced by our behavior, and morale is positively affected. We take responsibility for our actions and decisions because they are ours. All of the Ethical Principles for Hospitality Managers are simply ramifications of the first principle, which is honesty.

Remember the story about the boy who cried wolf all the time? When a real wolf actually appeared, no one paid attention to the kid and the wolf ate him. Though dishonest behavior does not necessarily result in being eaten by wolves, it is critical that we be honest so that people will take us seriously, trust us, and believe us. A conversation with a liar is a waste of time because it is comprised of pointless words that cannot be taken at face value. If our friends lie to us, cheat us, or steal from us, we generally stop being friends with them.

Our personal and business lives are not really separate. We want to be able to trust the people we do business with. If we have been lied to, cheated, or stolen from, we most likely will not continue to patronize that business. Instead, we will probably tell other people about our bad experience, perhaps even for years afterwards. We do not do business with corporations such as *The Olive Garden* or *Marriott*. We do business with Joe, or Cindy, or whomever the person is that serves us, cleans our room, or checks us in. They are the faces who flesh out and represent the business, although it is management who ultimately is responsible for their behavior. When we accept the principle that one leads by example, then it is logical to assume that if managers lie, cheat, or steal, their staff is likely to be influenced by such behavior. Managers are very visible. As managers, we must not only hire people who have the capacity to behave honestly, but then we must train them to behave honestly. The best way to go about this is to model honest behavior for them.

Honesty should not be looked upon as a chore. We should be honest because it is the right thing to do. Some of us, however, may need more practical reasons for being honest. The negative consequences for lying could be a loss of friends, a loss of respect and trust from our employees, and, ultimately, a loss of business from our customers. Obviously, in the final analysis it would result in less professional success.

When we think of people like former President Richard M. Nixon, what most of us tend to remember is that he was a liar; "I am not a crook," he said. Then, a generation later, Bill Clinton exhaled and assured us: "I did not have sex with that woman." Those claims seem rather hollow now. All the good these men did was overshadowed by their lack of honesty. Both did things that they did not want anyone to know about. They knew their deeds were reprehensible, but they did them anyway and then tried to lie their way out. These were public men who destroyed their reputations in very public ways. If they could go back in time would they do things differently? Probably.

At the start of our professional lives, it is sometimes difficult to care or even think about the state of our future reputation. The daily decisions we make determine how we turn out in the long run, and when we are old and gray it is too late to change the things we may be sorry for. Therefore, it is imperative

I SWEAR -- MONICA LEWINSKI DID NOT INHALE!!!

that we take the time now to think about whom we respect and why. Who have we chosen as our role models? Who is to lead us by example?

If recent events are any indication of the national state of ethics, it might be a better idea to look closer to home for these role models. Let us consider our experiences as students. While in school we may have been grateful for a good grade we really did not earn. Would this gift be something to be proud of? Would it not have been more inspiring to have a teacher who cared enough to take time to ensure we did the quality work deserving of that good grade? After all, what is the point of education? We live in what is essentially a civilized society, but we must strengthen our natural tendencies to do the right thing. It is a matter of setting higher standards for ourselves—standards of decency.

Ideally, we prefer politicians who stand up for what they believe rather than those who champion the causes of corporations they take money from. What standards of decency are ingrained in the latter? Religious leaders, who get caught stealing from their congregations, or having illicit sex and lying about it, do not usually engender our respect. Likewise, CEOs who become wealthy by bankrupting their companies and stockholders may fill us with disgust. As a people, though, we are mired in a laissez-faire attitude in terms of expectations of decency. The saying, "If you can't beat them, join them," has slowly and insipidly become our mantra. It is solely up to us to change things around, and that process starts from within.

We should consider how we would like others to think about us. We may need to start with an appraisal of our strengths and weaknesses and an honest look at our behavior and attitudes. Over time, will a continuation of how we are today result in who we eventually want to be? Now is the time to look and ask, and now is the time to make any necessary changes.

Most of us accept that we should be truthful, but to what extent and when? Perhaps we need to consider whether our truth is requested and/or helpful. Is any purpose served by telling someone with a huge proboscis that he or she has a really big nose? It may be true, but if the person did not ask for our opinion, and if our opinion was not offered to be helpful, but, rather, to be mean, then we are violating the ethical principle of Concern and Respect for Others.

On the other hand, if our purpose is to correct employees, thus helping them to be more successful in their positions, we might say to a server something like, "Your hair has gotten a little out of control; maybe you could tie it back?" This suggestion violates no ethical principles. It is about being helpful. If we do not bother to tell someone a truth and the omission causes him or her harm, while we have not lied, we have broken the ethical principle of Concern and Respect for Others.

The above examples are obvious. The problem, however, is determining our motivations and being cognizant of how we really feel deep down. We can justify our comments as "helpful" when they might not be. We must be able to look at ourselves honestly, and this can be painful. None of us are particularly thrilled to realize we have just acted like jerks. Some of us avoid that discomfort by not seeking the truth about ourselves. We justify and excuse our behavior, because, if we recognized our misbehavior, we would have to change. While change is difficult, not changing when we need to can result in stagnation and unfulfilled potential.

To be honest is to not lie, cheat, or steal. To be honest we have to be able to honestly look at ourselves and recognize our lies, our cheating, and our thefts—and to correct those behaviors.

INTEGRITY

Life would be so pleasant if everyone followed ethical principles. We could avoid war and all man-made catastrophes. Retaliation, the old "eye for an eye" idea, however, is far too appealing when we have been hurt. To refrain from cheating on an exam and get a lower grade than someone who did cheat can seem unfair. To do more than others yet still get the same pay or grade can make us angry and resentful. To have integrity is to do the right thing—follow all the ethical rules—no matter what anyone else is doing. To have integrity is to honestly appraise our own feelings and motivations, and then follow the rules regardless of any outside pressure.

Integrity is solid because it is built over the years by making ethical choices every time. Things that we do over and over become habits, so it gets easier as we have more practice, and, of course, we become what we practice. Decisions we make are based on the ethical principles we purport to live by (rather than by expedience) so people know where we are coming from. Because we make ethical choices every time, people can predict what we will do or say in most situations. We are consistent, and people can trust us.

Integrity implies wholeness—that our behavior matches our values. As managers, what kinds of employee conduct do we encourage? How do we deal with behavior that is inconsistent with the ethical policies of the company? If our behaviors do not match our values, employees will quickly learn what kind of actions get rewards and that is what they will do. Talk is cheap; our behavior tells employees what is really important.

Integrity also implies that our values are good, in that what we do takes into consideration what is good for others, not just ourselves. Integrity means that our actions are not selfish and that our decisions are made objectively without justifications and excuses.

TRUSTWORTHINESS

The American myth of the "rugged individual" is incorrect. We are social beings, and without each other we could not survive. Business is also about relationships. It involves relationships between employees, between managers, as well as those relationships that occur when both of these groups interact. There are also relationships between regional or corporate management and the local staff members. There is interaction with suppliers, with the competition, and the surrounding community. Without sound relationships, business could not survive.

Trust is the fundamental issue in relationships and relies on two components: the ability to predict behavior and the existence of similar values. To be able to trust people or organizations (that are comprised of people), we must be able to predict their behavior 85–90% of the time. This 10–15% margin of error is due to the fact that we are not machines. When someone's actions do not match his or her words, we should always choose to believe the person's actions. Talk is cheap unless backed by deeds.

We all have known people whom we felt uncomfortable around, as if we had to walk on eggshells. There was no telling from minute to minute how they might react. We cannot put our faith in people like that. We cannot trust them to refrain from hurting us. The same goes for organizations and/or management. Managers who are inconsistent—who one minute are nice, the next angry, who say something we do is fine one time and then say it is not fine the next time—cannot be trusted because we cannot predict their behavior.

For relationships to be successful, we need the ability to predict the other player's behavior most of the time. Trust implies something positive, that the behaviors we are predicting are not hurtful. We also need to have similar values. Marriages often dissolve because the participants have different fundamental beliefs. They clash over issues such as money, child rearing, or sexual fidelity because their values are not compatible. If we go to work for a company whose values are different from our own, we may find ourselves uncomfortable with our responsibility to model and enforce certain policies we do not agree with.

Trust is about honesty. If we enter into a relationship with a person or an organization that has not honestly represented itself, how can we determine if our values match? Trust is never guesswork or just a feeling, it is a matter of observation and thought. Is the person's behavior generally predictable? Do we have similar values? Understand that if we do not endeavor to answer these questions in our personal or business lives, the relationships we experience may end in pain and frustration.

LOYALTY

We cannot be loyal to someone with whom we have no trust. Feelings of betrayal and disappointment occur when we fail to recognize that someone is not worthy of our trust. It is our responsibility as thinking people to determine if someone is trustworthy or not. If someone has betrayed our trust—that is, we thought he or she was worthy of our trust, but then he or she did something that was opposed to what we thought we agreed upon—what then? In marital relations, if one spouse cheats on the other, should the couple split? If the husband gets in trouble through his own doing, should the wife stand by through adversity? Is that not what loyalty is all about?

Loyalty is similar to a contract: If you do this, I will be loyal. If the other person doesn't do what he or she agreed to, is the loyalty contract void? The key to this dilemma revolves around choosing our spouses, friends, employees, and companies carefully to begin with, and in that way we can be loyal without too much difficulty. The essence of loyalty is honesty. When we know and understand ourselves, and we know and understand the object of our loyalty, then we can behave in a trustworthy way.

Loyalty is the glue that bonds people together in communities, organizations, or families. There are times when we are angry with someone in our family, but if an outsider berates him or her, we jump to their defense. That is an example of loyalty. If we cannot trust our friends for support in times of need (if there is no sense of loyalty), we tend to cease considering these people as friends. We stop trusting them. We then look for others who are indeed worthy of our trust.

Companies are groups of people banded together for the purpose of reaching a common goal, like providing meals or hotel rooms. But if there is no loyalty between management and employees, or between employees and the company, self-interest and fear for survival can take precedence over the goal. Line workers or managers in fear of being laid off may feel pitted against one another to keep their jobs, and that supersedes working together to attain the goal. This lack of loyalty destroys the very point of the relationship.

When we are loyal, we are trusting that the organization has our best interests at heart. If we do not trust the organization, our loyalty will most likely dissipate, taking with it the sense of community and belonging that enables us to care about what we do. Trustworthiness inspires loyalty, and loyalty is the bond that holds organizations together so they can meet their goals.

Loyalties can be in conflict. If we were to discover that the company we work for is in some way adversely affecting members of our family, perhaps by opening or closing a facility they may have a financial interest in, what would we do? We are loyal to our company, but we are also loyal to our family. Whose interests come first?

Loyalty can sometimes be in conflict with other ethical principles. Say a friend tells us something in confidence, but our withholding of that information results in another friend's harm. Which principle is more important? *Loyalty? Concern and Respect for Others?* These are not easy questions, and proper ethical behavior is not always dictated by black and white, either/or considerations. That is one reason we need to delve deeper into the ethical decision-making process.

FAIRNESS

It would be interesting to know just how many times each of us has said, "That's not fair." We expect the same pay for equal work. We want the credit we feel we deserve. We want the same opportunity as others. We do not like it when authority figures have favorites (unless *we* are the favorite). We want our fair share, and when we don't get these things we say, "That's not fair!"

We are aware that it is illegal to discriminate against minority groups, women, elderly people, and so forth. We understand that it is unfair to be denied employment simply because we are female or African American. Conversely, we may feel that it is unfair if we are qualified but another person is given the job solely on the basis of his or her race. We all recognize what is unfair when it happens to us, but this can sometimes be a myopic reaction. We need to stand back and consider the larger picture: Does what one person deems fair treatment come at the expense of another?

The definition of Fairness (as stated in the beginning of the chapter) is clear. We want to deal with people who are fair and equitable. We do not want to be taken advantage of or treated poorly simply because of who we are. We want our individuality recognized as opposed to being stereotyped or pigeonholed because of some sterile demographic statistic. Most of us endeavor to treat others fairly and with an open mind. Once again, the key is honesty. Are we able to honestly see the underlying beliefs that affect our attitudes and behaviors?

Biases are built into us through our upbringing. We are socialized by our families, friends, and the networks of which we are a part. As children, we learn from the behavior and attitudes of those who care for us. Unless we seriously reflect on our beliefs and where these beliefs came from, we may not be aware that our beliefs and attitudes are biased. These unexamined beliefs and attitudes can result in unfair behavior, and when perpetrated by management can facilitate a reduction in employee performance. It causes resentment, lowered morale, increased turnover, and ultimately equates to less success for both the manager and the business itself.

When we have honestly identified our strengths, weaknesses, and beliefs, and then chosen a company whose values are compatible with our own (so that we can model and enforce the company policies comfortably), we must then manage with consistency. In that way our employees can learn to trust us and maintain a reasonable expectation of fair treatment.

CONCERN AND RESPECT FOR OTHERS

People will care for us about as much as we care for them. If we treat workers without respect or concern, it is unlikely that they will feel much loyalty toward us—and that can negatively affect performance and turnover. Inexperienced managers sometimes think that if they are too nice, their employees will take advantage of them. They make the mistake of identifying "professional" with "impersonal."

Companies that provide health care benefits demonstrate through policies that they take into consideration the needs of workers. Likewise, companies that avoid slashing payroll during hard times demonstrate concern and respect for their employees. When concern and respect is mirrored in all the company's policies and decisions, employees respond in terms of longevity and loyalty. Employees admire and respect the company and management and are ultimately more satisfied with their jobs. They tend to conduct themselves with more professionalism because they feel the respect of management.

We need to be aware that although we each have our own unique qualities, strengths, and weaknesses, we are more alike than not. We all have the same emotions and feelings. Because a person is uneducated and of a lower socioeconomic class does not mean that he or she does not feel joy, fear, love, anger, compassion, and so forth. In fact, emotional maturity does not have anything to do with job status.

None of us are immune to death, marital strife, unruly children, drugs/alcohol, and all of the problems that can touch our lives. If we fail to exhibit compassion to an employee in the midst of some personal crisis, we run the risk of losing an otherwise good worker, who, once through the crisis, may return to his or her prior consistent performance. If we simply replace the temporarily tormented employee with a new employee, it is very likely that the new employee will, at some time, experience his or her own life crisis. So we would have gained nothing. We, as management, have as much chance of finding ourselves in a life crisis situation as any of our subordinates.

We can think about managers we have had in the past for which we felt a great deal of respect. We can identify the qualities that made us want to work for them. What was it they did to bring out our best work? We can also think of managers who have had the opposite effect on us. We need to consider how we ourselves like to be treated. What kind of management strategy works best

IN THE TRENCHES

Kathryn Whitney, 21, Phoenix, AZ

"I am a line cook at an area hotel restaurant. It was one of those days when everything that could possibly go wrong, did. Tickets were coming out incorrect, guests were upset, and our manager in turn became upset. This was understandable, but this manager reacted by pulling a younger employee from the kitchen and then proceeded to yell at him in a very unprofessional manner. I believe that regardless of how upset a manager becomes, they should not use profanity towards any employees. It makes that manager the enemy rather than an ally you can bring problems to."

on us? Do we like to be ordered around and treated like incompetents, or do we like to be treated as important members of the operation?

When we hear about the Golden Rule ("Do unto others as you would have others do unto you"), some of us immediately think of hollow religious platitudes. The Golden Rule is promoted by all the major religions in the world. The Golden Rule, however, is also secular. Social psychologists call it the **reciprocity norm,** the learned expectation that we should return help to those who have helped us. The **social responsibility norm** states that we should help those who need our help, even if costs outweigh the benefits.

The Golden Rule may be the most important rule of life according to many moral philosophers. To live the Golden Rule means we must consider how our actions will affect others and then imagine ourselves as the others being affected by our actions. If we would not mind it happening to us, then we may go ahead with the action.

The ethical principle of Concern and Respect for Others is realized by living the Golden Rule. The benefits of living the Golden Rule are that our employees will not be retaliating or reacting negatively to our behaviors. They will feel better, work better, and be more loyal to the company.

COMMITMENT TO EXCELLENCE

People with integrity endeavor to do the right things all the time, no matter what. People who have a commitment to excellence do their best work regardless of circumstances. It does not matter if they like or do not like the job, or the reason for doing the job, or even for whom they are doing the job. It does not matter whether, or how well, they are getting paid. It does not matter what other people think about the job or the person doing the job. People with a commitment to excellence do everything to the best of their abilities, and with that commitment often comes personal satisfaction—not based on the outcome, but, rather, on the *effort.* Because they are giving their best, the end results are positive more often than not.

Sloppy, late, incomplete, and *poorly done* are words describing the work of someone who is not committed to excellence. In the absence of a commitment to excellence, this failure to do good work is not about ability or lack of ability, but, rather, it is about being lazy and/or not caring. It is an indication of low self-respect or lack of pride in oneself. As children, some people may not have been taught how to do good work. The expectations for these adolescents may have been very low. It might be necessary for some of us to "reparent" ourselves as adults. We may need to push and then reward ourselves for good work. We need to realize that we are capable and that we can and should do good work all the time.

We may feel resentful and disinclined to put our best efforts forward if we have suspicions about being taken advantage of by our superiors. Sometimes the fruits of our labors will be claimed by our boss as his or her own work. So, why should we bother? Sooner or later our good work will be noticed by others and could result in enhanced opportunities. That we are able to do good work (with a good attitude) under difficult circumstances inevitably comes to the attention of higher management, peers, and subordinates.

The choice to do our best at all times is ours and ours alone to make. We can do our best and expect the same effort from everyone else, and when we find that they do not follow our lead, it is easy to get angry and resentful about the unfairness of it all. To commit to excellence is a personal commitment, though, like integrity. It does not have anything to do with what anyone else is doing. It comes from us and is for us, and, while we are not doing good work for rewards, but, rather, a higher purpose, we often end up with plenty of rewards anyway, because good work is valued by many.

Excellent work is not, however, valued by everyone. Most of us have come across managers who seem threatened by the good work of subordinates. They fear that another person's efforts will somehow make them look bad, and so they discourage excellence in many subtle and not-so-subtle ways. Managers have a lot of influence over their employees and are responsible for bringing out the best in each. An excellent worker with a threatened manager, though, may find the going too rough under these circumstances and decide that they would be best served by finding employment elsewhere. Self-preservation is sometimes the only avenue open to us.

A commitment to excellence combines nicely with humility. Humility allows us to recognize our strengths and to be grateful for them—not boastful and obnoxious. As managers, our own commitment to excellence will influence our employees, and when excellence is part of the culture of a business, it is not only encouraged, but ultimately rewarded.

LEADERSHIP

A leader is someone who is followed by others. All managers are not leaders. Those who are not trusted or respected by their employees may fail when attempting to institute new programs. They can tell everyone to do something, and even show them how, but the employees do not embrace the new program and it may not succeed. Employees, on the other hand, will embrace a new program (even if they don't particularly like it) simply because they trust the manager's judgment and vision.

We have heard about military leaders who led their troops into dangerous, near-certain death situations. On the other hand, we heard about soldiers in Vietnam who assassinated officers rather than obey them. Why would soldiers in the first example follow the officer into battle knowing they would probably be killed, while those in the second case not only refused to follow, but actually went so far as to kill the officer? Was it because of the cause or because of the officer?

Leaders have tremendous influence over their subordinates, and with that comes the responsibility to be a *good* influence. Approximately 900 men, women, and children committed suicide in Guyana in 1978. They were followers of an American religious fanatic by the name of Jim Jones who brainwashed most of his followers into this act, and those that were not willing participants did so in the end at the point of a gun. This is an appalling example of leadership careening off in the wrong direction.

Leading is very different from forcing. We can force employees to do what we want by threatening them, but the resulting performance can lack enthusiasm and graciousness, which is particularly problematic in the hospitality industry. Employees who choose to follow a leader tend to be more positive. Again, we need to think about how we respond to various types of management styles. Which teachers or managers did we do our best work for? Why?

Charisma, which is the ability to influence people through charm, seems to have become more important to many of today's leaders than substance. Their positions flip-flop to whatever the most recent poll finds popular. When the focus is on the personality of the leaders, they become celebrities. Leadership should not, however, be about the leader, but, rather, it should be about the ability of the leader to bring out the best in his or her people.

Leaders help their people to mature and to reach their potentials. They teach their people skills and enable them to solve problems and handle work situations. Leaders help their people to excel and allow the credit to go to the employees, rather than taking it for themselves. Chinese philosopher Lao Tzu, no later than 400 B.C., said, "The existence of the leader who is wise is barely known to those he leads. He acts without unnecessary speech, so that the people say, 'It happened of its own accord.'"

Leaders must put the company's welfare before their own ambitions. The welfare of the company depends on its relationships with employees and customers, so leaders must consider the needs of their employees in order to produce a product that meets the needs of customers. The financial health of a company is, of course, vital. Without profit, there is no reason to stay in business. To that end, quality leaders provide the long-term vision and competence that enable the company to remain viable.

Leaders are only leaders because their employees trust them. Trust is possible because leaders' actions are consistent and based on ethical values and purposes that are for the good of the company. This provides stability for employees. It is essential for us to use care in selecting the companies for which we choose to work. Our personal values need to be in line with the company's or we will find ourselves at odds and unable to effectively lead our people.

REPUTATION AND MORALE

We cannot overestimate the value of our reputations. People have very long memories, particularly when recalling something scandalous or bad about us. Once a reputation has been tarnished, it is very difficult to correct the damage. The same is true for companies. When some of us, who are older, hear the brand name *Nestlé*, our first thought goes back to the 1970s when *Nestlé* gave free formula to Third World mothers so they would not be able to breast-feed their babies. Subsequently, they had to purchase formula that, of course, they could not afford, so their babies were put in serious jeopardy. For some people, no amount of chocolate can sweeten the tarnished image of *Nestlé*.

No number of good works will make people forget the one wrong move. We may be forgiven in time, but in business we can go bankrupt before enough time and good works result in a second chance. The obvious answer is to not do anything that might damage our reputation in the first place. And how do we do that? We adhere to the rules we have set for ourselves—rules that, when followed, will result in us being the kinds of people or organizations we wish to be.

In a way, companies are people. It is the combined identities of all the people that determine a company's identity. A company made up of good people will be a good one. An association of a bunch of crooks and lowlifes will not be. The practiced values of top management determine the way companies operate and their reputations ultimately are the result of those lived values. Companies are not moral or immoral. It is the morality of the people who run them that determines the morality of the companies.

ACCOUNTABILITY

Ethical managers take responsibility for their own actions and never try to shift blame onto others. Nor do they justify behaviors that were found to be less than satisfactory. Managers are also responsible for the actions of their subordinates. "I did not know," or, "I told him to do it, but he did not," are not acceptable excuses. The manager should have known, and, when we tell someone to do something, it is our responsibility to make sure the person knows how to do it, has the authority to do it, and then we must check to make sure it was done properly.

There have been so many instances lately of politicians and business executives denying wrongdoing that the term "stonewalling" has become commonplace. Taking responsibility seems to have gone out of style, yet management is ultimately about responsibility. When we are in charge of something, we are responsible for that which we are in charge. To be "in charge" means that there will be an accounting to see whether or not we met our responsibilities. If we are in charge, then we are accountable. We are accountable for the good and also for the bad.

When we accept positions of management, we also must accept that we are accountable for our decisions and our actions and the actions of our subordinates. Accountability belongs with management as much as the pay, perks, and power; it is part of the job.

CONCLUSION

We cannot separate who we are as individuals or managers when it comes to ethics. So while this text is about hospitality ethics, it is really about the ethics

LADIES AND GENTLEMEN OF THE PRESS: I CATEGORICALLY DENY ANY INVOLVEMENT WHATSOEVER WITH THE CHERRY TREE INCIDENT.

of individuals who are or will become managers in the hospitality industry. As human beings we are different in terms of our values, backgrounds, and our strengths and weaknesses. We put together teams of people whose strengths and weaknesses complement each other, and a variety of backgrounds expand the team's understanding and vision. However, to be effective, the team's ethical values need to be the same. That is the purpose of this textbook: to form us into a shared ethical belief system with the Ethical Principles for Hospitality Managers as the core.

KEY WORDS

Shared ethical values

Social responsibility norm

Reciprocity norm

Biases

Golden Rule

CHAPTER THOUGHT QUESTIONS

1. What are ethics and how do personal and business ethics compare?
2. Why do we need instruction or reinstruction in ethical decision making?
3. Why do we have to be ethical hospitality managers? What are some of the consequences for failing to behave in ethical ways?
4. What do we mean when we say that ethics are not relative? Back up your answer with some examples you may have personally encountered or read about.

5. Why do we want to avoid ethical dilemmas? How can we avoid ethical dilemmas? Give an example of a personal situation when you or someone you know avoided, or could have avoided, an ethical dilemma.

6. Discuss the relationship between honesty and integrity. Describe managers that you have worked for who had integrity and those who did not. Which did you prefer and why?

7. Discuss what relationships have to do with business. Identify the various relationships and why trust is necessary in these relationships.

8. Trust is the fundamental issue in relationships and has two parts. Please describe the two parts and then discuss how the two parts affected various relationships you have had with managers, friends, or family.

9. Discuss loyalty and leadership in terms of trust. Use personal examples to back up your discussion.

10. Define the Golden Rule, discuss why it is important, and describe how it affects business. Give personal examples of when you or someone else did and did not follow the Golden Rule, and how those examples affected you.

REFERENCES

Badaracco, J. J., Jr., & Ellsworth, R. R. (1989). *Leadership and the quest for integrity.* Boston: Harvard Business School Press.

Gensler, J. J. (1998). *Ethics: A contemporary introduction.* New York: Routledge.

Jaszay, C. (2002). Teaching ethics in hospitality programs. *Journal of Hospitality & Tourism Education, 14*(3), 57–63.

Myers, D. G. (1999). *Exploring psychology* (4th ed.). New York: Worth.

Romar, E. J. (2001, October). *Responsibility, leadership and personal ethics: A Confucian view of corporate social responsibility.* Paper presented at the Eighth Annual International Conference Promoting Business Ethics, Chicago.

Solomon, R. C. (1999). *A better way to think about business: How personal integrity leads to corporate success.* New York: Oxford University Press.

Starr, R. L. (1987). *Marion.* New York: Vantage Press.

The Tao Te Ching: A translation by Stan Rosenthal [Online]. Available at www.clas.ufl.edu/users/gthursby/Taoism/ttcstan3.htm

Van Hoof, H. B., McDonald, M. E., Yu, L., & Vallen, G. K. (1996). *A host of opportunities: An introduction to hospitality management.* Chicago: Irwin.

SUPPLEMENT

The following is a list of tips and considerations from Dean Ron Evans, former president and CEO of Best Western, for those who would like to be successful hospitality managers or CEOs. Many of the Ethical Principles for Hospitality Managers and issues discussed in this text are incorporated in this list.

1. Develop people skills. Work in and lead teams. Understand and appreciate diversity.

2. Now and forever, do everything as professionally as possible. All skills are transferable. Cream rises to the top, so, no matter what you do, do it well. It will be noticed.

3. Try to do more than asked of you. Be harder on yourself and expect more of yourself than anyone else. Look for areas to add value.

4. Understand the vision, mission, and strategies of your company and where your department fits.

5. Learn all facets of the company you work for (9 out of 10 won't and they won't be CEO). As you extend yourself into doing more and wider, you are the cream and will rise. CEOs don't give extra responsibilities to mediocre people. Good people are busy and get busier because they get things done.

6. Networking: Meet others and get involved. Boards of Directors appoint CEOs so make yourself known to the Board. Take any opportunity that comes along.

7. Hone financial and marketing skills. You must understand financial statements, cash flow analysis, ratios, and so forth. Boards notice and hire people with these skills.

8. You must be able to think and see things in both a micro and macro way. It is essential for you to be able to see the big picture.

9. Surround yourself with talented people. Hire only people who have a greater capacity for leadership than you did at their age.

10. Don't compromise morals or ethics to become CEOs. You cannot achieve your full potential with flawed morals and ethics.

11. Manage people by empowering them, mentoring them, and coaching them. Build in accountabilities. Remember Lao Tzu:

    - As for the best leaders: The people don't know of their existence.
    - As for the second-best leaders: The people honor the leader.
    - As for the third-best leaders: The people fear the leader.
    - As for the fourth-best leaders: The people hate the leader.

Luck comes when preparation meets opportunity. Start now! While there is no list of necessary characteristics to be a CEO, you would be well served to evaluate yourself by asking:

1. Why do you want to be a CEO?
2. Do you like to lead or follow?
3. Do you like dealing with many things at one time or one thing at a time? (There are many things going on at once.)
4. How do you respond to crisis and pressure? (There is a lot of pressure.)
5. Would you rather do things yourself or work through others? (CEOs do not have the time to micromanage and must delegate while remaining accountable for the work of others.)
6. How do you react to criticism? (CEOs take a lot of criticism.)
7. Are you willing to devote the time to be a CEO? (Family cannot be taken for granted, but you must marry well because your spouse will have to take care of things because you will be away much of the time.)

Chapter 2

Ethical Thought

A moral person lives according to principles of right and wrong. The study of these principles is called "moral philosophy" or "ethics." We often think of ethics in terms of business or medical ethics, which are basically codes of rules for members of a particular discipline. On the other hand, when we think of *morals* we envision guidelines for our personal behavior that have their origins in religious or family tradition.

Morals and ethics are basically the same thing, however, and it is senseless to attempt separation of our personal moral and business ethical behavior. Personal beliefs and behaviors extend into our business lives. When they do not match, we are conflicted and often frustrated and/or unhappy. That is why we are encouraged to investigate company philosophies during the job search process so that we can make wise employment choices.

Most of us know right from wrong. We know it is wrong to lie, cheat, and steal. We know that it is good to put forth our best efforts and be kind to others. For thousands of years, people have been giving serious thought to what it means to be decent and to live a good life. The purpose of this chapter is to give an overview of some of the various ways of thinking about ethics and to justify the approach we will be utilizing throughout the text.

The study of moral philosophy (ethics) is broken into two parts: **meta-ethics** and **normative ethics.** The former asks, "How do we determine what our moral principles are?", while the latter inquires, "What are the principles we ought to live by?" (In other words, where do we get the principles, and what should they be?) So, let us first look at the various ways of determining our moral principles.

META-ETHICS

Subjectivism

Subjectivism says that all moral beliefs are based on personal feelings. What we determine to be good or right is what we enjoy doing to begin with. If an individual likes to hurt people, then hurting people is good for that individual. Another person may have different feelings, and those feelings are good for that individual. Nothing is inherently good or bad—it is merely a matter of personal preference.

We may have similar preferences as we go through the socialization process, but that is not always the case. Few people adhere to strict subjectivism because it implies infallibility. (We are all correct, even if we disagree, but how could that be?) It is right to kill; it is wrong to kill. The two statements are totally opposite and cannot both be true at once.

Because we are thinking beings with the ability to reason, our thoughts and not just our feelings often guide behavior. When faced with dilemmas, we can analyze options and determine that our best response is perhaps something less personally desirable. For instance, if we find $1,000 at a bank ATM machine, we have the option of keeping it or leaving it with a bank employee so the money can be returned to the owner. We would probably like to keep the money and might think, "Finders keepers, losers weepers." Our capacity to reason, however, enables us to consider that while taking the money we could be recorded on the videotape at the ATM machine, and, as a result, caught taking something that is not ours. Through the application of reason, we may determine that our best interest lies in returning the money.

Incorporating our capacity for reasoning results in a variation of subjectivism. We can assess situations and consider everyone else's feelings along with our own, then make an informed and impartial decision as to the right thing to do. If we are impartial, do all people count the same? Should we consider a stranger's needs as equivalent to our own family's needs?

Of course, it is difficult to know the myriad future ramifications of any decision we make today, because it is difficult to be completely impartial. We can ask ourselves what the best decision would be if we did indeed know all the ramifications and were completely impartial. As humans, though, we may not always want to look at the truth, and, in that way, we avoid having to do a painfully right thing.

Emotivism

A variation of subjectivism is emotivism. It hinges on the principle that what we like is expressed emotionally and not considered either true or false. The statement, "I like to hurt people," does not mean that it is good to hurt people. With emotivism, if someone else says, "I do not like to hurt people," both can be true because they are merely exclamations of personal attitudes.

Emotivists believe that moral judgments are not scientifically testable facts, so there is little place for reasoning when it comes to moral discussions. A more moderate emotivism incorporates reason and requires that feelings (which are the basis of moral judgments) be impartial and informed.

Cultural Relativism

Another meta-ethical theory is cultural relativism, which holds that ethical principles are not universal, but, rather, determined by culture. Values are customs or preferences that develop over time within a culture. Whatever a society agrees is correct is deemed correct for that society. Another society may have a different idea of what is correct, and that is correct for that society. The suggestion, "When in Rome, do as the Romans do," is the concept behind cultural relativism.

Cultural relativists are tolerant of other cultures and do not judge one culture's ethical norms to be superior to others. They may prefer their own culture's norms, but only because they are used to them. They do not see theirs as better, just different.

For cultural relativists, what is good is what society approves of. Bad is what society does not approve of (the minority view). There is no inherent right or wrong; majority rules. The obvious problem with cultural relativism is this: what if society approves of enslaving blacks, exterminating Jews, putting young children to work in factories, or denying civil rights for women? Cultural relativists would not pass judgment on the policies of other societies.

The above examples may seem obvious to us. While bribery in our culture is not an acceptable business practice, how would we react if business dealings brought us to another culture where bribery was the accepted practice for getting things done? When in Rome, do as the Romans do? Are we cultural relativists only when it suits us?

Lawrence Kohlberg is an educational psychologist who studied the moral development of children. He identified the following six levels.

1. Stage of Punishment and Obedience: the right or good thing to do is to obey authority and *avoid punishment*.

2. Stage of Individual Instrumental Purpose and Exchange: the right or good thing to do is that which *gets us what we want*. At the same time, we allow others to do what they do to get what they want.

3. Stage of Mutual Interpersonal Expectations, Relationships, and Conformity: the right or *good thing to do is that which society expects us to do*.

4. Stage of Social System and Conscience Maintenance: the right or good thing to do is that which is good for society. Our personal needs are less important than the group's needs. We should *conform to society*.

5. State of Prior Rights and Social Contract or Utility: the right or good thing to do is that which upholds the values and rights of society. *Do what is best for the majority*.

6. State of Universal Ethical Principles: the right or good thing to do is to live the universal ethical principles such as the Golden Rule. We must do the right thing always.

It is good to have openness and tolerance for other cultures, but cultural relativity tops out at Stage 4 and is generally considered to be an immature approach to morality.

Supernaturalism

Subjectivists say that what is good or right is what we like. Cultural relativists say that good or right is what society approves of. Supernaturalists, on the other hand, say that good or right is what God wills us to do. The will of God is objective because it comes from a source outside of ourselves. So, assuming we believe in the existence of such an entity, how do we recognize and know the will of God?

There have traditionally been close ties between ethics and religion. All major religions espouse some version of the Golden Rule; do unto others as you would have others do unto you. Religious writings such as in the Bible or Koran offer behavioral suggestions, as do the leaders of various religions. The Ten Commandments, according to the Old Testament, are moral rules handed down from God. And so the thinking goes, God can enlighten us through prayer. There is always the risk, however, that our own desires may be confused with God's desires for us. There have also been unfortunate examples of religious leaders whose guidance was better for themselves than for their flocks.

Socrates posed this question: Is something right because God wills it, or does God will it because it is right? To wit, anything God wills is good, so nothing is good or right on its own. But, because God is good, He would only will that which is good or right to begin with. While religious people want to follow the **Divine Command** theory of right and wrong (will of God), the circular reasoning in the previous sentences makes it questionable.

The **Theory of Natural Law** says that everything in nature has a purpose, and this principle was incorporated into many Western religious traditions. God created us as rational beings so that we can figure out what we are supposed to do within the natural universe. St. Thomas Aquinas, a 13th-century philosopher, said we are to live our moral lives according to reason, conscience being the dictate of reason. Thus, atheists can also know moral truths.

Intuitionism

Intuitionism says that there are self-evident objective truths within us that any mature person can know. They cannot necessarily be proved or reasoned about; they are simply basic truths. We can assess moral theories by how well they fit with our own intuitions of what is right and good. Intuitionists, however, do not always agree on what the self-evident truths are.

The Golden Rule

The Golden Rule ("Do unto others as you would have others do unto you") does not tell us specifically what is right or good. Instead, it is a practical rule that helps us to ensure we are acting consistently with our beliefs. Following the rule requires us to imagine ourselves in others' positions and to think about how we would like to be treated. If we wish to be treated fairly, then we in turn must treat others fairly. If we want to be listened to, then we must listen to others, and so forth.

The Golden Rule is about our behavior, not the other person's behavior. If we treat others the way we would like to be treated, it does not necessarily follow that we will receive the same treatment. Morality is about how we choose to behave in all situations rather than merely reacting to another individual's behavior.

NORMATIVE ETHICS

We have looked at the various ways of determining our moral principles. Now we will look at four theories for determining how we ought to live.

Utilitarianism

Utilitarianism may be the most famous normative ethical principle in Western philosophy. John Stuart Mill built on the work of Jeremy Betham to develop utilitarianism. The general idea behind the utilitarian position is that right or good actions are those that result in happiness. Happiness is pleasure and the absence of pain. The best life, according to the Greatest Happiness Principle, is a life that has much enjoyment and little pain. The highest principle of morality for utilitarians is, therefore, that one should always act so as to maximize the greatest happiness for all people. Loving your neighbor as you would love yourself and practicing the Golden Rule can sum up the ideal perfection of utilitarian morality.

Some pleasures have more value than others. Human beings, according to Mill, need more than physical pleasure to be happy. A life of pleasure, as many of us may know, does not always result in happiness. Drug addicts may experience pleasure but the overall quality of their lives invariably becomes less than happy. No pleasure that conflicts with the sense of dignity inherent in all people will result in happiness.

Utilitarianism has two variations: act utilitarianism and rule utilitarianism. The principle of **act utilitarianism** requires that every time we act we ought to calculate and determine which among all the options open to us would promote the greatest net utility for all. The smallest things we do can have enormous consequences later. It may, however, be impossible for us to know the long-range consequences of our actions, and thus impossible to determine the correct action in every situation.

Mill believed that standards of morality should prescribe our duties or give us a way of determining our best actions in any circumstance, but why we do what we do has nothing to do with the morality of the act. Motive may, however, define the person doing the action. The best actions are those that promote the greatest good for all. Act utilitarianism *is*, perhaps, too difficult as criticized. It is too difficult to know all the consequences to all the people all the time, and too difficult to make timely good decisions.

Mill likened the difficulty problem to Christians not having to read the Old and New Testaments before making each decision. He stated that we have been living and learning and making decisions for all of history and can rely on rules that society has determined necessary for the ability of people to get along harmoniously. The principle of **rule utilitarianism** requires that every time we act we obey the set of rules that, taken together, promote the greatest utility for all. Thus, we only have to do the calculations (who are involved, what are the consequences, etc.) when two rules are in conflict.

Mill believed that people are social and have a natural need to "be in unity" with others. As civilization advances, education and the socializing influences of society tend to increase the conception that the individual is part of a whole— and what is good for the whole is good for the one. Society grows in health as people become more concerned with the good of the whole, and individuals grow to where they believe it is natural to consider the good of the whole and automatically make decisions for the good of all in every case.

Mill identified security as the most vital of all human interests. Security is instinctually sought for survival, thus the sentiments of self-defense and revenge are very strong. People, however, are capable of sympathy and have an understanding of the benefits that come along with being part of a larger community. Within this larger community, individuals have rights that must be agreed upon and protected by society in order to provide the essential security. Because people do not always agree on the rules, standards, or laws necessary to protect the rights of individuals in the community, the only way to decide is by determining what is best for the most people. Individuals agree to give up what may be simply expedient, their personal happiness, for the general expediency of the larger community, because it is ultimately individually better to live in a safe society where rights are protected equally and impartially.

There are few act utilitarians today because analyzing every single thing we do is too cumbersome, and it is difficult to identify all possible consequences in advance. Rule utilitarians accept a list of rules that have been shown to result in the overall best interests of the most people. In that way, they then only need analyze when there is a discrepancy between rules. The consequence of the action is more important to utilitarians than the means to reach the end. The statement, "He did it for the right reason," or, "She meant well," do not alone make an act good or right. The proper act, therefore, is one that turns out well for the most people.

Social Contract Theory

Adherents to the social contract theory believe that good or right is solely determined by the rules we need to make and follow in order for us to live together peacefully. In 1651, Thomas Hobbes theorized that the absence of a social contract would result in the *state of nature*, which he described as "lonely, violent chaos." Ergo, we voluntarily give up a few individual rights or freedoms and accept rules that everyone agrees to follow that permit equity and safety.

Governments exist to administer these rules, punishing citizens who fail to follow them. If and when the rules become slanted against any one group (so that members of that group fail to receive their fair share of the "mutual" benefits), the social contract will be violated and become void. This is the argument that was used to justify the American Revolution when the colonies broke away from England.

Categorical Imperative

Immanuel Kant believed that moral laws are absolute and do not change according to the situation. His categorical imperative of 1785 is the formula he devised to determine what the moral laws are. It states that there is only one law of morality and it is that we should act in ways that we would want our acts to become laws for everyone else's behavior.

Kant felt that for an act to be moral it must be done from a sense of duty without any selfish motivations. With the capacity to reason, we have the responsibility and opportunity to make moral choices that result in a will that is good in itself. A good will is a commitment to do what is morally required in all circumstances regardless of what other desires are present. Avoiding negative consequences, or doing good merely because we enjoy it, removes acts from being classed as moral.

As humans, we naturally desire to be treated well by others. As each of us has this desire, it is a universal desire, and the only way it can be realized is if everyone treats everyone else with respect. The second part of Kant's categorical imperative is that we should treat each other as ends and never as means. We must never manipulate or use people to get what we want, because people are rational beings and deserve dignity.

Self-love is not an adequate reason for doing our duty, because the motive behind self-love depends on the situation, and, when the situation changes, we may not feel compelled toward duty. Most of us know what is right and wrong. Kant suggests, however, that people tend to start fudging and justifying, so, therefore, they need the discipline of philosophy to keep morality on the straight and narrow. The categorical imperative gives clear guidelines for making decisions that benefit society, and, thus, individuals.

Virtue Theory

A virtue is a character trait that results in habitual good behavior, rather than a principle of action. Virtue theory requires that character traits considered virtuous be identified, defined, and justified. The challenge of virtue theory is, once again, identifying how we know which character traits are virtuous. Do the virtues come from God, are they determined by the particular culture; are they self-evident truths, or are they determined by individuals?

The pursuit of virtue was viewed by Socrates as the highest good. He believed that virtue is knowledge, and that to choose to do bad things is a consequence of ignorance. The ancient Greeks identified four cardinal virtues: wisdom, courage, temperance, and justice. To be wise is to have a rational understanding of how we ought to live. Courage is the trait that allows us to face danger or difficulty. Temperance means that we keep control of our emotions and appetites. Justice has to do with treating all people fairly. Others have added honesty, generosity, thoughtfulness, tolerance, and so forth. Faith, hope, and charity are additional theological virtues.

ETHICAL THEORIES AND DECISION MAKING

Consequentialism versus Nonconsequentialism

Utilitarianism and the Social Contract Theory focus on the outcomes or consequences of our decisions and acts. The acts themselves are only good if they result in favorable consequences for the most people. The Categorical Imperative and Virtue Theory, on the other hand, do not depend on the consequences of the act, but, rather, consider the rightness or wrongness of the particular act. An act that is inherently good is good whether or not it has the best consequences for the most people. Likewise, some acts are inherently bad even if they have good consequences for the most people. In other words, ends do not justify the means.

Philosophers attempt to supply grand theories to facilitate understanding and moral decision making. John Stuart Mill's Utilitarianism and Immanuel Kant's Categorical Imperative are two such theories. Mill's utility theory is **teleological** and focuses on the outcomes of acts (the ends justify the means), whereas Kant's Categorical Imperative is **deontological** and focuses on the acts themselves (the means are more important than the ends). Common goodness—both actions and results—may very likely fit in both theories. More than often, good acts result in good consequences, just as bad acts result in bad consequences.

Bad Decisions

Unethical business dealings are not some new phenomenon. The past few years, however, have been rife with corporate scandals. When we look at the following actions (of executives in charge of these huge corporations), greed seems to be the overriding motivation. At the same time, chief executives across all industries pocketed millions in cash bonuses and stock for 2003.

Enron   In December 2001, Enron, once the seventh largest U.S. company, filed the second largest bankruptcy in U.S. history and cost investors $68 billion. It is alleged that executives relied on accounting gimmicks and lies to deceive the government and investors about the financial health of the energy-trading giant. Former Chief Executives Kenneth Lay and Jeffrey Skilling and Chief Financial Officer Andrew Fastow are accused of creating partnerships to hide losses from shareholders. Fastow faces nearly 100 criminal charges including fraud, money laundering, conspiracy, and obstruction of justice. Michael Kopper, another former Enron executive, was convicted of money laundering and wire fraud. Executives sold off their own stock while prohibiting employees from doing the same until the company was bankrupted. In all, eighteen former executives have been indicted on charges related to falsifying earnings and manipulating energy markets. In June 2003, the Labor Department initiated a civil lawsuit against Enron and former executives and directors, attempting to recover hundreds of millions of dollars in retirement money that employees lost when the stock collapsed. More than 20,700 participants in Enron's 401(k) plan had nearly two-thirds of their assets invested in company stock. Private suits filed on behalf of the employees allege that they lost more than $1 billion. In September 2003, Ben Glisan, Jr., became the first executive to go to prison in the scandal as the former treasurer pleaded guilty to conspiracy and was led from the courtroom in handcuffs and ankle chains. Due to the ongoing nature of this scandal, it is impossible for this book to stay up to date, but rest assured that other prosecutions will follow.

Arthur Andersen   Arthur Andersen, as Enron's auditor, was the first accounting firm to be convicted of a felony and is no longer allowed to perform audit work. Corporations listed on the stock market are required to have independent audits. Arthur Andersen not only was responsible for the accuracy of Enron's financial statements and internal bookkeeping, but also created a conflict of interest by selling Enron millions of dollars' worth of consulting services. Arthur Andersen was found guilty of obstructing justice for destroying documents concerning Enron.

WorldCom   Chief Executive Officer Bernard Ebbers resigned after borrowing hundreds of millions of dollars from WorldCom. Corporate executives hid massive funds and then filed for bankruptcy protection with $3.85 billion of improperly booked expenses and another $3.8 billion in accounting errors. The $11 billion accounting scandal was the largest in U.S. history. Former Chief Financial Officer Scott Sullivan and former controller David Myers were arrested, with Myers subsequently pleading guilty to fraud charges. Former accounting director Buford Yates, Jr., also pleaded guilty to accounting fraud. In May 2003, WorldCom agreed to pay a $500 million fine to settle charges of securities fraud. In all, the company settled fraud charges with the Securities and Exchange Commission by paying out $750 million in cash and stock to victims. In August 2003, Oklahoma Attorney General Drew Edmondson filed the first criminal fraud charges against former CEO Ebbers and the beleaguered company. Also named in the complaint were Sullivan, Myers, Yates, and two other former executives, Betty Vinson and Troy Normand. Attorney General Edmondson alleges that Oklahoma pensions lost $64 million from WorldCom's collapse. If found guilty, the defendants face up to ten years in prison and a $10,000 fine. Federal prosecutors in New York have already charged all five with similar crimes, and, at this time, California, Oregon, West Virginia, and Indiana are also considering criminal charges against the company now known as MCI. (In November 2003, Oklahoma's attorney general temporarily dropped charges against Ebbers to avoid interfering with upcoming federal prosecutions.)

Tyco International   L. Dennis Kozlowski, the former chief executive of Tyco International, was indicted for tax evasion and evidence tampering related to Tyco's finances. Kozlowski, former chief financial officer Mark H. Swartz, and former general counsel Mark A. Belnick were accused of abusing loan programs and making unauthorized cash and stock awards of $600 billion.

HealthSouth   On November 4, 2003, former HealthSouth CEO Richard Scrushy was charged with 85 federal counts in an alleged $2.7 billion fraud that prosecutors say financed his lavish lifestyle. Charges include false certification of corporate statements, a new offense under the Sarbanes–Oxley law passed recently to target corporate wrongdoers. The indictment seeks the return of more than $278 million in alleged ill-gotten gains, and, if found guilty, Scrushy faces more than 650 years in prison and $36 million in fines.

ImClone Systems   Samuel Waksal, the former CEO of ImClone Systems Inc., was arrested for insider trading and accused of warning family members to sell off stock before the Food and Drug Administration announced the rejection of ImClone's star drug, Erbitux. Waksal was indicted on securities fraud, bank fraud, tax evasion, perjury, and obstruction of justice. In June 2003, he was sentenced to 87 months in prison and ordered to pay nearly $4.3 million in fines and back taxes for his role in insider trading. Waksal's friend, Martha Stewart, who also sold her ImClone shares before the FDA announcement, was found guilty of four counts of conspiracy, obstruction, and lying to federal investigators about her actions. Stewart was sentenced to 5 months in prison and 5 months of home detentions, although she is likely to appeal.

Adelphia Communications   Adelphia is under federal investigation and has filed for bankruptcy. Its founder, John Rigas, was arrested with his two sons for defrauding investors and using company funds as personal income. Various former Adelphia executives are indicted on charges of conspiracy, securities fraud, and wire fraud. Adelphia executives gave false documentation to hide debt and the real financial status of the company.

Global Crossing   Global Crossing is being investigated for possibly making deals with Qwest Communications designed to artificially inflate revenues through insider trading and questionable acquisitions of other businesses. The former chief executive, Leo J. Hindery, Jr., may have encouraged former chairman Gary Winnick to sell Global Crossing's assets to other companies before it went under. The Securities and Exchange Commission has charged Global Crossing with bookkeeping fraud. Shareholders are currently suing Winnick and the company. In addition, J.P. Morgan Chase & Co. is suing 23 former officers and directors of Global Crossing Ltd. for 1.7 billion, accusing them of hiding important financial information while running the fiber-optic network.

Wall Street   Merrill Lynch & Co paid a $100 million fine for encouraging investors to purchase stocks they referred to in-house as "dogs." The stock that was pushed came from companies who were paying large fees to Merrill Lynch for investment-banking services.

Mutual Funds   Investigations by the SEC into improprieties within this $7 trillion industry are expanding. In November 2003, Morgan Stanley agreed to pay a $50 million fine to settle charges that it steered investors to certain mutual funds in order to secure millions in commissions. In that same month, five former brokers and two former Boston branch managers of Prudential Securities Inc. were accused by regulators of fraud because of improper trading. Charges and civil complaints have been filed against several players in this industry, due to allegations that large investors or insiders receive preferential treatment in the timing of trades and other fund management practices.

Tech Boom/IPO   In June 2003, hundreds of companies that staged hot *initial public offerings* during the so-called "tech boom" agreed to pay $1 billion to investors under a tentative partial settlement. Litigation is ongoing against

55 brokerage firms accused of funneling huge payoffs to insiders through secret deals. The massive case involves 309 separate suits filed against 55 investment banks, more than 300 companies that went public between 1998 and 2000, and an unspecified number of their individual corporate officers and directors. The total number of defendants could be more than 1,000; companies involved include Global Crossing, MP3.com, Ask Jeeves Inc., and Red Hat Inc.

Cheating at Golf

Ford-Firestone, Kmart, Ahold. . . . Trillions of dollars in stock value has been lost in recent years, hundreds of corporate bankruptcies have been filed, and unemployment has burgeoned to unhealthy proportions. Every day we read about some new scandal, executives indicted, executives lying, cheating, and stealing. We may be relieved that none of these are hospitality organizations, but, as the largest industry in the world, are we more ethical or have we just been lucky and not gotten caught?

A survey of executives found that most do a lot of business on the golf course, and that golf behavior is a predictor of business behavior. Eighty-two percent of the surveyed executives admitted to cheating at golf. People with integrity do not become CEOs and suddenly turn unethical. It is the erosion of ethics over time that results in the unethical and sometimes criminal behavior of these top executives.

Most of the companies profiled above went into bankruptcy as a result of unethical decisions. The companies' employees, the stockholders, the communities where the companies are located, the customers—all of us are negatively affected when unethical management destroys companies. We must ensure that our own industry avoids the negative consequences of unethical leadership.

Avoiding Negative Consequences

The final result of getting caught hiding losses, hiding assets, using company money for personal spending, and lying to stockholders and employees will be extremely negative and costly. Executives with a lifetime of unethical behaviors behind them, however, may feel that the answer lies in simply not getting caught. They could certainly avoid the negative consequence of going to prison if they did not get caught.

The above corporate examples are obvious when we look at them *after* the executives were arrested or found out. It may be more difficult, though, to envision the "obvious negative results" while we are in the middle of situations. We may find that our ethical sensitivities have diminished as we have made questionable decisions over the years. We may not have started with a strong ethical sense to begin with, and may not have had ethical behavior modeled for us.

We can avoid negative consequences by doing the right thing. The problem with this prescription is that, with today's lack of shared ethics, too many

BOY GEORGE WASHINGTON

people do not know what the right thing is. We can make everyone memorize the ethical principles, but that will not necessarily result in anyone following them. Without a strong internal sense of right and wrong, we may not see any reason for following the rules.

Past performance is the best predictor of future performance. Hospitality students who cheat in college might later become hospitality managers. Will they no longer cheat? *Doing the right thing* and *avoiding negative consequences* can be different ways of expressing the same thing. It may be more convincing for hospitality students and managers to analyze decision options in terms of avoiding negative consequences than trying to convince them to do the right thing simply because it is the right thing to do.

Students tend to think in terms of outcomes of behaviors rather than the behaviors themselves. Teleological systems might have more application in the hospitality industry because managers can be taught to compare outcomes to the various stakeholders (customers, employees, the company, etc.) for each possible decision and then select the decision that has the best outcomes.

We can be taught the rules, but we must learn to live the rules. That may be possible only through the experience of calculating best outcomes for all options until a pattern becomes apparent, at which time we can accept and apply the rules without bothering with analysis. Perhaps the grand theories described in the beginning of the chapter are not all that important for people trying to decide what to do in their day-to-day lives. We will, however, be using a modified form of Utilitarianism to analyze a case study throughout the rest of this textbook.

ANALYZING CASES

Sometimes snap decisions are necessary. Mostly, however, they are not. Thoughtful decisions take into account all contingencies, and the risk of making bad decisions is reduced. Think about a snap decision to buy a new car while still a full-time student. It may seem like a terrific idea while looking at the car in the showroom. The dealer offers financing and affordable monthly payments. The student can picture driving around in the shiny new car and decides to just sign the papers. He or she leaves with a new car and drives off into the sunset.

The next day the student calls a car insurance company. He or she is shocked to find out how much the insurance is and that part of the money is due immediately. The student pays the bills and begins to realize that with the credit card bill, rent, utilities, and food, it will be necessary to work more hours. Working more hours affects school performance and leaves no time for important relationships. The student's romantic interest starts dating someone else who has more time and is not constantly worried about money. By semester's end, the student is way overextended—too tired and too stressed—and realizes that buying the new car was not such a hot idea after all.

The student could have avoided unhappy results had he or she thought about the possible consequences in advance of the decision. The student could also have considered alternate decisions. To buy or not to buy a new car are only two options. A third option might have been to buy a used car or a motorcycle or even a bicycle. The student could have considered how his or her decision might affect others, such as the girl- or boyfriend, work, school, perhaps even parents who might be called upon to bail the student out of financial difficulties.

Thinking ahead about how our decisions might turn out is not foreign to most of us. We think about whether or not we should go away for the weekend, weighing homework and other responsibilities. Sometimes we decide that under the circumstances it would be best to stay home and instead take care of business. Other times we may determine that we can, indeed, go away for the weekend and arrange to do our work while traveling or at some other time. Successful people think ahead and make sure their responsibilities are met.

Analysis

Analysis is a systematic way of thinking about something to reach a decision. We do analysis all the time. We use analysis when we want to buy a pair of shoes. We think about what we are going to use the shoes for—hiking, dancing? We consider the price, color, material, style, comfort, and so forth, and purchase the shoes that best match our needs. We use analysis to choose our clothing for the day. We consider our upcoming activities, the weather, comfort, our individual likes, and so forth, choosing the outfit that best matches our needs.

We could utilize a form to help us make important decisions such as buying a car. The form would have all the important features we desire. The form would also have factors such as cost, insurance, registration fees, resale value, gas mileage, and so forth. We would have spaces to enter the various models we looked at so that we could then determine which car was the best match for our particular needs. The form formalizes the analysis we do in our heads so that we can go through the same prescribed steps for every analysis we do.

Ethics Analysis

The idea of analyzing case studies may seem difficult. However, we have all been analyzing most every decision we make for all of our lives. We already know how to analyze. We will formalize the process so that we can become so familiar with ethical analysis that we will do it without thinking, just as we analyze what to wear without thinking. We will use the Ethics Analysis Form to help us organize and document our thoughts. The form has spaces for the decision option we are going to analyze, the **stakeholders,** the people who may be affected by our decision, the **ethical principles** that may be violated by the decision, and the **consequences,** which are the possible results of our decision.

Ethics Analysis Form

Decision Option:

Stakeholders	Principles	Consequences

Case Analysis Model

We can use the same process for analyzing every case study or situation. The Ethics Analysis Form provides a consistent format for our case analysis. Every case has a question that needs to be answered, a problem that needs to be solved, or a decision that needs to be made. Sometimes the most difficult task is simply identifying the problem. We must begin by reading the entire case, keeping the following questions in mind while doing so.

- What is the person in the case trying to accomplish? [This question is akin to the first step in the scientific process where we identify the problem. Actions without stated direction can lead us places we may not want to be in the end. We need to consider that the stated direction is the true direction we want to be going in.]
- Is what the person in the case is trying to accomplish ethical? [What we want is not always feasible and not always right. There is no point wasting time and energy on impossible goals. If the goal is feasible and also a good and appropriate goal, then we need to determine the best way to reach the goal.]
- What are the possible decision options? [There are usually several options. We often fail to consider alternatives. Which of the decision options is most likely to end in the desired results?]
- Where do the person's loyalties belong? Who or what is the person loyal to? [If a manager is being loyal to him- or herself instead of the company, there is a potential problem. Do we take positions in companies that we feel that we can be loyal to?]
- Who are the stakeholders who could be affected by the decision the person makes? [We are not alone. There are very few things we do that do not have some effect on someone. The key is to identify in advance just who all those parties are.]
- What are the possible consequences to all the stakeholders for each decision option? [It may be impossible to know exactly how what we do will affect others now and later. We can, however, identify likelihoods by thoughtfully considering the situation before acting.]
- Are there any ethical principles that might be violated by any of the decision options? [As we ascertain each possible consequence to each stakeholder for each decision option, we can run down the list of Ethical Principles for Hospitality Managers to see if any of them will be broken by the action.]

The Ethical Principles for Hospitality Managers (highlighted in Chapter 1) have been determined to hold true through countless analyses of situations. We can use these rules to help us make decisions. When a rule is violated, it has generally been found that problems will arise. Rule Utilitarianism allows us to learn from our collective experiences and establish rules so that we only have to analyze a situation when two rules are in conflict. We will, however, go through the entire analysis process for every segment of the case study as we go through the chapters of this text. After numerous analyses, we can more readily accept the rules and trust that following them is invariably the best strategy.

Case Study Analysis Example

We study ethics in order to be able to make good decisions—ones that result in the best consequences for the most people. What at first thought might seem good for an individual, may, upon contemplation, have some drawbacks that make it less good for the individual. Putting ourselves first is not always ultimately best for us. Let us look at a hypothetical situation that may be familiar to many students.

> Jason is a smart young man, but his grades are slightly below average because he works so many hours to pay for college. His friend Brian offers him a stolen copy of an upcoming midterm. Jason could probably do much better on the exam if he knew exactly what would be on it. What should he do?

We use the form and the questions above to get started. The decision options in the scenario are obvious: to take or not take the stolen exam from his friend Brian. We will analyze the first option, and start answering the questions.

- What is Jason trying to accomplish? *He is trying to get a better grade.*
- Is it ethical to try to get a better grade? *Yes.*
- Is it feasible to get a better grade? *Maybe. It may not be feasible for Jason to get a good grade without cheating if he cannot cut back on his work hours to study for the exam. This leads us to another option . . . he could try to get time off from his job. If he can't get time off, another option would be to give up the expectation of a good grade. Another option might be for Jason to take fewer classes.*
- What ways are available for Jason to get a better grade? *Studying or cheating.*
- Where do Jason's loyalties belong? *This question may not be applicable in this situation, or we may choose to come back to it later.*
- Who are the stakeholders who could be affected by Jason's decision? *Jason, Brian, other classmates, Jason's teacher, the school, his parents, maybe his fraternity, his friends, his employer, etc.* (We enter the stakeholders in the appropriate spaces on the Ethics Analysis Form.)
- What are the possible consequences to all the stakeholders if Jason takes the stolen exam? We start the analysis by asking ourselves questions and putting the answers to the questions in the appropriate spaces on the Ethics Analysis Form. One question leads to another question. We can determine what the questions should be by remembering what we're trying to find out. What can possibly happen to the stakeholder if the decision option is implemented? We will start with consequences for Jason.

1. What could happen if Jason takes the stolen exam? *Jason could get a high grade on the exam if he cheats by using the stolen exam. If Jason gets away with cheating this time, he may cheat again. Repeated cheating increases the chances of getting caught, resulting in painful consequences. Over time, the decisions we make determine the type of person we become.*

2. Will Jason feel proud of his high grade? *Jason might feel guilty or may not be able to feel pride in his work.*

3. If Jason cheats on the exam, will he have learned the material? *Jason may not have mastered the material covered on the test. He may subsequently be lost while trying to decipher material covered in the second half of the course. Is this material that Jason may need later to be successful on the job?*

4. Could any of Jason's classmates find out that he cheated on the exam? What might they think or feel if they find out? *Is it possible other students could find out? Word gets around. There could be several reactions: Some might feel resentful that Jason could get the same or better grade by cheating than they got after studying. Others might not care. Others could think that cheating might be a better strategy for them on the next exam.*

5. Could the teacher find out that Jason cheated? *Another student could tell on Jason, or perhaps the teacher might notice that several students (or at least Brian and Jason) had the exact same answers on the exam.*

6. What would happen to Jason if he was caught cheating? *Depending on the policy of the teacher and/or the school, the consequences could range from Jason receiving an F for the exam to Jason being expelled from the program or the university. Documentation of cheating could become part of Jason's permanent record. If he were expelled for cheating, "expelled for academic dishonesty" would probably be stamped on his transcript. If Jason tried to enroll in another university, they would request to see his transcripts. Would they be inclined to admit Jason with the stamp on his transcripts?*

7. If Jason got caught but was not expelled, how might this affect the rest of his time in school? *If Jason cheated in his major, the professor who caught him would most likely mention it to the other professors so they could keep an eye on him when he went into their classes. He would have a reputation with the faculty as a cheater. If recruiters asked a professor about Jason as a potential employee, he would probably not get a good reference. If other students were aware of Jason's cheating, they might not have a lot of respect for him. Jason would most likely not be nominated for any honors.*

It is possible that Jason might not get caught and no one but Jason and Brian would ever know. Even if no one ever found out, Jason might not learn important material and would have no reason to feel good about himself. If we go down the list of Ethical Principles for Hospitality Managers, we can identify principles that would be violated by his decision to take the stolen exam. Honesty, Integrity, and Commitment to Excellence would most certainly be violated. Fairness and Concern and Respect for Others, too, would be issues, and, of course, Accountability. We can ask the same types of questions for the other stakeholders, identifying possible consequences for them, and then enter them on the Ethics Analysis Form. (Please see below.)

Ethics Analysis Form

Decision Option: To take the stolen exam

Stakeholders	Principles	Consequences
Jason	Honesty Integrity Commitment to Excellence Fairness Concern and Respect for Others Accountability	• Jason could get a high grade on the exam if he cheats by using the stolen exam. • If Jason gets away with cheating this time, he most likely will cheat again. Repeated cheating increases the chances of getting caught, which will result in painful consequences. Over time, the decisions we make determine the type of person we become. • Jason might feel guilty or may be unable to feel pride in his good work. • Jason may not have mastered the material covered on the test. Is this material that Jason may need later to be successful on the job? • It is possible other students could find out. Word gets around. There could be several reactions. Some might feel resentful that Jason could get the same or a better grade by cheating than they get by studying. Others might not care. Others could think that cheating might be a better strategy for themselves on the next exam. • Another student could tell on Jason, or perhaps the teacher might notice that several students (or at least Brian and Jason) had the exact same answers on the exam. • Depending on the policy of the teacher and/or the school, the consequences could range from Jason receiving an F for the exam to Jason being expelled from the program or the university. Documentation of cheating could become part of Jason's permanent record. If he were expelled for cheating, "expelled for academic dishonesty"

(continued)

Stakeholders	Principles	Consequences
Jason		would probably be stamped on his transcript. If Jason tried to enroll in another university, they would request to see his transcripts. Would they be inclined to admit Jason with the stamp on his transcripts? • If Jason cheated in his major, the professor who caught him would most likely mention it to the other professors so they could keep an eye on him when he went into their classes. He would have a reputation with the faculty as a cheater. If recruiters asked a professor about Jason as a potential employee, he would probably not get a good reference. If other students were aware of Jason's cheating, they might not have a lot of respect for him. Jason would most likely not be nominated for any honors.
Brian	Honesty Integrity Commitment to Excellence Fairness Concern and Respect for Others Accountability	• Brian stands the same chance of getting caught as Jason and could suffer all of the same consequences. • His relationship with his friend Jason could suffer if they were caught.
Teacher	Integrity Fairness Commitment to Excellence Leadership Reputation and Morale	• If the teacher did not catch Jason and other students knew about the cheating, the teacher could lose the respect of students. • If the teacher finds out about the cheating, he or she would have to do something about it. No teacher likes to have to deal with cheating.
Other students	Honesty Integrity Trustworthiness Loyalty Fairness Concern and Respect for Others Commitment to Excellence Reputation and Morale	• If the exam is graded on a curve and Jason's grade is better than everyone else's, it could affect the curve and lower some of the other students' grades. • Students could feel resentment if they knew Jason was cheating and getting the same or better grades than they studied for. This could negatively affect the overall morale of the class. • Students might feel that they should tell on Jason but be very uncomfortable doing that. • Some students might be encouraged to cheat because they see Jason getting away with it.

(continued)

Stakeholders	Principles	Consequences
Parents, friends, employers		• Jason's parents could find out and be angry, disappointed, and humiliated. • Jason could lose some of his friends if he was caught cheating. • Jason's employer could find out and be afraid that Jason might try to cheat on the job.

The consequences of each of our actions can go far beyond the moment. In this situation, Jason loses nothing by not cheating. He doesn't deserve the good grade if he cannot earn it. It does not belong to him. It would be a stolen grade achieved by using a stolen exam. Jason would be unlikely to tell his teacher, parents, or employer that he cheated, because he would know they would think his action was wrong.

We can ask ourselves two questions when trying to make a decision: (1) Would I like to see a story about my decision printed in the newspaper for everyone to read? (2) Would I like it if everyone did what I am thinking of doing? In this situation, Jason would know that if what he did was printed in the newspaper, he would be in serious trouble. If he thought about cheating becoming the norm for all the students in his school, he could determine that his degree would become meaningless, and that the reputation of his school would suffer. He and his fellow students might have difficulty finding good management positions upon graduating. If they ever desired to go to graduate school, they most likely would not be accepted at any of the good ones.

There is a good chance that Jason would not be caught cheating this time. However, if he went ahead and was caught, he would most likely wish he had made a different decision. Even if he is not caught, there are enough negative consequences that could affect Jason and others directly and indirectly, whereupon, after analysis, the decision to take the stolen exam is not the best decision option. In the long run, Jason would be much better off by considering others.

CONCLUSION

We have looked at some of the best-known ways to determine moral principles and what the moral principles should actually be. We have reviewed some of the abuses of power that have resulted in bankruptcy filings, criminal prosecution, and personal devastation. We have utilized an Ethics Analysis Form and conducted an analysis of a decision most students have to consider at least once in their college careers.

Ethics or morals are not some "Sunday school" kind of thing that does not have anything to do with "real life." Throughout the course of this textbook, we will demonstrate the necessity of making ethical decisions in order to be successful business people. Many students will choose to make ethical decisions because they are the right thing to do. Others will make ethical decisions because they result in the best consequences for the most people. It really does not matter *why* we make ethical decisions. We just need to make them because it's good for all of us and our industry and our country.

KEY WORDS

Meta-ethics	Act Utilitarianism
Normative Ethics	Rule Utilitarianism
Subjectivism	Social Contact Theory
Emotivism	Categorical Imperative
Cultural Relativism	Virtue Theory
Supernaturalism	Teleological
Divine Command Theory	Deontological
Intuitionism	Analysis
Golden Rule	Stakeholders
Utilitarianism	Consequences

CHAPTER THOUGHT QUESTIONS

1. State your personal belief about one of the following topics: abortion, the death penalty, euthanasia, or eating meat. Why do you believe what you believe? Where did your belief come from? What makes your belief the correct one for you? What do you think other people should believe about the topic you chose? Should their beliefs be the same as yours? Why or why not?

2. Pretend you are a subjectivist and describe your idea of the perfect moral code for your society to adhere to. Discuss the pros and cons of this moral code.

3. What would cultural relativists think about the customs of other societies such as leaving old people or severely handicapped newborns out in the elements to die? Why would they think what they think? What are the pros and cons of cultural relativism?

4. Describe a situation where a utilitarian might think it was appropriate to kill someone. What could make killing appropriate for a utilitarian? Discuss pros and cons of holding a utilitarian view.

5. How would an act utilitarian determine what the moral act should be in a particular situation? How would a rule utilitarian determine what the moral act should be in a particular situation? Give specific examples from your own experience.

6. Describe the difference between the Categorical Imperative and Utilitarianism. Think of an act from your personal life that adherents to both theories would consider moral, and then explain why each would.

7. Which of the following ways of determining moral principles (Subjectivism, Emotivism, Cultural Relativism, Supernaturalism, or Intuitionism) best matches the way you determine your moral principles? Explain how and why.

8. The Golden Rule helps us to make sure we are acting consistently with our beliefs. Give an example when you did something according to the Golden Rule. How would you determine whether your act was moral? Choose a theory from this chapter to explain and justify your act.

9. Imagine that your boss wants you to work an additional shift. List all the reasons you might not want to work the additional shift. List all the reasons it might be good to work the additional shift. List all the people who might be affected by your decision to either work or not work the additional shift. What would be the best decision for you and why?

10. Using the Ethics Analysis Form, analyze a decision you made in the past. How did you originally make the decision? Did your analysis, after the fact, result in the same decision? Describe you feelings about the analysis process for decision making using the Ethics Analysis Form.

REFERENCES

CEOs' pay being watched. (2003, May 21). *The Arizona Republic.*

Corporate ethics [online]. (2003). Available at Washingtonpost.com

Executives made millions in bonuses. (2004, March 28). *The Arizona Republic.*

Executives say golf is vital to business [Online]. (2002). Available at http://www.hotel-online.com/New/News/2002Jun26/b.358.1025185192.html

Ex-HealthSouth CEO is indicted. (2003, November 5). *The Arizona Republic.*

Flew, A. (1979). *A dictionary of philosophy* (2nd ed). New York: Gramercy Books.

Gensler, H. J. (1998). *Ethics: A contemporary introduction.* New York: Routledge.

IPO investors to get $1 billion. (2003, June 27). *The Arizona Republic.*

Jaszay, C. (2002) Teaching ethics in hospitality programs. *Journal of Hospitality & Tourism Education, 14*(3), 58–63.

J.P. Morgan Chase & Co. (2003, December 12). *The Arizona Republic.*

Kagan, S. (1998). *Normative ethics.* Boulder, CO: Westview Press.

Kant, I. (1981). *Grounding for the metaphysics of morals: On the supposed right to lie because of philanthropic concerns.* Indianapolis, IN: Hackett.

Kreeft, P. (1999). *A refutation of moral relativism: Interviews with an absolutist.* San Francisco: Ignatius Press

Labor sues Enron, execs over pension losses. (2003, June 27). *The Arizona Republic.*

MacIntyre, A. (1998). *A short history of ethics: A history of moral philosophy from the Homeric age to the twentieth century* (2nd ed.). Notre Dame, IN: University of Notre Dame Press.

Mill, J. S. (1979). *Utilitarianism.* Indianapolis, IN: Hackett.

Morgan Stanley agrees to fine. (2003, November 18). *The Arizona Republic.*

Oklahoma charges WorldCom. (2003, August 28). *USA Today.*

Plato (1975). *The trial and death of Socrates.* Indianapolis, IN: Hackett.

Rachels, J. (1999). *The elements of moral philosophy* (3rd ed.). Boston: McGraw-Hill College.

SEC's inquiry gaining steam. (2003, November 5). *The Arizona Republic.*

Soccio, D. J. (1998). *Archetypes of wisdom: An introduction to philosophy* (3rd ed.). New York: ITP Wadsworth.

To avoid interfering. (2003, November 21). *The Arizona Republic.*

WorldCom's Ebbers to surrender in Oklahoma. (2003, August 29). *Bloomberg News.*

Chapter 3

Making Proper Employment Selections and Introduction to the Case Study

Chapter 1 introduced and described the Ethical Principles for Hospitality Managers we will be applying to segments of the case study. Chapter 2 was an overview of ethics—the history and various means for defining ethical behavior—and demonstrated usage of the Ethical Analysis Form. This chapter details how to make good employment selections and introduces the case study we will use throughout the remainder of the text. The case study is located after Chapter 15 and should be read in its entirety before moving on to Chapter 4.

FINDING THE RIGHT MANAGEMENT POSITIONS

Many of us have heard the phrase, "Do as I say, not as I do." Our employees, however, will do as we do regardless of what we say. Our attitudes and actions set the tone for the area we manage. We have a profound influence over our employees. They look to us for leadership. They expect us to know what we are doing and to do it right. When we are deficient, we lose their respect as well as our ability to lead.

The general manager of a property is responsible for everything that happens therein. None of us are capable of doing everything ourselves, so it is necessary to delegate authority and rely on subordinates. The management team we assemble must be able to work together. They must be in agreement and comfortable with company philosophy and values. If they are not, they may have difficulty living the philosophy and values, and, ultimately, may become "Do as I say, not as I do" managers. In the end, they will be far less successful.

As managers, one of our responsibilities is to ensure that we have adequate, well-trained staff, capable and willing to maintain standards set by the organization. Because managers must fit well with the existing culture, it is useful to identify the type of person who will be a good fit as an entry-level manager. Both upper management and those seeking management positions are best served by ensuring wise employment selections.

There are many entry-level hospitality management positions available, but not all of the positions will be a good match for us. Just as we all have our own personalities, likes and dislikes, attitudes and styles, so do companies. Aside from differences in target markets, services, and products, we find that companies' philosophies, values, and management styles are also dissimilar. Our best friends tend to be like us, mirroring our values and backgrounds. Marriages work best when the two partners are more similar than different. Likewise, we need to find management positions with companies that are compatible with who we are and what we like in order for the relationship to be a success.

This is not as easy as it sounds. Weary of poverty after 4 or more years of college, we may overlook differences in philosophies, attitudes, and management styles—due to our eagerness to garner a good wage. We may find that these differences become more important, though, after the newness of the job has worn off and we have become accustomed to having adequate funds. This is a textbook about how to be ethical. We are stressing making good employment choices because it is very difficult to be ethical and make ethical decisions in companies where ethical decision making is not supported by upper management. If companies expect us to behave in ways we are not comfortable with, make decisions we do not like, or treat us in ways we find hurtful, we will most likely choose or be asked to leave the company.

Many hospitality graduates change jobs within the first year out of school because they are unhappy with their chosen companies. Every time we make a job change it costs in terms of seniority, lost time, benefits, moving expenses,

IN THE TRENCHES

Kara Ledbetter, 20, Yuma, AZ

"I got a job working at a little mom-and-pop Italian place last year. On the second day I was given a task that required operating the meat cutter—this machine with a big revolving blade like you see in delis. Problem was, they gave me absolutely no training on it. So . . . I'm cutting some product and, wham-o! Off goes the end of my finger! It was cut down to the bone and looked pretty bad. I was worried that I'd have to go through life minus one fingerprint. So, I found mom and pop and they told me to put on a Band-Aid and keep it elevated, but *don't let the customers see it!* Then, of course, I had to continue working till my shift was over. Anyway, when I got home my parents took me to go to the hospital where I got several stitches. I filed for workman's comp because it was an accident on the job (and I couldn't afford to pay for the hospital visit myself), and then good ol' pop yelled at me for doing that. Yeah, and so I didn't work for mom and pop much longer."

relationships, and so forth. It might be a good idea to analyze potential employers with respect to salary and benefits, of course, but we should also identify how well they match our own attitudes, values, management styles, and philosophies before making an employment decision. Our chance for a long-term successful relationship with a company is increased dramatically when we make a good match.

Naturally, we must know ourselves before we can determine if a company is a good fit for us. It is necessary to honestly appraise our strengths, weaknesses, attitudes, values, and personal goals so that we can make the comparison. Ethics are part of our lives and cannot be looked at outside the context of our lives. In order to live as we believe we should, we must be in situations that allow us to do that. The following Personal Strategic Planning Model is a useful tool enabling us to become more aware of who we really are and what we really want. It is always helpful to answer the questions in writing because the task forces us to use complete thoughts.

Personal Strategic Planning Model

A. Personal Mission Statement
1. State your personal goals and objectives. Include:
   - Career
   - Financial
   - Family
   - Philosophy (values)
   - Other

B. Personal Strategic Planning Process
1. Perform *SWOT* analysis:
   - *S*trengths
   - *W*eaknesses
   - *O*pportunities
   - *T*hreats
2. Examine the environments in which you operate
   - Internal
   - External

C. Summarize Yourself and Your Situation

D. Analyze Prospective Positions and Companies

E. Select the Best-Fit Position

Personal Mission Statement.   Our personal mission statement says who we are, what is important to us, and how we plan to live our lives. It is essential that our mission statement convey these factors truthfully. Answering the following questions about our goals and objectives can help us to determine our own truths. These questions are posed to help us to discern our priorities. As we go through the process, additional questions may occur to us, which can then be incorporated.

Career

1. What job do you see yourself having 2 months after graduation? In 1 year? Five years? Ten years?
2. What level of responsibility do you want to have?
   a. Are you comfortable working for others (owners or supervisors) or would you prefer being your own boss?
   b. How much autonomy do you want and how much do you need?
   c. How patient will you be until you reach your preferred level of responsibility? Are you willing to "put in your time"?

Financial

1. In the same time frame, how much money do you want to be making? (2 months after graduation/1 year/5 years/10 years?)
2. What kind of lifestyle do you wish to have? (2 months after graduation/1 year/5 years/10 years?)
3. How important is money to you?
   a. Is your identity tied up with how much money you make?
   b. Do you need a large amount of savings to feel secure?
4. How much debt do you have now?
   a. What is your attitude toward debt, now and in the future?
   b. Will you buy things on credit? What kinds of things?
5. What do you want to spend your money on? (2 months after graduation/1 year/5 years/10 years?)
6. Is home ownership important to you?
   a. What kind of dwelling?
   b. How much would it cost?

Family

1. How important is family to you?
   a. How often do you want to see your parents/brothers/sisters/etc.?
2. Do you want to marry? By when would you like to be married?
   a. What type of person would you like your husband/wife to be?
   b. Do you want to be a dual-career couple? Would either career take precedence over the other?
3. Do you want to have children? When? How many?
   a. Who will take care of the children while they are very young?

    b. Will you put money aside for their college educations?
4. Will you want to stay in one place and put down roots or are you willing to relocate occasionally?
    a. How might moving affect your immediate and extended family?

Philosophical

1. What are your personal values? (Use the Ethical Principles for Hospitality Managers in Chapter 1 to help define your personal values.)
2. Can you comfortably accept other people's personal values if they are different from yours?
3. How able are you to differentiate between what you can and cannot control (such as other people's opinions and behavior)?

Other

1. What if physical/medical conditions (or other responsibilities) arise that need to be taken into consideration?

Personal Strategic Planning Process. Career or life planning involves looking ahead and determining where we want to be in the future. We consider long-range goals when making present decisions that will take us in the direction we wish to go. Accepting a position with a hospitality organization will move us closer to our eventual goal, move us away from our eventual goal, or put us in a holding pattern. If we have not identified the long-term goal, we will not know if we are going in the right direction.

    Goals must be feasible if they are to be reached. Particular skills and character traits are necessary for the various positions in the hospitality industry. The next set of questions is helpful in identifying our strengths, weaknesses, opportunities, and threats. This information is useful in determining the feasibility of goals and, ultimately, in finding a position with a good fit.

Strengths

1. What are you good at? What do you like to do? What are you willing to spend time on?

2. Are you an extravert or an introvert? (One is not better than the other—we must, however, make life choices that are in line with the way we are as individuals.)

3. Are you a good problem solver? (Can you look at a situation and figure out what's wrong, then devise a solution? How long will this take?)

4. Are you a good team player? Can you follow the directions of superiors?

5. Are you cautious or spontaneous? (Do you make decisions quickly or prefer to think things over? Are you driven or laid back?)

6. Are you a good communicator? How well do you get along with others? Are you comfortable with diverse types of people?

7. How do you rate on organizational skills? Time management? Attention span?

Strengths and weaknesses oftentimes are at the opposite ends of skill or character trait continuums. A successful entrepreneur may not have the interest, skills, and character traits necessary for long-term growth and management. The idea is to identify our particular strengths so we can look for a position that properly utilizes and honors them.

Weaknesses

What are you not good at? What do you not like to do? What are you not willing to spend time on? We can ask ourselves the same types of questions we pondered in the "Strengths" section above. We can identify any other weak points we may have. Some weaknesses can be strengthened. Other weaknesses must be identified so we can make sure our job performance will not be focused on them. Again, the idea is to identify our weaknesses and look for a position that utilizes and honors our strengths and not our weaknesses.

Opportunities

1. Which hospitality companies are recruiting at your school?

2. What positions do they make available for your hospitality graduates?

3. Are there other hospitality companies that do not recruit at your school?

4. Are there other opportunities available besides work in restaurants and hotels?

5. What career ladders exist within the hospitality companies? (Recruiters can be asked questions of this nature to determine future opportunities.)

6. Can you grow with the company? Are there tuition benefits and/or management development programs?

Threats

1. Recent downturns in the economy have resulted in hiring freezes and layoffs in some hotels. What is the state of the economy now and what is the prognosis for the future? How might this eventually affect you?
2. What is the financial status of the companies you are considering? Are they competitive today and will they be so in the future?
3. Are you considering a management career with a company that may lose its customer appeal as trends change?
4. Do you have any personal threats or impending disasters just waiting to happen in your life? What about any old business/personal baggage that might unpleasantly resurface?
5. Are you making lifestyle choices (drugs, alcohol, sex, gambling, compulsive shopping, etc.) that could interfere with your success?
6. Do you have health issues?
7. Are you too reliant on credit? Is your debt load manageable now and will it be so in the future?

The Environments in Which We Operate.   Companies do business in external environments they have no control over, such as competitors, suppliers, the economy, regulations and laws, social pressures, human resource availability, and so forth. They may have slightly more control over internal environments such as their own workers, organizational goals, and company policy. We also operate within external and internal environments that we most likely have little or no control over. It is useful to identify these environments so that we clearly and realistically understand the constraints we may be under.

Internal Environments

1. What expectations does your family have for you?
2. Do you belong to any social networks (churches or other personal organizations) that have expectations for you?
3. Do you have social, family, and/or other networks that support and care for you? Are there other people in your life that you care about?

External Environments

1. How do you intend to get to and from work? Do you own or plan to purchase a car? Are you close to freeways? What about public transportation? Is it sufficient for your needs?
2. How important is health insurance? Would its inclusion be an integral part of any prospective employment/benefits package?
3. How safe from economic forces is the prospective employer?

We all must live within environments where we have no immediate control such as the economy, rules and regulations, the legal system, the health care system, transportation system, insurance, and so forth. How might any of these external environments affect us now or in the future?

Summarize Yourself and Your Situation.   We may use our answers to all the above questions in constructing a summary profile of ourselves—who we are, what's important to us, our strengths and weaknesses, the type of position and company we would thrive in. The next step is to go through the same type of process to identify the mission, strengths, weaknesses, opportunities, and threats for each company we are interested in working for. Let us pretend we are interested in a fictional full-service hotel called the Freshwater Oasis Inn.

THE FRESHWATER OASIS INN CASE STUDY

Our case study involves a small full-service hotel. We will be analyzing situations that occur in the various departments of the hotel in the remaining chapters of the text. The situations, while occurring in a fictitious hotel, are real dilemmas hospitality managers must be able to deal with effectively. The Ethical Analysis Form affords us a systematic process for recognizing and dealing with ethical dilemmas.

Freshwater Oasis Inn Description

The Freshwater Oasis Inn (FOI) is a fictitious 100-room, full-service hotel. Our target market is upper-middle-class professionals who expect excellent service within a quiet, safe, and attractive setting.

FOI is located in Copper Hills, Arizona, just 20 minutes from Phoenix International Airport. Despite being newly constructed, great pains were taken to give the hotel an old Southwest kind of feel while incorporating the best that modern technology has to offer. Professionally landscaped gardens overlook the rugged desert from most vantage points on the premises. The *Lobby* is spacious with white painted adobe walls and vaulted ceilings. Highly polished sandstone covers the lobby floor and is continued on the surface of the Front Desk. Nearby, the *Sitting Room* welcomes guests with comfortable overstuffed chairs and a large, stone fireplace. Guests and visitors feel at home in this relaxed atmosphere. The *Oasis Lounge* is adjacent to the Sitting Room and provides beautiful garden views while offering a wide range of liquid refreshments, including our own private-label draft beers. An abbreviated menu is available from which guests can order appetizers or sandwiches while the kitchen is open.

A breakfast buffet featuring fresh fruits and home-baked pastries, along with cooked-to-order eggs, is served each morning in the *Garden Vista*. Weather permitting, a wall of Spanish-style arched doors can be opened, ushering in the soothing sounds of nature: water fountains, birds, and softly rustling leaves. Lunch is served either inside or on the patio where wrought-iron tables and chairs surround a meandering pool stocked with goldfish. Chef Eric prepares healthful, eye-catching dishes selected to delight our guests' palates and please their sensibilities. In the evening, the Garden Vista is filled with fresh flowers while small antique candelabras are lit on each table to set the mood. There are separate lunch and dinner menus, as well as daily specials with a Southwestern flare.

FOI has state-of-the-art audio/visual equipment and conference facilities perfect for small- to medium-sized groups. The patio is enchanting for weddings or special events. There is a large in-ground pool for guests. Amenities provided in each room include a TV, small refrigerator with mini-bar, hair dryer, BOSE radio, and Internet access. There is a safe at the front desk for guests' valuables, and, for a small charge, housekeeping will take care of their dry-cleaning needs. FOI provides agreeable accommodations for business travel or just an appealing time-out from the day's routine.

Freshwater Oasis Inn Organizational Chart

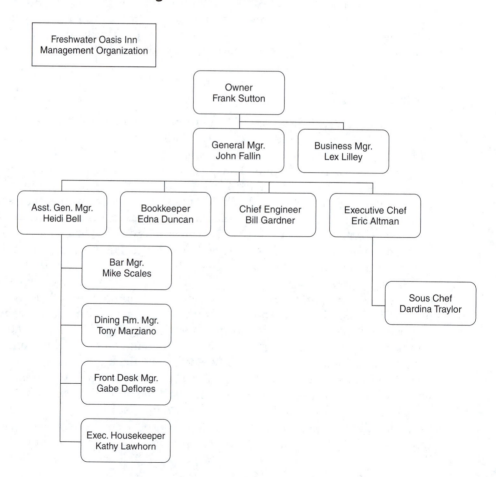

Freshwater Oasis Inn Management Profiles

General Manager: John Fallin, 46, was hired 6 years ago to open and manage FOI. He has an MBA from Stanford and for 5 years was food and beverage manager for a large, successful hotel in Los Angeles. His experience, combined with a refreshing vision for the inn, convinced owner Frank Stratton that John could make his business a success. As part of his contract, John has the opportunity to make a year-end bonus based on job performance and occupancy rates.

John compensated for his lack of comprehensive experience by hiring excellent people in top management positions. His emphasis is on FOI as a team. He allows them a certain amount of autonomy but provides guidance to ensure that the needs of the target market are met. His mantra is that managers be courteous, caring, and professional.

Assistant General Manager: Heidi Bell, 32, has been with John since opening. She has worked nearly every job in the hotel business over the past 14 years. Her last position was front desk manager at the elegant Bennett Arms downtown. Heidi felt her lack of formal education, however, was limiting her career and believed that FOI offered more responsibility, autonomy, and potential.

Front Desk Manager: Gabe Deflores, 26, has a degree in sociology but grew restless after 3 years in urban social services. He worked the front desk at two major hotels before coming to FOI. He supervises the AM and PM front desk employees and the night auditor.

Dining Room Manager: Tony Marziano, 31, began waiting tables at FOI 5 years ago. He has been supervising waitstaff the past 2 years. In addition to scheduling servers, he is also in charge of the host/hostesses and splits time between both positions.

Bar Manager: Mike Scales, 27, opened FOI as a server and moved behind the bar a year later. He was promoted 2 years ago and manages a staff of six along with his duties of inventory and ordering.

Bookkeeper: Edna Duncan, 57, is a close friend of Frank's who worked as a CPA at a major firm 25 years before embracing semi-retirement. Her limited duties at FOI amount to roughly 20 hours a week.

Executive Chef: Eric Altman, 39, received training at the Culinary Institute of Chicago and has worked some of the country's top hotels and restaurants. He wanted stability and less stress in a smaller operation and has been content at FOI these past 5 years. Similar to John's contract with Frank, Eric is also eligible for a year-end bonus based on performance and restaurant sales. He is responsible for all food service activities and supervises cooks and dishwashers on the day shift.

Sous Chef: Dardina Traylor, 22, was hired by Chef Eric 4 years ago to wash dishes. She began helping him with prep and soon moved into that position full time. She has been in formal training under Chef Eric for the past 2 years and was promoted in the last year to Sous Chef. Part of her responsibilities are to supervise cooks and dishwashers on the evening shift.

Executive Housekeeper: Kathy Lawhorn, 33, completed her hospitality degree and worked 10 years at a large hotel chain before coming to FOI. Kathy supervises housekeeping and the in-house laundry/dry-cleaning staff.

Chief Engineer: Bill Gardner, 53, worked 15 years as an assistant engineer at a high-rise apartment building in Phoenix. After completing union school and getting his license, Bill came to work for FOI at the hotel's opening. In addition to supervising a maintenance staff of four, he is also responsible for maintaining the in-ground pool and scheduling lifeguards.

Analysis of Freshwater Oasis Inn

We are allowed and need to ask questions and do research about prospective companies. We can find descriptions of the property, financial information, history of the property, plans for the future, mission statements, turnover rates, and so forth. We start by collecting any available information about the property. If we live nearby, a trip to the hotel (perhaps experiencing lunch) will enable us to observe how everyone works together and might be enlightening. We could also access the hotel Web page or do research at the library. We may know someone who works there or did so in the past, and we can contact that person for any information they could provide. And, of course, we can ask questions during a job interview.

The mission statement describes who the company is, what they do, and what they believe in. The Freshwater Oasis Inn's Mission Statement was found on its Web page and is as follows:

Mission of the Freshwater Oasis Inn

Our mission is to be successful as the most delightful, small, full-service hotel in Arizona. Our guests are valued and our gracious staff and facilities exceed their expectations. We value our staff and demonstrate it with higher-than-average wages, benefits, and respectful treatment within a teamwork environment. We promote from within whenever possible and have ongoing professional development for all employees.

We found that the Freshwater Oasis Inn is owned by Frank Stratton and appears to be financially stable. The 6 year-old establishment is located in Copper Hills, Arizona, and there are plans for expansion into other markets. There is little turnover among management, and it is reputed to be a good place to work. We were unable to visit FOI, but had friends who had stayed there who intimated to us that the staff was low key, polite, friendly, and very helpful. They described the visual impact of the inn as, "delightful."

If we knew an employee of FOI we could learn about management styles, pace, the working environment, how much autonomy was afforded management and staff, and so forth. While it is good to like the facility and its guests, it is the information mentioned above that enables us to determine whether or not we will enjoy actually working there. As prospective employees, however, we may have no way of obtaining this information prior to the initial interview.

If we are upper management hiring entry-level management, we can identify our company's management style, pace, working environment, level of autonomy, and so forth, because we too will need to know the type of person who fits well at our operation. A slow-moving, laid-back, casual person would not fit well in a fast-paced, highly structured, formal environment, even if he or she has all the necessary skills.

FOI has identified the culture and working environment as "family-like." That is, friendly, caring, and open with each other—but, as with families, sometimes one or more members can get out of sorts. Management at FOI never allows personal problems to interfere with guest service. They try to be sympathetic and helpful, realizing that all of us deal with life's ups and downs. While there is a hierarchal management structure at FOI, management is nonauthoritative and open to any and all suggestions from staff. Management recognizes the importance of every position and considers its role as another equally valuable part making up the whole.

Quality of life is the main reason several members of the management team are at FOI. The working atmosphere is generally relaxed. Employees and management are encouraged to enjoy their work and relationships with each other. Harassment of any kind, however, is strictly prohibited so that all employees can feel safe and comfortable while at FOI.

Summary Profile of a Freshwater Oasis Inn Manager

Managers of the Freshwater Oasis Inn will fit best if they are somewhat relaxed and able to deal with problems and changes without getting upset. They must put the guest's comfort and desires first, while at the same time caring about the comfort and desires of staff. They need to enjoy people and appreciate diversity. They should be teachers who enable all of their employees to be the best that they can be. Professional management at FOI means being committed to excellence.

Select the Best-Fit Position

Once we have summarized ourselves and our situations, and then analyzed prospective positions and companies, we will be ready to select the best-fit position as per the Personal Strategic Planning Model. We compare our own needs in terms of pay, benefits, location, promotion opportunities, and so forth, with those offered by the particular company. We compare the summary profile of ourselves with the summary profile of the type of person who will fit in well with the company. While the match does not have to be perfect, the closer it is, the better our chance for success.

It can be scary to be out of a job. We might be reluctant to turn down an offer from a company that is not a good match for us, fearing that we might not get another offer. There is a slight possibility that the position might work out better than our analysis led us to expect, but it would be naive to count on that. There will be consequences for the decision to either take or not take the ill-fitting job, and we can use the Ethical Analysis Form to systematically determine the possible consequences and thus be able to make an informed decision.

We often think in either/or terms. There are generally more options available if we take the time to consider them. In the case of the ill-fitting position (depending on the consequences), it might be advisable to take a temporary job to tide us over and keep up the job search for a better-fitting position. Another possibility might be to take a lesser position in a company that was a good fit, and, through good work, progress into management from within the company. Let us identify the stakeholders in our decision whether or not to take the ill-fitting position and the questions we might ask ourselves in order to determine possible consequences.

We begin our analysis by stating the decision option. In this case we will identify the consequences of taking an entry-level management position at the Freshwater Oasis Inn when it may not be a good fit. Then we note all the parties who may be affected by a newly hired entry-level manager. Obviously, a newly hired entry-level manager will be affected by whether or not he or she is a good fit for the culture of FOI. His or her family and friends, employees who will be supervised by the new manager, upper management, and FOI itself may all be affected by whether or not he or she is a good match for the inn.

Let us pretend that Jane applied for an entry-level management position at FOI. Jane did her Personal Strategic Plan and determined herself to be as follows.

Summary Profile of Jane

I am 23 years old and recently graduated from hospitality management school. I worked summers at a day-care center and lived at home with my parents who paid for my education. I had a full semester internship at a local hotel. I prefer structure and like to know exactly what I am to do, when, and how. I am very neat and do not like chaos. I want a career until I marry and would eventually like to have two children.

While this analysis is not directly about ethics, most everything may indirectly be about ethics. Are we honest to ourselves and to others? Are we committed to excellence? Are we being trustworthy? Are we honoring our own convictions? What about our own morale? Our respect and concern for others, and ourselves? We can use a modified Ethics Analysis Form to help us identify the possible outcomes to any decision we must make. In the "Consequences" column are questions that we can ask in determination of them.

Ethics Analysis Form

Decision Option: Take an entry-level management position at FOI when it may not be a good fit.

Stakeholders	Consequences
Newly hired entry-level manager (Jane)	• Jane is pleased with the salary and the location of FOI. • Will she like the other managers? Will they like her? Will she fit in with the other managers? • What if they don't like each other? What if she doesn't fit in? Will she like her job if she doesn't fit in? Will she enjoy going to work? Will she be willing to put in overtime? • Will she be able to work effectively with the other managers? Will she have to put up with behavior or attitudes she finds offensive? How will she do this?
Jane's family and friends	• If Jane is unhappy at her job, how will this affect her family and friends? Will they get tired of listening to her complain? Will it affect Jane's relationship with them? • If Jane has a boyfriend and is always frustrated and/or unhappy about work, could this have a negative effect on their relationship?
Employees supervised by Jane	• What will employees think of Jane? Will they appreciate that she is different from other managers? How might they react to her management style? • Will Jane be able to inspire and get the best work from her employees? Will they follow her?
Upper management	• What will upper management think of Jane? Will upper management know if the other managers do not like her? How could this affect upper management's attitude toward Jane? • If need be, will upper management take the time to help Jane get along with everyone and be more effective? What if they will not? Will Jane be promoted?
FOI	• How will Jane feel about FOI if she is not getting along well there? How might this affect her work? • If Jane does not like FOI, would others know? Could this affect FOI's reputation? How? • If the employees she supervises are not happy with Jane, how might this affect the guests? FOI?

It is quite possible that Jane will get along just fine. She may be a bit uncomfortable at first but could grow to like many of the managers and they her. If she is too rigid, however, it is more than likely it will not work out, and Jane, and everyone around her, will be miserable. She might be better off considering another option. From upper management's perspective, Jane is probably not the best choice for the position at Freshwater Oasis Inn. We can avoid problems as managers and/or prospective employees by analyzing both the company and the applicant to determine if the match is good.

We cannot know for sure whether or not a position will be a good match for us. Some positions may begin as very good matches and then a change in administration or policy can alter the fit. Just as it is good to know someone before you marry him or her, it is a good idea to get to know a company or an employee before making an employment commitment. Dating is the means for determining whether we want to marry someone and analysis is the means for determining whether a person is a good match for a position. Neither means is failproof, but we can reduce the risk of a bad match and all the torment that goes with it.

CONCLUSION

Mistakes in choosing a position in a company or in hiring an employee can be costly in terms of time, money, and pain. It behooves employers and job applicants to pay close attention to both the needs and characteristics of the company—and the needs and characteristics of the applicant—in order to make a good match for the person to the job.

The Freshwater Oasis Inn, the hotel in the continuing case study, was described, and the management team of FOI was introduced in this chapter. We presented an example of the job match analysis process for an entry-level management position at the inn using a modification of the Ethics Analysis Form.

This is a textbook about ethics and how to make ethical decisions in the hospitality industry. Ethics, however, do not stand alone and are part of most every situation in which we are involved. It is much easier to be ethical and to do the right thing when we are part of an ethical community or organization, because doing the right thing is part of the culture. When doing the right thing is not part of the culture, we may have to buck the system to make the ethical choice, and bucking the system often results in problems for both the organization and the employee.

Our goal is that all hospitality managers make ethical choices every time. However, to do that with the least amount of pain requires that we make good employment choices to begin with. We must choose companies where ethical decisions are expected and honored. If we are hiring managers, we must choose people who will be able to make the ethical decisions our companies require. We do not just guess and hope for the best when considering management positions for ourselves, nor do we cross our fingers and rely on luck when considering the hiring of management applicants. The analysis process described in this chapter is a means that can facilitate good employment selections. It is through these good employment selections that we can avoid the pain of having to buck the system.

CHAPTER THOUGHT QUESTIONS

1. Think about the various managers you have worked for in the past (or teachers you have had). Which manager had the most beneficial influence on you? Describe this influence and discuss why and how the particular manager was able to affect you.

2. Which manager or teacher had the least beneficial influence on you? Discuss why.

3. Think about the various jobs you have held. Describe the one that was the best match for you. What made it so? How did this job differ from other jobs that may not have been such good matches?

4. Discuss the difference between a good match between a person and a job and a good match between a person and a company. Illustrate your discussion with examples from your own working life or from someone you know.

5. Why is it important for companies and individuals to write mission statements? How do mission statements affect decision making?

6. Use the Personal Strategic Planning Model and write you own personal mission statement.

7. Perform SWOT analysis on your own life and put it in writing.

8. Examine the environments you operate in as per the Personal Strategic Planning Model.

9. Write a summary of yourself and your situation as per the Personal Strategic Planning Model.

10. Describe organizations and positions you believe you are best suited for.

REFERENCE

Jaszay, C. (2002). Finding the right management position. *Hosteur, 11*(1), 17–21.

Chapter 4

Ethics and Front Office Management

The first three chapters of the text served as an introduction to ethics. The next seven chapters will analyze ethical dilemmas within various operations departments of the Freshwater Oasis Inn. This chapter will analyze a situation that arises and must be dealt with by front office staff. We will also take an in-depth look at courtesy and civility, because the way we comport ourselves relates to our ability to be ethical.

FRONT OFFICE

The front office is oftentimes described as the "heart" of the hotel. Its desk is located in the lobby and is where guests check in and out. Front desk personnel have direct contact with the guests and this is where problems, complaints, and/or requests are handled. In addition, much of the interdepartmental communication flows through the front office, and about 66% of hotel revenues generate from the rooms division, which the front office manages.

The front office may be called the *front desk* or perhaps *guest services*. No matter how it is referred to, it is the primary contact point for guests at the hotel and, thus, of primary importance.

FRONT DESK AT FRESHWATER OASIS INN

An elderly guest at FOI, Meta Adams, called the front desk to complain about noise coming from a nearby room. (Please see "No Ifs, Ands, or Butts," in the case study at the back of the text.) The front desk manager, Gabe Deflores, answered the call.

Gabe was introduced in the last chapter. He is 26 and has a degree in sociology, but grew restless after 3 years in urban social services. He worked the front desk at two major hotels before coming to FOI. He supervises the AM and

IN THE TRENCHES

John Henley, 22, Little Rock, AR

"The summer after 9/11 I was working front desk at the Embassy Suites in Little Rock. A suspicious looking man came in with a letter for a local anchorman who was staying at the hotel. I thought nothing of it and accepted the letter. Later, though, my boss (the AGM) asked about the letter. He was worried about *anthrax*. Having no recourse, I gave him the letter and he opened it with the housekeeping manager and myself as witnesses. Turns out there was nothing life threatening (phew) . . . so he directed me to repackage the letter. I can understand his concern, but tampering with people's property seems a bit over-the-top. And handling anthrax is a job better suited for the HASMAT guys anyway."

PM front desk clerks as well as the night auditor (same duties as desk clerk, but also responsible for running day's end reports). Gabe reports to the Assistant General Manager, Heidi Bell.

After verifying the location and validity of the complaint, Gabe asked the guest, Seymore Butts, to turn down his music. Mr. Butts responded by offering Gabe a $100 bribe to overlook the noise. This segment of the case study requires that Gabe, as Front Desk Manager, make a decision. We will use the Ethics Analysis Form and work our way through the case to determine which decision results in the least possible negative consequences for the most people.

STATE THE PROBLEM

We cannot figure out solutions if we have not identified the problem we are trying to solve. We cannot make good decisions if we have not identified the purpose of the decision. To analyze for best solutions or decisions the first thing we must always do is *state the problem*. Starting with stating the problem seems obvious, yet many of us skip this step or have difficulty identifying the real problem. Some of us have a tendency to act before thinking. We may feel that it is our responsibility to do something and to do it immediately, but when we skip the analysis step we run the risk of acting in an ineffective and, perhaps, detrimental way. We may discover that we are in worse shape than before, and ultimately find ourselves having to correct the correction.

Others of us may tend to react to situations. For example, Bob gets angry at Mary. The initial reason for Bob's anger is lost to Mary as she reacts to Bob's tantrum by getting angry in return. Had Bob taken the time to precisely define what he was angry about and what he wanted from Mary, he could have presented his feelings in a way that did not block Mary's reception of his message. Thinking ahead about reactions we wish to elicit from others can help us to better phrase our requests. When we react to whatever another person says or does, we are in essence giving that person control over our behavior.

The opposite of reactive is **proactive.** To be proactive is to think in advance how we will handle situations that could arise in the future. If we have a **contingency plan,** we will simply employ whatever actions we have predetermined to be appropriate when the situation arises. If *this* happens, then we will do *that*. To be proactive is to be in control of our own behavior.

Some of us may experience feelings such as anger, sadness, or annoyance, and we may act on the sensation without identifying why we feel the way we do. If we do not know why we are angry at someone and yet strike out in anger, perhaps over something unimportant, we will most likely have to deal with the other person's reaction to our inappropriate anger. We may find ourselves apologizing for getting angry at the person for no good reason, but still be angry because we never addressed the real reason for our anger, and it remains unresolved.

Our ability to state the problem is sometimes related to whether or not we feel that we have control over our lives. If we sense that we have no control over our lives and find ourselves asking, "Why me?" every time something happens, we may not see any need for identifying the problem. If, on the other hand, we feel confident about the direction of our lives, we must identify any problems in order to determine how to correct them.

Again, to Mary in our previous example. She has been out of work for a while and feels scared. Her car will not start before a very important job interview. If Mary feels that she has no control over her life, she might react by crying: "Everything is ruined! I'll never get a job! Nothing ever works out for me! Even my car hates me!" If, however, Mary feels that she has control over her life, she might be more rational and instead think to herself: "Why won't this car start? Am I out of gas? Is the battery dead? Can I fix this in time to get to the interview? What is an alternative way to get to the interview if I can't fix it in time?" And so forth.

Mary, in the second reaction to her car not starting, began by stating the problem: "The car will not start." She then tried to figure out why that was the case—no gas, dead battery. She weighed possibilities within the context of the short time she had to make the interview, and, if she could not get the car started in time, she began thinking of alternative ways to get to the interview. Mary's **internal locus of control,** in the second reaction, allows her to consider solutions, try them out, and devise other possibilities if those solutions do not work. In the first reaction, Mary's **external locus of control** makes her a victim of circumstances and gets in the way of her ability to even consider possible solutions.

To identify the problem, we may have to ask ourselves specific questions such as: "What do I feel? What do I want? What is the problem here?" When Mr. Butts proposed the $100 bribe for Gabe to forget about the noise complaint, and then said, "Whadaya say?" Gabe was forced into an immediate decision. This is a situation where it would be nice to have a contingency plan in place: If someone offers me a bribe, then I will _____. That is the point of this textbook, so that when a situation arises we know how to handle it.

Because this is a case study, we are able to step back from the situation in which Gabe finds himself. We can take time to identify the problem and come up with the best possible decision. The obvious dilemma is whether or not to take the bribe. There is, however, the other problem of what to do about Miss Adams's complaint. We can analyze the various decision options using the Ethical Analysis Form. Let us begin with the option to take the $100 and disregard Miss Adams's complaint. We enter the selected decision option on the blank Ethical Analysis Form. Other decision options would be to take the $100 while attempting to satisfy Miss Adams at the same time, refuse the $100 and satisfy Miss Adams instead of Mr. Butts, or refuse the $100 and try to satisfy both Miss Adams and Mr. Butts.

Without a contingency plan in place, we might not be prepared to deal with this situation. We might, in a split second, think that nobody would ever discover that we took the $100. Most of us would be delighted to have an unexpected influx of cash. We might think Miss Adams is just some crabby old lady who is nowhere near as important as a rock star. We might go ahead and take the $100 for fear of insulting Mr. Butts. A predetermined contingency plan allows us the time, while not under pressure, to adequately think through all the possible consequences for this decision.

IDENTIFYING THE STAKEHOLDERS

Our decisions affect other people. We identify all those whom our decisions might affect in order to be aware of possible consequences to them that, if we know, might influence our decision. A decision made to accept a job in another state, without considering the desires of a spouse, could result in marital difficulties. Marital difficulties could adversely affect the person's performance on the new job, which then could result in . . . and so on.

Gabe's decision will most certainly have professional and personal ramifications for himself, as well as the two guests, Miss Adams and Mr. Butts. His decision could also affect FOI employees and even the financial health of the inn. We enter these identified stakeholders on the blank Ethics Analysis Form. This exercise constitutes a format that will aid us in systematically asking questions as to how each stakeholder will be affected by the decision option we are analyzing. We enter answers to the questions as we go down the list of stakeholders. A completed Ethics Analysis Form follows the upcoming discussion of possible consequences if Gabe takes the bribe and ignores Miss Adams's complaints.

ANALYSIS OF POSSIBLE CONSEQUENCES FOR GABE

We begin our analysis by asking questions. What is the best thing that could happen to Gabe if he takes the money? What is the worst thing? What will Mr. Butts expect of him if he takes the money? Will there be additional special service requests by Mr. Butts if he accepts the bribe? How will his taking the money affect Miss Adams, other guests, and his staff? Are the wishes of one guest more important than those of another? Will the noise complaint go any further than Gabe? Could Gabe's boss get involved? How could this affect Gabe? Could Gabe's staff ever find out that he took the $100? How would this affect Gabe? How would this affect the behavior of Gabe's staff? How would this affect Gabe's ability to manage his staff?

We have identified the $100 correctly as a bribe. Gabe, however, in the heat of the moment, might not perceive the $100 as so. He could think of the sum as payment for having to deal with an unwanted noise problem—a tip from a guest with special needs. We have a human tendency to justify doing things we might know deep down are not right. To determine if an action is right or not, we might want to ask ourselves what our boss would think of it. Gabe would probably not even dream of telling his boss, Heidi, because she most certainly would not perceive the $100 as a tip.

We humans sometimes try to protect ourselves from truths we might not want to accept. Taking a bribe is wrong. Taking a tip is not wrong. If we identify something as wrong, we either refrain from doing it or we knowingly do something wrong. Most of us think of ourselves as ethical people, so to maintain this self-identity we might not want to look too hard at the action. We can accept a "tip" and still consider ourselves to be ethical. Perceptions are not necessarily reality.

Gabe is paid a salary by FOI and is expected to handle guest complaints as part of his job. Managers generally do not accept tips. If under special circumstances they have occasion to do so (private parties, weddings, etc.), they would in turn be dispersed to appropriate tipped employees. It is unlikely that Gabe would be giving the $100 to other employees in this case. If Gabe does not take the $100, he is not losing anything because he did not deserve the money to begin with. If he accepts the money, it may be easier for him to take a bribe at another time. Practice allows us to become desensitized to questionable behavior.

Mr. Butts considers the $100 a payoff, not a tip, enabling the continued playing of his radio at full blast. Gabe, by accepting the money, would be agreeing to prolong the disturbance. If the loud music continues, Gabe or his staff may have to deal with other guest complaints. Some guests may be bothered by the noise but will not complain. Dissatisfied customers do not come back, and they usually tell their friends about their experience.

Miss Adams could confront the rock star directly if Gabe does not address her complaint, and a nasty scene might occur. She could take her complaint to the general manager if she felt that she was being ignored by Gabe. His superior might question Gabe as to why the complaint was not addressed to the satisfaction of the guest. Gabe could find himself in trouble for not doing his job adequately. At the very least, he could lose the trust of upper management.

In time, if Gabe learned that one of his front desk clerks also took a bribe from a guest, he might be more inclined to overlook the offense. If offenses are overlooked by management, they tend to increase. Gabe's ability to effectively manage his staff could be reduced, as his employees become aware that he does not seem to care what they do. Gabe's failure to deal with the noise complaint will be noted by his employees, and they could also become resentful if they have to deal with his unfinished business.

ANALYSIS OF POSSIBLE CONSEQUENCES FOR MISS ADAMS

We must keep in mind what we are trying to accomplish with this analysis. We are attempting to anticipate all possible consequences for making the decision to accept the $100 from Mr. Butts and ignoring Miss Adams's complaint. We began by asking questions about how this decision could affect Gabe. Next, we ask questions to determine how the decision could affect Miss Adams. How might Miss Adams feel? What might Miss Adams do if she is ignored?

Miss Adams is obviously upset and unlikely to drop the matter if her complaints are not addressed. She will most likely continue to complain and could ask to speak to the general manager if the noise does not cease. It is possible she could go to Mr. Butts and personally request that he be quiet. Mr. Butts could refuse or even tell Miss Adams that he "took care" of the noise complaint with the desk guy (Gabe).

Miss Adams is elderly, and, while she is unlikely to become violent, she could have a stroke or heart attack due to the stress of the situation. If she survived the ordeal, though, she would probably relate her dissatisfaction with FOI to friends and family, which could negatively affect the inn's reputation. If her complaints were ignored, Miss Adams might feel that management did not care whether or not she was enjoying her stay. She could assume that her business was not appreciated and that FOI management put Mr. Butts's pleasure before her comfort. She might even leave before her anticipated departure date.

SEYMORE BUTTS

If Gabe accepts the $100, Mr. Butts would assume it is okay to continue playing his music as loud as he likes. He would think that a bribe ensured that his comfort was more important than that of the other guests. His behavior could actually get worse as the night progresses. This possibility would pose additional problems for other guests and the front desk staff.

Mr. Butts could tell his friends about FOI being a cool place to stay, where his identity was protected and a payoff to front desk employees took care of any problems. Mr. Butts, however, does not match the target market of FOI, and his friends may not be the guests of choice either. On the other hand, the worst thing that could happen if Gabe did not take the $100 is that Mr. Butts could get angry, cause a scene, trash his room, and either check out or be asked to leave.

ANALYSIS OF POSSIBLE CONSEQUENCES
FOR OTHER EMPLOYEES

What effect will Gabe's handling of the noise complaint have on other staff members? Employees of FOI will surely notice that Mr. Butts is allowed to continue making noise. They may be aware of Miss Adams's complaints. They might wonder why the front desk manager is not doing something about the problem.

After Gabe has gone home for the day, his own staff might be called on to do something about the noise. They might feel resentment that Gabe left them with this problem. The front desk staff could lose respect for Gabe for not controlling Mr. Butts's behavior. If another of the desk clerks went to Mr. Butts's room later to ask him to turn down his music, the rock star might mention that he already took care of the noise problem with Gabe. Or, he might figure that everyone at FOI has his or her hands out—and offer the new desk person a bribe as well.

Gabe's employees could feel uncomfortable that their supervisor is not handling guest problems properly. If they found out about the bribe, they might feel that they should either confront Gabe directly or bring this matter to the attention of his superior. Some employees might take another route and determine that it must be okay for them to take bribes too. Gabe's staff could become less cooperative, and turnover and productivity could be negatively affected.

ANALYSIS OF POSSIBLE CONSEQUENCES
FOR FRESHWATER OASIS INN

FOI has the reputation of being a safe and quiet place to stay. If Gabe does not make sure that guests are protected, FOI's reputation could be harmed. Guests who are bothered by noise during their stay may not come back to the inn again. They could tell family and friends that FOI is not a quiet place to stay. Word of mouth could decrease new and repeat business, resulting in a loss of customers and revenue.

Gabe could lose the respect of his staff for not taking care of problems. His staff might find out about the bribe and this could affect morale. Lowered morale affects job satisfaction and turnover. Front desk employees might need to be retrained in desired appropriate behavior. Gabe's boss could find out that he did not handle guest complaints satisfactorily. John or Heidi could learn that Gabe took a bribe. In either situation, Gabe could be disciplined and/or terminated. Termination would incur expenses to recruit, hire, and train a replacement front desk manager.

ETHICAL PRINCIPLES VIOLATED BY THIS DECISION

As we go along, we record answers to the questions we ask about each of the stakeholders in the "Consequences" column on the Ethics Analysis Form. We can now go back over each of the answers and determine if any of the ethical principles would be violated by any of the consequences. We can simply go down the list of ethical principles starting with Honesty and ask: "Do any of these consequences violate Honesty? How about Integrity?" And so forth. We enter the violated principles in the "Principles" column on the Ethics Analysis Form.

Taking a bribe is not an honest thing to do. Gabe is paid by FOI to ensure guest satisfaction. FOI would not want Gabe taking $100 from a guest to overlook the guest's noise, which is disturbing another guest. Gabe also assured Miss Adams that he would take care of the noise problem. To not take care of it would be tantamount to lying to Miss Adams, so we can write "Honesty" as a violated principle on the Ethics Analysis Form.

Integrity involves doing the right thing no matter if anyone knows or not. Accepting a bribe is not an act of integrity, so we can enter "Integrity" on the Ethics Analysis Form. Upper management may or may not know that they can "Trust" Gabe to handle a guest complaint in an appropriate manner. Gabe's employees may feel they cannot trust Gabe to do his job the way they would expect. Management's trust is violated by the act of taking a bribe, and his poor handling of the complaint violates his employee's trust.

Management's "loyalty" is to be with the company. Gabe, in taking a bribe to overlook a guest's noise, was being loyal to the offending guest rather than to the company. As the front desk manager, Gabe would be required to discipline any employees who would take a bribe from a guest to overlook inappropriate behavior. It would not be "fair" to punish an employee for doing what a manager does.

If Gabe chooses to ignore Miss Adams's noise complaints, he will be exhibiting a lack of "concern and respect for others." Also, "a commitment to excellence" requires that we do our best work always. Taking $100 and allowing Mr. Butts to ruin Miss Adams's peace and quiet works against the mission of the inn and would not constitute an example of Gabe doing his best work.

We lead by example. Taking a bribe is not a good example and could have the effect of encouraging employees to do things that would hurt FOI. The "reputation" of the inn and the "morale" of employees could be harmed if Gabe chooses to take the $100 from Mr. Butts. Managers are "accountable" for their actions. It is unlikely that Gabe would tell his boss that he took the $100 from Mr. Butts. He would pocket the bribe with the hopes that no one would ever know.

So, taking the money is not a good idea. Every single ethical principle will be violated if Gabe decides to take the $100 and ignore Miss Adams's complaint. To take the bribe and ignore the noise complaint is clearly unethical and could result in numerous negative consequences for all parties involved. There is the slim possibility that Gabe could take the bribe and Miss Adams would not pursue the complaint. She might fall asleep, and perhaps no other guests would be bothered by the noise. It is also possible that no one would ever find out about the bribe.

It is more likely, however, that Miss Adams will pursue her complaint, and Gabe will be responsible for a lot of problems that could have been avoided. At worst, this choice could result in Gabe's termination. We can all imagine how Gabe would be ruing his acceptance of the bribe if the worst-case scenario cropped up. It is likely there would be at least some negative consequences from the decision to take the bribe, outweighing by far the benefit of an undeserved $100. If Gabe's management ability is reduced due to loss of respect and/or decreased morale and increased turnover, he could lose more than $100 in merit raises alone.

Our integrity is built up or torn down by every decision we make. To make an unethical decision and not get caught makes us less sensitive to the next time we have an ethical dilemma. The more times we do something wrong, the more chance we have of getting caught. One unethical decision can lead to other distressing situations. Violating any of the ethical principles generally results in trouble and torment that can be avoided. Doing the ethical thing is much easier and better for everyone in the long run.

OTHER DECISION OPTIONS

Taking the $100 to overlook a noisy guest's behavior is unethical and will most likely result in negative consequences. Ignoring Miss Adams's complaint is also unethical and will probably result in negative consequences. Obviously, not taking the $100 and not ignoring Miss Adams's complaints is the least potentially painful decision. It is not unreasonable for Mr. Butts to be quiet. FOI does not advertise as a wild party property. FOI knew that Mr. Butts was the pseudonym for a rock star who did not want to be recognized. It could have been stressed at the time the reservation was made that FOI was a very quiet property and that noise and partying were not permitted. He might have been discouraged from making the reservation in the first place. Then there would not have been a problem.

It is possible that Mr. Butts would finally respond to Gabe's request that he turn down the radio. Another option might be to move Mr. Butts to a room that was away from the other guests, if such a room was available. Take no bribe and make both guests happy. The worst that can happen if Gabe does not take the bribe is that Mr. Butts refuses to be quiet, there is no place to move him to, and Gabe is forced to ask that he leave. Mr. Butts could cause a huge disturbance and the police might be called. However, even if the worst happens, the other guests would most likely forgive FOI because Gabe ultimately responded to the parties who were in the right. Apologies could be made for the disturbance and some sort of gift extended.

Ethics Analysis Form

No Ifs, Ands, or Butts

Decision Option: Take the $100 and disregard Miss Adams.

Stakeholders	Principles	Consequences
Gabe (Front Desk Mgr.)	Accountability Integrity Concern and Respect for Others Commitment to Excellence Loyalty Leadership Honesty Trustworthiness Fairness Reputation and Morale	• Gabe gets an undeserved $100 and Mr. Butts is happy. • It could be easier for Gabe to take bribes in future situations. • Front Desk receives more complaints from Miss Adams and perhaps other guests. Other guests may also be bothered but not complain. • This can result in dissatisfied customers. • Miss Adams could complain directly to Mr. Butts, and Gabe could have to deal with a nasty confrontation. • Miss Adams could complain to the general manager and Gabe could be disciplined or even terminated. • If other front desk employees were caught taking a bribe, would Gabe be able to discipline them? His management effectiveness could be damaged.
Miss Adams		• Miss Adams could feel unimportant, angry, and frustrated. (She is elderly and could be so upset she could have a stroke or some other physical reaction.) • Miss Adams could check out early. She would perhaps never come back, and she could tell other people how dissatisfied she was.
Seymore Butts		• Mr. Butts may return expecting to bribe FOI management to allow inappropriate behavior. • Mr. Butts's behavior could get worse if he is allowed to continue disturbing Miss Adams.

(continued)

Stakeholders	Principles	Consequences
Other Front Desk Employees		• Employees could lose respect for Gabe when they see him not control Mr. Butts's behavior. • Employees could be less cooperative and turnover and productivity could be negatively affected. • Some employees could suspect or find out that Gabe took the $100 bribe and feel that it is okay for them to do the same thing. • Some employees may be uncomfortable with Gabe (their boss) not handling the situation or taking a bribe (if they find out) and wonder what to do about it. (Should they confront Gabe or go to the general manager?) • Other front desk employees could feel resentful at having to deal with Miss Adams's continuing displeasure.
Freshwater Oasis Inn		• Reputation of FOI as quiet and safe could be damaged. • Word of mouth could decrease new business and repeat business, resulting in a loss of customers and revenue. • Working environment could deteriorate as trust is lost. • If Gabe is eventually terminated, FOI would incur costs for recruiting/training a new front desk manager and for reinstilling desired appropriate behaviors for remaining employees.

CIVILITY

Civics, the study of how to be good citizens, does not seem to be part of all high school curriculums anymore. In civics classes we learned about our local, state, and federal governments, but also we may have learned about the necessity of putting the whole of our society before our own self-interest, and, in essence, becoming aware that our self-interest lies in the overall health of our society. In civics classes, we learned, in part, how to be civilized.

Life is comprised of relationships. We enter relationships with our families and friends, with the companies we work for, and with the communities and organizations we belong to. Civility is far more than superficial good manners. Courtesy and good manners are like the oil that keeps machinery working smoothly. Civility is more like the machinery itself. **Civility** is a determination to behave in ways that are a positive influence on society as a whole. Civility in business is being profitable without cheating, stealing, or lying. Civility in our personal relationships is about accepting people as they are without trying to manipulate, take advantage of, or use them for some selfish purpose.

IN THE TRENCHES

Kathryn Whitney, 21, Phoenix, AZ

"I am a line cook at a local restaurant. I was sitting with coworkers at a pre-shift meeting. The professional business end of the meeting had very obviously ended because the conversation degenerated into a discussion of who amongst the males at the table would make out with a certain singer. Being the only female present, I began to feel uncomfortable, especially when they described her body and the bodies of other females in great detail. I asked to be excused from the table and was then ridiculed for my desire to not be part of that particular conversation."

Ethics are the rules civilized people live by. If we are not taught the rules, how can we hope to be civilized? It is necessary for us to understand what civility means, what it looks like, and how it feels, because our management positions in society come with responsibilities to foster civility.

Civility requires self-knowledge and knowledge of others. We must understand our motivations and openly communicate with others, enabling us to understand theirs. We may not be in agreement and may never be in agreement, but we graciously accept others' opinions and feelings.

Civility has to do with how we handle dissension. In management, we may find it necessary to make decisions that everyone is not in agreement with. If we use our management power to crush and humiliate opposition, we make it too dangerous for peers or subordinates to offer differing opinions. Morale can suffer, and we will find ourselves making decisions without all sides being considered. This avenue can lead to mistakes being made.

Civility has respect for others at its base. While good manners are part of civility, they alone do not equate to civility if we are only being polite to someone we have no respect for. Peoples' behavior does not always deserve our respect. All people, however, deserve our respect simply because they *are* people.

ETIQUETTE

Etiquette is the combination of attitude, behavior, and grooming that meets the conventional standards required for acceptance in polite society. We understand intuitively that we are the same person whether or not we are dressed professionally and our hair is combed in a conservative manner. We know that it is wrong to judge people on the basis of their looks or their manners. However, the reality is that we are all initially judged on the basis of our appearance, so, it behooves us to learn and practice the rules. We can buck against the rules and be right and unsuccessful, or we can follow the rules and not be excluded or misunderstood because we do not look or behave like others expect us to.

It is very difficult to undo first impressions. A first impression can negatively or positively affect the way we are perceived. A great first impression will eventually be forgotten if there is a lack of substance over time. A poor first impression is, however, difficult to overcome. Good work may not be noticed or will be assumed to be mediocre. If we truly believe that looks are unimportant, then we should ask ourselves why we might be so resistant to modifying our style to better match the status quo.

Dress has become more casual and less differentiated over the past 20 years. Children, teens, and adults all appear decked out in jeans, tee shirts, running shoes, and baseball caps. Dressing the same across age and class lines may or may not be a good thing. However, in business, where we want our performance to be recognized, professional attire is still recommended. The following are some basic dress and grooming rules that we may want to use as a grooming checklist.

1. Be very clean and neat. Keep perfumes or colognes subtle.
2. Have clean, short, and well-manicured nails. No brightly colored nail polish.

3. Hair should be neat and clean. No elaborate or unusual hairstyles.
4. Teeth must be clean and well cared for.
5. Makeup should be minimal and subtle.
6. Clothes should be clean, neat, in good shape, and fit well. They should be conservative, not too brightly colored, and not too stylish. They should be comfortable and appropriate for the season. It would be better to wear one or two excellently made business "uniforms" than to have many cheaper outfits.
7. Shirts/blouses should be clean and ironed.
8. Shoes should be polished and in good shape. Run-down heels can be replaced at a shoe repair shop. Heels should be low and styles conservative.
9. Jewelry should be minimal and not flashy.
10. The general rule is that nothing should be "too" anything—not too stylish, not too flashy, not too big, too small, too short, too long, too anything.

These rules relate to being ethical in that they allow us to be taken seriously so that we can influence those around us. Following the rules is part of our commitment to excellence. We cannot do excellent work if our dress or behavior offends customers or makes us less effective with our employees. Our dress and behavior demonstrate the dress and behavior we expect from employees. We lead by example.

It is true that the above rules are more like window dressing than about substance. But, if we wish others to recognize our substance, we do not want to put up a barrier that others may not be able to see through. We want to make sure that we are giving our companies and our customers the messages we really mean to give them. Messages such as: "I am a professional. I know what I am doing. I can be trusted. I am responsible. I can take care of business." And so forth. We do not want to be giving our companies and customers messages like: "I am a rebel. I do not care what you think. I do whatever I want, whenever and wherever I want. If you do not like my clothes or my attitude, it is because you are not as cool as I am." And so forth.

Our attitude is about civility. A civil attitude is one that is indicative of caring about others and respecting them and their differences. A respectful attitude is not obsequious. It is instead, truly interested and considerate. We listen and pay attention to others and their opinions. We say what we really mean and only if it is necessary and useful. We may not agree and we may voice objections, but they are voiced with civility—that is, with respect for others and ourselves.

Courtesy means that we use good manners in all our social encounters. Good manners allow us to move comfortably in and out of whatever personal or professional situations we may find ourselves. We were probably all taught to be courteous as children, but unless we remind ourselves of the rules and practice them we can get out of the habit. If we want to move up in the business world, we must have and use good manners. We must practice lest we can forget to use them, and someone notices. The lack of good manners will get in the way of what we are trying to express or do.

Good table manners are essential. It is probably a capital idea for most of us to review an etiquette book occasionally just to make sure we have not unconsciously slipped into bad habits. If we do not know a specific rule, we can always think to ourselves, "How would I like to be addressed or treated?" and then act accordingly. The following are some general rules for courteous behavior.

1. Always say please and thank you. "Please" makes an order a request and makes most people more willing to comply.
2. Do not speak too loudly, too quietly, too slowly, or too quickly.
3. Listen to what others have to say without interrupting or finishing their sentences for them. Be a patient listener. Respect others' opinions.
4. Do not use inappropriate or off-color language.
5. Smile and make eye contact.
6. Do not stand too close or too far from others when conversing.
7. Do not inappropriately touch others.
8. Do not point at people or use a harsh tone of voice.
9. Do not try to impress others with your superior intelligence. Use simple language. Do not be a name-dropper.
10. Do not flirt.
11. Do not smoke.

The rules of etiquette help us to fit in and get along in any society. The statement, "Hey, gimmie that book!" says the same thing as, "Bob [or whatever the person's name is], would you please pass me that book?" One is an impersonal order while the other is a personal request. The result may be the same, but the latter request will leave no residual resentment with the passing of the book. We can be well served by following the rules of courtesy alone, but, when civility underlies the courtesy, we are better people.

CIVILITY AT FRESHWATER OASIS INN

If we all practiced civility we would have very few problems. Mr. Butts would not have turned his music so loud because he would have been concerned about the comfort of the other guests staying at the inn. Miss Adams would not have been so rude to Gabe had she not been disturbed in the first place. Gabe would not have been thinking disrespectfully about both Mr. Butts and Miss Adams. Miss Adams and Gabe reacted negatively to Mr. Butts's behavior. While they are responsible for their own behavior, Mr. Butts is the main problem in the scenario. Gabe's behavior was, however, outwardly courteous to Miss Adams and Mr. Butts.

Management sets the tone and the tone should be civil. To allow ourselves to think disrespectfully about guests can spill over into our attitudes and behavior. Our behavior models for our employees how we want them to think and behave. Civility needs to be more than skin deep. We as management or students must begin practicing civility in all our affairs so that it becomes who we are, and not just something pasted on to our outsides.

CONCLUSION

Effective living does not come naturally. There are a multitude of skills that we must master to be successful human beings. The same skills are also needed to be successful hospitality managers. The way we choose to present ourselves and behave affects our ability to manage effectively. If we are rude or offensive to others, we are not being ethical, because ethical people are concerned for each other, and they are committed to excellence.

One of the few areas where we have any control is in the way we choose to think and behave. It is useful to have rules we can follow that will result in behavior that can lead us to success. It is through practice that following the rules becomes habit. When we make the right choices we build integrity.

KEY WORDS

Proactive

Contingency plan

Internal locus of control

External locus of control

Civics

Civility

Courtesy

Etiquette

CHAPTER THOUGHT QUESTIONS

1. Discuss the importance of having contingency plans in place. Describe an incident at your work where a contingency plan was or should have been in effect. How did or would a contingency plan affect the outcome of the incident?

2. Describe your locus of control. How do you typically handle problems? Describe a recent situation and how you handled it. If you could do it over, how would you change things?

3. Based on the analysis of the front desk case study, write out a policy for what to do and say when a bribe is offered. Please define the difference between a tip and a bribe in your policy.

4. Managers are role models for their employees. Discuss the consequences when managers do not do what their employees are expected to do. How can being role models be used to our management benefit?

5. Describe a situation where a manager you worked for did not model the correct behavior. How did the manager's behavior affect the employees' behavior?

6. Discuss the difference between civility and courtesy and describe how they work together.

7. Think about growing up in your family. Were you taught and required to use good manners in your home? Give examples of what and how you were taught. Would you teach your children the same things in the same ways? What might you do differently and why?

8. Compare the civility level at various jobs you have held. How did the civility level affect how you felt about working at the various jobs? Describe, in terms of civility, the way you would like people to interact when you are the manager. How will you make this happen?

9. Why might it be useful to conform our appearance and behavior to the commonly accepted rules of etiquette? Evaluate your own appearance and behavior against the rules listed in this chapter. Why do you or do you not follow the rules? What affect does your appearance and behavior have on your business and personal life?

10. Describe the type of person in terms of civility and etiquette you would like to be in 10 years. Will your current habits result in what you would like to become? What changes might you make now to result in what you would like to be later?

REFERENCES

Burgess, G., & Burgess, H. (1997). *The meaning of civility.* Conflict Research Consortium, Colorado.

Hesselbein, F. (1997). The power of civility. *Leader to Leader, 5,* 6–8.

Mercedes, M. (2001). *A book of courtesy.* San Francisco: Harper.

Peck, M. S. (1993). *A world waiting to be born: Civility rediscovered.* New York: Bantam Books.

Post, E. L. (1992). *Emily Post's etiquette.* New York: HarperCollins.

Vallen, G. K., & Vallen, J. J. (2000). *Check in check out.* Upper Saddle River, NJ: Prentice Hall.

Wagner, E. B. (2001). Good manners are good for business. *The Business Journal of Phoenix.*

Windsor, P. (1999). Politeness and civility are missing in business. *Baltimore Business Journal.*

Chapter 5

Ethics and Housekeeping Management

In Chapter 4 we addressed an ethical dilemma involving a noisy guest and the front desk. In this chapter we will look at a situation occurring in the housekeeping department that is related to that very same incident. As managers of hotel/restaurant-type operations, the effects of most things we do are far-reaching and cut across departmental boundaries.

HOUSEKEEPING

While professional housekeeping has expanded over the years, the primary responsibility is still cleaning guest rooms. Few people grow up with aspirations of becoming a housekeeper, and, instead, they take these low-paying jobs because they have no other options. Housekeeping departments are generally culturally diverse, and many employees may be educationally, economically, and/or socially disadvantaged. A large proportion of housekeeping employees may not be able to read or speak English.

Demographics within housekeeping departments pose supervision challenges requiring that managers understand employees who may be very different in terms of social backgrounds. It is the responsibility of managers to facilitate ethical awareness and behavior among employees; however, before this can be done, certain individuals may need to learn basic work ethics involving punctuality, attendance, how to get along on the job, and how to communicate courteously with guests. This is made more difficult when underlying commonalties do not include even a shared language.

Housekeepers come in contact with guests and have access to their rooms and belongings. As in all hospitality positions, it is essential to make good hiring selections. Not all people will make good housekeepers, and not all people should be trusted with access to guest rooms. We, as managers, are ultimately responsible for our guests' safety and security.

HIRING AND SUPERVISING A DIVERSE WORKFORCE

Obtaining and retaining a qualified staff are primary duties for hospitality managers. We hire only those who are willing to do the job, capable of doing the job, and then we must train them to do the job as required. Each employee must be willing, capable, and trainable—or else the relationship will not succeed. Our task is to recruit appropriate applicants, and then to select the most suitable for that particular job's specifications.

Opportunities are supposed to be equal in the United States, but, unfortunately, they are not. The ratio of white male managers to ethnic minority and/or female managers does not mirror the makeup of the population. It is human nature to prefer people who seem more like us. We gravitate toward that which is familiar. Accordingly, white male managers tend to hire young, white male workers. We have laws that make it illegal to deny employment based solely on race, religion, age, and gender, but the equal opportunity laws have not been put fully into practice at every workplace.

Even if it was not the law, there are nowhere near enough white male workers to fill all the available management positions in the hospitality industry. We have no choice but to consider African Americans, Hispanics, Native Americans, Asian Americans, immigrants, the elderly, and women for management positions. Variations in culture, education, language, and so forth, require us to recognize differences without judging and to develop understanding and appreciation of **diversity**, in order to benefit from the realities of today's workforce.

All ten of the Ethical Principles for Hospitality Managers apply directly to managing diversity. We cannot be ethical people if we are discriminating against individuals who differ from us. The first step is determining our own biases. All of us have been socialized as children and may have beliefs that we are unaware of. If we fail to identify these beliefs, we could unconsciously be acting on them, which might in turn be detrimental to our success. Do we blindly assume the stereotypes laid out for us by our possibly misinformed elders? Are we to perpetuate bigotry? Intellectually we may know better—but, until we root out these ingrained biases, we might be unintentionally oblivious to our discrimination based on **stereotypes** absorbed as children.

As prospective managers, we seek the wisdom to view each person individually and then make hiring decisions based on how well he or she matches job specifications. We cannot evaluate prospective employees through lenses that distort who they really are and how well they might perform. If we believe that certain ethnic minority groups are less capable, we may pass on hiring extremely capable members of that particular group. Or, if we do hire them, we may not notice when they do exceptional work. Conversely, we may incorrectly assume that an applicant, who seems much like us, will do a terrific job based solely on that biased similarity. We could end up hiring a person based on what we think of ourselves rather than on whom he or she really is. **Discrimination** on the basis of race, ethnicity, age, gender, or religion is not only illegal, but closes us off from potential employees that we need.

IN THE TRENCHES

Olga Berrelleza, 29, Casa Grande, AZ

"I worked at this one restaurant as a head line cook for 18 months. One busy Friday night I was training a new employee, a female like myself, and the kitchen supervisor turned to us and said, 'If you don't watch out, you will get raped on the line.' I was dumbfounded and asked him to repeat himself . . . and he did so. I told him to go to hell to which he just laughed. I was very angry and hurt because I thought I had his respect and I could not believe he would say such a thing. The next day I told the general manager what had happened and how upset I was and demanded that he do something. He said he would talk to the supervisor, and the next day the kitchen manager teased me about the incident. When I got angry he said, 'That's why girls don't belong in the kitchen: they get too emotional.' I talked to the general manager again and advised him I would quit without notice if something wasn't done about this right away. He responded by suspending me for 2 weeks for threatening to quit. I then went to the district manager and explained what had happened. A meeting was called for all parties involved and I got apologies and was allowed to return to work with a $1.50 an hour raise. Upon my return, though, the general manager called a meeting to announce the opening of my head line cook position. I'd been demoted. I confronted him afterwards and he said he no longer wanted to deal with me and that I should just go talk to the kitchen manager. I quit."

Can we honestly appraise our own thought systems and rid ourselves of discriminatory beliefs? It is unfair to discriminate against people based solely on our own unrealistic perceptions of them, disregarding what actually does or could take place in reality. Managers with *integrity* do the right thing in all situations whether they want to or not. We cannot be *trustworthy* if we retain stereotypical beliefs about people. We must have *concern and respect* for our workers because of who they are and not in spite of whom we think they are. Our *commitment to excellence* requires us to do our very best and to bring out the best in all our workers. We can only accomplish this by eliminating biases from our hearts and minds.

Most of us like to be known individually and not as anonymous members of a group. "All college students are . . ." prefaces a statement that by design generalizes wide swaths of people. When directed at us, most of us find assertions like this somewhat frustrating and offensive. "The rest of them may be, but not me," is often our response to being clumped together in a group and labeled. To be ethical means to be honest in our appraisal of ourselves as well as other human beings.

As managers our job is to assemble, supervise, and retain a qualified, trained team that is capable of getting the job done according to facility standards. The challenge in today's work environment is to build teams from people who may be very different from each other. Though we are not social workers, these same communication skills, interpersonal/social skills, and cultural awareness and appreciation are essential for us to be effective in our chosen profession.

HOUSEKEEPING AT FRESHWATER OASIS INN

Maria, one of the housekeeping workers at FOI, found a black leather dress left behind when a guest registered as Seymore Butts was asked to leave because of repeated noise violations. The dress was bagged and left in the restroom of the housekeeping office. (Please see *First Ya Seymore, Then Ya Don't* in the case study at the back of the text.)

The Executive Housekeeper, Kathy Lawhorn, asked Trini (the only housekeeper fluent in both English and Spanish) to fill in for her while she was out sick. Subsequently, Trini was on duty when Sheena Williams (a guest of Mr. Butts) called to ascertain if the dress had since been turned in. Trini did not locate the dress in the Lost & Found bin, and it was agreed upon that she would notify Sheena if the dress eventually showed up. A few minutes later, though, Trini came across the dress in the office sink where Maria had dropped it the night before.

STATE THE PROBLEM

Trini found the missing black leather dress and noticed it was just her size. The ethical dilemma in this situation is obvious. Trini knows the dress belongs to Sheena and now must decide whether or not to take the item home for herself. Taking someone else's property is theft and obviously unethical. While this is not a management ethical dilemma, it could become one depending on what Trini decides to do.

Trini has two choices in this situation. We can analyze both options and make our decision based on which has the least number of negative consequences. We start by analyzing Trini's decision to take the dress. We enter the decision option on an Ethics Analysis Form.

As managers we can identify our decision options, analyze them, and make sound decisions based on that analysis. Our workers can also be taught to identify and analyze decision options. Avoiding negative consequences does not require us to be moral people. What we discover, however, is that we end up behaving morally/ethically in order to avoid the negative consequences. Trini may or may not be concerned about doing the right thing, but she would most certainly avoid being harmed in any way.

While we might prefer that everyone make ethical choices because it is inherently good, what we really need is for employees to behave ethically regardless of why they do so. Teaching our workers to analyze for negative consequences is an effective way to enable them to make ethical decisions. Some of us need to be reminded to think before we act, because thoughtless acts can result in unfortunate consequences for ourselves and others.

IDENTIFY THE STAKEHOLDERS

We identify and enter all parties who may be affected by Trini's decision to take the dress. A completed Ethics Analysis Form follows the discussion of this segment of the case study. Trini would be the first party entered on the form. In essence, she is contemplating stealing a guest's dress. She could be disciplined or terminated if caught. Sheena's dress will either be returned or it will not, so her name is also entered on the form. Kathy Lawhorn will be affected by her employee's action, and, if Trini gets caught, Kathy will personally have to discipline or terminate her. Additional housekeeping staff might also be affected, and FOI as a whole could find itself negatively impacted by word of mouth in the community.

ANALYSIS OF POSSIBLE CONSEQUENCES FOR TRINI

If Trini takes the dress and gets caught, she could lose her job. She could experience difficulty finding another position without positive references and a reasonable way of explaining her whereabouts during time covered by the nonexistent reference. It is possible that Trini would not get caught, or, if caught, would not actually lose her job—but, if any negative consequence occurred, we can assume that she would most likely wish she had not taken the dress in the first place. Many problems can be avoided by simply thinking through possible consequences before we act.

We begin the analysis of possible consequences for Trini by asking if any good could come out of taking the dress. We note that Trini would get an expensive dress for free. The big question is whether or not she will get caught, because, if she does, the cost to Trini would be considerably more than the value of the dress. The dress somehow ended up in the housekeeping office restroom, so at least one other person knows about it. Sheena Williams could call back again and talk to Kathy about her missing dress. Kathy would probably remember Gabe's message about Maria cleaning up the mess in Mr. Butts's room and ask Maria about the dress. There is a pretty good chance that Kathy could figure out that Trini took the dress.

If no one discovers that Trini took the dress, she might be tempted to take other things. We get less sensitive to wrongdoing each time we commit another infraction. Every time Trini steals something, she increases the risk of getting caught and suffering negative consequences. Trini might also feel nervous or guilty while wearing the dress, fearing quite naturally that someone might recognize it.

Analysis is not difficult. We start by asking ourselves questions about what could happen. One question leads to another, and the answers can lead us to the conclusion that Trini will likely suffer negative consequences, if not now, then later, for taking the dress. On the other hand, if Trini returns the dress she does not lose anything because it was not her dress to begin with. If we stayed at a hotel and left something behind, would we like our belongings returned? If we were Trini's supervisor, what would we prefer Trini's decision to be? When it comes to personal items left behind by guests, it is highly unlikely that the policy of the FOI housekeeping department is: "Finders keepers, losers weepers."

ANALYSIS OF POSSIBLE CONSEQUENCES
THE CUSTOMER (SHEENA WILLIAMS)

If Trini does not go through with the theft, Sheena will get her dress back. If Trini takes the dress, Sheena could lose her expensive dress. Obviously it would be best for Sheena if Trini returns the dress. We can ask ourselves what Sheena might do if she does not get her dress back. Would she suspect that an employee of the hotel stole her dress? As we mentioned above, Sheena might call back about her dress and talk to Kathy, and then Kathy would question Trini.

ANALYSIS OF POSSIBLE CONSEQUENCES
FOR OTHER EMPLOYEES

Maria most likely put the dress in the housekeeping office restroom. If Maria ever saw Trini in the dress, she might know that Trini stole it. If Sheena calls back again, Maria and others might be questioned about the dress. It is quite possible that other employees could find out that Trini took the black leather dress. And, if they did, what would they think about it? How might it affect their behavior? We can put ourselves in the situation and think how we would feel if we knew a fellow worker stole something from a guest. What would we think about that worker? Would we maintain trust for him or her in the future? Most likely, we would not.

If Kathy was unaware of Trini's theft, but another employee knew, would it be his or her responsibility to tell on Trini? How might he or she feel about that? We generally do not like to tell on people and might be afraid of reprisal. Honest housekeepers could feel resentful if Trini is allowed to get away with taking the dress. Some housekeepers might assume that it is okay to steal things from guests if Trini gets away with it. Trini's unethical action could have negative effects on the other employees' attitudes and behavior. The old saying, "One bad apple can spoil the barrel," sums up the relationship between Trini and her fellow housekeeping employees.

ANALYSIS OF POSSIBLE CONSEQUENCES FOR KATHY LAWHORN

Kathy Lawhorn, 33, completed her hospitality degree and worked 10 years at a large hotel chain before coming to FOI. Kathy supervises housekeeping and the in-house laundry/dry-cleaning staff.

It is very likely that Kathy will suspect that Trini took the dress. Kathy would then have to confront Trini. Few of us find this kind of encounter anything but uncomfortable, and what if Trini merely denies any involvement with the dress in question? Regardless of the voracity of Trini's denials, at the very least Kathy's trust in her would disappear and she may even wonder if other staff members are also stealing. Gabe, the front desk manager, and at least one other employee know about the dress. Other employees could find out too. Employees would expect Kathy to do something about the situation and would lose respect for her if she failed to take responsibility. Kathy's ability to manage would be compromised. Her employees could become less cooperative and might even question Kathy's judgment for putting Trini in charge in the first place.

Kathy's boss (John Fallin, the general manager) could become aware that Kathy's employees were stealing guests' property. We are responsible for the behavior and actions of our staff, and we must be aware of what they are doing while on the clock. Kathy put Trini in a position of authority, primarily because Trini speaks both Spanish and English, and she is ultimately accountable for the results of her decision. Kathy could be humiliated, appear less competent, and face disciplinary action herself.

ANALYSIS OF POSSIBLE CONSEQUENCES FOR FOI

Sheena Williams does not fit the profile of the target market for FOI. She could, however, tell friends or relatives who then might spread the word that Sheena had an expensive dress stolen while staying there. This could damage the reputation of FOI as a safe place to stay.

If housekeeping management deteriorates, a reduction in employee satisfaction might cause morale to fall and performance to suffer. Turnover and absenteeism might also increase. All of these things cost money and harm the reputation of FOI as a quality place to work.

ETHICAL PRINCIPLES VIOLATED BY THIS DECISION

We have identified as many of the consequences for Trini taking the dress as we could think of. We knew from the onset that taking the dress was unethical, but let us now go through the list of ethical principles to identify which principles in particular are violated by this decision. We enter these violated principles on the Ethics Analysis Form.

Honest people do not steal. Trini knew the dress belonged to Sheena and considered taking it anyway. We enter *honesty* on the form. Trini would show a decided lack of *integrity* by doing something unethical when she thinks no one would find out. Dishonest people with no integrity are not *trustworthy*.

Trini's action would not be good for FOI, so the principle of *loyalty* is violated. Taking the dress would indicate a lack of *concern and respect* for Sheena and her property. It would also disrespect the FOI housekeeping rules and Kathy, her supervisor. A *commitment to excellence* is violated when any of the ethical principles are compromised while performing a job. Excellence means we do our best work, and stealing a guest's dress would not be indicative of Trini being "at her best."

The *reputation* of FOI as a safe place to stay could be harmed by this action. The staff's *morale* could suffer if one employee (Trini) does not follow the rules others do. Morale declines when trust and respect between employees, and between employees and management, are diminished. The executive housekeeper, Kathy, is responsible for the actions of her employees. Each individual, however, is personally responsible for his or her own action. Saying, "My boss made me do it," does not excuse our behavior. Trini is accountable for her action (should she decide to take the dress), and, by extension, so is Kathy, her supervisor.

The decision to take the black leather dress violates nine of the ten Ethical Principles for Hospitality Managers. Trini is not a manager, although she was acting as manager when the ethical dilemma came up. Management is responsible for modeling ethical behavior for employees, for hiring employees who are capable of being ethical, and for facilitating employee ethical awareness and behavior. These ethical principles are not just for managers but for everyone, and must be abided to if we are to successfully run our hospitality concerns.

OTHER DECISION OPTIONS

The other decision option in this dilemma is for Trini to call Sheena Williams and inform her that the dress was found. There are no negative consequences for calling the guest and arranging to return the dress like management at FOI

Ethics Analysis Form
First Ya Seymore, Then Ya Don't

Decision Option: Trini takes the leather dress

Stakeholders	Principles	Consequences
Trini (Housekeeper) [Decision-Maker]	Honesty Integrity Trustworthiness Loyalty Fairness Concern and Respect Commitment to Excellence Reputation and Morale Accountability	• Trini gets an expensive leather dress. • If the owner calls back, Kathy might question housekeepers and find that Maria put the dress in the office. Trini could be questioned. She can either lie or admit she took the dress. • If Trini lies, she may find it easier to steal again. • Fearful of getting caught, Trini might feel nervous or guilty every time she wears the dress. • Trini could get terminated for stealing.
Sheena Williams (friend of guest)		• Sheena loses an expensive dress. • Sheena might call back and talk to Kathy about her missing property. • Sheena might miss the next tour bus because of a wardrobe shortfall.
Kathy (Manager)		• Kathy may have to deal with Trini. If Trini admits taking the dress, she will have to discipline or terminate her. If Trini lies, Kathy will still lose trust in Trini and may also wonder if other employees are stealing. • If other employees know what Trini did, they could lose respect for Kathy for not knowing or for knowing yet still doing nothing. They could become less cooperative. They might question Kathy's judgment for putting Trini in charge and be less trusting in the future. • It was Kathy's choice to put Trini in a position of authority that day, and, if her superior found out, Kathy could be humiliated and appear less competent. Kathy is responsible for the actions of her employees and would be held accountable. She might even face disciplinary action herself.
Other Employees		• Other housekeepers might think it is okay to steal and be tempted to do so if Trini gets away with it. • If another employee finds out, he or she would be faced with the dilemma of whether or not to tell on Trini.

(continued)

Stakeholders	Principles	Consequences
		• Other housekeepers could feel resentful if they knew Trini was getting away with stealing.
Freshwater Oasis Inn		• The customer could tell other people that an employee of FOI stole her dress. This would damage the reputation of FOI as a safe place to stay. • Employee dissatisfaction with housekeeping management could increase turnover and create hiring and retention problems.

would prefer. Most of us knew this before going through the analysis process, but we may not have realized the extent of the consequences for not doing the right thing.

The analysis process can be eye-opening and save us from any unpleasant results of a decision or action we might make without thinking. Every action and/or decision we make can have long-term repercussions. The past is inexorably linked with the future. One unethical decision can lead to other distressing situations. There is no "just this once" exemption when it comes to compromising one's ethics. It is all about setting precedents, and a person must decide which fork of the road he or she wishes to take. There is no turning back.

SEQUEL TO THE WRONG DECISION

In *Enter the Potty Planner* (see case study, back of text), Trini is observed by John Fallen and Gabe Deflores leaving FOI wearing the dress in question. After being appraised of the situation by Gabe, John can either let Kathy Lawhorn deal with the employee in her own department, he can deal with Trini himself, or he can forget about the entire episode. What might seem amusing to Gabe is not so funny to a person charged with the responsibility of running a large operation, one whose decisions affect the livelihoods of a great many people. John does not really have a choice. One of the most difficult aspects of management/supervision is never being able to let anything or anyone slide—not ever. We are sometimes inclined to look the other way so as not to confront an employee about a misdeed. To not address a misdeed is to validate that wrong behavior, and that validation is likely to inspire others. Infractions invariably get worse and spread throughout the staff.

An analysis of the decision option *To not tell Kathy that Trini took the dress* can be done by identifying the stakeholders and asking how the decision will affect each one. We can go down the list of Ethical Principles for Hospitality Managers and note on the Ethics Analysis Form any principles that are violated by the decision. The following analysis leads us to the conclusion that Kathy must be notified of Trini's offense.

Ethics Analysis Form

Enter the Potty Planner

Decision Option: To not tell Kathy that Trini took the dress

Stakeholders	Principles	Consequences
John (General Manager) [Decision-Maker]	Integrity Loyalty Leadership Accountability	• Maria is aware of the leather dress, and other employees could also become aware that Trini took the guest's dress. If Trini is not disciplined, other employees and managers could assume that theft and similar wrongdoings are okay. John could lose his leadership authority. • John's ability to control Gabe could be diminished and his authority reduced if Gabe were to witness him doing nothing about Trini's theft.
Gabe (Front Desk Mgr.)		• If any of Gabe's staff became aware that Gabe knew and didn't tell Kathy (Exec. Housekeeper), they might conclude that it is okay to steal, and, in the future, it might be more difficult for Gabe to control and discipline his own staff. • If Trini is not disciplined, Gabe would be sent a strong message by the general manager that theft or other wrongdoings can be overlooked. • If Gabe overlooked future incidents and neglected to inform the general manager, his loyalty could be in question. This could have a negative effect on Gabe's career at FOI.
Trini (Housekeeper)		• If Trini is allowed to steal, it is quite likely that she will steal again.
Kathy (Exec. Housekeeper)		• If Kathy is not informed of the theft and does not find out on her own, her staff could lose respect for her and her authority could be diminished. • If Kathy is unaware that Trini took the dress, she might be considered by John and Gabe as less capable and not in control of her department.
Other Employees		• If other employees find out that Trini took the dress, and then observe how management knew and did nothing, they might reason that it is okay to steal. They might also conclude that it is fruitless to tell on other employees committing bad acts on the job, and refrain from doing so in the future. • Some employees might find themselves in the very uncomfortable position of knowing they should tell

(continued)

Stakeholders	Principles	Consequences
Other Employees		on their colleague. The struggle is made more difficult if they find out that a manager and/or the General Manager knew and did nothing.
FOI		• Employee theft decreases profits, destroys trust, and breaks down teamwork and relationships. It can have a negative effect on the working environment. • Word of mouth about the incident might harm FOI's reputation in the community.

OTHER DECISION OPTIONS

Generally we go through proper channels in management. Kathy is Trini's supervisor, so it is appropriate for John to let Kathy deal with Trini. There are no negative consequences for John if he tells Kathy about Trini wearing the missing dress. Kathy will, of course, have to deal with a problem and could be less than thrilled to do so. However, there are fewer negative consequences for Kathy to deal with Trini than if she does not know.

In *More or Less Black Leather Dress* (see case study), John turns the Trini problem over to Kathy Lawhorn, who in turn informs Trini during a meeting that she would be fired on the spot if she ever took anything from the Lost & Found again.

ANALYSIS OF KATHY'S DECISION TO NOT DISCIPLINE TRINI

Kathy already made her decision, so we are going to do an "after the fact" analysis using the Ethics Analysis Form. We identify and enter stakeholders on the form and begin asking the questions necessary to think through possible consequences of her decision. Kathy, Trini, other employees, and FOI could all be affected and are entered on the form. A completed Ethics Analysis Form follows this discussion.

ANALYSIS OF POSSIBLE CONSEQUENCES FOR KATHY

Whatever we do or fail to do sends our employees a message. We need to ask ourselves if the message we are giving our employees is the message we really want them to have. If one employee is not disciplined for stealing, it would be unfair to discipline another employee for a similar offense. Our management actions override any written policies. What we do is what they believe. In the end, Trini was not seriously disciplined for stealing a guest's dress from the housekeeping office. This could lead other staff members to the conclusion that theft is permissible and will not merit punishment.

If Kathy's employees sense that she is shirking her managerial duties, they could lose respect for her. Their trust in Kathy could diminish, and with it Kathy's ability to manage her staff. John would most likely check to see what Kathy had done about the Trini situation. He would be unimpressed with the threat to fire Trini if it ever happened again. He would probably discover the real reason behind Trini's light punishment for stealing, the truth being that Kathy Lawhorn uses Trini's bilingual capabilities to bridge the gap between herself and the non-English-speaking workers on her staff. This, in particular, would be most unimpressive to John.

ANALYSIS OF POSSIBLE CONSEQUENCES FOR TRINI

We may have heard mothers yelling threats at their out-of-control children. Children and adults learn very quickly how much they can get away with. Trini got away with stealing a dress from a guest of the inn. She did not have a lot of respect for Kathy before this incident and will most likely have less after it. Trini is obviously not very good at self-control, and, without discipline, is very likely to misbehave again.

ANALYSIS OF POSSIBLE CONSEQUENCES
FOR OTHER EMPLOYEES

Our employees are generally well aware of what is going on in the department. They would know that Trini took the dress and received no disciplinary action. They might think that it is all right to take things from the inn since Trini did not get in trouble. Kathy would very likely lose the respect of her staff because she is not keeping Trini in line.

They would probably be aware of the fact that Kathy depends on Trini's ability to speak both English and Spanish, and that more than anything else is the reason behind why Trini was allowed to steal. They might resent this double standard, suspecting that a similar infraction on their parts would most likely be dealt with in a much harsher manner. Eventually another employee might actually be tempted to steal something from the inn, get caught, disciplined, and feel unfairly treated by Kathy. When management is inconsistent and unfair, morale suffers.

ANALYSIS OF POSSIBLE CONSEQUENCES FOR FOI

If more employees are tempted to steal from guests of the inn, the reputation of the inn could suffer, which could hurt sales. Management is responsible for the morale of the staff, and, if the morale is low, turnover could increase. FOI could lose its reputation as a good place to work.

Ethics Analysis Form

More or Less Black Leather Dress

Decision Option: To not discipline Trini for taking the leather dress

Stakeholders	Principles	Consequences
Kathy (Exec. Housekeeper) [Decision-Maker]	Integrity Loyalty Leadership Accountability	• If Kathy does not discipline Trini for stealing the dress, she will be sending a strong message to her staff that theft is okay, and that they should not expect any punishment if caught. • Kathy's ability to discipline any other employee's theft would be diminished. • Kathy could lose the respect and trust of her employees, which could negatively affect her ability to manage. • John, the general manager, could think Kathy is not in control of her department.
Trini (Housekeeper)		• Trini, although warned of dire consequences if it ever happens again, got away with theft. • Trini might not believe Kathy's threats and steal again. • Trini did not have much respect for Kathy in the first place, and may have less after this.
Other Employees		• Other employees would know that Trini was not disciplined for theft and could think that it is okay to steal from the hotel.

(continued)

Stakeholders	Principles	Consequences
Other Employees		• They could lose respect for Kathy for failing to do her job. • If they got caught stealing, Kathy could discipline or terminate them.
FOI		• Employee theft could rise. • Morale and trust could fall. • Turnover could increase.

OTHER DECISION OPTIONS

Kathy told Trini that she would be fired on the spot if she ever took anything from the Lost & Found again. Trini was not really disciplined for stealing the dress, just threatened. We know that taking the dress was wrong, and our analysis of all three case study segments indicated numerous negative consequences if Trini is not disciplined. This behooves us to consider in depth why Kathy only threatened Trini.

Kathy is managing a culturally diverse department where several of the staff can barely speak English, and her Spanish is inadequate. Most college hospitality management programs strongly encourage or require Spanish as a second language. We may have heard people say, "This is America—so if people want to come here, they should learn to speak English." Regardless of how some people may feel, people with limited English language skills will continue to fill many entry-level positions in the hospitality industry. As managers, we must be able to communicate with them in the language they understand.

Kathy did not want to terminate Trini because she is bilingual and Kathy can only speak English. Kathy's deficiency put her in the difficult position of losing the only person in her department who could communicate with everyone. She may have felt that she had to tolerate Trini's behavior in order to function in her management position. In short, Kathy's lack of Spanish language skills disadvantaged her and jeopardized her ability to effectively manage her department.

Not disciplining Trini further decreases her management effectiveness and we can rest assured that there will be more problems involving Trini in the future. Also, in terms of her relationship with John Fallen, the general manager, he is now aware of Kathy's shortcomings as a manager of a culturally diverse housekeeping department.

CONCLUSION

Decisions made in each subsequent dilemma determine the life of the problem. Wrong decisions continue the torment. Doing the ethical thing is much easier and much better for everyone in the long run. If Kathy could communicate in

Spanish, she would not have had to depend on Trini. A more trustworthy Spanish-speaking housekeeper could have filled in for Kathy while she was out sick, with phone calls being temporarily rerouted to the front desk. If Trini had not been alone in the housekeeping office, she would not have stolen the dress. The entire incident could have been avoided. This whole dilemma comes down to Kathy not being appropriately qualified to manage a diverse workplace. Her failure to take the proper action (when one of her employees was caught stealing) is a direct result of these shortcomings.

KEY WORDS

Demographics	Stereotypes
Diversity	Discrimination

CHAPTER THOUGHT QUESTIONS

1. Think about the jobs you have held. Describe the racial, ethnic, and gender makeup of the employees of one or several of the jobs. Which category were you in? Did people in the various categories stick together or mix with others? Why or why not?

2. Describe and compare your closest friends with yourself in terms of demographics. Discuss the difference between making friends and choosing employees in terms of discrimination.

3. What biases did your parents or caregivers hold about races, ethnic background, or gender? List statements you heard as a child that are examples of stereotypical thinking. Write at least one example for each where the statement is incorrect.

4. There is a large proportion of kitchen and housekeeping employees who do not speak or write English. What do you think about this? Aside from being illegal, what would the ramifications be for refusing to hire kitchen and housekeeping personnel who were not fluent in English?

5. How does having a staff that does not speak English affect your ability to manage? Why should the manager of such a department be able to communicate with his or her employees in their own language?

6. In *More or Less Black Leather Dress*, Kathy thinks, "After all, you don't need Mother Teresa for cleaning a hotel room." What did Kathy mean by this? Is she correct? Discuss safety/security issues involving housekeeping staff.

7. If you were the general manager of a property and were hiring a manager for a housekeeping department with a diverse staff, list the qualifications the manager candidate would have to possess in order to be hired. Why are these qualifications necessary?

8. List some of the problems management might have to contend with when managing a diverse workforce.

9. Describe how managers you have worked for have dealt with issues related to managing diversity. Use specific examples.

10. If you were the general manager of FOI, how would you deal with Kathy and her management of the housekeeping department? (Hint: Outline a program to help Kathy to be a better manager.)

REFERENCES

Davis, B. G. (2001). *Tools for teaching.* San Francisco: Jossey-Bass.

Jaszay, C., & Dunk, P. (2003). *Training design for the hospitality industry.* New York: Delmar.

Martin, R. J. (1998). *Professional management of housekeeping operations.* New York: Wiley.

Singer, P. (1993). *Practical ethics* (2nd ed). Cambridge, UK: Cambridge University Press.

Chapter 6

Ethics and Sales and Marketing

MARKETING

Marketing involves selecting whom we wish to serve, determining what they would like, and then how, when, and where they would like it. Once we know that all this is feasible through market research, we must let the **target market** (the people we have selected to serve) know that we have what they want, and then we must show them how to get it. This is accomplished through **promotion** and **sales**.

Many hotels and restaurants earn revenue from providing space and services for special events, conferences, parties, and so forth. Sales people locate potential customers and attempt to match customer needs with appropriate hotel or restaurant services. The satisfaction of the guests and the people who planned the event, conference, or party will determine whether or not they will hold their next meeting at the property and what they will tell others about the experience.

Both buyers and sellers of space and services for their organizations are acting as go-betweens for hotels and prospective guests. The hotels want the groups' business and the planners want suitable sites for their groups' events. The sales people are working for the hotel, while the meeting planners may either be working for the particular group on a full-time basis or be independent contractors hired by the group to plan their meeting or event.

The abuse of familiarization trips (FAM, the complimentary on-site visits to properties by planners), hotel rebates pocketed by planners, and covert commissions demanded by planners for booking with properties, are types of questionable ethical practices professional meeting planner organizations have been very concerned with. Hotels have been criticized for offering meeting planners expensive personal gifts and other incentives such as free rooms, limo service, and entertainment to encourage planners to book meetings at their properties.

To that end, some hotels offer meeting planners points that can be redeemed for free rooms, vacations, and/or frequent flyer miles. Even though *Meeting Professionals International* and the *Society for Government Meeting Planners* prohibit accepting points and gifts, the incentive programs are nonetheless widespread.

Sales people and meeting planners are often tempted to compromise personal ethical standards to make profitable deals, but unethical behavior can ruin the reputations of both wrongdoers and those who have been wronged. Without an industry-wide ethical standard, however, unethical actions may seem to be the norm. Organizations are realizing that values may have to come from the organizations rather than individuals (in the organizations), and, to that end, they are establishing written codes of ethics.

ETHICS CODES

Like a building code is a list of regulations that must be followed in any kind of construction, and the legal code is the list of laws citizens must obey, an **ethics code** is a list of moral rules that members of particular groups or professions agree to follow. More organizations today are writing ethics codes because managers are often more inclined to respect and prefer having company rules when making difficult ethical decisions.

Lest they become useless, rules must be enforced and lived by. It is the responsibility of upper management to see that policies and procedures are designed reflecting the moral tone set by the company. Having this in place enables managers and staff to adhere to the company's ethics code. A tangible ethics code that is modeled by management can have a powerful impact on the behavior of all employees.

There are managers who mouth ethical principles but push and reward sales staff for doing whatever it takes to get the sale. These individuals undermine ethics codes with actions that do not match their words. If upper management honors and rewards ethical practices, sales managers will find it easier to follow the ethics code and to model the ethical rules for their sales staff. Selling involves building relationships with clients. Trust is the basis of relationships. If a hotel's sales department promises something but does not deliver, the client will be dissatisfied, will most likely not come back, and they will tell others of the breach. This, of course, can have a very negative effect on a property's reputation and future sales.

When hotels have written ethics codes in place that preclude making empty promises, misleading clients, downgrading the competition, stealing clients, and so forth, it is safe for sales staff to do that which is required and ethically correct. By behaving ethically, sales staffs build trusting relationships with clients who are more satisfied and tend to be loyal. Companies discourage unethical behavior in their employees when they define and penalize lying, cheating, and stealing, and when they model and reward honesty and integrity.

All managers and staff will not be on the same page ethically. It is the responsibility of top management to set the ethical tone and then to ensure that everyone in the company is made aware of the rules, and how and why to follow the rules. The long-term benefits of ethical sales policies and practices far outweigh short-term unethical results that may backfire and ultimately hurt sales.

Hotels generally want the business meeting planners can bring to their properties. While meeting planners represent particular organizations or companies, they are usually working independently and often find themselves in situations where the line between acceptable and unacceptable behavior is fuzzy and temptation ever present. Because meeting planners may have more loyalty to their profession than any particular company, professional codes may be more effective than corporate codes of ethics for addressing ethical issues facing individuals in the meeting planning industry.

The following "Principles of Professionalism" is an example of an ethics code that Meeting Professionals International's (MPI) 17,000 members are expected to agree to and follow.

PRINCIPLES OF PROFESSIONALISM

The *Principles of Professionalism* provide guidelines recommended for the business behavior of its members that impact their perceived character and thus the overall image of MPI. Commitment to these principles is implicit to membership and is essential to instilling public confidence, engaging in fair and equitable practices, and building professional relationships with meeting industry colleagues. As members of MPI, we are responsible for ensuring that the meeting industry is held in the highest public regard throughout the world. Our conduct directly impacts this result.

Maintaining Professional Integrity:

- Honestly **REPRESENT AND ACT** within one's areas of professional competency and authority without exaggeration, misrepresentation or concealment.
- **AVOID** actions which are or could be perceived as a conflict of interest or for individual gain.
- **OFFER OR ACCEPT** only appropriate incentives, goods and services in business transactions.

Utilizing Professional Business Practices:

- **HONOR** written and oral contracts, striving for clarity and mutual understanding through complete, accurate and timely communications, while respecting legal and contractual rights of others.

- **ENSURE** rights to privacy and protect confidentiality of privileged information received verbally, in writing or electronically.
- **REFRAIN** from misusing solicited information, proposals or concepts.
- **COMMIT** to the protection of the environment by responsible use of resources in the production of meetings.
- **ACTIVELY PURSUE** educational growth through training, sharing of knowledge, expertise and skills, to advance the meeting industry.

Respecting Diversity:

- **EMBRACE AND FOSTER** an inclusive business climate of respect for all peoples regardless of national origin, race, religion, sex, marital status, age, sexual orientation, physical or mental impairment.
- Adherence to the Principles of Professionalism signifies professionalism, competence, fair dealing and high integrity. Failure to abide by these principles may subject a member to disciplinary action, as set forth in the Bylaws of Meeting Professionals International. (Reprinted with permission)

Corporations and professional organizations that have developed codes of ethics, model ethical behavior, and design policies and procedures in line with the codes of ethics make it easier for all of their employees or members to be ethical. Talk is cheap. Supporting ethical behavior is more difficult and more expensive. However, the long-term benefits, in terms of profits, customer satisfaction, and employee satisfaction, make the commitment to support ethical behavior necessary for future success.

SALES AND MARKETING AT FRESHWATER OASIS INN

John Fallen, 46, was hired 6 years ago to open and manage the inn. He has an MBA from Stanford and for 5 years was food and beverage manager for a large, successful hotel in Los Angeles. His experience, combined with a refreshing vision for the inn, convinced owner Frank Statten that John could make his business a success. As part of his contract, John has the opportunity to make a year-end bonus based on job performance and occupancy rates.

John compensated for his lack of comprehensive experience by hiring excellent people in top management positions. His emphasis is on FOI as a team. He allows managers a certain amount of autonomy but provides guidance to ensure that the needs of the target market are met. His mantra is that managers be courteous, caring, and professional. While most properties have at least one person who is solely responsible for sales and marketing, up to now John has been handling sales and marketing with the help of his assistant general manager, Heidi Bell.

Mr. and Mrs. Bob Grobbins and their two children checked into the Freshwater Oasis Inn to determine whether the property would be a good site for the upcoming conference for the Greater Phoenix Association of Funeral Home Operators. John gave them a tour of the inn while Kip, the bell person, took the children and luggage to their comped rooms. (Please see *Meet Blob Grobbins* in the case study at the back of the text.)

On the way to the room, Bob Grobbins lit a cigar in the elevator and alluded to his expectation of free golf that weekend at the expensive Timberlanes Golf Course. He basically threatened not to book with FOI if golf was not included in his comped package. "(You don't have an) arrangement with Timberlanes?" he said, "Jeez, The Abbey at Copper Hills does. What's goin' on here, John?" The cost of a round of golf at Timberlanes is $450 per person and too rich for the blood of a smallish hotel like FOI. John is put on the spot and has to decide what to do. Because this is a case study, we can step back and do a quick analysis using the Ethics Analysis Form.

STATE THE PROBLEM AND IDENTIFY THE STAKEHOLDERS

When faced with a difficult question, it is inconvenient to take time to do the analysis that would help us to give a satisfactory answer. If we were to analyze the question in advance, we would be able to give Mr. Grobbins a well-considered answer. Because this is a case study we can step out of the picture and analyze the consequences of paying $900 for Mr. and Mrs. Grobbins to play golf at Timberlanes.

The stakeholders in this situation who may be directly affected by the decision include John Fallin, Bob Grobbins, and FOI. We enter the decision option and the stakeholders on a blank Ethics Analysis Form. A completed form follows the discussion of this segment of the case study. We can begin by asking ourselves what is the worst thing that can happen if John does not give the Grobbins free golf at Timberlanes. The obvious answer is that Bob could choose another property for the funeral home operators conference. Although unfortunate, that would not be the end of the world for FOI.

ANALYSIS OF POSSIBLE CONSEQUENCES FOR JOHN

To find out possible consequences for John, we start asking questions such as: Does Bob really intend to book the funeral directors conference with FOI? If he gives Bob the free golf at Timberlanes, as Bob requested, will that be all it takes for FOI to get the booking? How might John feel if he gives them the free golf and then does not get the booking? How would he feel if he does get the booking? Can he get the booking without the free golf? One question leads to another. We are not mind readers and can never know for sure what the outcome will be, but we can make well-thought-out, educated guesses based on our experience in the business and interaction with other individuals.

John would be delighted to have a big party in the slowest time of the year. The $900 golf fees for the Grobbins would be a small payment for the money the conference would bring in. There is no guarantee, however, that Bob

Grobbins will book his conference at FOI if he is given free golf at Timberlanes. John would most likely feel rather disgusted about the whole thing if Grobbins did not book with FOI after receiving the free golf.

There is a risk of not getting the booking no matter what John does; however, it is probably a greater risk if he says no to Bob's demand for free golf at Timberlanes. If he gives Bob the golf, though, Bob might demand more free services, which could put John in an awkward position. Where do we draw the line? How might this demand for more free services make John feel?

ANALYSIS OF POSSIBLE CONSEQUENCES FOR BOB GROBBINS

Bob is getting a free deluxe vacation for his entire family. Meeting planners do need to check out properties to see if they are appropriate for their meetings or conferences. Hotels often provide free accommodations and services for the FAM (familiarization) trips. Professional meeting planners, however, do not abuse FAM trips and they do not appreciate "amateurs" giving the meeting planning industry a bad reputation.

Bob is taking advantage of FOI. Could his family be aware of this? What message is he giving his children? Parents (like managers) show their children (employees) what is important by their actions. Bob would probably not counsel his children to lie, cheat, or steal. Through his actions, however, he is demonstrating that it is acceptable to lie, cheat, or steal—if done in the name of business.

ANALYSIS OF POSSIBLE CONSEQUENCES FOR FOI

FOI could get a large booking in the slowest month of the year. Or they could end up without the booking and be out of the money for the Grobbins' stay plus the cost of the golf excursion. A bribe is a secret payment to get something. Bob was essentially asking John to give him a secret payment (the free golf at Timberlanes) in return for Bob possibly choosing FOI for their conference.

If FOI gets the booking after giving the Grobbins free golf, Bob might expect and/or lead his group to expect more than the hotel is willing to provide. This could cost FOI a lot of money and turn the experience into an unpleasant one for all stakeholders.

ETHICAL PRINCIPLES VIOLATED BY THIS DECISION

The buyer in this case, Bob Grobbins, is holding the power. John wants Bob's business and has to more-or-less bid for it along with the other property, The Abbey at Copper Hills. We can look at the decisions and behavior of both Bob and John, buyer and seller, and determine if either are violating ethical principles by asking for or granting free golf at Timberlanes.

Free golf at Timberlanes has nothing to do with the funeral home owners conference. FOI does not have an arrangement with Timberlanes, so if any of the conference attendees wanted to play golf, they would probably be playing at one of the courses FOI does have an arrangement with. So to give or receive free golf at Timberlanes should be unnecessary for the booking decision. John would be giving in to Bob's selfish personal demands.

John would be violating Integrity, Commitment to Excellence, Leadership, and Accountability, while Bob would be violating Honesty, Integrity, Trustworthiness, Fairness, Concern and Respect for Others, Commitment to Excellence, Reputation and Morale, and Accountability. Bob's behavior is unethical in asking for the free golf. John's behavior is only unethical if he gives Bob the free golf.

Ethics Analysis Form
Meet Blob Grobbins

Decision Option: To give Bob and his wife free golf at Timberlanes

Stakeholders	Principles	Consequences
John (General Manager) [Decision-Maker]	Integrity Commitment to Excellence Leadership Accountability	• If John gives Bob free golf, Bob may choose FOI for the conference. This would be a lot of business in a slow time. • It is also possible that Bob might not choose FOI, and John would be out the cost of Grobbins' stay plus $900 for Bob and his wife's golf. • Bob might demand more free services, which puts John in an awkward position. If he says no to Bob's demands, he risks not getting the booking.
Bob Grobbins (Conf. Planner) [Decision-Maker]	Honesty Integrity Trustworthiness Fairness Concern and Respect for Others Commitment to Excellence Reputation and Morale Accountability	• Bob gets a free deluxe vacation for his entire family. • Bob is taking advantage of FOI. He is teaching his children that this behavior is okay.
FOI		• FOI could get a large booking in the slowest month of the year. Or they could end up without the booking and be out the money for the Grobbins' stay plus golf.

(continued)

Stakeholders	Principles	Consequences
FOI		• If FOI gets the booking, Bob might expect and/or lead his group to expect more than the hotel is willing to provide. This could cost FOI a lot of money and turn into an unpleasant experience for all stakeholders.

CHOOSING THE DECISION OPTION

Which decision option, to give or not give Bob the free golf, has the most negative consequences? Which decision violates ethical principles? Not every ethical dilemma is clear-cut or obvious. In the Bob Grobbins dilemma we are looking at a variety of fairly negative consequences with either decision. We might be very tempted to simply give Bob the golf in hopes of getting the conference. When we analyze the decision, however, we can see that there are perhaps more negative consequences to honoring Bob's demand for the bribe.

The dilemma could be avoided if FOI determined in advance what they care to use as incentives for potential conference bookings. They could be upfront with what is and what is not included at the time of the FAM trip scheduling. While certainly desiring the extra business in a very slow month, FOI may be better off in the long run by only offering incentives directly related to the potential booking and for the meeting planner alone. In the pursuit of business, FOI's property and services must be able to stand on their own without reliance on unrelated incentives (bribes).

CLOSE THE SALE

Toward the end of *Edna Bumpkin* John books twenty-five rooms for the Phoenix Philatelist's Club. (Please see *Edna Bumpkin* in the case study at the back of the text.) A discount is always given to large groups, but John failed to mention it and instead used the discount to maneuver the club to a later, less desirable date. The president of the Phoenix Philatelist's Club thought he got a good deal for his group by being willing to change their date to later in June.

We might think, "no harm, no foul." FOI will have a big party during a slow time at the inn, and the president of the Phoenix Philatelist's Club is happy. It might be insightful to analyze the possible consequences of this questionable sales tactic. We will analyze the decision option to use the automatic 10% discount to maneuver dates and close the sale. The stakeholders are the Phoenix Philatelist's Club, John Fallin, and other customers. Once again, we begin by entering the decision option and the stakeholders on a blank Ethics Analysis Form. (A completed form follows the discussion of this segment of the case study.)

ANALYSIS OF POSSIBLE CONSEQUENCES FOR THE PHOENIX PHILATELIST'S CLUB

The Phoenix Philatelist's Club is changing its conference dates to a less desirable time of the month in order to get the 10% discount. The discount is, however, actually given to any large party regardless of what time of year they are booking rooms. So the club could have had the discount *and* the preferred dates. In essence, John misled them.

If the members and/or president of the club discovered John misled them, they could feel resentful, demand redress, or even cancel the booking. They could feel that they were taken advantage of and that John betrayed their trust. Their opinion of FOI would be lowered. There is a good chance that they would never find out, but we must ask ourselves if we are willing to take the risk. People talk, and, even in big cities, it is remarkable how word can get around.

ANALYSIS OF POSSIBLE CONSEQUENCES FOR JOHN FALLEN

John might have to deal with a large party that felt they were misled. They could even cancel the booking and go elsewhere. It would be John's fault. If the club does not discover John's slight of hand, FOI will retain the booking and his questionable method of securing the sale will be validated. He will then be encouraged to repeat this unethical sales technique and perhaps might get caught later.

John's integrity is at issue here. Some less-than-ethical managers think unethical practices are acceptable so long as they do not get caught. Integrity is about doing the right thing because it is the right thing to do, regardless of whether anyone notices. If John figures he is unlikely to get caught and then misuses the 10% discount to maneuver the club into a less desirable date, then what does this say about his character? How will this affect John and his character growth down the road? Integrity is nurtured and built through every decision we make. Fudging here and there tends to desensitize us, and over time we may find it increasingly easy to be dishonest.

ANALYSIS OF POSSIBLE CONSEQUENCES FOR OTHER CUSTOMERS

This is another of those ethical dilemmas where it depends on whether or not anyone finds out. There is a chance that no one ever will. Yet, there is also a possibility that any of the club members, at any time in the future, could be talking to someone else who booked or was going to book a large party at FOI, and it could be realized that all large parties get the automatic 10% discount. Club members could feel embarrassed that they were fooled into thinking they got a good deal. This could negatively affect their perception of FOI, they would never return on their own, and they could share this negative perception with potential customers forever. This could hurt FOI's reputation and affect sales for years to come.

ETHICAL PRINCIPLES VIOLATED BY THIS DECISION

John's decision to use the automatic 10% discount (to maneuver dates and close the sale) violates many of the ethical principles. Misleading customers violates *honesty*. Dishonest actions are not marks of *integrity*. John is not *trustworthy*, and it is not fair to make the customers think they have to accept less desirable dates to get the discount. He showed little *concern and respect* for customers.

To do anything that violates any of the ethical principles is not indicative of a *commitment to excellence*. John's actions as General Manager were not ethical, and, thus, his *leadership* suffers. The *reputation of the inn* could suffer, which could have a negative effect on employee *morale*. As general manager, John is *accountable* for his behavior and the behavior of everyone under his management. We enter the violated principles on the Ethics Analysis Form in the space provided for Ethical Principles for the decision-maker, John.

Ethics Analysis Form

Edna Bumpkin

Decision Option: Use the automatic 10% discount to maneuver dates and close the sale

Stakeholders	Principles	Consequences
Phoenix Philatelist's Club (stamp collectors)		• If they found out they were misled by John, they could feel resentful and demand redress. • They could feel taken advantage of and that their trust was betrayed. • It is possible they would never find out.
John (General Manager) [Decision-maker]	Honesty Integrity Trustworthiness Fairness Concern and Respect for Others Commitment to Excellence Leadership Reputation and Morale Accountability	• John might have to deal with a large group that felt they were misled. They could even cancel the booking and go elsewhere. It would be John's fault. • If the club does not find out, John will get the booking and his less-than-ethical method of securing the sale will be validated. He will then be encouraged to use it again and could get caught later.
Other Customers		• If the club finds out, they will tell other people and potential customers might choose not to stay at FOI. This could hurt business for years to come.

OTHER DECISION OPTIONS

Hotels have a rack rate, and only customers who do not know better actually pay full price. None of us would be too happy to discover we were too unsophisticated to get a good rate. The whole idea of "negotiating" rates might be, perhaps, unethical. We could do an ethics analysis of the choice to use negotiable room rates. We might discover that using negotiable room rates violates the same ethical principles that John violated by employing his questionable sales tactic.

There is a good chance that the Philatelist's Club would never detect John's unethical manipulation of the discount, and the consequences, even if it was discovered, would be minimal. However, the long-term effects to John's character and our industry as a whole (when other hospitality operations are doing the same thing) could be negative.

PROFESSIONALISM

A **profession** is an occupation that requires specialized knowledge and skills and is generally looked on with respect by most people. Professions usually have established entrance criteria and rules of right practice. Making large salaries can be a benefit of being in a profession; however, making money cannot be the point of the profession. For business to be thought of as a profession, it must have goals other than simply making money. In other words, business must be good for the community and society to be considered a profession.

We need business if we are to sustain life as we know it today. It is a huge integrated enterprise to manufacture and distribute all the goods we are used to having. Logging, mining, corporate farming, building, manufacturing, and so forth are all entities managed by business people. If the individuals who are running corporations think of themselves as professionals, then they must be concerned with the long-term good of the community rather than mere profits.

Physicians and surgeons can make large salaries, but their primary focus is on healing people rather than making money. When the focus veers from that higher purpose, professions begin to lose their standing. The legal profession has in recent years been the butt of jokes alluding to the greed of certain attorneys. Likewise, the business community has also taken its fair share of hits. When CEOs put short-term profits ahead of concern for the long-term health of the company, or when they make additional profits by failing to spend the money necessary to handle toxic waste or pollution (resulting from the manufacturing process), these too are examples of unprofessional management.

To behave professionally means we continue to study and grow within our profession, we take responsibility for ourselves and our work, we conduct our personal and business lives with integrity, and we are ethical. Throughout this text we have examples of unethical behavior encountered by hospitality students working entry-level positions in the hospitality industry (see *In the Trenches*). These examples are not headline-making scandals. They are, instead, the everyday sort of management behavior many workers have come to expect.

While thousands of highly professional individuals have management positions in hospitality, there are still far too many nonprofessional ones who continue to damage the reputation of the biggest industry in the United States.

The reputation of our industry can encourage or discourage good people from considering careers in hospitality management. What is the perception of college students, majoring in academic areas other than hospitality, of the hospitality management major? We may really like our hospitality major and know it is a good match for ourselves, but is it not perceived as an easier major? Is it considered less important than, say, math or business or biology? Why is this?

Maybe it is because so many people have held unsatisfactory low-level jobs in the hospitality industry. Perhaps they have waited tables or tended bar to help pay their way through college before moving on to careers of interest. The hospitality industry is often not thought of as a career destination, but only as a means of getting to something better. As professionals, we take pride in our industry and our good work in the industry, but it is painful to have the overall reputation of the industry (we are devoting our working lives to) perceived as unprofessional.

It is becoming more difficult to move ahead in hospitality management without a college degree. The industry has become so competitive that good quality management is necessary. The "seat-of-the-pants" school of management was never more than adequate, but adequate is no longer adequate. We compete for employees, and today's employees expect to be treated with respect. They go elsewhere if they are dissatisfied, and unprofessional managers are unable to hire and retain the best employees.

The reputation of the hospitality industry is dependent upon the behavior of its management. If we want our industry to be respected, if we want our own career choices to be respected, then we must make our industry respectable. It is up to us. There are over 500 college hospitality management programs in the United States. The graduates of these programs are filling entry-level hospitality management positions all over the country. Within 20 years, most of the top-level hospitality management positions will be held by our graduates. The decisions our graduates make, and the way they behave in management positions, can make the reputation of our industry one we can all be proud of.

Profits are obviously important. The industry must prosper in order to continue providing the jobs and services that have become vital in our economy and our way of life. An industry of this magnitude cannot, however, exist for the sole benefit of stockholders and top management. This giant industry provides the livelihood for millions of workers. It has an important place in the overall scheme of life in the United States. It is our responsibility as educated leaders, as professionals, to manage this industry in ways that are good for the workers, the customers, the community, and the country. That requires specialized knowledge gained in hospitality management programs and ethical professionals who manage with integrity.

Hospitality managers must understand what professional management involves and embrace the responsibilities. Those who disregard their duty do a

grave disservice to the reputation of the industry. If all hospitality graduates are steeped in and committed to the Ethical Principles for Hospitality Managers, we, in essence, would have an industry-wide code of ethics. Whether in food and beverage, sales, marketing, human resources, housekeeping, meeting planning, or any of the myriad career options in the hospitality industry, we should all work together for the good of all, with trust and integrity.

Line workers new to our industry would soon be socialized in ethical behavior, which might affect other areas of their lives. Life is better when we can trust everyone we do business with (and have contact with) to behave ethically. It is easier to make ethical decisions and behave ethically when it is part of the culture. It is management's responsibility—our responsibility—to make ethics part of the culture. We could avoid all of the negative consequences found in the case study simply by being ethical.

CONCLUSION

In this textbook, we are looking at doing the right thing because it is less painful. However, the mark of an ethical person is to do the right thing out of duty. David Rockefeller said, "Duty is liberating. It forces you to transcend your own limitations and makes you do things that may not come naturally but must be done because they are right."

Ethics codes spell out the rules that members of organizations agree to abide by. Adherence to the rules raises the level of corporate behavior and results in the trust and respect of the community.

KEY WORDS

Marketing   Sales

Target market   Ethics code

Promotion   Profession

CHAPTER THOUGHT QUESTIONS

1. Think of your favorite restaurant. Describe its target market. Compare yourself to the target market of the restaurant. Are you part of this target market? What does the restaurant do to specifically meet the needs of the target market? Describe the menu items, decor, style of service, and so forth, and then explain how or why they meet the needs of the target market. Could they alter anything to better meet the needs of the target market? If so, what could they change?

2. Have any of the places you have ever worked had an ethics code? If yes, describe what was on the ethics code and how you knew about it. If none of the places you have worked had an ethics code, what was the unwritten code of ethics? What was expected of you in terms of ethical behavior (good or bad), and what did management do to model this behavior?

3. List and describe the benefits of having written ethics codes in place in companies. Have you ever been in trouble for something you did not know was wrong? Describe the situation. How does this incident compare to situations that could arise in companies without written ethics codes?

4. Compare the "Principles of Professionalism" of the *Meeting Professionals International* with the Ethical Principles for Hospitality Managers. Are there any principles that are not included in both documents?

5. Describe the relationship between hotel sales people and meeting planners. Discuss the ethical temptations inherent in both positions and possible ways to decrease the temptations.

6. What are the characteristics that make an occupation a profession? What characteristics does the hospitality industry have that might qualify it as a profession? Should the hospitality industry be regarded as a profession? Why or why not? Explain.

7. Describe professional behavior. Discuss if it is possible to behave professionally in a job that is not considered a profession. Give personal examples to back your discussion.

8. Think about all the jobs you have held. Which ones did you like and which ones did you not like? Why? Were the various managers you worked for professional or unprofessional? Is there a relation of professional management to jobs you liked? Discuss.

9. Before you gave serious thought to a career in the hospitality industry, what was your perception of the industry? Has it changed? What is the perception of the industry by your friends or relatives? Are you satisfied with our own and others' perception of the hospitality industry? Why or why not?

10. Discuss the relationship between company reputations, ethics, and written ethics codes. Use examples from your work experience to describe situations where a written ethics code might have had a beneficial effect on the workplace.

REFERENCES

Coughlan, R. (2001). An analysis of professional codes of ethics in the hospitality industry. *International Journal of Hospitality Management, 20*(2), 147–162.

Jaszay, C. (2002a). Company values and ethical leadership. *Journal of Human Resources in Hospitality and Tourism, 1*(3), 47–55.

Jaszay, C. (2002b). Ethical behavior in the hospitality industry. *FIU Hospitality Review, 20*(2), 439–445.

Jaszay, C. (2003). Review of hospitality ethics in research in 2000 and 2001. *Isbell Hospitality Ethics Web Page.* Available at http://www2.nau.edu/~clj5/Ethics/

Manning, G. L., & Reece, B. L. (1998). *Selling today: Building quality partnerships* (7th ed.). Upper Saddle River, NJ: Prentice Hall.

Solomon, R. C. (1999). *A better way to think about business: How personal integrity leads to corporate success.* New York: Oxford University Press.

Starr, R. L. (1987). *Marion.* New York: Vantage Press.

Van Hoof, H. B., McDonald, M. E., Yu, L., & Vallen, G. K. (1996). *A host of opportunities: An introduction to hospitality management.* Chicago: Irwin.

Chapter 7

Ethics and Facilities Management

Facilities management is an area that many of us are less familiar with. We know about serving and housekeeping and checking guests in and out. Facilities management, instead, concerns keeping the building and operating systems working and in good repair. It includes engineering and maintenance and may be closely related to security. Facilities management personnel rarely deal directly with guests and need entirely different skill sets. They must be able to repair and maintain electrical, water, lighting, energy and waste systems, laundry and foodservice equipment, heating and air conditioning, ventilation, and safety and security systems.

In this chapter we will consider ethical issues in both engineering and security, addressing the overlap between the two management areas. Very small properties may not have engineering and/or security departments. The owner may do all the maintenance him- or herself and hire experts to work on the various systems when necessary. Large properties, however, need engineering in-house because the maintenance and repair requirements are enormous. Keeping our guests safe from violence and physical danger also becomes more complex as the size of the property and the number of employees and guests increase.

While engineering is responsible for the repair and maintenance of the building and its systems, the general manager is responsible for the entire operation, which includes engineering. Most of us probably have a better grasp of engineering in terms of our own homes. We know that if we buy a house there is a certain amount of preventative maintenance required—tasks such as cleaning gutters, changing furnace filters, and keeping the chimney flue clear of ash buildup. We must fix anything that breaks, such as a window or a light switch. It is important that we see to the upkeep of the premises, with tasks such as painting and lawn work. If we overlook these responsibilities, the beautiful house becomes dilapidated within a very short period of time.

In the case of a house, it is the homeowner's responsibility to do the upkeep. In the case of a hotel or restaurant, it is the general manager's responsibility to do the upkeep, and he or she will often hire an engineering manager or "chief engineer" to head up the department. Facilities or engineering managers are rarely ever recruited from university hospitality management programs. Instead, they often come from the building and maintenance trades. A large property may need numerous maintenance staff, so supervisory expertise is necessary along with building systems knowledge.

FOSTERING A SHARED ETHIC

We all have our own ethical standards. They may or may not match the ethical standards of the property. One of our tasks in management is to foster a shared ethic among our employees. We accomplish this in the following ways.

1. We hire people who will be willing and able to accept the property's ethical standards.
2. We clearly state the ethical standards so employees know what they are and what they mean in specific behavior terms.
3. We develop policies and procedures that are in line with the ethical standards.
4. We reward ethical behavior while punishing behavior in conflict with the ethical rules we have set.
5. Any time we make decisions, we incorporate questions that concern the ethics of each possible decision option.
6. The general manager makes sure that all of his or her department heads are addressing the ethical aspects of decisions they make within their various management areas. Then the general manager must support these decisions, while taking into consideration ethical concerns.

The above steps enable us to unify our beliefs into a working ethic that elicits predictable and appropriate behavior from all employees. In engineering, however, ethical concerns often cost money. Upgrading fire and safety systems, security windows and doors, and performing the preventive maintenance necessary to avoid safety hazards can be very expensive. Because things of this nature are not all that noticeable, the general manager may decide on a less expensive, less safe option. If upper management talks about ethics but then chooses short-term financial savings above guest safety, engineering will have been shown what really matters and might conclude that concern for guest safety is unnecessary.

MORAL AND LEGAL REQUIREMENTS

We are morally and legally required to keep our guests and employees safe from fires, accidents, and injuries. Fire codes and the Occupational Safety and Health Administration (**OSHA**) set mandatory safety regulations. *Concern and respect* *for others, trustworthiness, commitment to excellence, reputation and morale,* and *accountability* are the ethical principles violated if we fail to take proper care of equipment and systems that, unmaintained, could expose guests and employees to danger. Working fire alarms, sprinklers, evacuation plans, and emergency trained staff all cost money. However, the unnecessary loss of lives in a fire costs considerably more.

We are also responsible for keeping our guests and employees safe from violence at our properties. The courts have awarded large cash settlements to hotel guests who have been assaulted, raped, or robbed while staying at the particular property. We are required to provide **reasonable care** that foreseeable incidents will not cause harm to our guests. We have no control over criminals. What we do have control over is a criminal's opportunity to reach our guests and do them harm. A guest cannot be assaulted in his or her room if there is no way for a criminal to get in. Windows and doors must be made secure. Employees who have access to guest rooms must be carefully selected and then supervised. Engineering and housekeeping staff should be required to wear photo identification badges, and special attention must be paid to key-making machines and who has access to them. Who can utilize this machinery to make keys, who has keys already, and who can get keys are all potential security issues that can be dealt with preventively.

Eighty-five percent of all guest protection incidents involve employees. In other words, our guests are far more likely to be hurt by criminals employed

IN THE TRENCHES

Justin Garber, 23, Winchester, VA

"I used to work for a subcontractor who made food deliveries for five different restaurants. The one in question here was a fine-dining, expensive, and popular steak/seafood joint. When I would go back into the kitchen to receive the food orders, the head chef/part owner would always be smoking cigarettes while cooking. Sometimes he'd be drinking Wild Turkey and the smoke would be dangling out of his mouth, the ash building up, and every so often it would actually fall on the food. When I finally asked one day why it was he smoked while cooking, he just made this sort of 'Ehhhhh' noise. That was it. The restaurant is still in business and the food's good and everyone loves it, but I don't understand how someone could operate in such a manner."

by the hotel than those passing through it. Theft of guests' property and assault by hotel personnel is a management problem that must be solved. At the same time, we, who have chosen to be in the hospitality industry, are generally "people people" who enjoy serving and making our guests happy. We think of ourselves as gracious hosts. We do not like looking at guests and employees with suspicion, but *we* are not *everybody*. It is similar to the act of not locking our car, trusting that people are good and will not attempt to steal it. A better approach would be augmenting these rosy feelings with the realization that there are those out there who might be tempted to steal an unlocked automobile. Therefore, we lock our car all the time in order to lovingly spare our fellow citizens the temptation to do something bad. The former example is good and naive; the latter is good and realistic.

FACILITIES MANAGEMENT AT FRESHWATER OASIS INN

Chief Engineer Bill Gardner, 53, worked 15 years as assistant engineer at a high-rise apartment building in Phoenix. After completing union school and getting his license, Bill came to work for FOI at the hotel's opening. In addition to supervising a maintenance staff of two, he is also responsible for maintaining the in-ground pool.

In *Locked Up or Tight?* (see the segment of the case study in the back of the text), one of Bill Gardner's employees, Milt, who is handicapped with a severe stutter, suggested that they should install security bars on the lower floor guest room windows to protect guests from attack by a rapist who has been terrorizing the city. Bill dismissed the idea as too expensive. There are several issues, aside from the obvious security versus money issue, which this segment of the case study brings to light. The plight of handicapped people on the job, Bill's caveman attitudes toward technology and women, and his somewhat obsolete handyman approach to running the maintenance department at FOI (i.e., assigning frivolous "fix-it" tasks at the expense of other, perhaps more important uses of his staff's time and energy). These issues will all be addressed within the analysis of the guest safety dilemma.

We will take an Ethics Analysis Form and enter Bill's decision option: *To not install security bars on ground floor guest room windows*. We will also enter the stakeholders this decision may directly affect: *Bill, Milt, Guests, Employees, John*, and *FOI* may all be affected by Bill's decision. A completed form follows discussion of the case.

ANALYSIS OF POSSIBLE CONSEQUENCES
FOR BILL GARDNER

Bill recognized the possibility that guests at FOI could be in danger from the rapist. Yet he summarily rejected Milt's suggestion for placing security bars on the ground floor guestrooms, saying that such devices were unattractive and would eat up his entire budget for the next year and a half. While his statement may be true, Bill did not research the actual cost of security bars or consider any number of other more attractive options. He did not discuss the matter any further with Milt, and did not bring the issue of guest safety to the attention of John, the general manager. He simply let it drop.

Bill actually joked that one of the rape victims could have avoided the attack had she stayed home and baked cookies for her husband. His statement indicated disagreement with the proposition that women have the same financial need and right as men to work and travel, and that women should not be subjected to violence because of their gender. Sex discrimination and sexual harassment are illegal. If his attitude and statements were made more public, they could be found offensive, affect his behavior as a manager, and could open FOI to legal action.

FOI will be held accountable if a guest is assaulted while staying at the inn and reasonable care was not taken to keep them safe. In the first case of this kind, Connie Francis, in 1974, was raped in her room at a Howard Johnson property. She was awarded $2.5 million because the sliding door the rapist entered was found to be insecure. "Reasonable care" is not spelled out and often gets defined by juries. When Bill is alerted to an obvious breach in security, to simply do nothing is unlikely to be considered reasonable care. Because John is the general manager of FOI, he would have to take responsibility for the actions or nonactions of his staff. General managers expect their department heads to keep them apprised of departmental problems and issues. Bill Gardner could be disciplined or even terminated if a guest is harmed because guest room windows or doors were not secure. He would have difficulty obtaining another position where security is a job responsibility.

If Bill researched security options for the ground floor guestroom windows, he could present a proposal to John requesting additional funds for security. Bill's assertion to Milt that his budget would be eaten up for the next year and a half is most likely untrue. John would most certainly consider his chief engineer's proposal and then would make the decision—and the responsibility for the decision would be off Bill. True security professionals are often frustrated by operations that say they care about guest safety but then refuse to budget funds to maintain and update security measures.

The lack of communication of guest safety standards and communication between the chief engineer and the general manager are problems that become apparent in Bill's decision to do nothing about guest safety in this situation. It is John's responsibility as general manager to know what is going on in all the departments and to foster open communication lines between all of the departments and with him. It is John's responsibility to hire department heads capable of embracing and modeling FOI's standards, and these department heads should alert him to problems and help him to effectively run FOI.

John may or may not be aware that there have been assaults on guests at properties close to FOI. However, he would expect his chief engineer to be on top of safety issues related to the physical plant. If Bill offered no information about safety, it would be up to John to inquire about what provisions Bill was considering in light of the recent violent attacks against women in the area. If the chief engineer has done nothing, and has no plans to do anything, and, after acknowledging the existence of a breach in security that he is and was aware of, Bill could lose the trust of the general manager, which would not bode well for his future at FOI.

ANALYSIS OF POSSIBLE CONSEQUENCES FOR MILT

Milt is rightfully concerned about the safety of guests in ground floor rooms. He told his supervisor, Bill Gardner, that the ground floor windows were not secure and suggested they put bars on them. Bill said the bars were too expensive and Milt was expected to drop the subject. Milt's communication disorder makes conversation very difficult, so he could not effectively argue his point of view with Bill. Neither would he relish the idea of pursuing the issue on another level with, perhaps, John Fallin (the general manager).

At any rate, FOI would not hold Milt responsible if a guest were harmed because engineering neglected to secure ground floor windows. Milt, however, would feel personally responsible because he knew something was unsafe and still did not pursue it. To take personal responsibility Milt would be required to tell Bill's boss, John Fallin, that the ground floor windows were not secure and that Bill said it was too expensive to do anything about it. The thought of going over his supervisor's head might be stressful. After all, it is entirely possible that John could agree with Bill about the unfeasibility of installing security bars. Bill could discover that Milt went over his head, be vindictive about it, and endeavor to make life miserable for him. Milt could lose his job or feel pressure to seek a position elsewhere.

ANALYSIS OF POSSIBLE CONSEQUENCES FOR GUESTS

There would be negative publicity in the media if a guest was attacked at FOI. The guest (and people who know the guest) would tell others about the incident, tarnishing the reputation of FOI as a safe place to stay. Obviously, business could be harmed. When we go to restaurants, we expect the food to be safe. When we stay in hotels, we expect the rooms to be secure. When they are not and we suffer the consequences, we can and usually do sue. And we win.

The chance of a guest being assaulted in this situation is greater than usual. There is a known rapist breaking into ground floor hotel rooms in the vicinity of FOI. If there was a rapist breaking into homes in our neighborhood, it would be reasonable to lock our doors and windows at night. We would take reasonable precautions to keep ourselves safe. If we had an overnight guest in our home, we would take steps to ensure our guests' safety as well. As professional hospitality managers it is our responsibility to keep guests safe, and the courts agree.

There is a chance that the rapist would skip over FOI and no guest would be harmed even without additional safety precautions, *this time*. To not take safety precautions would increase our risk of having an incident at some point, however, and the cost of an incident would be far more than the cost of the safety precautions, not to mention relieving management and guests of the worry.

ANALYSIS OF POSSIBLE CONSEQUENCES FOR EMPLOYEES

Anything that harms FOI harms the inn's employees. Employees count on FOI for their incomes. If business decreases because a guest was assaulted, some employees could have their hours reduced or be laid off. If Milt was to voice his guest safety concerns to another employee, it could get around that FOI puts profits ahead of guest safety. This could negatively affect employees' attitudes about the state of guest safety, the maintenance department, and about management at FOI.

If the company does not care about guest safety, why should employees care? Employees might wonder if the company cares about their safety. If employees do not think the company cares about them, they will be less satisfied with their jobs, job performance could suffer, and turnover could increase. Trust in management could decrease, which then affects the ability of management to lead the employees.

ANALYSIS OF POSSIBLE CONSEQUENCES FOR JOHN FALLIN

The general manager's job is to run the operation effectively, ensuring customer and employee satisfaction and financial success. If a guest is harmed, John, as general manager, is held accountable. FOI could be sued, and John would most likely face disciplinary actions or lose his position altogether. He would have a difficult time finding a comparable position. If a guest is not hurt at this time, but safety precautions have not been taken, the risk of harm to a future guest would be viable, and could result in similar outcomes.

The general manager is responsible for the actions of his or her department heads. John must rely on his managers to keep him informed and to take care of business in their respective departments. John is responsible for hiring capable managers and supervising them. It is John's responsibility to infuse a sense of right and wrong in his management team that is appropriate for FOI. Adherence to the shared ethics is made possible by policies and procedures that are compatible with the ethical principles held by FOI. John's chief engineer is making decisions that may or may not be in line with the ethical standards of FOI. John is being held accountable for the decisions Bill Gardner makes, so John must know what Bill is doing.

If John allows Bill to work without communicating with him, or, if John allows Bill free reign to make decisions incompatible with FOI's mission, philosophy, and ethical principles, John could lose leadership authority with his other managers. Communication could break down further and the shared ethics could be lost. It is the general manager's responsibility to set the standards, get everyone to accept and work the standards, and maintain the standards through effective supervision.

ANALYSIS OF POSSIBLE CONSEQUENCES FOR FOI

If a guest is harmed now or in the future, FOI could be sued and would suffer reputation damage that could reduce business. Reduced business could result in fewer hours for employees and some might even be laid off. If John's leadership authority deteriorates, adherence to standards could diminish, resulting in less satisfied customers and further reduction in business. While it is possible that a guest would never be harmed, the risk of that occurring should be eliminated as much as possible. Reasonable care should be taken to protect guests so that FOI in turn is protected from harm, which ultimately protects the livelihoods of employees.

ETHICAL PRINCIPLES VIOLATED BY THIS DECISION

Bill Gardner's decision not to install security devices on ground floor guestroom windows, or pursue other means of security, violates several of the Ethical Principles for Hospitality Managers. Bill knows there is a security risk but still chooses to do nothing. *Integrity* is doing what we know is right no matter what. Bill does not have integrity. He is not *trustworthy*, in that John cannot trust him to do what is right and best for the inn. To do nothing when guests are at a safety risk is to show no *concern and respect for others*.

Bill does not have a *commitment to excellence* since he has no problem ignoring a safety risk. As manager of his department, part of Bill's job is to model behavior that supports the standards of FOI. His employees may be influenced by his inappropriate behavior, so for that reason he violates the principle of *Leadership*. *Reputation and morale* could also suffer as a consequence of Bill's decision not to take safety precautions. He is *accountable* for his decision and will bear the consequences.

Ethics Analysis Form

Locked Up or Tight?

Decision Option: To not install security devices on ground floor guestroom openings

Stakeholders	Principles	Consequences
Bill Gardner (Chief Engineer) [Decision-Maker]	Integrity Trustworthiness Concern and Respect for Others Commitment to Excellence	• Bill could lose his job if a guest is harmed because he failed to alert the general manager of a possible security breach. • Bill could lose John's trust for the same reason.

(continued)

Stakeholders	Principles	Consequences
Bill Gardner (Chief Engineer) [Decision-Maker]	Leadership Reputation and Morale Accountability	
Milt (Engineering Employee)		• Milt could feel personally responsible if a guest was harmed because he failed to pursue his concerns about insecure ground floor windows. • Going over his supervisor's head could be stressful. John might side with Bill on the issue, and Bill could then be vindictive. Milt might experience hassles on the job, or lose the job itself.
Guests		• A guest could be harmed, which could negatively affect the rest of his or her life. • Negative media attention could tarnish the reputation of FOI as a safe place to stay. • Word of mouth from an injured guest (and his or her acquaintances) could tarnish the reputation of FOI. • Business at the inn could suffer as the property's reputation falls. • An injured guest could sue and would likely be awarded a large sum of money.
Employees		• If business decreases, employees could suffer reduced hours or layoffs. • Employees could discover that FOI put short-term profits ahead of guest safety. This could negatively affect attitudes and job performance. • Employees could lose trust in management. • Turnover could increase.
John Fallin (General Manager)		• If a guest is at some time injured due to John's turning a blind eye to security concerns and then sues, John could lose his position. • He could have difficulty finding a comparable position if he is terminated at FOI. • John is accountable for Bill's decisions, so it is assumed that he must know what Bill is doing. And he *should* know what Bill is doing. • His leadership authority could be undermined if he allows Bill, or any manager, to operate outside of the FOI ethical principles.

(continued)

Stakeholders	Principles	Consequences
FOI		• If a guest is at some time injured, FOI could be sued and suffer reputation damage that could reduce business. • Reduced business could result in fewer hours for employees, who might later be laid off as a result. • If John's leadership authority deteriorates, adherence to standards could diminish, resulting in fewer satisfied customers and a further reduction in business. • Employee dissatisfaction could cause increased turnover.

OTHER DECISION OPTIONS

Bill Gardner's decision not to propose to his general manager the installation of safety devises on ground floor guestrooms is unethical. It puts guests in unnecessarily dangerous positions. The consequences could be horrible for the guest and his or her family and friends. We do not have the right to take that type of risk with our guests. Furthermore, FOI could be damaged financially, which would jeopardize the livelihoods of all its employees.

Bill did not bother to pursue the issue of guest safety with the general manager who has the power to authorize expenditures. Bill failed to research any other options that might have been equally effective and more attractive and acceptable to guests. He could have had Milt look into security options instead of wasting time fixing broken equipment that would most likely never be used again. Bill's offhand dismissal of the issue of guest safety in effect jeopardizes John Fallin's position as general manager at FOI. John is ultimately responsible for everything that takes place during his watch, so Bill, as his hand-picked choice to manage maintenance and security at FOI, has failed him greatly with his inability to recognize potential disaster when it stares him in the face. It is not Bill who will have to answer questions if and when the worst-case scenario occurs, it is John.

SWIM-UP POOL FRANK

Most of the ethical dilemmas we are looking at are fairly clear-cut. We know what is right and wrong from the beginning. While it might be initially tempting to make the unethical choice, we have found, through the analysis process, that the wrong choice results in avoidable negative consequences. In *Swim-Up Pool Frank* (see the segment of the case study at the back of the text), Frank

Stratten, the owner of FOI, paid the inn a surprise visit to initiate a construction project in the pool area. He spoke with John Fallin (general manager) and Bill Gardner (chief engineer) about "getting the ball rolling" on the addition of a swim-up bar in the pool at FOI.

John applied for a building permit and Sam Riley came out from the city to inspect. Riley said John should pay him $500 to "get around snaggles with the permits." Riley implied that he had the power to hold up paperwork indefinitely if John failed to make the payment. The $500 is not a legitimate payment to the city. Riley would pocket the money, and the city would know nothing about it. Every single ethical principle is violated by Sam Riley's demand for a $500 payment. Bribery is illegal, and it is certainly unethical for Sam Riley to request it.

John is disgusted by such a demand but now must decide whether or not he should pay Sam Riley the $500 bribe. We can use the Ethics Analysis Form to help us arrive at the best decision. We enter the decision: *To go ahead and pay the bribe,* and then we list the obvious stakeholders as: *John Fallin, Sam Riley, Heidi Bell,* and *FOI.* A completed form follows this discussion.

ANALYSIS OF POSSIBLE CONSEQUENCES FOR JOHN FALLIN

We begin by considering the timeline John has on the pool project. Most tourists choose Arizona as a vacation destination in the winter months to avoid the cold, so having a heated pool on the premises is a definite plus. Eventually the summer weather makes having a pool a necessity, but there is no real concern about that in this case. Summer is the slow season in the Phoenix area. Winter is king. So construction during this period would have to be done quickly because the pool cannot be out of commission. If the city holds up the permit, John would be unlikely to have the swim-up bar open in time for the seasonal rush.

John needs the building permits quickly in order to get construction started and finished in the shortest time possible. If he pays the $500, he will get the permits quickly. If he does not pay the $500, he will not. The extra $500 payment would not cause FOI financial hardship, and John may feel that $500 is a small price for avoiding the aggravation Sam Riley could most certainly cause. Sam Riley has probably extorted money successfully from other companies for just that reason: it is easier to simply knuckle under and pay the $500.

Can John go to the agency and complain? Does he have any proof? Will he be able to get his permits in time if the agency decides to investigate the allegations? It will be John's word against Sam Riley's. John may not be able to resolve this to his satisfaction. However, the agency most likely would be aware of his allegations, and, hopefully, make it possible that undue delays in his permits be avoided. We know that Sam Riley is abusing his authority and doing something illegal and wrong. To do the right thing in this situation—refuse to pay the bribe—could cause John untold aggravation and a costly delay on the building permit.

ANALYSIS OF POSSIBLE CONSEQUENCES FOR SAM RILEY

Sam Riley has probably extorted a lot of money over the years and damaged the reputation of the agency he works for. He could be fired and even prosecuted for extorting citizens, *if he gets caught*. Sam Riley is not an upstanding citizen. He is raising children and may not in turn be teaching them to be good citizens. He is not behaving in ways that are good for society or the community in which he resides.

Riley is responsible for his actions. His superior at the agency is also responsible for those actions taken by employees under the auspices of city government. He or she should have had policies and procedures in place, along with better supervision, to facilitate the prevention of these sorts of illegal activities. As managers, we are accountable for the actions of our employees. If we did not know they were acting inappropriately, we *should* have known. That is our responsibility.

ANALYSIS OF POSSIBLE CONSEQUENCES FOR HEIDI BELL

We respect people with integrity. To have integrity means we demonstrate the courage of our convictions by doing what we know is right even when there is pressure to do otherwise. Heidi will learn from the way John handles this situation and will most likely handle similar situations in ways modeled to her by her superior. Heidi does not have to make the difficult decision in this situation. She will most likely understand John's reasoning if he decides to pay the bribe, but she may also lose a little respect for him in the process.

ANALYSIS OF POSSIBLE CONSEQUENCES FOR FOI

FOI has a duty to provide guests the full array of services. The inn has no control over the weather, but it does have control over pool construction (which could spoil a guest's stay if the pool were not available). The $500 payment would not hurt FOI, while the delay in construction would.

ETHICAL PRINCIPLES VIOLATED BY THIS DECISION

We all know that Sam Riley is a despicable crook abusing his position as a government official. This is a difficult case because FOI would most likely be better off if John just went ahead and paid the $500. John would avoid all sorts of aggravation, and the swim-up bar would be up and running for the busy season so guests could enjoy it without the inconvenience of ongoing construction.

If John pays Sam Riley the $500 bribe, his *integrity* will be violated because he knows bribery is wrong. He would be choosing to pay the bribe, not because it is right, but because it is expedient. Paying bribes hardly comes under the principle of *commitment to excellence*. John instructs his managers through his own actions, so the principle of *leadership* is violated because, if John chooses to pay the bribe, he is modeling unethical behavior for his staff. And, of course, as general manager, John is *accountable* for his behavior and the behavior of his staff.

Ethics Analysis Form
Swim-Up Pool Frank

Decision Option: To pay the city inspector a $500 bribe to get a permit

Stakeholders	Principles	Consequences
John Fallin, (General Manager) [Decision Maker]	Integrity Commitment to Excellence Leadership Accountability	• To not pay the $500 could hold up the permit, and John could have the pool torn up when guests need it most. • Frank the owner might think John was incompetent if he could not get the pool done in time for the busy season. • Paying the $500 may be expedient, but he would be going along with something unethical, which ultimately damages his integrity. • John could report Sam Riley for extortion.
Sam Riley (City Inspector)		• If he gets caught, Sam Riley could be fired and even prosecuted for extorting citizens. • Riley has probably extorted a lot of money over the years, and damaged the reputation of the agency he works for. • Sam Riley is not an upstanding citizen. He is raising children and may not be teaching them to be good citizens. He is not behaving in ways that are good for society or the community.
Heidi (Assistant General Manager)		• Heidi will learn from the way John handles this situation. She will most likely handle similar situations in ways modeled to her by her superior. • Heidi does not have to make the difficult decision in this situation. She will probably understand John's reasoning if he decides to pay the bribe, but she may also lose a little respect for him in the bargain.
FOI		• FOI has a duty to provide guests the full array of services. FOI has no control over the weather, but it does have control over pool construction. Permit problems could spoil a guest's stay if the pool was subsequently not available. • The $500 payment would not hurt FOI, while the delay in construction would.

MAKING THE DECISION

Whenever we do anything in violation of ethical principles we are chipping away at our own integrity. We are making it easier to do the wrong thing next time. Do we have a responsibility to report wrongdoing, or is it okay to simply ignore it? Think about news stories you have read where bystanders did nothing when someone was being violated. How does one go about reporting wrongdoing of this nature? Perhaps John could write to Sam Riley (and make copies available to city officials) expressing his view that paying Riley $500 under the table does not seem to be the right thing to do—or for a building inspector to request.

All of the dilemmas we have analyzed so far have resulted in choosing ethical decisions because they had the least negative consequences. Our analysis of *Swim-Up Pool Frank* shows us that opting for the right decision (to not pay the bribe) could actually hurt FOI in the short term. All along we have been encouraging students to analyze situations to determine the least painful option. In this case, doing the wrong thing is in fact the least painful decision. There are, however, some larger, long-term consequences we need to address in order to understand why we might want to suffer negative consequences for making the ethical decision in order to avoid doing something wrong.

- John and Heidi would both know they allowed Sam Riley to extort money from FOI. They would think less of the local authorities. They would know they did the *expedient* thing instead of the *right* thing. Their integrity would be compromised.
- The community's business environment is allowed to deteriorate because everyone will know that local officials need bribes to facilitate getting things done. The business environment becomes less civilized. Excellence, integrity, honesty, and so forth are not in the equation.
- It hurts all of us when we stand by while someone acts improperly and undermines the system.

This is a difficult case because doing the wrong thing is easier and good for John and FOI in the short run. The long-run consequences are not all that obvious, and it might be appealing to just ignore the whole thing—that is, to let someone else worry about the corrosion of society. This is a situation where the organization has to support doing the right thing. And why do the right thing? As educated professionals, we have a responsibility to care for our workers, our businesses, and our communities. Who else will perform this function if we do not? Each unethical decision, each decision to look the other way and just go along because it is expedient, breaks down the trust and respect that holds societies together. In the big picture, if no one paid bribes to city officials for building permits and licenses and whatnot, then crooked city officials would not even think to ask for bribes. They would just do their jobs and the world would be a much more pleasant place.

You will be in top management positions within the next 20 years. It is you who will set the tone for your organizations. It will be *you* who is charged with the task of guiding managers to the point where they can make ethical decisions even when difficult and not obviously beneficial in the short run. Not everyone has integrity because integrity is built over years spent making ethical choices, oftentimes difficult choices, hard choices, unpopular choices, and not always expedient choices. That is why we respect people with integrity, because they had the courage and the strength to do the right thing.

CONCLUSION

We might not ordinarily think of facilities management as being wrought with ethical dilemmas. We have seen, however, that this "nonhospitality" department ultimately concerns the welfare of guests and employees, and that a strong ethical sense is essential to keep them both safe. If facilities deteriorate, business will suffer and jobs could be at risk. If a guest is hurt, either by human intervention or something unsafe in the building, we open ourselves to a lawsuit. Our reputation might in turn be tarnished, which would affect the business as a whole.

There are no independent departments within hospitality operations. They need to be totally integrated. Intercommunication between departments and the general manager is of the utmost importance. The general manager is accountable for the entire operation and must know or be made aware of what everyone is doing. Lapses are ultimately his or her responsibility. By fostering an ethical climate based on clearly stated ethical principles and policies and procedures (that support the ethics), managers are better able to make decisions in line with the standards, mission, and philosophy of the operation.

KEY WORDS

OSHA   Reasonable care

CHAPTER THOUGHT QUESTIONS

1. Discuss why it is essential for new hires to be able to accept and work within the operation's ethical standards. Describe problems that may arise if they cannot.
2. As managers we are to hire people whose ethical standards are either compatible with the facilities' standards or who will be able to accept and work within those same ethical standards of the facility. How can we determine in job interviews what prospective employees' ethical standards are, or if they will be personally capable of embracing the facilities' standards?

3. Assess the presence or absence of a shared ethic in a current or past work-place. What did management do to foster a shared ethic? What affect did this have on employee behavior? What could the manager have done to foster a shared ethic?

4. Think of examples from your personal experience where you did what you thought you were supposed to do and then got in trouble for it. Why did you think you were doing the right thing? Were you doing the right thing? How could this situation have been avoided? Answer the same questions about a personal experience where someone else did what they thought you wanted him or her to do and then you were upset with them for doing it.

5. Reconsider any big decision you had to make or are currently considering. State the decision option you were or are considering and list the questions you can ask to determine whether any ethical principles will be violated.

6. Describe what you would consider to be *reasonable care* for a trip into the forest with several small children; a field trip to a public zoo; an afternoon at the beach.

7. Describe any measures that have been taken to keep either guests or employees safe from accidents or violence at any hospitality operation at which you have worked. Do you foresee any possible dangers that have not been addressed at your place of work? What are they, and what measures could be taken to avoid harm?

8. Describe the communication between departments and between departments and the general manager at any job you have worked. Did the departments feel connected to each other? Were the employees of the various departments friendly with each other? Did the general manager know who you were? Did he or she address you by name? Could or should the general manager have known you? Discuss why or why not and describe how you would like to be treated at a job. Is this feasible; why or why not?

9. Discuss what you believe are our personal responsibilities for the good of our society and communities. Mention such things as government, the environment, natural resources. Give examples of choices you make that are for the greater good. List things that you think you ought to be doing.

10. Discuss the differences and similarities between personal responsibility and the responsibility of people in management positions for the good of our society and communities.

REFERENCES

Burstein, H. (2001). *Hotel and motel loss prevention: A management perspective.* Upper Saddle River, NJ: Prentice Hall.

Gray, W. S., & Liguori, S. C. (2003). *Hotel and motel management and operations* (4th ed.). Upper Saddle River, NJ: Prentice Hall.

Hall, S. S. J. (Ed.). (1992). *Ethics in hospitality management: A book of readings.* MI: Educational Institute of the American Hotel & Motel Association.

Homan, D., & Pratt, L. C. (2002). *Radical hospitality.* MA: Paraclete Press.

Newland, L. E. (1997). *Hotel protection management: The innkeeper's guide to guest protection and reasonable care.* Washington: TNZ.

Van Hoof, H. B., McDonald, M. E., Yu, L., & Vallen, G. K. (1996). *A host of opportunities: An introduction to hospitality management.* Chicago: Irwin.

Chapter 8

Ethics and Foodservice Management

Almost every hospitality organization has some sort of foodservice component. There are over 9 million foodservice workers in the United States and many of them are in low pay, no experience necessary type positions. While there are many foodservice management opportunities for hospitality graduates, the field is complex and requires special skills in several areas. Ethical concerns are particularly evident in managing diversity, employee safety on the job, food safety, and purchasing, all of which are areas that will be addressed in this chapter.

MANAGING DIVERSITY IN FOODSERVICE

We can expect to have employees from a wide variety of backgrounds in our foodservice operations. Many of the positions are entry level without education or work experience requirements. As a result, many of our employees will have little education or work experience and may need additional training in workplace etiquette and work ethics.

Some of our foodservice employees may not be able to communicate in English, and some may not be able to read or write in any language. Twenty percent of American adults are functionally or totally illiterate. Illiteracy is mostly hidden, and, because it is often not a result of low intelligence, it is not unusual to find that many illiterates have devised sophisticated means of functioning while keeping the deficiency hidden. Unless we actually see job applicants fill out applications or ask them to read something aloud, we could easily be hiring people who cannot read, write, or compute adequately.

We have to recognize our employees' cultural differences to ensure that we are communicating in effective ways and do not create barriers for understanding and compliance. We may need to make some concessions for the needs of single parents and older workers in terms of time off for sick kids and/or medical problems. The ethics of managing a diverse workforce were discussed in Chapter 5.

WORK ETHIC

A **work ethic** is the sense that work is necessary and good for us, and it manifests itself in good work habits such as timeliness and being on task while on the clock. A good work ethic helps us to enjoy our jobs by finding value in the simple act of working. People with good work ethics tend to be sons or daughters of hard-working people with those same good work ethics. We as children learn what we see.

Our employees, however, may not have had the work ethic instilled in them as children, and their attitudes at work may be less than joyful. We can go ahead and blame their unenthusiastic work performance on a poor work ethic, or we can ask whether or not their jobs and working conditions allow for a sense of pride. We can look at our management strategies and determine if we are providing positive incentives to reinforce good feelings about their efforts on the job.

Just as we may not all have the same personal ethics, we may not all have the same work ethic. We can hire people who are willing and able, and then we can instill an appropriate work ethic in them by providing good training, good working conditions, a sense of personal ownership in the product and place of business, and positive ongoing supervision.

Poor management can destroy an otherwise strong work ethic in employees. There are many hard-working foodservice employees who care and take pride in their work, but there are also far too many managers who fail to notice the good efforts of their employees. Instead, these managers criticize their employees unnecessarily, are disrespectful and unappreciative of their work, and do not take into consideration their employees' feelings. Poor management is the single biggest reason for 30% of restaurants going out of business in their first year of operation.

FOODSERVICE WORKER SAFETY

The foodservice industry has more than twice as many accidents as other industries. Workers suffer falls, burns, cuts, and strains, most of which could be avoided because accidents are primarily caused by the careless actions of people. Our responsibility as managers is to foster a safety-conscious workforce and working environment. We are responsible for identifying and correcting potential safety problems, and for training and supervising our employees in safe work habits.

Foodservice equipment is very powerful and we must never assume employees know how to safely use the equipment. Employees must be trained to properly use foodservice equipment such as slicers, mixers, and food processors. Teenagers are particularly at risk for accidents because most have not lived long enough to have gained the painful common sense experience that teaches us to be careful. We are responsible for the safety of our workers while they are in the workplace.

FOOD-BORNE ILLNESS AND FOOD SAFETY

We will go out of business if our guests are not satisfied with the food or service. Their gratitude for merely surviving the dining experience will probably not be enough to bring them back. This might seem like an oversimplification, but the bottom-line reality for foodservice managers is that, no matter how delicious and attractive the food is or is not, it must not make guests sick or kill them.

Most food-borne illness is caused by contamination or unchecked bacterial growth. Both of these sources of food-borne illness can be avoided if foodservice workers are following safe food-handling practices such as keeping cold food cold, hot food hot, and washing hands and utensils frequently. It is management's responsibility to make sure food-handlers are using safe practices. This requires that we be communicating standards and procedures effectively—and then supervising and monitoring to ensure that standards are being met and procedures are as specified.

FOODSERVICE AT THE FRESHWATER OASIS INN

Executive Chef Eric Altman is 39 years old, received training at the Culinary Institute of Chicago, and has worked some of the country's top hotels and restaurants. He wanted stability and less stress in a smaller operation and has been

IN THE TRENCHES

Joey Schultz, 20, Tempe, AZ

"I'm an associate manager at a local Italian fast-food place. One night while working at the drive-thru register, another manager risked contamination and poor food quality in order to save time on a customer's order. It was one of the busiest hours of the night and this manager was preparing orders for my rush. I had an order that called for food needing to be microwaved then placed on top a pasta dish. Rushing to prepare the order, the manager grabbed the bag from the microwave and dropped it on the floor. Several chicken pieces spilled onto the tile. This manager simply picked up the bag and scooped all the chicken back in it, then proceeded to serve it up for me. I was shocked and told her to make another, but she insisted it was too busy and she 'didn't have the time.' Instead of just handing out the dish, though, I took the extra time to prepare another one regardless of whether or not the remaining drive-thru guest were served in the advertised 5-minute time frame. This was a situation where I felt the integrity of the food product outweighed the speed of service."

content at FOI these past 5 years. Similar to John Fallin's (general manager) contract with Frank (the owner), Eric is also eligible for a year-end bonus based on performance and restaurant sales. He is responsible for all foodservice activities and supervises cooks and dishwashers on the day shift. Chef Eric also supervises Dardina Traylor, who began at FOI a few years ago and has worked her way up to the position of sous chef.

Eric purchased thirteen 4-pound beef tenderloins from Tate Brothers to run filets as a special. (See *The Best-Laid Plans* segment of the case study at the back of the text.) Dardina dropped three trays containing the filets they had just cut up. The filets landed on the floor amidst the fragments of ramekins broken in the process. Eric has to decide what to do with the filets. Should he serve them or not?

If Eric does not serve the contaminated filets, his food cost is going to increase and he will have to decide on and prep another special. We can assume that our guests would not order filets if they knew they had been on a dirty floor amidst the remnants of broken ramekins. To counter this, Eric could rinse the filets off, pick out any ceramic particles stuck in the meat, and the guests probably would not know the difference. We can enter *serve the contaminated filets*, along with the stakeholders, *Eric, Dardina, Customers,* and *FOI,* on a blank Ethics Analysis Form and conduct an analysis to determine possible consequences for the decision to serve the filets. A completed Ethics Analysis Form follows the discussion.

ANALYSIS OF POSSIBLE CONSEQUENCES FOR CHEF ERIC

We begin the analysis by entering the answers to the following questions on the Ethics Analysis Form. What is the likelihood of someone getting sick or injured from eating the contaminated filets? What would happen if someone did get sick or injured? Could Eric be held responsible? What could happen to him? His reputation? His position? Each time Eric serves contaminated food, he runs the risk of an outbreak of foodborne illness. If he serves the contaminated meat this time, will he be more inclined to serve contaminated food again?

It is quite possible that if he goes ahead and serves the contaminated filets his guests will never know, and his food costs will not take the subsequent hit. He could lose the respect of his staff, however, which could in turn reduce his management effectiveness.

ANALYSIS OF POSSIBLE CONSEQUENCES FOR DARDINA

If he serves the contaminated filets, how might this affect Dardina and her future performance? Could other employees discover that FOI was serving the filets Dardina dropped? Would employees tell other employees? What might the waitstaff think about serving contaminated meat? Would they steer customers away from the filet special? How might this affect other employees' performance? How might very ethical employees feel about the manager or other employees who behaved in questionable ways? What would Dardina's decision be if an employee she was supervising dropped food on the floor? Can a manager enforce rules he or she does not follow?

ANALYSIS OF POSSIBLE CONSEQUENCES FOR CUSTOMERS

Could customers find out that contaminated meat was being served? How? If a customer(s) got sick or injured from the contaminated meat, what could happen? What might they do?

ANALYSIS OF POSSIBLE CONSEQUENCES FOR FOI

What are the consequences to the inn if customers are sick or injured from the contaminated steaks? Could this become a story in the local news and print media? What if no one gets sick or injured, but customers hear "rumors" about contaminated food being served? Is this possible? How could this affect FOI? If employees know about the contaminated meat, how can this affect the reputation of FOI as a good place to work?

ETHICAL PRINCIPLES VIOLATED BY THIS DECISION

To analyze the decision option (to go ahead and serve the contaminated filets), we ask and answer questions to ascertain the possible consequences—that is, what will happen if we do this or that? We enter the answers to our questions on the following Ethics Analysis Form. We can then consider our answers and go down the list of Ethical Principles for Hospitality Managers and enter violated principles on the form.

Withholding contamination information from customers is *dishonest*, because the information would probably change their menu selection decisions. Eric knows that the meat is contaminated and knows it is not right to serve contaminated meat. To go ahead and do something we know is wrong is the act of a person without *integrity*. To serve the contaminated meat puts customers at risk. The person who would knowingly put customers at risk cannot be *trusted* and shows a lack of *concern and respect for others*.

A *commitment to excellence* means that we always do our best work. Serving contaminated meat is wrong. Eric would be setting a bad example for his employees if he serves the contaminated meat, and his *leadership* ability would be diminished. FOI's *reputation* could be damaged and the *morale* of the staff could deteriorate. As Executive Chef, Eric is *accountable* for everything that goes on in foodservice and for his decisions.

Ethics Analysis Form

Best-Laid Plans

Decision Option: Eric decides to serve the contaminated meat

Stakeholders	Principles	Consequences
Eric (Exec. Chef) [Decision-Maker]	Honesty Integrity Trustworthiness Concern and Respect for Others Commitment to Excellence Leadership Reputation and Morale Accountability	• If Eric serves the meat (that mixed with shattered ceramic on the floor), his food cost would not go up. • If people get sick or injured from the contaminated meat, Eric would be responsible. He could face disciplinary action and/or termination. • If people get sick or injured from the contaminated meat, Eric's reputation as a chef would be tarnished.
Dardina (Sous Chef)		• If the contaminated meat is served, Dardina might feel that it is okay to serve contaminated food, and it could happen again. Other employees might think it is okay and be less careful as well. • Though it was Dardina's carelessness that caused the problem, Eric will still be held responsible. • Dardina's supervision of staff might be less careful and her ability to manage could be reduced.
Customers		• Someone could get sick or injured. • More than likely no one would get sick or injured from eating the contaminated meat. They might never know their steak had been on the floor with broken ramekins. • People talk, and it is possible customers could hear that contaminated meat was being served. This could damage FOI's reputation and result in lost sales.
FOI		• If people get sick or injured from the contaminated meat, FOI will be held responsible for medical costs and could be sued. • The restaurant could be investigated by the health department and cited for unsanitary practices, perhaps even shut down. This is public record. • The bad publicity could result in loss of business, and FOI's reputation as a quality place to dine would be tarnished. • Employee morale could go down, and turnover could increase. FOI could become less desirable to potential employees.

OTHER DECISION OPTIONS

If Eric does not serve the filets, he will have to change the special. What will customers' reactions be to the change of special? Some may be disappointed, but most would probably rather not eat contaminated meat. Customers will probably be pleased to know FOI would rather take a loss than endanger their welfare. That can enhance the reputation of FOI, making customers feel good about coming back, and causing them to remark favorably to others about their experience at FOI.

Dardina and other employees will notice that Eric always does the right thing even when it affects the bottom line. How might that influence Dardina's behavior? Other employees? They may all be more careful. The manager's behavior is always more influential than what he or she says. Doing the right thing becomes the norm and what is expected and modeled. Trust and loyalty could increase and turnover and absenteeism could decrease.

Other than a temporary rise in food cost, FOI is not in any way harmed by not serving the contaminated steaks, and no ethical principles are violated if Chef Eric does not serve the meat in question.

We might be very tempted to serve the contaminated steaks in order to keep food cost down. When we analyze the decision, however, we uncover some very negative consequences that could have far-reaching negative effects on both our ability to manage and the success of FOI. Why take the chance?

Obviously we should not be wasting food, and Eric's food cost will go up if he does not serve the contaminated filets. No problem would have arisen had Dardina not dropped the filets in the first place. She placed one tray on top of another separated by ramekins. The load was too heavy and unstable for her. It is not surprising that the top tray slid off and Dardina dropped the whole thing. It is always easy to look back and say what should have been done. Our management task is to think about possible consequences before we take action. Accidents are costly and avoidable. It is the chef's responsibility to make sure mistakes like this do not happen, and this is accomplished through proper training and supervision.

THE ETHICS OF PURCHASING

Foodservice operations can have huge budgets for purchasing all the food and supplies necessary to prepare menu items. Purchasing is either handled by the kitchen manager, the executive chef, the food and beverage director, or, in very large operations, a purchasing agent. The higher the food cost, the lower the profit, so careful purchasing is extremely important to ensure that costs stay low as possible. The purchase of too much food can result in spoilage and waste. The purchase of too little food can result in inconvenient trips to grocery stores or other suppliers, increased stress, or customer dissatisfaction. And, of course, it is necessary to monitor prices to ensure we are getting the best deal for specified products.

Because there are large amounts of money involved, suppliers are eager to have our business. Ethical issues may arise if suppliers offer incentives to encourage us to order from them. When we are given the responsibility of purchasing food and supplies, our loyalty must remain with the organization we represent. We are using the organization's money to purchase food and supplies, and not our own resources. So, gifts (before or after the purchase) or incentives do not belong to us, but rather to the foodservice organization whose money we are spending. There are fine lines between gifts, bribes, and kickbacks. We should insist on good products, good service, and fair prices from our suppliers, foregoing any of these unrelated incentives and gifts. There are opportunities for theft and unethical behavior all along the chain of supply, and we must resist any temptation to behave unethically.

For many years, purchasing agents have worked toward professionalizing the purchasing component of foodservice management. Over 45,000 supply managers belong to the Institute for Supply Management, which is a nonprofit association dedicated to professional development and promotion of the profession of supply management. ISM members agree to live by the following ethical code.

Principles and Standards of Ethical Supply Management Conduct

LOYALTY TO YOUR ORGANIZATION
JUSTICE TO THOSE WITH WHOM YOU DEAL
FAITH IN YOUR PROFESSION

From these principles are derived the ISM standards of supply management conduct.

1. Avoid the intent and appearance of unethical or compromising practice in relationships, actions, and communications.
2. Demonstrate loyalty to the employer by diligently following the lawful instructions of the employer, using reasonable care and granted authority.
3. Avoid any personal business or professional activity that would create a conflict between personal interests and the interests of the employer.
4. Avoid soliciting or accepting money, loans, credits, or preferential discounts, and the acceptance of gifts, entertainment, favors, or services from present or potential suppliers that might influence, or appear to influence, supply management decisions.
5. Handle confidential or proprietary information with due care and proper consideration of ethical and legal ramifications and governmental regulations.
6. Promote positive supplier relationships through courtesy and impartiality.
7. Avoid improper reciprocal agreements.

8. Know and obey the letter and spirit of laws applicable to supply management.

9. Encourage support for small, disadvantaged, and minority-owned businesses.

10. Acquire and maintain professional competence.

11. Conduct supply management activities in accordance with national and international laws, customs, and practices, your organization's policies, and these ethical principles and standards of conduct.

12. Enhance the stature of the supply management profession.

Each of ISM's standards are defined and discussed in detail in their "Guidelines," which can be found in Appendix A at the back of the text. The Guidelines are relevant and useful for purchasing personnel in the hospitality industry, but may also be useful as a model for ethics code development.

PURCHASING AND RECEIVING AT FRESHWATER OASIS INN

In this segment of the case, the substitute driver for Tate Brothers (one of FOI's food suppliers) offers Chef Eric tenderloins at a 50% discount if he pays with cash. (Please see *Aardvark Takes a Holiday* at the back of the text.) To analyze this dilemma, we enter the decision option *to take the tenderloins at half price* and the stakeholders *Eric, Tate Brothers, FOI,* and *Other Employees* on the Ethics Analysis Form. A completed form follows the discussion of this segment of the case study.

We can start the analysis by asking ourselves how the driver can offer Eric the tenderloins at such a low price. If we were Tate Brothers, would we think it was okay for the driver to be offering product to Eric at a 50% discount if he pays with cash? It is obvious that the substitute driver is running a scam on Tate Brothers and selling their goods for personal gain. In other words, he is stealing the tenderloins from Tate Brothers and attempting to sell them to Eric for a low cash price. The driver said, "I got some tenderloins just fell off [the truck]." Eric is not naive and would certainly know that the driver is trying to sell him stolen product, and not just some clumsy steer that lost its footing.

We might like to pretend the tenderloins are not stolen and that we are just being offered a really good deal because it is our lucky day. As professionals, however, we must face reality and question this good deal. Buying stolen property makes us an accessory to the crime of theft. Period. When we are in doubt about the rightness of an action, we can ask whether or not we would like our

(Reprinted with permission from the publisher, the Institute for Supply Management™, *Principles and Standards of Ethical Supply Management Conduct,* approved January 2002.)

boss to know we acted in such a way. Eric's boss, John Fallin (general manager), would probably not be pleased that Eric was buying stolen tenderloins.

ANALYSIS OF POSSIBLE CONSEQUENCES FOR ERIC

The dilemma for Eric in this segment of the case study is this: *should he resist the temptation to buy stolen tenderloins?* If Eric refuses to buy the meat in question, the worst thing that can happen is that the driver will leave and never offer Eric stolen products again. In that case, Eric will get only what he ordered and at the prices he was expecting to pay. He loses nothing and cannot be harmed.

If Eric buys the half-price tenderloins and uses them at the restaurant, his food cost will be reduced. If he pays for them with his own money and takes them home, he reduces his personal food costs. Eric would be unlikely to inform John because he would not want John to know he was involving FOI in criminal activities.

Every time we do the wrong thing, it is easier to do the wrong thing again the next time. If Eric succumbs to the temptation of buying the tenderloins, his sensitivity to right and wrong will be diminished and he will be more tempted the next time to also do wrong. The more wrong one does, the better the chance of getting caught. His employees could easily notice that he is buying tenderloins for cash and would likely presume the tenderloins are stolen.

Our employees look to us for direction and would prefer to respect us if given the choice. If Eric's employees realized he was buying stolen tenderloins from the driver for cash, he would lose moral authority in their eyes. They might reason that if it is okay for Eric to behave questionably, then it is also okay for them to behave in the same manner. They might be more inclined to steal food and supplies from the kitchen. It would be more difficult for Eric to control the behavior of his employees. He would be trying to use a "Do as I say, not as I do" management strategy, which is far less effective than modeling correct behavior.

It is possible that Tate Brothers could figure out that Eric had the missing tenderloins. They could call Eric and question him about the tenderloins. This would be humiliating, and Eric would most likely be inclined toward lying in order to protect himself, compromising his ethics even further. The suppliers might not believe Eric's denials and might subsequently refuse to do business with FOI in the future. John then would most certainly find out that Eric bought the stolen tenderloins, and Eric could face disciplinary action and/or lose John's trust.

It is also possible that no one except the driver would ever know that Eric bought the stolen tenderloins. The driver could, of course, tell other drivers about his scam (that Eric will buy stolen food and supplies). Eric's reputation in the food industry could be tarnished, and he could find himself with additional offers of stolen food and supplies. His risk of eventually being caught increases, and all the negative consequences he avoided the first or second time might later come home to roost.

ANALYSIS OF POSSIBLE CONSEQUENCES
FOR TATE BROTHERS

We ask the same type of questions for Tate Brothers. Such as, how will the missing tenderloins affect Tate Brothers' costs? Where were the missing tenderloins supposed to go? How might Tate Brothers deal with the customer who actually ordered the meat and might not have gotten it delivered? How would that affect Tate Brothers' reputation?

Workers for Tate Brothers loaded product on the truck that was supposed to be delivered to its customers. The tenderloins in question were to have been delivered to the customer who ordered them. We place orders with suppliers for food that we need to prepare the menu for our guests. If we do not receive some of the ordered items, we will either have to make a trip to the grocery store, or perhaps not be able to serve the particular menu item. The trip to the grocery store costs money in terms of time and aggravation, as well as the added cost of higher retail prices for the product itself. To not have a menu item available costs money in terms of guest dissatisfaction. The customer who does not receive the ordered tenderloins could tell other restaurateurs, which would damage Tate Brothers' reputation. If it was discovered that this was not an isolated incident, the customer might decide to get a more reliable supplier and Tate Brothers would lose the business.

It is very unlikely that Tate Brothers put the tenderloins on the truck accidentally. Even if it were so, the product belonged to Tate Brothers and they would want it back for resale to another customer. Because Tate Brothers originally purchased the tenderloins and never got compensated for their sale, the company's food cost would increase.

The customer who did not receive the tenderloins could call Tate Brothers to complain. An in-house investigation by supervisors might uncover the substitute driver who stole and sold the tenderloins. They would have the unpleasant task of having to deal with the substitute driver, most likely firing him, and they would also incur additional costs through the recruitment and training of a replacement driver.

Even if Tate Brothers never found out about the substitute driver stealing and selling the tenderloins, it is possible that other drivers would. As a result, they might be encouraged to try the same thing, or be put in the uncomfortable position of having to decide whether or not to tell on the substitute driver.

ANALYSIS OF POSSIBLE CONSEQUENCES FOR FOI

It is possible that Tate Brothers could suspect or know that Eric bought the stolen product from their driver. They could pursue the matter, calling Eric, and perhaps even John. If John became aware of the problem, he would have to confront Eric and maybe discipline him. If Tate Brothers suspected Eric of buying the tenderloins, they could feel that Eric took advantage of them, and this would in turn affect Eric's and FOI's reputation as good people to do business with.

If Eric's ability to manage and/or his reputation in the foodservice community is damaged, morale in the department could suffer. Turnover could increase, which ultimately negatively affects FOI's reputation as a good place to work and incurs recruiting, selecting, and training expenses.

ANALYSIS OF POSSIBLE CONSEQUENCES FOR OTHER EMPLOYEES

If Eric paid cash for the tenderloins for use at FOI, he would have to be reimbursed by the company, which would require some type of receipt. So, if he chooses to buy the tenderloins, they would most likely be for his personal use. Employees would not be directly affected unless they found out that Eric was buying stolen tenderloins from the Tate Brothers' substitute driver. How likely is it that employees would find out? It is quite possible that one or more of the kitchen employees would notice Eric conferring with the driver, paying the driver, and taking possession of the tenderloins. One or more employees might notice Eric going home with a Tate Brothers' package.

Some employees with knowledge of Eric's action might assume that it is okay for them to do the same thing, or they might be more tempted to steal other food or supplies from FOI. Employees caught doing what Eric is doing could be punished or terminated, which, of course, creates another ethical dilemma: can a manager who does not follow the rules enforce the rules for the rest of the staff?

Other employees might find it disturbing that the chef is buying stolen property. They might wonder if they ought to say something about it, and to whom? This could put employees in an uncomfortable position, especially if their supervisor is Eric himself. They could fear reprisals from Eric. Some employees could feel resentful that Eric and other dishonest sorts seem to get more in return than what they get for their own hard, honest work. They could lose respect for both Eric and the company that maintains his position of authority (FOI), and, in turn, the quality of their own work and/or job satisfaction could deteriorate.

ETHICAL PRINCIPLES VIOLATED BY THIS DECISION

We can go down the list of Ethical Principles for Hospitality Managers and see that every principle is directly violated by the decision to buy the tenderloins. *Honesty* and *integrity* are obvious. To buy stolen tenderloins is not honest and we cannot claim to have integrity when we do dishonest things. Eric can lose the *trust* of the supplier, his employees, and also his boss if they find out he bought the stolen tenderloins. FOI pays Eric's salary and he would not be demonstrating *loyalty,* because he would be getting a personal gain in a way that harms FOI.

Eric's employees would see it as *unfair* if he punished them for doing something he himself did. They might find it unfair that Eric, or employees like him, seem to be more successful through dishonesty than what they get in return for their honest hard work. Eric shows no *concern and respect* for Tate Brothers if he takes advantage of them by purchasing stolen tenderloins from their dishonest driver. A *commitment to excellence* never includes buying stolen property under the table from a supplier.

Eric would lose his *leadership* authority. Employees must trust and respect a manager to follow him or her. When employees no longer trust and respect the manager, *morale* falls, which can negatively affect job satisfaction and turnover and the *reputation* of FOI as a good place to work. Eric is *accountable* for the success of the foodservice at FOI, and it is his responsibility to carefully consider the consequences of actions before he takes them.

Ethics Analysis Form
Aardvark Takes a Holiday

Decision Option: Take the tenderloins at half price

Stakeholders	Principles	Consequences
Eric (Exec. Chef) [Decision-Maker]	Honesty Integrity Trustworthiness Loyalty Fairness Concern and Respect For Others Excellence Leadership Reputation and Morale Accountability	• Get tenderloins at a very discounted price and lower food costs, or take them home for personal consumption. • Eric knows that the driver stole the tenderloins. FOI has a policy against buying stolen property. Eric will have to hide his actions if he buys the tenderloins and could feel guilty. • This decision will make future questionable decisions easier. • If other employees notice, he will lose their respect along with his ability to manage them should they get caught doing something similar. • When Tate Brothers realize their tenderloins are missing, they could trace them back to FOI and Eric. Eric could face future humiliation, discipline, and possible termination. He could lose the trust of FOI top management.
Tate Brothers		• The customer who was supposed to receive the tenderloins would be dissatisfied with Tate Brothers. This could have a negative effect on Tate's reputation and business. • If Tate Brothers find out, they would have to discipline or terminate the substitute driver. This would result in additional hiring and training costs. • If other Tate Brothers drivers find out what happened, they could be tempted to try and do the same thing.

(continued)

Stakeholders	Principles	Consequences
Freshwater Oasis Inn		• Tate Brothers could feel that Eric took advantage of them, and FOI's reputation with suppliers could be damaged. • The administration could have to discipline Eric, which could result in extra expense.
Other Employees		• If other employees realize that Eric is making questionable decisions, they might think it's okay for them to do the same thing. • Ethical employees could feel upset that less ethical decisions are making people more money than their hard, honest work is getting them. They could lose respect for Eric and the quality of their work could deteriorate. • Questionable decisions that are modeled and reinforced by the manager could result in employees not trusting management, perhaps making them less trustworthy employees as well. Turnover and absenteeism could increase. • Employees caught doing what Eric is doing could be punished or terminated. • If Dardina (the sous chef) or any other employee discovered what Eric did, should he or she say something, and to whom? This quandary might cause apprehension and discomfort.

OTHER DECISION OPTIONS

This dilemma is not about whether it is right or wrong to buy the stolen tenderloins. Instead, Eric is dealing with a temptation to do what he already knows is wrong. It is possible that no one will find out that Eric bought stolen tenderloins from the Tate Brothers' substitute driver. If he gets by with this he will be more apt to do something similar again, and his chances of getting caught increase each time he does something wrong.

It is more likely, however, that someone will find out, and the consequences could be painful and cost him much more than the savings on the tenderloins. We noted in the beginning of the analysis that there were no negative consequences if Eric refuses to buy the stolen steaks. He pays exactly what he is supposed to pay for the items he actually ordered. He does not lose anything.

We might be tempted to buy the stolen tenderloins, but when we analyze the decision we can see that there are some very negative consequences that could have far-reaching negative effects on us, on our ability to manage, and on the business. By doing something we know is wrong, we risk damaging our department within the operation, our ability to manage it, and we put in jeopardy our professional future.

Any time we make a decision in violation of the ethical rules, there will be negative consequences that could have been avoided. It is in our best interest to analyze decision options ahead of time, and then choose the decision that has the least amount of negative consequences to stakeholders. We should do the right thing because it is good for business and because it is ultimately good for us.

CONCLUSION

We have to communicate effectively with a diverse workforce so that they understand the importance of food and work safety standards. We must provide training that enables them to meet the standards, and then we must supervise them to maintain the standards. We will have to manage in ways that encourage the development and/or maintenance of a strong work ethic among our employees. Purchasing requires a healthy sense of right and wrong along with specific technical skills. These are some of the special skills that managers must have in order to successfully manage their foodservice employees.

We can go down the list of the Ethical Principles for Hospitality Managers and note that all of the principles are involved with good management. We must look at our management strategies and styles *honestly* to ensure that they have only positive effects on our employees' work ethic and that they are not discriminatory in any way. We train and supervise our employees to work safely and to handle food safely so that no one is hurt or made ill, because we are *concerned* and have *respect* for our guests and employees.

Our employees *trust* us because they know that we are *fair* and are *accountable* for the success of the operation, which their livelihood is dependent upon. Our employees are *loyal* to us because we treat them with respect and model the type of behavior we expect from them. *Morale* is high among the employees, and our *reputation* as a good place to work is known in the labor pool. We are *committed to excellence* and are able to *lead* our employees because they trust us to do what is good for the operation and for them. We live our lives and manage our employees with *integrity*.

KEY WORD

Work ethic

CHAPTER THOUGHT QUESTIONS

1. The next time you go to the grocery store be aware of which products you would be able to select if you were illiterate. Many products have pictures of the food on the label, but some do not. Describe how a foodservice employee could be illiterate and how he or she might hide that fact from management. Discuss the possible problems that could arise from illiterate foodservice workers.

2. Describe your own work ethic. Where did it come from? How does your work ethic differ from fellow employees'? Describe the work ethic you would like all your employees to have when you are the manager.

3. What are some of the causes or reasons why some people have a poor work ethic? What are some things you could do to improve or strengthen the work ethic of the people you manage?

4. Identify potential safety problems or risks at your current or past workplace. If you were manager, what could you do to ensure that your employees do not get hurt on the job? Discuss the various reasons, including ethical reasons, why we are responsible for keeping our employees safe.

5. Discuss the importance of management modeling correct behavior. Use examples from *The Best-Laid Plans*. Describe managers you have worked for who practiced what they preached and other managers whose philosophy was "Do as I say, not as I do." Which manager did you prefer? Why? Which manager was more effective? Why?

6. Compare and contrast the "Principles and Standards of Ethical Supply Management Conduct" in this chapter with the "Principles of Professionalism" in Chapter 6. How do they both compare with the Ethical Principles for Hospitality Managers in Chapter 1?

7. Why is purchasing particularly ethically challenging? Foodservice suppliers may offer incentives and give gifts to encourage foodservice managers to buy food and supplies from them. Pretend you are the general manager of a hotel. Develop a purchasing policy for your foodservice manager that spells out what he or she should do about gifts and incentives from suppliers.

8. Think about any work situations where you have seen another employee do something wrong. How did you feel about it? Did you think you should tell on the person? Did you want to tell on the person? Did you tell on the person? Why or why not? In the last few segments of the case study, employees and managers might have known things other employees were doing that should have been brought to the attention of management. Think about and then discuss what you think you should do when you see an individual do something unethical on the job.

9. Continuing with the discussion in question 8, is there a difference between what managers and line employees should do if either see someone doing something unethical on the job? Do managers and employees have the same or different responsibilities for bringing unethical behavior to the attention of responsible management? Discuss.

10. In both case study segments in this chapter, Eric essentially knew the difference between right and wrong, but was faced with the temptation to do wrong because of financial concerns. Think about and describe when you have been tempted to do something wrong (such as take too much change when a cashier makes a mistake). What did you do and why? Would you do it the same or differently today? Why? If you were the other person (such as the cashier), what would you prefer the other person do in the situation? Why?

REFERENCES

Jaszay, C., & Dunk, P. (2003). *Training design for the hospitality industry.* New York: Delmar.

Payne-Palacio, J., & Theis, M. (2001). *West & Wood's introduction to foodservice.* Upper Saddle River, NJ: Prentice Hall.

ServSafe coursebook (2nd ed.). (2002). National Restaurant Association, Educational Foundation.

Walczak, D. (1997). The proletarian gourmet [ethics and chefs]. *FIU Hospitality Review, 15*(2), 27–34.

Chapter 9

Ethics and Dining Room Management

The service of food is one component of foodservice management. We have chosen to address the front-of-the-house service function separately from the back-of-the-house kitchen management that was the focus of Chapter 8. Poor service can put a restaurant out of business regardless of how good the food is. Poor service is the main reason guests stop patronizing restaurants.

Not everyone can be good servers. Servers need to come into the job with certain characteristics in order to be successful. They must enjoy working with and serving people, enjoy a fast pace, be able to see their position as "sales," and be able to allow customers to be right even when they are not. If potential servers have these characteristics they can be trained in the procedural parts of the job, such as how to take orders and put down plates properly. It is much more difficult to train someone to like people and to not fall apart in a rush.

The dining room is where foodservice employees meet the guests. Server–guest interaction in large part determines the success of foodservice. It is essential that front- and back-of-the-house employees work together as a team to produce and serve what guests want and expect. This supportive team effort is the result of good management where employees are carefully selected, trained, supervised, and treated with respect.

Professional dining room management requires skills in communication, human resource management, and service. In this chapter we will analyze a case study segment in the dining room at the Freshwater Oasis Inn, and, later, focus on communication.

THE DINING ROOM AT FRESHWATER OASIS INN

Tony Marziano, 31, began waiting tables at FOI 5 years ago. His job title is Dining Room Manager, though he also has other responsibilities. Tony has been supervising wait staff (servers and bussers) the past 2 years. In addition to

I'M SORRY, BUT THIS RESTAURANT IS BLACK TIE ONLY... YOU PENGUINS WILL HAVE TO LEAVE IMMEDIATELY.

scheduling servers, he is also in charge of the host/hostesses and splits time between both positions.

Tony served a party of nine and was given an $80 tip on top of the automatic gratuity. (See *Tony Marziano and the Infamous Double Tip* in the case study at the end of the text.) He was uncertain if the guest knew that there was an 18% tip automatically added (for parties of eight or more) and that the guest in fact meant for the $80 amount to be extra because of his good service. Tony has to decide whether or not to question the guest about the additional $80.

If he asks the guest, the worst thing that can happen is that the guest will take back the $80. Tony will, of course, still get the automatic 18% tip that amounts to $126 on a $700 check. He would probably like to have the additional $80, which would be equivalent to a 30% tip of $206. When in doubt, we can ask ourselves what we would like if we were the other person. Would we want Tony to ask us if we meant to leave an additional $80? Most likely, we would.

We can enter the decision option to *not ask the guest* on the Ethics Analysis Form. We can also list the stakeholders who could be affected by the decision Tony makes. They will be *Tony,* the *customer, other employees,* and *FOI.* A completed form follows this discussion.

ANALYSIS OF POSSIBLE CONSEQUENCES FOR TONY

If Tony does not ask the customer if he meant to leave an additional $80 on top of the 18% tip, Tony will get a huge tip. He will not know for sure that the customer meant for him to have the additional $80, so there will always be that little nagging doubt that he took advantage of the customer. If he made this decision this time, it will be easier to make the same questionable decision the next time.

The customer could later realize he left an additional tip and demand it back, which would be humiliating to Tony. It is also possible that the bookkeeper could catch the error. Tony is dining room manager, and if it was discovered that he did not follow FOI rules by clarifying the guests' intentions (with regard to the additional $80), he could find himself facing disciplinary action, termination, or at the very least he could lose the trust of his supervisor.

If other servers see what Tony does, they may try to do it themselves. Tony may have difficulty later disciplining employees for what he himself is doing. He could lose their trust and respect, which would negatively affect his ability to manage.

ANALYSIS OF POSSIBLE CONSEQUENCES FOR THE CUSTOMER

If the customer did not mean to give Tony the additional $80, he could notice the mistake later and call FOI and demand it back. The customer might not pursue the matter of the $80 but would probably feel disgust, would probably not come back, and might say negative things about FOI. It is possible the customer would never notice if it was mistakenly given. However, if it was not a mistake, would he feel adequately appreciated for such a big tip if Tony never said anything?

ANALYSIS OF POSSIBLE CONSEQUENCES FOR OTHER EMPLOYEES

If other servers are unaware that he took the extra $80 without asking the customer, they might not suffer any negative consequences. However, there are several employees in the dining room who could somehow see the check and find out what Tony was doing. One employee might tell another employee, and Tony's behavior would constitute a message that it was unnecessary to follow rules. Tony's employees might emulate his behavior and feel that it is okay to take advantage of customers, and the ethical climate of the department would decline. When employees know that customers cannot trust Tony, they might wonder if *they* can trust Tony. If they do not trust Tony, absenteeism and turnover could increase.

Tony is responsible for enforcing the rules. He might later have difficulty disciplining employees for doing the very same thing that he has done. If he did attempt to discipline an employee, the staff as a whole could perceive the act as unfair and their attitude and performance could decline. Employees who do not take advantage of guests might be resentful that less ethical employees make more money. They could feel that they should inform on these dishonest employees, yet fear reprisals from Tony and the others.

ANALYSIS OF POSSIBLE CONSEQUENCES FOR FOI

Tony suspects that the customer did not know he was automatically assessed an 18% tip and is reticent to ask him for fear of losing the additional $80. When we get away with doing something wrong, we are more likely to commit the offense again. Each time we do something wrong we increase the risk of getting caught, and all the negative consequences would eventually befall FOI.

The customer could figure out that he mistakenly double-tipped Tony and tell other people of his negative experience at FOI. This would damage the inn's reputation and possibly result in loss of sales. Tony's employees could find out and lose respect and trust for Tony, which could eventually result in increased turnover and lowered morale. If employees begin emulating Tony's behavior, the ethical climate of the department would deteriorate, and employees could find less satisfaction in their work, and this could affect the reputation of FOI as a good place to work. Business can suffer if employees are dissatisfied because their performance can deteriorate, resulting in dissatisfied guests who do not come back and warn their friends to do the same.

ETHICAL PRINCIPLES VIOLATED BY THIS DECISION

We found numerous possible negative consequences if Tony decides to skip questioning the customer about the extra $80 tip. We can now go through the list of Ethical Principles for Hospitality Managers to determine which, if any, are violated by this decision. We find that *honesty* is violated because Tony suspects that the customer does not know that an 18% tip was automatically added. To not mention this to the customer is to allow the customer to be misled. Tony knows that it would be right to question the customer. *Integrity* is doing what is right even if we do not want to. Tony could lose the *trust* of both his employees and supervisor if they find out he did not follow the rules he is supposed to enforce.

Tony is not being *loyal* to his company if he chooses to personally benefit by doing something that could hurt FOI. His employees would think he was not being *fair* if he were to punish them later for doing the same thing he did. To not question the customer as to whether he really intended to give Tony an extra $80 shows a lack of *concern and respect for others*.

Tony is the dining room manager, and his job is to supervise employees and enforce the standards. A *commitment to excellence* is demonstrated by taking the standards seriously and modeling them for his employees. His *leadership* will be harmful if he does not follow the rules he expects his employees to follow, and this can have a negative impact on the *reputation and morale* of FOI and the staff. As manager he is *accountable* for his behavior and the behavior of his employees.

Every ethical principle will be violated if Tony does not clarify the guests' intentions regarding the extra $80 tip. It would be unethical for any of his employees to operate in such a way, but it is worse for the manager to not follow rules he is charged with enforcing. Our employees can be influenced by our behavior, and we have the responsibility to always be a positive influence. When we are put in positions of authority, we must take our responsibilities seriously and behave with integrity.

Ethical Analysis Form
Tony Marziano and the Infamous Double Tip

Decision Option: To not question the guest about the extra $80 tip

Stakeholders	Principles	Consequences
Tony (Dining Room Manager) [Decision-Maker]	Honesty Integrity Trustworthiness Loyalty Fairness Concern and Respect Excellence Leadership Reputation and Morale Accountability	• Get 18% tip plus $80 but battle with uncertainty as to whether the customer actually intended for him to have the additional gratuity. • This decision will make future questionable decisions easier. • It is possible that the customer could realize his mistake later or that the accountant might discover it while doing the books. Tony could face future humiliation and possible demotion/termination. • Tony's employees could learn about and then emulate his actions. He would have difficulty enforcing rules and could lose the respect and trust of his employees, negatively affecting his ability to manage.
Customers		• If the customer actually meant for Tony to have the additional $80, and Tony never acknowledged it, then the customer might not feel adequately thanked for the huge tip. This might give the customer a queasy feeling that perhaps Tony thought it was a mistake, and was, in effect, endeavoring to rip him off through his silence over the matter. • The customer could realize later that he mistakenly put the additional $80 tip on the charge. At that point he could either demand it back or just accept his feelings of having been taken advantage of. He might never come back, and he might advise his friends to avoid FOI as well.
Other Employees		• If other employees realize that Tony is making questionable decisions, they might feel that they should be doing the same thing. If customers feel taken advantage of, the ethical climate could deteriorate and business could be negatively affected. Questionable decisions that are modeled and reinforced by the organization's leadership could result in employees not

(continued)

Stakeholders	Principles	Consequences
Other Employees		trusting management and perhaps make them less trustworthy themselves. Turnover and absenteeism could increase.
		• Ethical employees might get angry that other less ethical employees are making more money.
		• Employees could lose respect for Tony and be less cooperative, loyal, and the quality of their work could deteriorate.
		• Employees caught doing what Tony is doing could be punished or terminated, which, of course, creates another ethical dilemma: can a manager who does not follow the rules enforce these rules for the rest of the employees?
		• If another employee discovered what Tony did, should he or she say anything, and to whom should he or she say it?
Freshwater Oasis Inn		• The reputation of the restaurant and the inn as a whole could be damaged if the customer felt he had been taken advantage of. He would most likely never come back and probably tell everyone he knows, at every opportunity, how much he does not like FOI.
		• If the customer meant for Tony to have the extra $80, or never noticed he made the mistake, the inn's reputation could also suffer in that Tony would have made a questionable decision. This seemingly minor gaffe would enable him to make other questionable decisions in the future, and the employees he supervises would be influenced by his behavior. The whole ethical climate could be diminished, ultimately resulting in less than happy guests, tarnishing the reputation of the operation, etc., the gist of which could result in less business.

OTHER DECISION OPTIONS

The other decision option in this situation is for Tony to ask the customer whether he actually wanted to leave him an additional $80 tip. We noted earlier that the only negative consequence of taking this route is that Tony could lose the extra $80. He would still have the $126, so this is not a terrible prospect. Plus, he may ascertain that the customer wanted him to have the additional $80. Tony would feel very good about accepting the $206 tip for his excellent service, and he would have made that money honestly.

If Tony asks the customer about the additional $80, the customer will probably be pleased that Tony cared enough to ensure he was not making a mistake. The customer would probably feel appreciated and tell others about his pleasant experience. Other employees will notice that Tony invariably does the right thing. The manager's behavior is always more influential than what the manager says. Doing the right thing becomes the norm and what is expected and modeled. Trust and loyalty could increase and turnover and absenteeism could decrease.

We might be very tempted to just take the $80 without involving the customer. But, when we analyze the decision, we can see that there are some very negative consequences that could have far-reaching effects on our ability to manage and on the business as a whole. On the other hand, none of the ethical principles are violated by the decision to ask the customer whether or not he meant to leave an additional $80 tip. To the contrary, there are numerous positive consequences.

THE SEQUEL TO THE $80 TIP

In *$80 Takes On a Life of Its Own* (see case study at the back of the text), Jimmy the bus boy spots the check for Tony's nine-top with the additional $80 tip. Although the charge had not yet been closed out, Jimmy assumed that Tony was taking advantage of a guest, probably because that is what he would have done. Later, Jimmy tells Tony that he will not tell on him—provided he gets promoted to waiter soon as possible.

Tony, unbeknownst to Jimmy, had already asked the customer about the $80 (while serving coffee) and was told it was a bonus for exceptional service. While Jimmy's assumption is incorrect, Tony finds himself in a nasty situation because of an imagined unethical act. In *The Tip That Keeps on Giving* (see case study), Tony goes to his supervisor, Heidi Bell, the Assistant General Manager, and tells her he wants Jimmy fired for trying to blackmail him.

Jimmy's behavior is unethical. Attempting to blackmail his supervisor into giving him a promotion violates all the ethical principles. Tony violated no ethical principles. What we have in this situation is a management dilemma.

IN THE TRENCHES

Tom Gready, 20, Tuscon, AZ

"While serving at a local restaurant, I ran into an ethical problem regarding tip policy. This was not a personal experience but involved a fellow server. For parties of eight or larger we add an 18% gratuity. The server in question returned with the signed credit card authorization and realized that the guest had added another $50 on to the automatic service charge. The manager on duty told the server not to inform the guest, though, and to just keep the money instead. This manager has since been fired, due to unrelated events, but is it ethical not to tell customers about a service charge when it is clearly labeled on the check and explained at the time of reservation?"

Perhaps there might have been a better way for Tony to handle it. Let us look at this situation in retrospect and attempt to define the problem and a course of action that can avoid putting Tony, the dining room manager, in the position of cross-accusations with a busboy in front of Heidi.

To start this analysis, we must consider why Jimmy would assume that Tony is taking advantage of the customer. Jimmy was fairly new on job. It is unlikely that he had seen Tony doing other unethical things because Tony was a long-term trusted employee/manager. If Jimmy was disturbed about a possible rule violation, he could have spoken to Heidi about his suspicions (please see *Falcon Crust* in the case study). Instead, he tried to use the information to blackmail Tony into giving him a server position. It appears as though Jimmy might be a person without much moral fiber.

That describes Jimmy but does not explain why he would make what turned out to be an incorrect assumption about Tony. We often assume that others think like we do. Judging from Jimmy's behavior, it might be logical to assume that he would not have questioned the guest about the $80, and thus he reasoned that Tony would not either. Our perception of the world and the people we encounter is often colored by lessons we may have learned as children. Those who are raised in healthy, loving families are more likely to feel that the world is a safe place and that most people are good. We become what we are taught.

We originally learn right from wrong by watching and emulating those who raise us. As adults, we are capable of identifying the standards we were taught as children. We can choose to let go of those standards and incorporate and practice new standards that might be a better fit for who we would like to be. Jimmy's standards do not match the standards of FOI. It is generally better to hire people whose personal standards are similar or who will be able to accept and live by the standards of the organization. Jimmy may not have been a good hire.

At this point, it seems apparent that a shared ethic is lacking at FOI. It has been demonstrated by their actions in various situations that John Fallin, Gabe Deflores, and Tony Marziano have chosen to do the right thing. Bill Gardner and Kathy Lawhorn have not. When everyone is operating according to the same set of rules, individual behavior decisions are more likely to conform to the group. Conforming behavior is rewarded, while behavior that does not conform is punished. The present assortment of personal ethical standards (held by various FOI employees) ultimately determines individual behavior within the group. This is ethical chaos. It is better for an organization to decide beforehand on the appropriate ethics that everyone must accept and practice. We find that this approach results in more consistently correct behaviors from everyone.

Had there been a shared ethic in the form of an ethics code that all FOI employees were expected to accept and practice, and had Tony been instructed on how to identify applicants with the ability to adhere to FOI standards, Tony probably would not have hired Jimmy in the first place. This problem could have been avoided. Even if Jimmy had still been hired, had there been an ethics code (that all new hires were trained and rewarded to follow) he may not have assumed that Tony would ignore the rules, and this situation might have been avoided.

Tony did not handle Jimmy's blackmail threat. Instead he went to Heidi, his supervisor, and demanded that Jimmy be fired for trying to blackmail him. Tony did not inform Jimmy that he asked the customer if he really meant to give him the extra $80. Tony did not take the opportunity to *instruct* Jimmy, and that is part of a manager's job. All Tony did was get *mad*. Jimmy's behavior was reprehensible, of course, but Tony, as manager, did not effectively manage. That is his job, and he failed.

Tony's lack of management expertise is common in the hospitality industry where line workers are often promoted without any specific management skills. Being an excellent waiter does not mean that Tony is automatically an excellent manager. The two positions require totally different skill sets. Tony has the service skills but is lacking in communication and human resource skills. The real question we need to ask is this: who was it that promoted Tony without making sure he was trained to manage?

Every hospitality operation is a system where all the parts work together to put out a product. Everything we say or do affects other parts of the system. John, the general manager, is responsible for determining and implementing the preferred culture at FOI. This includes, as its foundation, a shared ethic. Every manager must be immersed in the culture and taught how to convey it to employees. John is responsible for the entire operation and the work of all his managers. Tony was promoted into management without being given the skills to properly do the job. Tony, in turn, hired Jimmy and did not socialize him into the culture. He failed to effectively communicate with Jimmy, so the problem ballooned. Obviously the busboy can be fired, but nothing will change in that present management still lacks the skills necessary to avoid these and other kinds of ethical and personnel problems.

ETHICAL PRINCIPLES VIOLATED IN THE SEQUEL

The three segments of the above case study illustrate trouble and torment that could have been avoided. Doing the ethical thing is much easier and better for everyone in the long run. Although not directly involved, as general manager John still played a key role in the lapse of ethics here. By not instituting an FOI ethics code from the get-go, one detailing the type of behavior required at FOI, he violated *commitment to excellence, leadership, reputation and morale,* and *accountability.* He allowed everyone to operate on their own individual codes of ethics, resulting in frustration and inconsistency. He avoided having to teach his managers how to enforce and model an ethics code by simply not having one.

An ethics code embodies knowledge of psychology, philosophy, behavioral organization, and management. A general manager can be successful if he or she abides by the ten Ethical Principles for Hospitality Managers, and has technical hospitality and organizational skills required for development and implementation of management systems incorporating ethics in every aspect of the operation.

COMMUNICATION

To be ethical means that we abide by all the Ethical Principles for Hospitality Managers. *Fairness, concern and respect for others, commitment to excellence, leadership,* and *reputation and morale* are all violated if we are unable to communicate successfully with employees. Just because we have eardrums and vocal cords does not guarantee we can communicate. Effective communication is the result of possessing learned skills. If we grew up with ineffective communicators we are most likely to be ineffective communicators ourselves, unless we have evaluated our skill levels and taken steps to improve them.

In the dining room segments of the case study, Tony's communications skills were negligible. While he was able to communicate beautifully with guests, his communication with Jimmy unnecessarily aggravated an unfortunate situation. Tony reacted to Jimmy overdoing it with Tony's customers with a mean-spirited order: "You just clear the plates, Laddy." Jimmy reacted to Tony's belittling words with anger and attacked Tony in his imagination: *"What a jerk. Dining room manager. Hah! Tony's nothin' but a waiter sits people on the weekends."* Jimmy then noticed the additional $80 tip, made the false assumption, and tried to use the information to blackmail Tony into promoting him to server. How much of this was a direct result of Tony's flippancy is up for debate, but it certainly did not help matters any.

This is a perfect example of ineffective communication. Tony did not exhibit *concern and respect for* Jimmy. Tony's negative reaction resulted in a nasty order rather than an appropriate managerial directive such as, "Thanks, Jimmy, but I'd prefer to finish off this party myself. Why don't you coffee tables 17 and 18, because Kelly is busy in the kitchen and that would help her out." He could explain later who serves whom, when, how, and where, teaching Jimmy how to work as a team member. Jimmy would have gone off to serve the coffee without being angry at Tony, and most likely would not have even noticed the $80 tip.

When Jimmy winked and assured Tony that he would not tell provided he is promoted to waiter, Jimmy responded by saying, "You have *got* to be kidding." At this point, Tony could have laughed it off and calmly informed Jimmy that he had already asked the customer and the tip was in fact extra. Better yet, before the question of the $80 tip even came up, Tony could have used it as an opportunity for training. He could have showed the check to Jimmy while explaining the FOI honesty standard and procedure for questioning the guest and why it was important. These are examples of communication and human resource management skills that could have not only avoided the blackmail threat, but further indoctrinated Jimmy into the appropriate FOI ethical behavior.

EFFECTIVE COMMUNICATION BASICS

We are told over and over that we must have excellent communication skills to be effective managers. Management is about relationships: manager to top management, manager to manager, manager to employees, and so forth. In fact, we need excellent communication skills to be effective in any relationships. The divorce rate is an indication of our lack of personal communication skills. We can use the following communication basics in our personal and professional lives.

If we are with another person, we are communicating whether we are talking or not. A silence between two people can communicate comfort, acceptance, ease, or it can communicate anger, disgust, or disinterest. Whether we are tense or relaxed, our breathing pattern, posture, and facial expression all communicate on a nonverbal level that we are all quite adept at understanding. The way we communicate in most situations has become habitual. We may know teenagers who are always sullen with their parents, no matter what is being discussed, or someone who always seems to be whining. They are oftentimes unaware of the way they appear.

To be an effective communicator we first must know what we want to communicate, and, second, we need to know how to say it in a way that it will be heard and elicit the desired response. Sometimes in our personal relationships we may be feeling grumpy and take it out on someone we are close to. Behavior of this kind, if often occurring, can result in the end of a relationship. In management, however, we do not have the right to act on undefined feelings. Our position of authority comes with the responsibility to control our personal feelings and behave in ways that are good for the company.

In *$80 Takes On a Life of Its Own*, Tony was peeved with Jimmy for horning in on his party and told him, "You just worry about clearing tables and keeping the bus station clean. Comprendo?" As manager, Tony is responsible for everything that goes on in his department, and he did not have the right to act on his feelings when it was detrimental to the company. We can imagine Jimmy's reaction to such an order. He most likely felt anger, embarrassment, and/or resentment. He could have thought that Tony was being unfair to him when he was merely trying to help. Jimmy will probably be less enthusiastic about looking after Tony's tables in the future, and may dislike Tony and be less cooperative.

If Tony wanted to create ill will between himself and Jimmy, he said precisely what was needed to get that outcome. Tony was angry and reacted in anger. The consequences of his anger, however, are most likely not what Tony really wants.

Had Tony given the situation with Jimmy a little thought before responding, he could have determined that what he wanted was for Jimmy to understand and work appropriately within the relationship between server, busser, and the server's party. He could then have thought about how best to get that across to Jimmy. A reasoned explanation of who does what, how, and why, with the intent of instructing and helping Jimmy to be a better busser (so that he could become an FOI server), could have given Tony his desired results.

We have to ask ourselves what we are feeling, why we are feeling it, and whether it is reasonable to be feeling it. If it is not reasonable we have to drop it. Jimmy was in Tony's territory, and Tony was feeling a little threatened by it. Had Tony identified his feelings he could have acknowledged them and realized that Jimmy, perhaps, was just trying to help. Or he was trying to show Tony that he would make a good server at some time in the future. Tony did not make the effort to recognize that his anger was unreasonable, and, if acted on, would have a long-term detrimental affect on Jimmy and his performance and future at FOI.

Communication Barriers

Kathy Lawhorn in Chapter 5 had the most obvious communication barrier. She was unable to speak Spanish well enough to adequately communicate with her staff. There are other barriers, however, that can block communication. We need to examine our own communication habits or patterns. We must ensure that we are not communicating in ways that make it difficult or impossible for the intended target to receive the message.

Receiving Barriers.   We tend to hear what we want and expect to. We each come from different backgrounds and have different experiences that flavor our perceptions of much of what we see and hear. While our perceptions may not be reality, they are real enough to us to effectively block incoming messages when they are not consistent with our own belief systems. It is useful to understand where people are coming from so that we can tailor our delivery of the message in terms that will be acceptable to them.

Any kind of physical discomfort can get in the way of receiving the intended message. If an employee is focused on a sick child at home, or some other personal problem, he or she might not hear the message. If it is too noisy, or, if the person we are trying to communicate with is very busy, he or she might let the message "go in one ear and out the other." We can notice if the listener is distracted, then either address the distraction before delivering the message, or wait until a better time.

Some of us simply do not listen. We might be nodding our head in agreement with a certain statement, yet in actuality be thinking about lunch. Our employees might pay no attention if they find what we have to say boring. We must make sure that our employees are getting the message, however, so we ask them to repeat it back to us in their own words, or show us that they understand by either an example or a demonstration. As managers, we must practice listening carefully to what our employees have to say. We listen to their words and notice their tone of voice, posture, facial expression, and movements. If we fail to listen, they will think we do not care about what they have to say, and we lose their trust and/or we may not get information that might have been important. If we do not listen to our employees, they will eventually give up attempting to communicate with us.

Communication is two-way, made up of talking and listening. Listening takes energy and discipline, and is not easy. We need to evaluate how well we listen and make improvements if necessary. The body language that goes along with listening includes eye contact with the speaker, head nodding, an alert expression and posture, and an absence of squirming and fidgeting. The body language should accompany actual listening, which is enhanced by asking questions and restating important points in our own words. In personal relationships, listening is a gift. In managerial relationships, it is a necessity.

Sender Barriers. We must be aware of and take into consideration the possible barriers receivers might have that can block our message getting through to them. We can use a language they can understand, be attuned to cultural or personal differences, deliver our message when they are not distracted or too busy, and keep their attention by asking them questions or asking them to repeat back what we are saying. Asking if they understand is usually not the best way to ensure acceptance of the intended message. People may say they understand when they do not because they are embarrassed, afraid, or disinterested.

We must also be aware of their perceptions of us. How do we look and sound to the people we are talking to? What is our body language saying to them? Is the tone of our voice and our facial expression appropriate for the message? People can tune out our words, but it is difficult to tune out the nonverbal communication. How much our employees trust and respect us also affects how well they will hear our message.

In the Tony/Jimmy situation, Tony did not have a thought-out message to deliver. Instead, he went with his feelings and was sarcastic and patronizing, and Jimmy reacted to it negatively. Oftentimes when we are communicating, particularly in business, we are looking for a specific response. Obviously we have to know in advance what the specific response is and then we tailor our demand in terms that will result in obtaining the desired response. We are allowed to use our brains in communication. We can think to ourselves how the other person will react to our demand. We can change the delivery style and wording until we come up with a delivery that *will* result in the desired response.

Most people tend to react with anger when addressed in an angry tone and manner. Our business communication is not personal. There is very little place for anger in our business communication. Anger begets more anger, and that anger can become the focus while the real message is lost. We must identify our motivation behind our delivery style and the words we choose. If our motivation is to make someone feel bad or stupid, or in any way subpar, then our message will be lost. We have to let go of blame and anger if we want the other person to be able to hear our message.

Messages that are too long, too complex, or too general may not result in the desired response. If we talk too fast, or the message is ambiguous or contains incorrect information, we may end up frustrating the person we are talking to and make it difficult for him or her to do what we want. We must never assume that the other person knows what we want or expect and not bother telling him or her. We must clearly and specifically state what it is we want, and how, when, and why the person is to do it.

It is our responsibility to be sure that our messages are being received as they were intended. As managers, we are also responsible for understanding the intended meaning of messages from our employees. These are learned skills. There are numerous excellent books available that can help us to close any communication skill gaps we may have. The majority of problems, business and personal, are the result of poor communication. To be successful managers, we have to be able to get our messages across in ways that employees will be able to understand, accept, and implement.

CONCLUSION

The dining room manager, Tony, mishandled a situation with an employee because he did not have the necessary communication and human resource management skills. He was further hampered by a lack of guidance from the inn's top management. While Tony is responsible for his own behavior, John, the general manager, is responsible for everyone's behavior. John failed to put in place an ethics code that all managers and employees could use as a behavior guideline.

CHAPTER THOUGHT QUESTIONS

1. Describe a situation you have experienced where a manager spoke to you in a way that made you angry or hurt your feelings. What did the manager say? What did the manager want? Did he or she specifically state what he or she wanted? What was your reaction? Did the manager get what he or she wanted?

2. In the example above, rewrite what the manager should have said to you to get what he or she wanted.

3. Discuss why good communication skills are so important in your personal life.

4. Discuss why good communication skills are so important in your current or future professional life.

5. Evaluate your communication skills. How well do you listen? Who are the people you listen to carefully? Who are the people you tend to just pretend to listen to? Why do you listen to some and not to others? What characteristics need to be present for you to listen?

6. What changes do you need to make in order to listen better? Why is it important to make these changes? If you do not feel you need to make any improvements in your listening skills, please discuss why not.

7. When you want something from someone close to you, how do you ask for it? Describe a recent situation, what you wanted, what you said, and the results. What changes might have made the interchange more effective? Please incorporate the chapter suggestions.

8. Discuss how effective communication differs and is the same in both your personal and business life. Discuss management responsibilities. Are you a better communicator in your personal or business life? Why?

9. Ask someone you know how he or she perceives you. What kind of person do they think you are? How would they describe your personality (i.e., are you aggressive or passive, how easy you are to be with and to deal with, and so forth)? Write your perception of yourself and then compare the two. How are they similar? How are they different? Which is right?

10. Think about a past or current job you have held. Was or is there a sense of continuity? Did the general manager seem to be in control of the operation? Compare your perception of your experience with the problems that John Fallin seems to be experiencing at FOI.

REFERENCES

Bolton, R. (1979). *People skills: How to assert yourself, listen to others, and resolve conflicts.* New York: Simon & Schuster.

Cullen, N. C. (2001). *Life beyond the line: A front-of-the-house companion for culinarians.* Upper Saddle River, NJ: Prentice-Hall.

Lussier, R. N. (1989). *Supervision: A skill building approach.* Chicago: Irwin.

Martin, W. B. (2003). *Providing quality service: What every hospitality service provider needs to know.* Upper Saddle River, NJ: Prentice-Hall.

Chapter 10

Ethics and Bar and Beverage Management

Managing a bar is similar to managing a foodservice. It is the *differences,* however, that make a separate chapter on bar and beverage management necessary in a textbook on ethics. There may be fewer people involved in bar transactions in that the bartender usually takes the order, makes the drink, serves the drink, and acts as cashier. With fewer people involved, the opportunities for employee theft are greater.

The other big difference between food and bar service is that alcohol, the primary focus of the bar, is a drug that is often abused. We who are in the business of serving alcohol to customers need to be acutely aware of the potential for abuse by customers and employees. We must also know how to control the possible negative consequences.

THE BAR AT FRESHWATER OASIS INN

Mike Scales is 34 and has been at FOI since it opened. He has been promoted from bartender to bar manager. Mike has a high school education, is streetwise, and a little rough around the edges. He knows he has a good job, however, so he takes it seriously and works hard. In *Slick Rudy* (see the segment of the case study at the back of the text), Mike dealt with a customer who tried to scam FOI by switching the $20 bill he originally had in his hand with a $5 bill, then claiming it was a $20 bill when Mike returned from the register. Mike was familiar with this trick and was somewhat rude with the customer while explaining FOI's policy on cash transaction change disputes.

This is not an obvious case. The first thing we always do is state the problem, the ethical dilemma. What is the problem here? Is there a problem here? Sometimes it is difficult to tell. Has Mike done anything wrong in this situation? Something does not seem quite right, but it is hard to pin down, so we can work through it and see what happens. The "decision option" entry does not really apply, as Mike simply followed the FOI policy. The stakeholders are *Mike*, the *customer*, and *FOI*.

ANALYSIS OF POSSIBLE CONSEQUENCES FOR MIKE

FOI had a policy (take the customer's name and address, then return the disputed change by mail if the bartender's bank is over at shift's end) that Mike followed to protect FOI from getting scammed. If we go down the list of Ethical Principles for Hospitality Managers, we find that none were directly violated. Mike followed the policy and was straightforward, although somewhat impolite.

When the customer first sat down, Mike pegged him, albeit correctly, as shifty and a potential problem. His assessment of the customer made him alert so that when the customer switched the bills, Mike noticed. What if the customer did not do anything wrong? Could Mike's initial assessment affect the quality of service he gave to the customer? What if the customer had been African American, Native American, Hispanic, or any other minority group that has suffered discrimination? The police stop cars driven by African American males more often than whites because they "look suspicious." Is what Mike did to the customer—profiled him as "shifty"—the same?

Mike's previous experience made him wary, which ultimately saved FOI money. While Mike did nothing technically wrong in this situation, we might want to be more cognizant of our own tendencies to make judgments, and to be sure that our judgments are not based in prejudice. Prejudicial judgments could affect our behavior and violate many of the ethical principles.

ANALYSIS OF POSSIBLE CONSEQUENCES FOR THE CUSTOMER

In this situation, the customer did in fact try to cheat FOI out of $15. Mike did not mistreat or harm him in any way. The customer's behavior was unethical and violated *honesty, integrity, trustworthiness, fairness,* and *concern and respect for others*. Other than possible humiliation, he did not suffer any negative consequences in this situation. He could, however, experience negative consequences in a future situation.

ANALYSIS OF POSSIBLE CONSEQUENCES FOR FOI

Mike would have come up short $15 at the end of his shift if he had not noticed the switch of bills. FOI would have lost $15 but avoided a conflict with the customer. Handling the situation as Mike did, by following FOI policy, the customer could possibly say bad things about FOI, which could damage FOI's reputation amongst grifters, and be ultimately *good* for business.

The customer was the only person who violated ethical principles. There were no negative consequences for Mike. Negative consequences for the customer and FOI were negligible. Mike did the right thing when he caught the customer in the bill switch in *Slick Rudy*. This situation, however, brought up memories of a former job of Mike's when a fellow employee, Maggie, came up short at the end of her shift and was required to pay back the shortage.

The Federal Fair Labor Standards Act states: "Deductions made from wages for such items as cash or merchandise shortages, employer-required uniforms, and tools of the trade, are not legal if they reduce the wages of employees below the minimum wage or reduce the amount of overtime pay due under the FLSA."

Maggie, at Mike's previous job, was a tipped employee and most likely received minimum wage ($5.15/hr) or less for her hours worked. It would have been illegal for her employer to make her pay back the shortage. It is possible that her employer did not know it was illegal to make her pay back the $40. Ignorance of the law, however, does not mean we do not have to follow the law. Whether or not the employer knew it was illegal, the decision to make her pay back the money raises ethical questions that can be answered through analysis.

We can analyze the manager's decision to make Maggie, a tipped employee, pay back a shortage due to either a mistake or being cheated. *Maggie, other employees*, the *manager, customers,* and *FOI* could be affected by this decision so we will enter the decision option and the stakeholders on an Ethics Analysis Form. A completed form follows the discussion.

ANALYSIS OF POSSIBLE CONSEQUENCES FOR MAGGIE

Maggie accepted traveler's checks without asking for identification. She may or may not have been trained on the procedure for accepting traveler's checks. We might assume that she would ask someone if she did not know how to do it, but whenever we make an assumption, we risk being wrong. Even though this is the United States and we believe in equal rights and equal access, Maggie should have noticed that the woman was a bag lady sitting at the bar alone, drinking $40 worth of drinks using traveler's checks. She should have mentioned this to her manager. We do not know the details in this situation, but questions that come to mind are: why did Maggie not say anything to anyone? Was she oblivious or was it unsafe to ask questions?

Maggie should have been able to assess the situation and register some concern. This is similar to the situation where Mike noted the customer looked "shifty" and then was on guard. Though we just explored the ethics of "profiling," it would be unrealistic to say that generalizations do not play a role in the way we approach certain customers. There is a big difference, however, between profiling winos and an entire race of individuals based solely on the color of their skin. We have to be careful to not unnecessarily hurt our customers by making incorrect assumptions. That having been said, Maggie in this situation did not follow a procedure that may or may not have been in place, and was then punished by being forced to pay back the $40 loss.

Maggie was angry, crying, and said it was unfair to have to pay back the $40. She, of course, would most likely never again let a bag lady drink at the bar and pay with bogus traveler's checks. Expensive lessons are usually very effective, but they often can have negative side effects. As a result, Maggie's attitude could become less positive, and she might even resort to stealing. She could complain to other employees and/or take another job.

ANALYSIS OF POSSIBLE CONSEQUENCES FOR OTHER EMPLOYEES

Other employees would find out that Maggie was required to pay back the shortage. They would probably be more careful about shortages themselves so they would not have to pay them back. If none of them had received specific training in serving bag ladies and/or cashing traveler's checks, they could feel that Maggie's treatment was unfair or too severe, which could affect morale and/or turnover. It is unwise for management to unfairly take money from the pocketbooks of bartenders, because, as was stated earlier, they have a much greater opportunity to steal. It would be akin to insulting the brake mechanic just before leaving our car with him for repair work.

IN THE TRENCHES

Maricelyn Seaton, 31, Kayenta, AZ

"I've worked in the hotel industry for quite some time and have had many crazy experiences involving questionable ethical practices on the part of management. The worst, however, occurred one day while in my position as front desk agent at a local hotel. I was working the 3–11 shift and my manager usually left @ 5:00 or 6:00 PM. At shift's end I made my cash drop, including $400 in one hundred dollar bills. I filled the drop sheet in properly and a coworker witnessed the event and double-checked the count. The owner was making a deposit the next day and noticed that the envelope was opened and $100 was missing. The manager insisted he did not take the money. The only people with access to the safe were the manager and the owner himself, yet I was blamed for the shortage and required to pay it back."

ANALYSIS OF POSSIBLE CONSEQUENCES FOR THE MANAGER

Employees might be more careful in the future if they knew they would have to pay back any shortages. The manager, however, might have lost employees' trust or loyalty if employees think Maggie was treated unfairly. This could affect his or her ability to manage effectively and could lead to headaches due to less cooperation and increased turnover. Some bartenders could rationalize that if it was okay for management to "steal" from them, then they should steal from the company. As a result, liquor costs could rise and profits could fall, these barometers directly affecting a manager's performance rating.

ANALYSIS OF POSSIBLE CONSEQUENCES FOR CUSTOMERS

If employees are unhappy, service levels and cheerfulness could decrease. If employees take all this in stride, determined to not let this happen to them, they could become more suspicious and less gracious, which could negatively affect the bar's reputation and business. Mismanagement can create a wedge of hostility between customers and employees, or can cause employees to talk negatively about management in front of customers, which negatively impacts the overall service experience for the customer.

ANALYSIS OF POSSIBLE CONSEQUENCES FOR THE BAR

The bar could lose its reputation as a good place to work, and unhappy employees could be delivering a lower quality service, which could negatively impact business. There will be recruiting, selection, and training costs incurred if employee morale decreases and turnover increases. Employee theft could increase, causing liquor costs to rise, and overall profitability would be lessened.

ETHICAL PRINCIPLES VIOLATED BY THIS DECISION

Making Maggie pay back the $40 shortage at the end of her shift is probably illegal in this situation and violates several of the ethical principles. If Maggie was not trained or informed ahead of time that she was responsible for shortages, she could feel she was treated *unfairly* by the manager. She would perhaps lose her *trust* for the manager and might be less *loyal* in the future. Maggie's own *commitment to excellence* may not be as strong as we might like.

This situation was something that happened at a place Mike Scales worked before FOI, so we do not have all the details. It is unclear whether or not Maggie had been trained how to handle traveler's checks and guests who do not fit the target market. If she had not, *fairness* and *concern and respect for others* would also have been violated.

Many of the principles could be involved in this situation such as *commitment to excellence, leadership, reputation and morale,* and*accountability.* Because we do not have all of the details, it is entirely possible that the other employees thought it was okay for management to require Maggie to repay the shortage. However, in this situation, it was probably illegal to force her to repay the shortage. The illegality of the policy, combined with the chance of negative consequences due to violations of the ethical principles, should lead us to the conclusion that there might be a better decision.

Ethical Analysis Form

Slick Rudy / Maggies Payback

Decision Option: To make Maggie pay back the $40 shortage

Stakeholders	Principles	Consequences
Maggie	Commitment to Excellence	• Maggie was angry and said it was unfair to have to pay back the $40. • She would most likely never again let a bag lady drink at the bar and pay with bogus traveler's checks. • Maggie's attitude could be less positive and she might even resort to stealing to get back at management. • She could complain to other employees and/or take another job.
Other Employees		• Other employees would probably be more careful about shortages to avoid having to pay them back. • They could feel that the treatment of Maggie was unfair or too severe, which could affect morale and/or turnover, or lead some to thievery.
The Manager [Decision-Maker]	Fairness Trustworthiness Loyalty Concern for Others Commitment to Excellence Leadership Reputation and Morale Accountability	• Employees might be more careful in the future if they knew they would have to pay back any shortages. • The manager could lose employee trust and loyalty, which could affect his or her ability to manage effectively. • Employees could be less cooperative and turnover could increase. • Employees could resort to stealing because of what they might consider similar behavior on the part of management (with regards to their unfair shortage policy). This could lead to higher liquor costs and lower profits, which would reflect negatively on the manager's performance.
Customers		• Employees could be more suspicious and less gracious and polite to customers. • Service levels and cheerfulness could decrease.

(continued)

Stakeholders	Principles	Consequences
Customers		• A detectable rift between employees and management might negatively affect customers' experience at FOI.
FOI		• FOI could lose its reputation as a good place to work. • Unhappy employees could be delivering a lower quality service, which could negatively impact business. • There will be recruiting, selection, and training costs incurred if employee moral decreases and turnover increases. • Employee theft could increase, affecting profits.

OTHER OPTIONS

The $40 loss is an indication that employees are not being adequately trained and supervised in at least one area, which could be improved upon immediately. Perhaps Maggie was trained and should have known what to do, or at least had the common sense to alert the manager on duty. Perhaps she should be retrained and/or disciplined for failure to follow procedures. If she does not improve, she might need to be terminated or put in a position that better matches her strengths. If Maggie cannot be trained, perhaps she should not have been hired in the first place.

Avoiding problems is good management. We call it being **proactive.** Because we deal with people, there will be surprises—some that will be unpleasant. Professional managers, however, make sure that they are not inadvertently causing problems or failing to take the necessary precautions to avoid them.

STAR-TENDER

In *Star-Tender* (see the segment of the case study in the back of the text) we have another situation involving Mike Scales, the bar manager. Mike's rough management style and categorizing Floyd as a "type," determining to get rid of him, is similar to the *Slick Rudy* segment in the way Mike dealt with the crooked customer. As manager, Mike must make sure Floyd is doing his job correctly and working as part of the bar team. His management style for dealing with Floyd may be problematic, even though he may not have violated any of the ethical principles.

Sometimes ethical violations are obvious. Sometimes they are not. Sometimes we might suspect that something is wrong, but after the analysis process we find that it is not an ethical dilemma, but, rather, a management or leadership problem. Mike's actions in both *Slick Rudy* and *Star-Tender* were somewhat questionable, but not necessarily because of ethics violations. The flashback situation about the bartender named Maggie in Mike's previous job did turn out to be an ethical dilemma. Regardless, the analysis process practiced throughout this book is a useful way to predetermine best decisions whether they concern ethics or not.

Not all ethical dilemmas present the opportunity for heinous behavior on the part of management. However, little infractions can lead to bigger infractions. Any deviation from the rules can tend to desensitize us. Integrity is developed over time by consistently making ethical decisions. Not all consequences of our decisions are immediate. It is difficult to consider every ramification of every decision we make. We can, however, rest assured that ethical decisions are far less likely to have negative consequences—now or later.

ALCOHOL AND THE HOSPITALITY INDUSTRY

In *To the Rescue of Jim Dandy* (see the segment of the case study at the back of the text), Eddie, one of the FOI bartenders, does not want to serve Jim Lansing, a regular customer, because he has already had way too much to drink. Eddie is worried, however, that to refuse Jim one last drink could result in losing the tip on what has built up into a large tab.

It is illegal to serve alcohol to intoxicated guests. The reason there are liquor liability laws is that people under the influence of alcohol do not always make rational decisions. They may think they are perfectly capable of driving, yet their intoxicated driving performance may be erratic and dangerous and could hurt other people. To keep other people safe from drunk drivers, it has become the responsibility of the bartender or server to recognize when customers are nearing intoxication. It is their prerogative and also their responsibility to refuse service of any additional alcohol to a customer they consider intoxicated. Both bartender and drinking establishment can be held liable if intoxicated guests get in accidents and hurt themselves or others.

Eddie knows the law, but he is working alone, and following the law could upset the customer and cost him his tip. He must choose between right and wrong, so this is an ethical dilemma. We will begin by analyzing the decision for Eddie to *give Jim the last drink* he requested. *Eddie, Jim, other employees, FOI,* and *other drivers or pedestrians* are the stakeholders who could be affected by Eddie's decision to serve Jim one last drink. We enter the decision and the stakeholders on an Ethics Analysis Form. A completed form follows this discussion.

ANALYSIS OF POSSIBLE CONSEQUENCES FOR EDDIE

If Eddie goes ahead and gives Jim one last drink, Jim will be pleased and will probably leave him a large tip. Jim is a regular customer with a drinking problem. If Eddie serves him this time, Jim will most likely expect Eddie to serve him on other evenings when he is equally intoxicated. Other customers witnessing the event would also expect the same treatment. So Eddie could be faced with the same dilemma over and over again.

Eddie can weigh the risks. How likely is it that Jim will get in an accident on the way home when he is already "hammered" *before* having one final drink? What kind of damage could an accident cause? In 2002, 17,970 people were killed in alcohol-related car accidents in the United States. Most of the people hurt or killed in the more than 25,000 alcohol-related accidents each year are innocent bystanders. Eddie and FOI could be sued if Jim causes an accident.

Jim is already intoxicated. Mike, Eddie's supervisor, is responsible for the decisions Eddie makes on the job. He would probably not be pleased to discover that Eddie was putting FOI in jeopardy to facilitate a bigger tip. Eddie could face disciplinary action even if Jim made it home safely—this time. If Eddie serves one intoxicated guest, he will be more likely to serve other intoxicated guests, and this increases the risk that someone will have an accident and Eddie and FOI will be held liable.

ANALYSIS OF POSSIBLE CONSEQUENCES FOR JIM LANSING

There is a good chance that Jim could cause an accident and hurt or kill himself and/or others. If Jim survives an accident, he would be charged with driving under the influence. He could lose his driver's license, he could be sued by anyone he hurt, and/or he could go to prison. The negative publicity could harm his car dealership and his family. Jim could also sue FOI and Eddie for overserving him and causing his accident. He would most likely win such a case.

ANALYSIS OF POSSIBLE CONSEQUENCES FOR OTHER EMPLOYEES

Other employees might witness Eddie serving the obviously intoxicated guest. They could assume that they too could serve intoxicated guests. Others might find it disturbing and wonder if they should report Eddie's reckless behavior, which could cause stress and discomfort. Any increase in serving intoxicated guests raises the accident risk factor, and thus increases the risk that FOI and/or an FOI employee could be sued. It would be a personal disaster for Eddie if he were sued for serving an intoxicated guest, but it could also have a negative effect on staff morale.

ANALYSIS OF POSSIBLE CONSEQUENCES FOR FOI

Serving customers additional drinks brings in more revenue to FOI while increasing servers' and bartenders' tips. If Jim got in an accident, though, FOI could be sued and possibly lose its liquor license. A resort that cannot serve alcohol most likely would go out of business. Any legal action taken against Eddie and/or FOI would become known in the community and negatively affect FOI's reputation and sales.

ANALYSIS OF POSSIBLE CONSEQUENCES FOR OTHER DRIVERS OR PEDESTRIANS

Drunkenness has become socially unacceptable. Laws have tightened as the public's attitude toward drunk driving has hardened, and law enforcement has become less tolerant. We may not like the idea that servers can be held responsible for drunken customers' accidents, but that is the reality we must deal with as hospitality professionals. The families of people Jim might injure or kill in a drunk driving accident would be devastated, and they would most likely sue Jim, Eddie, and/or FOI.

ETHICAL PRINCIPLES VIOLATED BY THIS DECISION

If Eddie was the bar manager instead of just the bartender, his decision to serve an already intoxicated guest would violate all ten of the Ethical Principles for Hospitality Managers. As a bartender, his decision would be to break the law and put someone's life in imminent danger for a mere $30 tip. Eddie knows Jim is intoxicated, and he knows it is illegal to serve him another drink. To knowingly break the law is to be *dishonest*. It is unlikely that Eddie would tell Mike, the bar manager, about the fact that he continued to serve an intoxicated guest. *Integrity* would be violated because he would have chosen to do the wrong thing.

Eddie would jeopardize FOI's liquor license and open the inn to possible lawsuits for a possible $30 tip, so he is not *trustworthy* and would be *disloyal* to the company that pays him to do a job. To allow Jim to get in a car and possibly hurt or kill himself and/or others violates *concern and respect for others*. He is not *committed to excellence* if he breaks the law and endangers other people and FOI for a tip. The *reputation and morale* of FOI and its employees could suffer from negative publicity if an accident should occur. Eddie may ultimately be held *accountable*, so he needs to think about the possible consequences in advance.

Ethics Analysis Form
To the Rescue of Jim Dandy

Decision Option: Eddie gives Jim a last drink

Stakeholders	Principles	Consequences
Eddie Bates (Bartender) [Decision-Maker]	Honesty Integrity Trustworthiness Loyalty Concern and Respect for Others Reputation and Morale Commitment to Excellence Accountability	• Eddie gets a big tip and avoids hassling with Jim. • Jim is happy and satisfied and Eddie will see Jim more often because Jim knows he can get unlimited drinks out of Eddie. • If Jim gets in an accident, Eddie could feel guilty and/or get sued. • If FOI management discovers Eddie is serving more drinks to already intoxicated customers, Eddie could face disciplinary action or be terminated.

(continued)

Stakeholders	Principles	Consequences
Jim Lansing (Customer)		• Jim could have an accident and hurt or kill himself and/or others. • If Jim gets into an accident as a result of drinking, this could negatively affect his reputation in the community and the health of his car dealership. • Jim could have his license revoked and possibly go to jail.
Other Employees		• Other employees seeing Eddie get away with serving an intoxicated customer might be encouraged to do the same. That would, of course, increase the risk of an accident and damage the morale of the entire staff.
FOI		• Selling Jim more drinks produces more revenue for FOI. • If Jim is in an accident, FOI could be sued and they could lose their liquor license. This would jeopardize the entire operation. • The reputation of FOI could be damaged by adverse publicity.
Other Drivers or Pedestrians		• Other drivers and pedestrians are at risk when a drunk driver is on the road. • If injured or killed by Jim, they or their families could sue Jim, FOI, and/or Eddie.

OTHER DECISION OPTIONS

The other decision option in this situation is for Eddie to not give Jim the extra drink. Eddie might not get the tip because Jim will most likely get mad, but all the other consequences remain the same because Jim was already intoxicated before the last drink. This situation was about serving an intoxicated guest *more* alcohol. The guest should not have been served alcohol to the point of intoxication to begin with. Even without a last drink, all of the ethical principles and the law were already violated. If Jim had been cut off at a more appropriate time, the bar tab would not have been as high and Eddie would not be worried about losing such a large tip.

We might be tempted to just keep serving customers even if they are becoming intoxicated. But when we analyze the decision to do that, we can see that there are some very negative consequences that could have far-reaching negative effects on our life and on the business. Imagine Eddie in court getting sued, wishing he had skipped the $30 tip and avoided ruining his own life. Of course, it is possible that Jim would not get in an accident, but he would most likely be back and Eddie would then be dealing with the same risk over and over. Are we willing to risk our lives for $30?

Our employees might not bother to think out the possible consequences of their actions before taking them. We as managers, however, must be sure that our people are doing the right things—the ethical things—because our business depends on it.

ALCOHOL ABUSE AND ALCOHOLISM

Alcohol accompanies many events. We toast the bride and groom, ring in the New Year, and christen ships with champagne. We drink cold beer at ball games, have tropical drinks at pool parties, and many religious ceremonies include wine. We serve wine with dinner and often bring a bottle when we go to someone's home for dinner. Alcohol is served on airlines, at sporting events, and at the theater. Alcohol can enhance many occasions when used in moderation. Most of us are familiar with the positive attributes of alcohol. It is the negative side of alcohol, however, that we must clearly recognize.

If all our friends are heavy drinkers, if we spend our leisure time in bars where everyone is drinking, we can come to think that it is normal to drink a lot and acceptable to become intoxicated. That perception is further reinforced when we also work in or around a bar. We can categorically state, however, that it is not normal to drink a lot, and it is unacceptable to become overly intoxicated.

Alcohol is an addictive drug that, when used in moderation, can reduce inhibitions and enhance relaxation. When abused, it can and does destroy lives. **Alcohol abuse** or problem drinking can develop into the more severe **alcohol dependence** or **alcoholism.** Close to 15 million Americans abuse alcohol while 8.1 million are alcohol dependent. Alcoholism in the United States costs more than $185 billion a year due to lower productivity, illness, and premature death.

One third of the U.S. adult population abstains from the use of alcohol, and many others are **social drinkers.** Alcoholism is a progressive disease that ends in insanity or death unless treated. Through time and continued drinking, a small percentage of social drinkers become alcohol abusers. At this stage drinking becomes more important in their lives and they may exhibit unbecoming behavior and suffer frequent hangovers. Drinking may cause personal and work problems, which are alleviated/aggravated by more drinking. Continued drinking progresses into alcohol dependence where the need to drink is overwhelming.

Alcoholism runs in families, so some of us may be physically predisposed to become alcoholics. Parental behavior, peer pressure, cultural attitudes, and the availability of alcohol all factor into the risk of alcoholism. People who start drinking when they are kids are four times more likely to become alcohol dependent than those who wait until they are age 21 or older. Many alcohol abusers are in **denial.** They will not recognize their drinking as problematic and insist that they can stop whenever they want.

Prolonged heavy drinking can result in liver damage, heart damage and heartbeat irregularities and hypertension, all of which can cause death. Alcohol impairs judgment and physical reflexes, which can result in accidents. Large amounts of alcohol can cause stupor and death. Excessive drinking during pregnancy can cause fetal alcohol syndrome, which results in physical and mental defects to the baby.

Treatment for alcoholism can be effective but is uncertain. Alcohol-dependent people can suffer physical withdrawal symptoms when they quit drinking and may need medical help. It is possible but extremely difficult to recover from alcoholism on one's own. Individual counseling, group therapy, alcohol treatment programs, and drug treatment can help alcoholics to stop drinking, but the rate of recidivism is high. Alcoholics Anonymous and other similar but secular self-help programs are shown to be effective support sources.

ALCOHOL ABUSE AT FRESHWATER OASIS INN

Those of us in the hospitality industry are particularly at risk for alcoholism because alcohol is available at all times, and because we are often around people who are drinking. Frank Stratten in *Palmas No Coconutus* (see the segment of the case study at the end of the book) has taken to hanging out at the new swim-up pool bar, what he refers to as his "office." Frank hired John Fallin to manage FOI, so he has no management duties or responsibilities beyond getting a tan.

All the employees are aware that Frank is the owner of FOI and they treat him with respect. Frank, however, is taking up one of only eight barstools almost every day and is not tipping the bartender, Jorge, for making all his banana daiquiris. As Frank gets intoxicated, he makes fun of Jorge's Mexican heritage. So Jorge is working harder, making less money, and is offended by Frank's comments. As a result of being flustered by the owner's presence, he takes a shortcut in not tying the garbage bag and Judy the cocktail waitress slips on a banana peel that fell from the untied bag.

Prior to Judy's accident, Frank in his drunkenness called Gabe at the front desk to inquire why the palm trees did not have coconuts. He then demanded that Gabe track down the building engineer, Bill Gardner, and see to it that they are cut down immediately and replaced with coconut-bearing palm trees. So, what we have here is Frank being an offensive nuisance, getting in the way of the employees' work, and causing accidents. Because Frank is the owner, employees feel like they have to take him seriously.

Let us look at Frank's behavior in ethical terms. Frank is in the way, wasting staff time with ridiculous questions and demands, and negatively affecting Jorge's income and time. While he is not directly responsible for the banana peel falling out of Jorge's garbage bag, he was the reason Jorge was aggravated and pressed for time and subsequently less careful. If Frank could *honestly* look at himself and his behavior, he would know that he is causing problems. A person of *integrity* does not put selfish desires before the good of the rest.

Jorge said he liked Frank well enough when he was sober, but, when he was drunk, Frank made offensive remarks to Jorge. People who say offensive things when they are drunk tend to lose our *trust* even when sober, because we may suspect that what they said are their real feelings. Jorge works for Mike, who works for Heidi, who works for John Fallin. That none of the managers are addressing the problem that Frank has become leaves the problem to Jorge who is in no position to handle it. Jorge's manager is to take care of problems on the job that affect Jorge. Jorge's sense of *loyalty* could shrink.

It is not *fair* that Frank takes up space at the bar and then does not tip Jorge for making his drinks. This negatively affects Jorge's income and demonstrates a lack of *concern and respect* on Frank's part. Other employees will notice that Frank does not tip, word will get around, and Frank's *reputation* will be further ruined. *Morale* suffers when employees are expected to wait on people without being tipped.

When we are *committed to excellence* we are at our best at all times. We do what we are supposed to and then some. Frank is not at his best after six or seven banana daiquiris, slinging ethnic slurs at Jorge who is making Frank's drinks and not getting tipped. *Leadership* is compromised when behavior is less than desirable. Frank's presence should be positive, and, if it is not, he should not hang around at FOI. John is the only person at FOI who can appropriately speak to Frank about his behavior. John's *leadership* is also compromised when the employees see that he does nothing about Frank. We are all *accountable* for our own behavior, but top management is held *accountable* for everyone's behavior in an operation. Therefore, it is John's responsibility to do something about Frank.

ETHICS AND OUR LIVES

There are many things in this world that we have no direct control over—the weather, the government, what other people say or do, and so forth. What we do have control over is our own behavior. We can control what we say and do. When we are under the influence of alcohol, however, our ability to control ourselves is diminished. While the bartender or server can be held legally responsible if we go out, drink too much, and have an accident, we are morally responsible. If we are to be men and women of integrity, we must be accountable for our own decisions and behavior at all times.

We have choices and can choose to take good care of ourselves or not. We can choose to eat healthy food, sleep adequately, exercise regularly, work to the best of our abilities, and take care of our families, homes, and communities. We need to balance our work with healthy pleasure and relaxation. We need to take time to nurture familial relationships and friendships. Our physical and mental health is dependent upon the choices we make.

This is a textbook about ethics in the hospitality industry. Ethics are rules that people choose to follow. So, for an industry to be "ethical" means that the people who make up the industry must be ethical. To be successful managers, it is necessary for us to make ethical choices in our managerial roles, but also in our personal lives. Our *commitment to excellence* at work is impeded if we make decisions in our personal lives that hinder our performance on the job.

Drinking too much, staying out too late, failing to give our families the time and care they need, all interfere with our ability to excel.

Abraham Maslow theorized that the highest level of human need is to actualize our full potential. Who we are inside, outside, on the job, and at home is consistent and our best. To be successful in business takes hard work, and it requires us to make the difficult decisions that will shape us into people of integrity. *Integrity* means we do what we know is right even when there is pressure to do otherwise. That means we *honestly* analyze our motivations, desires, and behaviors to determine if they are in line with the Ethical Principles for Hospitality Managers. We enlarge the scope of our responsibility beyond the job to include our families and our personal lives because they impact our professional lives.

None of us are perfect. We all have weaknesses and faults. We must, however, strive to be our very best. We will fail occasionally, and we will make mistakes, but we keep on trying and will continue to grow and improve if we wish to be successful managers and successful people.

CONCLUSION

Managing any department in a hotel requires particular technical knowledge plus human resource skills. Managing a bar may be more challenging because we are serving alcohol. Alcohol is a legal drug that is part of our culture. Some guests, employees, and managers, however, can be negatively affected by alcohol. Alcohol abuse is a major public health problem. We can be held liable if we overserve alcohol to a guest who later has an alcohol-related accident.

In this chapter we explored ethical issues involved with serving alcohol to guests and looked at the problems caused by an owner abusing alcohol at the property. We also addressed the necessity of making good personal behavior decisions in order to be successful.

KEY WORDS

Fair Labor Standards Act	Alcohol abuse
Proactive	Alcohol dependence/alcoholism
Social drinker	Denial

CHAPTER THOUGHT QUESTIONS

1. List and describe the particular problems associated with serving alcohol as compared to just serving food.
2. Describe a time when you made a judgment about a person and how your judgment affected your behavior. Discuss how our judgments can help us, but, also, how they can sometimes be incorrect and harmful.

3. How can we determine if something is an ethical dilemma when it is not obvious? Give an example of a work situation that was a management dilemma rather than an ethical dilemma.

4. Use the Ethical Analysis Form and analyze the management dilemma in question #3 to determine the best solution.

5. Describe a time when you were away from home and you, or someone you were with, or someone you noticed was intoxicated. Who was serving the alcohol? Did they continue to serve the person after he or she was noticeably intoxicated? How did the person who was intoxicated get home?

6. Discuss how you feel about the bartender being held responsible if a guest leaves the establishment drunk and has an accident. If you serve alcohol in your home, what would you do if a guest was starting to get intoxicated? What would you do if your guest wanted to drive him- or herself home?

7. What are your personal feelings about alcohol? Describe your personal drinking habits. If you do not drink, describe the drinking habits of someone you know. Categorize their drinking as social, abuse, or dependence.

8. Discuss whether or not it is possible to be an ethical manager yet be unethical at home. Why or why not? Use examples. How might a person be affected if he or she is ethical at home, but expected to be unethical at work?

9. Describe the kind of person you really are deep down. How does this compare with the way friends and family, coworkers, strangers, bosses, and any others you can think of see you? Which perception of you do you prefer? Why? How could you make it so everyone sees you the same? Discuss why it might be good to have a consistent personality and how it applies to ethics.

10. Is the way you think you are in question #9 the way you want to be? Why or why not? If you would like to be different than what you think you are, how could you become the way you would prefer?

REFERENCES

Alcoholism. (2003). *Microsoft Encarta Online Encyclopedia*. Available at http://encarata.msn.com.

Myers, D. G. (1999). *Exploring psychology* (4th ed.). New York: Worth.

Rande, W., & Valentino, L. (2001). *The beverage service world*. Upper Saddle River, NJ: Prentice-Hall.

Van Hoof, H. B., McDonald, M. E., Yu, L., & Vallen, G. K. (1996). *A host of opportunities: An introduction to hospitality management*. Chicago: Irwin.

Chapter 11

Ethics and Human Resource Management

Ethics concern people—how we think, feel, and behave. While we may have some contact with guests in hospitality management, our primary responsibility is managing the people who are delivering the service product to our guests. The way we think, feel, and behave can have a profound effect on our employees and determine whether or not we are successful managers.

Adequate staffing of well-matched people for the various positions, scheduling, training, and evaluating employees' performance require specific management knowledge that may be gained in hospitality management programs. It is essential to hire candidates who match the job specification for the particular positions. They must first be willing to do the job, and then we must train them to do the job.

Hiring appropriate people requires us to *honestly* identify any biases we may hold that could interfere with our ability to see the match or mismatch between a candidate and the job specification. Our *loyalty* to the company is demonstrated by our careful selection of potential employees, ensuring that new employees will be assets with the ability to meet company standards. We show *concern and respect* for job applicants by taking them seriously and appreciating their time, interest in our positions, and their needs. We show *concern and respect* for our staff by only hiring individuals who will be able to pull their share of the load and work well with others.

Providing formal training to new employees allows them to be competent on the job from the beginning. Training demonstrates *concern and respect* for new employees, continuing employees, and also for guests. Our *commitment to excellence* becomes tangible when we not only expect excellence from our employees, but show them how to perform excellently. *Leadership* is not fearing that employees will surpass us, but, rather, giving employees the tools to excel. The *reputation and morale* of the workplace and the staff rise as we make it possible for our employees to do their very best.

It is in the day-to-day supervision of our employees, however, where people skills are most necessary. **People skills** are the combination of communication skills, social skills, and **empathy,** that when working together enable us to be positively effective with our employees. Because we all have the same feelings, we are capable of empathizing or understanding how other people feel in particular situations. Some of us may need to practice tuning in to others' feelings by asking ourselves how we would feel if we were in the other person's shoes.

SUPERVISION

Supervision is ongoing training where we make sure that the standards reached in training are maintained on the job. The "I'm the boss" management style is ineffective with today's workforce. **Coaching** is a supervising technique that encourages and rewards adequate (meets the standards) performance and discourages and corrects inadequate (does not meet the standards) performance. Managers act as coaches by making sure directions are clear and specific and then giving frequent positive corrective feedback. If we take what we say seriously, our employees will be more likely to take it seriously, and, thus, follow through as expected.

To coach our employees, we have to be "out on the floor" with them. We must be able to see what they are doing. Just like the coach of an athletic team, we must be aware who is doing what, when, where, and how, and we must positively reinforce that which is good and correct that which is not. Because everyone knows that the coach's *loyalty* is with the company, and there are no hidden agendas, employees can *trust* the coach to be *fair* with them. Employees are more satisfied when they are treated with *concern and respect,* and *reputation and morale* rises.

Our *leadership* is enhanced when our employees want to follow us because they know we are leading them in a direction that is good for the company, and, in turn, good for them. Our *commitment to excellence* requires us to use the coaching technique because employees prefer it to being ordered around. We can think about how we like to be managed; our employees are no different. Most of us prefer the more positive coaching approach.

Supervision is the most time-consuming part of human resource management. Effective supervision requires us to have communication skills, problem-solving skills, negotiation and conflict management skills, and personal management skills. In order to manage our employees, we first need to be able to manage ourselves. The following topics are areas where we can, perhaps, make some personal improvements. If we are behaving and living in a healthy way, we will be more successful managers and our employees can learn from our example.

IN THE TRENCHES

Tina Poley, 20, Phoenix, AZ

"I work the front desk at a residence hall. We recently hired a new office manager who has since missed three shifts, all of which were considered unexcused absences. She doesn't register equipment when it's checked out (so we can track who has it), and gives out room keys without checking ID or verifying information. We are allowed one emergency missed shift but are put on probation as a result, and any further infractions are grounds for termination. If any other desk worker had done what this manager has, they would have been fired long ago. Despite knowledge of all these infractions, though, the hall director has not taken any action whatsoever against this manager. As a result, morale amongst the desk workers has plummeted."

STRESS MANAGEMENT

A little stress is good. A lot of stress can make us sick or even kill us. We need to take steps that will reduce the amount of unnecessary stress. Members of Twelve-Step programs say the Serenity Prayer: God, grant me the Serenity to accept the things I cannot change, the Courage to change the things I can, and the Wisdom to know the difference.

Seems simple, however, many of us are not even aware that things we may be doing are creating stress and could be avoided. The key is, of course, to recognize what we can and cannot control. There are very few things we can control. We have no control over what other people say, do, and think. We have no immediate control over the government, society, the weather, housing availability, the economy, the job market, and so forth.

The only thing we really have any control over at all is our selves. We can choose what we think, feel, and do. If we fail to make a choice, that in itself is actually a choice. We can control the types of foods we eat. Nutritious, balanced diets are better for our health and can reduce the risk of heart disease, diabetes, and other diet-related problems. We can choose to get adequate sleep. If we are well rested and well fed, we are more able to cope with things that tend to come up in life. If we are poorly fed and tired, we have less resistance to illness, and we all are aware that life is hard enough when we feel good. When we are sick and tired, it can be very difficult.

We have the choice to control the amount of alcohol, nicotine, caffeine, and other drugs we allow in our bodies. Too much of any of these drugs can either increase stress or create other problems that increase stress. While drug abuse increases stress, exercise decreases the stress response and can reduce other health risks. Prayer, meditation, and deep breathing have also been shown to reduce stress. If we choose to exercise regularly and allow regular quiet times for ourselves, we can reduce the amount of stress in our lives.

We need a balance between work and play to be healthy, functional adults. Workaholics tend to have strokes and heart attacks. Their relationships are often either poor or nonexistent because they may have failed to give their relationships the amount of time necessary to nurture and grow them. Lives of decadence are devoid of meaning and can result in despair. We can choose how we use our time. We can choose to find meaningful activities, and we can choose to develop good relationships that help us to enjoy the good times and sustain us in the not-so-good times.

When we identify what we have control over and no control over, we can then choose to let go of worry, anger, or grief when it is pointless. We can use our energy to make changes that are possible and helpful instead of wasting energy "pounding our heads against brick walls." Recognizing that we have control over ourselves—what we do, think, feel, and say—allows us to seek solutions to problems rather than feeling like leaves tossed by the wind.

We have control over how we take care of ourselves—how much sleep we get, what and how much we eat and drink. We can make a point of nurturing good relationships. They take time and effort. If we do not put time and effort into our relationships, we will not have any. If we blame all our problems on others and look to others to solve our problems, we will ultimately be disappointed in life, others, and ourselves, and be less successful people. Life is meant to be joyous. If we are not experiencing joy much of the time, then we need to look at how we are living and thinking and make some changes.

TIME MANAGEMENT

Management can be stressful. We must make sure we are eliminating unnecessary stress, because if we don't, we will most likely get burned out, be less successful managers, and/or suffer some physical ailment, such as a stroke or heart attack.

There is only so much time in a day and we can only do so much. If we say *yes* to everything, we may find ourselves overloaded and set up for failure. As managers, we may feel that work has to come first because if we do not do our jobs, we could lose them, and then our families could be in jeopardy. That is certainly true. However, if we are overloaded, something has to go and it more often than not is our family time. When we do not give our families adequate time and attention, they leave us. And this, of course, creates more stress in our lives. So, it is essential that we effectively manage our time.

First we must determine our priorities. What is really important to us? What isn't very important? How are we actually spending our time? It is helpful to keep a detailed log of our activities in a day. We might seem to never have enough time, but by detailing the things we actually do, we often find that we are spending more time on things that have no priority in our lives. Time-consuming things such as watching television, or, at work, we might be shuffling papers or doing easy or less important tasks rather than what we need to do.

We tend to spend the most time on things we like rather than the things we do not. Students tend to spend more time studying favorite subjects, and the time they spend studying their least favorites—such as math—is often spent thinking about how stupid and useless math is instead of actually learning it. It is no wonder that we are not very good at what we dislike because we have spent very little quality time practicing it. And, practice makes perfect.

We simply have to bite the bullet and do the top priority first, move to the second priority next, eliminate the things that have no priority, and, when we are finished, then we can play. Unsuccessful people tend to work that order backwards.

Rarely will anyone ever take care of us. People will keep asking us to do things so long as we keep saying yes. Before saying yes, however, we must consider how much time it will take, how important the activity is, and what we will have to eliminate if we agree to do it. There is a limited amount of time. If our time is already full, then we will have to give something up in order to accomplish the new task. If it is our boss asking us to take on another task, we may have to explain what we have to do and negotiate some extended deadlines on other tasks. We must not sacrifice our family or our health for another task.

DELEGATION

A third related area is delegation, which is the process of assigning responsibility and authority to employees in order to accomplish an objective. Delegation will give us more time and less stress, it can develop employees' capabilities, and, as it demonstrates trust and confidence, it can lead to better human relations and job performance.

Some harried managers resist delegating tasks because they can do them better and faster themselves. That is often true. However, it is only true once. If we take the time to show someone how to do the task, and give him or her authority to do the task, we will never have to do the task again. And that is a lot less time consuming.

To be truly successful managers we need to hire capable people and then help them to excel. If we are threatened by employees who do their jobs better than we could do them, we will end up with a mediocre operation and be less successful managers. The better our people are and the more they excel, the better we are as managers. Our people will appreciate that we enable them to reach their potentials and to improve. They will be more loyal, more productive, and do better work.

There are some tasks that should not be delegated because they are either confidential or require our particular expertise. It is inappropriate to delegate tasks that are rightfully ours simply because we dislike them. As managers we must also consider the workloads of the people we are delegating tasks to. They may not be inclined to admit they do not have enough time. The tasks have to be done properly so we must ensure that the person is adequately trained to do the task, has the authority to be able to do it, and has the time to do it. We are ultimately responsible for the work of all our people, so we must have adequate controls in place and check that the task has been done in a timely and correct fashion.

Personal management skills are learned. They do not come naturally. Those of us who had perfect parents learned the skills as children and have matured into expert communicators who lead well-balanced, successful lives. The other 99% of us have stumbled and been made painfully aware of the gaps in our personal management skill inventories.

College is the one time in our lives where we are electively taking time out to learn and grow. It is in the college years where, if we wish to, we can become aware of our personal strengths and weaknesses. If we do not identify our weaknesses, how can we possibly hope to improve? Most universities have personal development programs for students, and there are numerous self-help books available so we can learn and practice new behaviors that will replace the old, ineffective ones. With practice these new behaviors can become skills.

Personal management skills are often learned later in life, for instance, after a heart attack. We can save ourselves, our families, and the people we manage a lot of time and torment if we do not wait for our bodies to force us to improve our communication, delegation, and time management skills. We can also reduce the harmful stress levels in our lives by making good life choices and taking good care of ourselves.

We cannot attain and maintain the success levels we desire if we do not have personal management skills. There is no point in waiting until later. Now is the time to look at ourselves and identify any personal management skill deficiencies. Now is the time to begin learning and practicing new, more effective behaviors. Having well-developed personal management skills results in more successful personal and business lives.

HUMAN RESOURCE MANAGEMENT AT FRESHWATER OASIS INN

Heidi Bell, 32, is the Assistant General Manager and has been with FOI since it opened. She has worked nearly every job in the hotel business over the past 14 years. Her last position was Front Desk Manager at the elegant Bennett Arms downtown. Heidi felt that her lack of formal education, however, was limiting her career and believed that FOI offered more responsibility, autonomy, and potential.

In *New Kid on the Block* (see the segment of the case study at the back of the book), Heidi hired Nancy in reaction to being understaffed. She has now realized that Nancy does not physically fit in—she does not have "the look." Therefore, she has decided to get rid of her. She made a thoughtless snap decision to hire Nancy and has now made another thoughtless snap decision to get rid of her. On Nancy's first day of training, she became painfully aware that Heidi, Tony, and another employee were laughing at her. This was her initiation into the FOI family.

Heidi did not carefully select Nancy and now wants to get rid of her. It is obvious that the whole problem could have been avoided by taking the time to make sure Nancy was a good match for the position. We can analyze the consequences of getting rid of Nancy to help us make the best decision in this unfortunate situation. *Heidi, Nancy, other employees,* and *FOI* will all be affected by the decision to get rid of Nancy and can be entered on an Ethics Analysis Form along with the decision option. A completed Ethics Analysis Form follows this discussion.

ANALYSIS OF POSSIBLE CONSEQUENCES FOR HEIDI

John and the other managers will notice the new server and may wonder why Heidi hired her. That Heidi is not defending Nancy and is instead making fun of her suggests that Heidi does not know why she hired Nancy. This odd behavior makes Heidi look incompetent, cruel, and could be harmful to Heidi's future at FOI.

It will become obvious to everyone that Heidi made a hiring mistake. Employees can lose confidence in a manager who makes mistakes and then mishandles the aftermath. Heidi could experience less cooperation and acceptance from other staff members, which could undermine her ability to implement future decisions.

ANALYSIS OF POSSIBLE CONSEQUENCES FOR NANCY

We can imagine how awful Nancy must feel with the assistant general manager, the dining room manager, and another employee laughing about her. Management's behavior influences the behavior of other employees. Nancy is being poorly treated by staff *and* management, and she is also not being given parties to serve, which means she is not making any tips.

Nancy is being abused on the job and could sue for discrimination and/or wrongful discharge if she is terminated. She may tell people about her negative experiences, and that could harm FOI's reputation in the community and amongst the labor pool.

ANALYSIS OF POSSIBLE CONSEQUENCES FOR OTHER EMPLOYEES

In the past, some of the employees may have been hurt by other kids or adults. They might be able to relate to Nancy's discomfort. Since Heidi is treating Nancy so poorly, employees could fear that Heidi might treat them poorly too. Heidi is allowing other employees to make fun of Nancy and this could cause some employees to lose trust and respect for Heidi.

Managers have tremendous influence over their workers. A manager's actions speak louder than his or her words. Heidi was laughing over "accidentally" hiring Nancy, and this gives everyone the message that it is okay to abuse fellow workers. No matter where it originates, abusive behavior is unethical and destroys the civil working environment. As this environment deteriorates, attitudes sour and turnover can increase.

ANALYSIS OF POSSIBLE CONSEQUENCES FOR FOI

If Nancy is forced out by abusive treatment or terminated, she could decide to sue. Nancy did nothing wrong and could possibly win a wrongful discharge or discrimination suit. This information would become public and could harm the reputation of FOI. Even if there is not a lawsuit, employees talk, and job satisfaction could suffer. FOI's reputation as a good place to work could also be damaged.

ETHICAL PRINCIPLES VIOLATED BY THIS DECISION

Heidi did not demonstrate *integrity* when she laughed about Nancy, and, by her behavior, encouraged other employees to also mistreat her. She is not *trustworthy*, because if she can hurt some employees, she could easily hurt other employees. Employees' *loyalty* could be shaken if they fear that Heidi could treat them in a similar manner. It is *unfair* to single out an employee for abuse. Nancy did not deserve to be ridiculed. Heidi showed no *concern and respect* for Nancy, failed to have any empathy for Nancy, and she hurt her and allowed others to do the same.

Heidi violated *commitment to excellence* by not making a good selection for the server position to begin with. She further violated this principle by her uncivil behavior, which has negative effects on all of the stakeholders. Employees expect managers to do the right thing and will not follow a manager who does not—thus, Heidi's *leadership* ability is weakened. As the workplace becomes less civil and trust is diminished, the *morale* of the staff goes down, and the *reputation* of FOI as a nice place to stay and a good place to work is harmed.

Heidi is *accountable* for her behavior and the behavior of her staff. The only principle Heidi did not violate was *honesty*. She, in fact, merely abused the principle of honesty by being openly critical of Nancy's appearance, which at this point served no useful purpose and only hurt Nancy and allowed the other employees to behave poorly at Nancy's expense.

Ethics Analysis Form

New Kid on the Block

Decision Option: Heidi made a hiring mistake and wants to get rid of Nancy

Stakeholders	Principles	Consequences
Heidi (Asst. General Manager) [Decision-Maker]	Integrity Trustworthiness Loyalty Fairness Concern and Respect for Others Commitment to Excellence Leadership Reputation and Morale Accountability	• Heidi's action could come to John's attention (General Manager), and her management competence could be questioned. • Heidi could lose the trust and respect of the staff, and this could undermine her ability to implement future policies and decisions.
Nancy (New Server)		• Nancy's feelings could be hurt and her livelihood endangered. • Nancy could decide to sue FOI for discrimination and/or wrongful discharge if she is terminated.
Other Employees		• Other workers might fear similar treatment from management. This could affect their loyalty and trust of FOI and Heidi in particular. It could negatively affect their attitudes on the job and possibly increase turnover. • Other workers might feel that it is okay for them to abuse a fellow worker if they see management doing the same. This can destroy team effort and the overall working environment.
FOI		• FOI could be sued for wrongful discharge or discrimination. They could be forced to rehire Nancy and pay her back wages. • FOI's reputation as a good place to work could be damaged. This could affect the quality of future job applicants.

OTHER DECISION OPTIONS

Obviously Heidi should have been more careful in selecting a new server. Not every person is a good match for a specific job. Once we select someone, though, we are stuck with him or her. It is our responsibility as managers to make careful selections, hiring only people who are capable, willing, and trainable. They must have all the characteristics necessary to handle the position. If Heidi had done her job properly to begin with, this dilemma would not have come up.

Once Heidi realized her mistake, however, she did not consider other options. There are almost always other options; we just have to take the time to consider what they might be. Perhaps Nancy could be transferred to another position at the inn. Heidi made the mistake, so maybe FOI could pay for a "makeover" that would align Nancy's appearance with the preferred "look" for FOI servers. Any other options could then be analyzed for consequences and violations of ethical principles.

To get rid of Nancy by either terminating her or making her life miserable (and hoping she will quit) is unethical and a very bad decision. It is unconscionable to make up for a hiring mistake by punishing or abusing the individual in question, and there are numerous negative consequences that would be very likely to result.

This dilemma is an example of hiring out of desperation without taking the time and effort to ensure that the worker is a good position match. It illustrates problems that almost always arise from poor management. If we make a mistake we must figure out an ethical way to correct it. It is about being responsible for our actions and decisions, and we had best think about their consequences ahead of time to ensure that we are making the right ones. It is almost always easier and less painful to do the right thing, and, at the same time, it is far better for our careers and the business we are in.

CHAIN OF COMMAND AT FRESHWATER OASIS INN

Tony Marziano began waiting tables at FOI 5 years ago. He has been supervising waitstaff the past 2 years. In addition to scheduling servers, he is also in charge of the host/hostesses and splits time between both positions. In *Shrinkage* (see the segment of the case study in the back of the book), Heidi has made a decision and acted without taking the time to consider consequences. Without informing Tony, she reduced the size of the dining room stations in response to a couple bad spotters' reports. Tony and his staff are incensed.

Heidi may have had good reasons for reducing the number of tables in the stations, but she ignored Tony's place in the chain of command and did not prepare the staff for the change. Thus, the change was not well accepted. Had she analyzed her decision before acting on it, she might have anticipated the consequences and either made a different decision or implemented the decision in a more effective manner. We can look at her decision option in retrospect and

IN THE TRENCHES

John Banker, 20, Show Low, AZ

"I was scheduled to work immediately after Thanksgiving and came back early from visiting family for the shift. The following Monday I called for my schedule and was told to come meet with the owner. When I showed up for this meeting, I was laid off. A couple weeks later I discovered that my bank account was overdrawn $500 because my last paycheck from the company had bounced. This, of course, caused lots of stress and time wasted recovering these wages and finding a new job. Plus, I didn't get any pumpkin pie."

enter *Heidi ignores Tony in the chain of command* on an Ethics Analysis Form along with the stakeholders, *Heidi, Tony, FOI*, and *other employees*, who will be affected by the decision Heidi makes. A completed Ethics Analysis Form follows this discussion.

ANALYSIS OF POSSIBLE CONSEQUENCES FOR HEIDI

How we implement changes in what we want our people to do determines whether or not they will enthusiastically embrace the new way. Heidi made a decision and expected it to be done without making any effort to introduce it to Tony and his staff. In fact, Tony was the last to find out about the new station sizes, so, rather than encouraging his staff to accept them, he felt angry and left out of the decision process. This only fueled further dissension amongst the ranks.

We can ask ourselves how the people affected by our decisions will feel. The servers would naturally be concerned about loss of income and could feel that Heidi does not care about their livelihood. She should have anticipated that Tony would be unpleasantly surprised, and, perhaps, angry and insulted that the stations had been changed without his knowledge. Tony could even decide to leave FOI because of Heidi's thoughtless slight.

The **chain of command** is graphically depicted in organizational charts. At FOI, the servers report to Tony, Tony reports to Heidi, and Heidi reports to John. When someone goes over our head we may feel resentment because we are not given the opportunity to deal with whatever problem the other person had with us. In this situation, Heidi bypassed Tony and issued orders directly to his staff. Tony's authority was undermined by Heidi's failure to go through proper channels. Employees learn from managers, so they might conclude that it is appropriate to forego the chain of command, which would ultimately damage Heidi's and other managers' authority.

Heidi's decision to reduce the size of server stations may not be successful because Tony and his staff may not accept it graciously. If the dining room staff is up in arms, John most likely would get wind of the situation. He would see that Heidi did not go through the established FOI chain of command and therefore created a problem. Her level of competence would be decreased in John's eyes, which would obviously be bad for Heidi's standing at FOI.

ANALYSIS OF POSSIBLE CONSEQUENCES FOR TONY

Tony was given no chance to consider the pros and cons of reduced server stations before an angry staff assailed him. That his servers saw how it was probably humiliating to Tony, and because he was unprepared, he was unable to support and positively implement the decision.

Heidi undermined Tony with his staff, so Tony is not only angry but will most likely become less cooperative and trustful of Heidi. In the future he might not bother with the chain of command, since Heidi did not, and this would further undermine the organization of FOI. His attitude toward working could change if he is feeling offended and insulted by Heidi. He could begin looking for another job and perhaps even leave FOI or worse, remain as an ineffective manager with a bad attitude.

ANALYSIS OF POSSIBLE CONSEQUENCES FOR FOI

If Tony feels that Heidi has treated him poorly, and it was supported by FOI, he will probably talk about it with family and friends. Word of mouth has a tremendous impact and could negatively affect FOI's reputation as a good place to work. It could become difficult to recruit and hire the best people. There would be recruiting, selection, and training costs incurred if Tony or other servers decide to leave FOI.

Employees who feel that their opinions and needs are not considered in policy changes may become less cooperative and customer service could suffer. Employee satisfaction could lessen and turnover could increase. Upper management might be forced to step in and deal with the morale/service problems caused by Heidi.

ANALYSIS OF POSSIBLE CONSEQUENCES FOR OTHER EMPLOYEES

What managers do has far more impact than what they say. When Tony's staff sees Heidi trample all over him, they could lose confidence in his ability to manage and champion their interests at FOI. Their perception of Heidi could be very negative and they most likely would no longer trust her. Her ability to institute changes or programs would be diminished.

In the future they might be less apt to use the chain of command, and that can weaken the organization of FOI and create chaos. The servers are at FOI to make money. If they feel that management decisions are jeopardizing their livelihoods, they could become less satisfied with their jobs, service levels could go down, and turnover could increase. As trust in management deteriorates, the working environment becomes less civil and less desirable.

ETHICAL PRINCIPLES VIOLATED BY THIS DECISION

There are some very negative consequences as a result of Heidi's failure to consult with Tony before reducing the size of server stations. We can go down the list of Ethical Principles for Hospitality Managers and identify Heidi's ethical violations. Heidi is certainly not *trustworthy* in that she bypassed Tony, undermined his authority, and put him in a difficult position with his staff.

Her lack of *concern and respect* for both Tony and his staff's feelings—in particular, their fear of reduced tips—destroys *trust* and employee *loyalty* to FOI. John's *trust* in Heidi's ability to manage effectively may be lowered. Employees could feel that Heidi's action was *unfair* to them, and her failure to deal with their perceptions violates *leadership. Reputation and morale* will be harmed. Heidi is *accountable* for her decision and her behavior, and John is *accountable* as well.

Ethical Analysis Form

Shrinkage

Decision Option: Heidi ignores Tony in the chain of command

Stakeholders	Principles	Consequences
Heidi (Asst. General Manager) [Decision-Maker]	Trustworthiness Fairness Concern and Respect for Others Loyalty Leadership Reputation and Morale Accountability	• Heidi's decision was not well accepted and implemented because she failed to include Tony, her dining room manager, in a major decision that involved his staff. • Staff members could lose respect for Heidi and think that she does not respect their feelings. • Tony may feel Heidi does not trust or respect him, and he could decide to find another job. • Heidi's example might lead other staff to forego the chain of command, which would undermine her and other managers' authority. • When Heidi's new policy is not embraced, Heidi could face humiliation and questions by upper management regarding her failure to go through the usual chain of command.
Tony (Dining Room Mgr.)		• Not being informed or included made it difficult for Tony to support and implement the change. • Tony could feel offended and become less cooperative and less supporting of management. • Tony could feel betrayed and decide to find another job. • Tony could feel that since Heidi did not follow the chain of command, he does not have to either, further harming the chain of command.

(continued)

Stakeholders	Principles	Consequences
Freshwater Oasis Inn		• If Tony tells people he has been poorly treated, this could negatively affect FOI's reputation as a good place to work. • Employee satisfaction could diminish if staff input is not considered in policy changes. Productivity and service quality could decline, which could harm guest satisfaction and the reputation of FOI. Less business and higher turnover rates could result. • If Tony or other servers quit, FOI would have additional hiring and training costs. • Upper management may have to deal with Heidi and the dissatisfaction caused by her failure to work with Tony.
Other Employees		• If the chain of command is not followed by managers, employees might not feel they have to follow it either. This can cause management problems. • Employees who feel that their livelihood is in jeopardy may look for other jobs. • Employees who feel they are being taken advantage of may lose respect for management. Productivity can diminish and turnover can increase. • Questionable decisions that are modeled and reinforced by the organization's leadership (managers) could result in employees not trusting management and perhaps making them less trustworthy employees.

OTHER DECISION OPTIONS

Heidi's objective was most likely to improve the quality of service in the dining room. Her task was to figure out the best way to meet her objective. Smaller server stations could give servers more time for each party, which could improve service. She should have analyzed that option, considering how it would affect the servers, Tony, and the guests. She could have anticipated that servers might fear making less money if they have fewer parties to serve. This would be an unacceptable option if servers would indeed make less money. Server *morale* would suffer, which could affect their *loyalty* and the rate of turnover.

Heidi could have conferred with Tony as to whether smaller stations were really the answer to the service problem. If they agreed that they were, they could have, perhaps, shown how servers could increase check totals and tip percentages by more concentrated service, so as to increase rather than decrease tips. Tony could have then set up a servers meeting to introduce the new stations and allieviate fears. If this was not possible, then other decision options (such as additional training or incentives) could have been considered and analyzed. At the very least, Tony's insight would have been valuable in terms of just how far they could pare station sizes down without causing undue financial hardship on the servers.

Every decision we make, and every action we take, has repercussions. One thing leads to another and another and another. It is a good idea for us to consider possible consequences before we make a decision or take an action. Read *The Eagle Has Landed* (see the segment of the case study at the back of the book) for a follow-up on the Heidi/Tony fiasco. Heidi can see, after the fact, that she made a mistake. Her boss, John, was then required to deal with Heidi's mess that was a direct result of her thoughtless action.

CONCLUSION

To be a successful manager requires technical, organizational, and relationship skills. It also requires stamina and good health. We cannot separate who we are at home from who we are at work. Compartmentalizing our lives into separate independent segments can close us off from the support we all need to be whole. About the only thing we have any control over is ourselves—how we think, feel, and behave. It is our responsibility to make life decisions that will result in good consequences. We can choose healthy food and drinks, exercise, and relaxation all in moderation. We can make time for family and friends and use our time at work efficiently, setting realistic priorities. As managers, we are teachers. We take the time and make the effort to enable our workers to reach their potentials on the job, which, in turn, decreases our workloads. We can get help when we need it and offer help to others when they need it.

We have looked at two situations in this chapter caused by Heidi's thoughtless decisions. We are seeing a pattern at FOI where individuals are making decisions that are not based on a consistent company philosophy. Heidi does not know how to analyze decisions in advance of action. It is ultimately John's responsibility to recognize her management skill gaps and do something about them.

KEY WORDS

People Skills	Time Management
Empathy	Delegation
Supervision	Chain of Command
Coaching	

CHAPTER THOUGHT QUESTIONS

1. Define "empathy" and discuss why it is an important characteristic to have when making decisions that affect others.
2. Think about a work situation where a manager made a decision that affected you. What was the decision? How did it affect you? Do you think your manager thought about how his or her decision would affect you before it was made?
3. Define "coaching" and discuss why it is a more effective management strategy in today's work environment. Use personal examples from your work experience.

4. Make a list of the stress reducing strategies described in this chapter. Which of the strategies do you utilitize, and how well? Which do you not, and why not? What could you change in your life that would reduce unnecessary stress?

5. Make a list of your current priorities in order of their importance. Keep a time log for a few days, writing down precisely how you spend your time. Total the time spent in categories that emerge from your log. How does your actual use of time compare to your priorities? What changes could you make to better use your time?

6. When you look at your list of priorities in question #5, are there any that could be delegated to someone else? Are any of your priorities not really necessary? Could you take any of them off your list? Why or why not?

7. Describe a time when you did not show someone else how to do something because "it is faster if I just do it myself." Describe a time when someone did not take the time to show you how to do something that could have relieved him or her of the responsibility thereafter. How did it make you feel? How did it make you feel about the person who did not take the time and effort to show you?

8. Consider managers you have worked for in the past. If you have not held a job, consider parents, teachers, or anyone who was in a position of authority over you. Which of the managers did you like best? Least? Why? Which seemed to be the most effective? Why? Describe them in terms of stress management, time management, and delegation. Is there any connection between their personal management skills, their effectiveness, and how well you liked them?

9. Discuss why it is so important for us to hire people who are a good match for the position. Have you or someone you know ever been hired for a job that you/they were not a good match for? What characteristics/skills were necessary for the job and which ones did you or your acquaintance not have? How did the job work out? Did you/him/her work successfully and for how long?

10. Draw an organization chart for a current or previous job. Describe the chain of command and where you fit in the chain. Did everyone follow the chain of command? Give instances where the chain of command was followed and where it was not. Why is it useful to have a clearly defined chain of command in an operation?

REFERENCES

Iverson, K. M. (2001). *Managing human resources in the hospitality industry.* Upper Saddle River, NJ: Prentice Hall.

Jaszay, C. (2002). Personal management skills. *Hosteur, 11*(2) pp. 15–18.

McQuade, W., & Aikman, A. (1993). *Stress: What it is, what it can do to your health, how to handle it.* New York: Penguin Books.

Van Hoof, H. B., McDonald, M. E., Yu, L., & Vallen, G. K. (1996). *A host of opportunities: An introduction to hospitality management.* Chicago: Irwin.

Chapter 12

Ethics and Technology

Property management (PMS) and **point-of-sales (POS)** systems are the comprehensive computer software programs that make almost every aspect of day-to-day hospitality operations more efficient, convenient, and accessible. The technology itself cannot be ethical or unethical; it is merely a tool that can be used at the operator's discretion. Most of us have become very familiar with computers and the technology that has become an ordinary part of so much of what we do. We have included a separate chapter on technology because, as technology expands into so much of our lives, the ethical issues involving privacy, personal use, purchasing, and implementation need to be addressed.

Using the company computer for personal business (or to surf the Web) is a form of theft if the company expects employees to be on task with company business. It is not much different from stocking our home office with company supplies. Both acts constitute theft and are not activities we would be likely to inform our boss of. At the other extreme, some companies use their computer systems to monitor employees' every moment and ensure they are on task. The power of technology cuts both ways. It makes our jobs easier, and, yet, it brings our jobs home with us and lessens our personal freedom. The downsides of this equation are in the hands of management, however, and it is management's responsibility to ensure that the rights of employees are not being abused.

Many of us are annoyed on a daily basis by junk mail, phone solicitors, and computer spam. Companies we have done business with have sold our names, addresses, phone numbers, and/or e-mail addresses to marketers who assail us with offers to buy things or donate money. Many of us would prefer to not receive these unwanted offers and may feel that our privacy has been violated.

In *You Reap What You Sow* (see the segment of the case study in the back of the book), Sheri Eggmeyer, FOI's new bookkeeper, informs John, the general manager, that a direct mail advertising broker will pay a very lucrative sum for FOI's customer database. When John asked Sheri's opinion of the sale, she said, "Money is money. What's not to like about it? Who are these people to you?" We can figure out *what's not to like about it* by doing an analysis of the consequences for selling the customer list to a direct marketer.

We can enter the stakeholders, those parties who may be affected by the decision to sell the customer list, on a blank Ethics Analysis Form, along with the decision option. *Customers, FOI, John,* and *Sheri* may be directly affected. A completed Ethics Analysis Form follows this discussion.

ANALYSIS OF POSSIBLE CONSEQUENCES TO CUSTOMERS

Customers coming to FOI trust that their personal information will not be released to anyone. If they were to be asked, most customers would decline permission to have their names released to direct marketers. Very few of us enjoy the unsolicited mail, calls, and spam, and we know that most of our customers will also not enjoy it. We betray the *trust* of our customers by releasing their personal information. We would be displaying a lack of *concern and respect* for our customers by exposing them to information abuse.

Customers could suspect that the new rush of unwanted solicitations were a result of staying at FOI and either complain directly to FOI and/or not return and tell their friends what they think we did.

ANALYSIS OF POSSIBLE CONSEQUENCES FOR FOI

It is possible that some customers could suspect FOI released their information and the inn could lose their return business and good will. Word of mouth from dissatisfied customers can have a long-term negative effect on business and harm the *reputation* of FOI. Our *loyalty* must be with the company and requires that we not do anything that could harm the company. We would probably like to have funds from the sale of the customer database, but it would not be worth the possible long-term ill will our action might create.

ANALYSIS OF POSSIBLE CONSEQUENCES FOR JOHN FALLIN

John is being encouraged by his bookkeeper to accept the lucrative direct marketer's offer for the FOI customer database. John knows his customers would probably not appreciate him releasing their personal information to a direct marketer broker. He is most likely aware that customers' annoyance will far outweigh any positive benefits realized by their receiving unwanted solicitations.

John would be violating *honesty* because he would be keeping this information from his customers. He would be violating *integrity* because he would be doing something that he knows is not in his customers' best interest. Selling customers' personal information is not indicative of a *commitment to excellence*, and he could feel guilty.

John *leads* by example and, if he chooses to sell the customer database, would be modeling unethical behavior for Sheri, the new bookkeeper. John is *accountable* for his decisions and the decision to sell the FOI customer database is unethical.

ANALYSIS OF POSSIBLE CONSEQUENCES FOR SHERI EGGMEYER

If John agrees to sell the customer database, Sheri would be given a clear message that it is okay to be unconcerned about the welfare of guests—and that short-term profits are more important than doing the right thing. Since Sheri in fact lobbied for the deal, it is likely that she already conducts her business life this way, but John's acquiescence could confirm and/or make worse Sheri's future behavior and decisions. John is being given a training opportunity to promote appropriate ethical decision making if he chooses to make the right decision, which is to turn down the direct marketer's offer.

ETHICAL PRINCIPLES VIOLATED BY THIS DECISION

We found nine out of ten Ethical Principles for Hospitality Managers would be violated if John opts to sell the customer database. This is a decidedly unethical decision. Sheri's future behavior could be negatively influenced by John's decision, and John would know he acted unethically when given a choice to do otherwise.

If is quite possible that none of the customers will suspect that FOI is to blame for the increase in their unwanted solicitations. It is also possible that there would be no negative consequences to John or FOI from customers as a result of this decision. The decision remains, however, unethical. It is not all right to hurt people so long as they do not know we are hurting them. Integrity is built over the long run by making often difficult yet correct decisions—even when no one knows the difference.

Ethics Analysis Form

You Reap What You Sow

Decision Option: To sell the FOI customer database to a direct marketer

Stakeholders	Principles	Consequences
Customers		• Customers would receive unwanted junk mail, phone calls, and e-mails.
		• They could suspect FOI released their information and could direct complaints to the inn.
		• They might tell their friends that FOI released their information, causing ill will within the community.
		• They might not return to the inn.

(continued)

Stakeholders	Principles	Consequences
FOI		• If customers suspected FOI released their personal information, FOI's reputation could be harmed and sales could be lost. • A devious act like this (on the part of management) could affect the way they *think* about customers, which would eventually trickle down to the way they *interact* with customers. This would, in turn, impact the way customers *think* about FOI.
John (General Manager) [Decision-Maker]	Honesty Integrity Trustworthiness Loyalty Concern and Respect for Others Commitment to Excellence Leadership Reputation and Morale Accountability	• John knows it is wrong to sell the database and could feel guilty for doing so. • John models behavior for his staff and would be modeling unethical behavior for Sheri, the book keeper. • If customers get wind of the fact John sold them out to direct marketers, he would be held responsible for any negative repercussions of this act.
Sheri (Bookkeeper)		• Sheri will be shown that short-term profits are more important to FOI than customer welfare. This message could negatively affect her future behavior and decisions.

TECHNOLOGY AT FRESHWATER OASIS INN

FOI owner Frank Stratton's business manager, Lex Lilly, has secured a big discount on "Point-of-Order Micros" for FOI from one of her other clients. John Fallin as general manager must decide whether or not to adopt the new technology. (Please see *Lex Luther* in the case study at the back of the book.) John is not impartial. He does not want the new system because he tried one like it before and the technology at the time was a total failure. The other problem is that there could be a conflict of interest in Lex recommending FOI purchase a system from one of her clients.

John is not a technology expert so he does not really have the expertise to know if it is a good deal or not. John most likely could not tell if it was a good system by reading the specs. Frank, the owner, is not a technology expert. He is relying on Lex's opinion, and Lex does not appear to be a restaurant technology expert either. Lex's other client, Hank, is the technology expert, but Hank is the supplier. Do we buy things simply on the advice of a supplier? And, more to the point, who is qualified to actually make the determination? No one is!

So, how can John figure out if it is, indeed, a better system at a good price? We can begin by analyzing how buying or not buying the new system would affect the various stakeholders, *employees, customers, John,* and *FOI*. We enter the decision and stakeholders on a blank Ethics Analysis Form, the completed version of which follows the discussion.

ANALYSIS OF POSSIBLE CONSEQUENCES FOR EMPLOYEES

How will the employees initially feel about a new system? How do we get employees to embrace it? How do we make the transition to the new system go smoothly? If it is a good system and is implemented successfully, what positive results could it have? If it is a bad change and does not work well, how might employees feel?

Most of us are not wild about change. We are usually more comfortable with what we are familiar. New systems take time to learn and to become adept at. There is usually an initial period where our performance is hampered by the new system. Because our employees may not enthusiastically embrace the new technology, we may want to involve them in the decision-making process. We could, perhaps, have employees try out several systems before deciding. We could send several employees to other operations using similar systems. We could present the various systems at an employee meeting with time for testimonials and questions.

When employees can see a reason for changing the system, such as increased convenience, efficiency, and accuracy, they can become more interested in making the change. High-quality, user-friendly, formal, paid training conducted *before* employees are expected to use the new system with guests can cut down on frustration, anger, and reduced tips. If the new system is not an improvement or was not implemented effectively, it could negatively affect attitudes and turnover.

ANALYSIS OF POSSIBLE CONSEQUENCES FOR CUSTOMERS

If the new system is better, accepted by the staff, and smoothly implemented, the guests might not be aware that there is a new system. It is possible that the new system could even improve service, allowing guests additional access to servers with fewer mistakes. If the new system is not better or is poorly implemented, decreased employee morale and increased turnover could negatively affect customer satisfaction, which could affect how much they tip servers, word of mouth, and repeat business.

ANALYSIS OF POSSIBLE CONSEQUENCES FOR JOHN FALLIN

Leadership is evidenced by employees' willingness to follow. If John decides to purchase a system that is not an improvement or fails to effectively implement the system, employees could blame John for their frustration and difficulties and be less likely to go along with any future new ideas. John could lose the trust and goodwill of his employees if he subjects them to unnecessary torment.

As general manager, John is accountable for FOI. If the system is not an improvement, he is responsible. If the system costs more than it should, he is accountable for the money spent. If the system is not implemented smoothly and morale goes down, business will suffer, and he could lose his job. It is essential for John's welfare that he makes an educated and thoughtful decision as to whether or not to purchase the new system. This is the real problem: does John have the expertise to make an educated and thoughtful decision regarding this matter? Not really.

ANALYSIS OF POSSIBLE CONSEQUENCES FOR THE FRESHWATER OASIS INN

If, after implementation, the new technology turns out to be a bad match for FOI's needs, they might have to go back to the old system. Employees would most likely be irate and disgusted over their wasted effort and frustration, morale would decrease, and service could suffer. FOI would be out the $50,000 and in chaos. If it turned out to be a well-implemented and preferable system, however, it could result in happier employees, customers, and perhaps might lead to greater profits for FOI.

John would have to determine, in advance, whether the new system (if it is, indeed, better) would be more cost effective to own than to lease the old system. If the new system is not an improvement or is poorly implemented, employee morale could decrease. Turnover could increase and result in a staffing shortage and increased selection and training costs. FOI could also lose its reputation as a good place to work.

ETHICAL PRINCIPLES VIOLATED BY THIS DECISION

We can go down the list of Ethical Principles for Hospitality Managers to see if any are violated by John's decision to buy or not buy the new system. There is a lot at stake with this decision. The new system costs $50,000 and employees will have to accept and learn how it is used. If the system is not a good match for FOI's needs and/or is poorly implemented, a lot of time, money, and goodwill with employees and customers will be lost.

Honesty is indirectly violated in this situation if John makes the decision without recognizing he does not have the expertise to properly evaluate the technology. **Humility** has to do with recognizing both our strengths and weaknesses. None of us knows everything, and no one expects us to. There is, however, a specific body of knowledge that managers must have in order to be effective. That is why hospitality management programs are becoming more of a necessity in preparation for hotel or restaurant management positions.

John will lose the *trust* of his employees if he fails to make the correct decision on whether or not to purchase the new system. Employees may not want

IN THE TRENCHES

Justin Bozoian, 22, Phoenix, AZ

"While working for a prominent Mexican food restaurant in Phoenix, I observed a very questionable situation. One of my coworkers, Mike, was a bartender/server who also had trainer duties. Mike was then promoted to lead-hourly (hourly paid manager). On nights when Mike closed the restaurant, it was necessary for all hourly paid employees to be clocked out in order for him to run the end-of-day reports. Being an hourly paid employee himself, Mike had to guesstimate his clock-out time (as per assistant and general managers' instructions). Mike was fired one day when the regional manager compared the clock-out times with the alarm record and noted that they did not coincide. The reason given for Mike's termination was that he was "stealing hours." The sad thing is that Mike was not paid for his time training for this new position, and he had also been working for free on numerous occasions over the last month in order to get the bar ready for a new roll-out of well liquors and drink recipes. The fact is, even if he did overestimate his time on closing nights, he still wasn't compensated for the time he'd spent there overall. What's worse is that none of the other managers informed the regional manager that they had in fact told Mike to clock out and guesstimate his time. In short, nobody stuck up for Mike."

to learn a new system. It will be imperative that John implements the system carefully, realizing that the success of a good system is only possible if employees accept it and want to make it work. *Concern and respect* for his employees' feelings and needs will be violated if the system is poorly implemented, causing unnecessary frustration and loss of tips.

Commitment to excellence requires that we do our best work and do what is best for the company and our employees. Making the correct decision and implementing it properly is John's responsibility. His *leadership* ability will be in question if he fails to implement the new system properly and staff finds themselves in chaos. The *morale* of the staff could plummet if the system is not an improvement or is poorly implemented. FOI's *reputation* as a good place to work could be tarnished as could John's *reputation* as an effective manager. John will be held *accountable* for his decision because he is the general manager of FOI.

Ethics Analysis Form

Lex Luther

Decision Option: To buy or not to buy the new technology

Stakeholders	Principles	Consequences
Employees		• No one likes change. Employees may not enthusiastically embrace the new technology. • If it is a good change, how do we get employees to embrace it? How do we make the transition to the new system go smoothly?

(continued)

Stakeholders	Principles	Consequences
Employees		• If it is a good system implemented successfully, it could result in increased convenience, efficiency, and accuracy. • If it is a bad change and does not work properly, employees could be frustrated, angry, lose tips, and it could negatively affect attitudes and turnover.
Customers		• If the new system is better and smoothly implemented, customers could remain satisfied. • If the new system is not better, customer service could suffer, which could reduce tips. Customers tell friends and family, and repeat business could be lost. • If the system is not implemented smoothly, employee morale and increased turnover could negatively affect customer satisfaction, which could affect word of mouth and repeat business.
John (General Manager) [Decision-Maker]	Honesty Trustworthiness Concern and Respect for Others Leadership Commitment to Excellence Reputation and Morale Accountability	• Employees might not trust John's future decisions if this was a bad one. They would be less likely to go along with any more new ideas. • As general manager, John is accountable for FOI. If the system is not an improvement or is actually less efficient, he is responsible. • If the system costs more than it should, he is accountable for the money spent. • If the system is not implemented smoothly and morale suffers as a result, business will suffer and he is accountable. • It is essential for John's welfare that he makes an educated and thoughtful decision regarding purchase of the new system. (This is the real problem: John does not have the expertise to make an educated and thoughtful decision as to whether or not to purchase the new system.)
FOI		• If the implemented system is not a good match for FOI's needs, they could be out the $50,000 and have to reinstate the old system. • If it is a good, well-implemented system, it could result in happier employees and customers and perhaps bring more profits to FOI. • It could be more cost effective to own the new system (if it is, indeed, better) than to lease the old system. • If it is a good system, but poorly implemented, employee morale could decrease and turnover increase, which could be costly to FOI.

(continued)

Stakeholders	Principles	Consequences
Lex Lilly		• Lex works for and is trusted by Frank, the owner of FOI. She is not, however, employed by FOI nor does she have any formal position at FOI. She, technically, is not a stakeholder in this decision. • Depending on what kind of person Lex is, she could take offense if John questioned her and, subsequently, work against him with Frank. On the other hand, she could be a very fine, professional person and not have any problem with John doing his homework. We simply do not know. • John will ultimately be held accountable for the success or failure of the new system, not Lex.

OTHER DECISION OPTIONS

The decision to purchase the new technology is very important and will affect a lot of people and the business. John does not have the technology expertise to be able to recognize the best-fit system. His attitude about the hand-held wireless system may not be realistic because so many years have passed since his initial negative experience with the technology.

John is accountable for his decision and should not trust that Lex knows what is best in this situation. She is not a restaurant technology expert and she may or may not be financially benefiting from FOI purchasing a system from one of her clients. John does not know that he can trust Lex to do the cost accounting to determine if the new system is, indeed, a good deal. So, John has a very important decision to make about something he has no expertise in, and, the owner's business manager, who may have a conflict of interest, is proposing the technology.

John needs some objective expert help to handle this decision properly. Because the stakes are so high, he cannot afford to make a mistake. Professionals do not take unnecessary risks. In this situation, John should hire a consultant to do an independent evaluation. The consultant could put out an **RFP** (request for proposals) and evaluate possibly three different systems including Hank's. (Consultants can be found through hotel-restaurant university programs or through hospitality consulting firms.) The several-thousand-dollar expense could save untold money/torment and is a necessary price for risk reduction.

The other problem involves implementation of the new system, if one is purchased, so that it does not result in chaos and frustration for employees and poor service for customers. Employees will be using the new system and should have input in the selection. They could be allowed to try the consultant's chosen system before it is purchased. A comprehensive implementation plan would need to be developed that includes formal training and employee input.

We need to think about our decisions before we act on them. This was a very important decision, and the wrong decision could be very costly and painful to many people. This was a little different situation than many of the other case studies. What we had to determine here was how to make the decision—not what decision to make. John had to be able to assess his own ability to make a decision regarding technology. He also had to assess whether or not Lex knew what was best for FOI.

Sometimes the smart and ethical thing to do is to recognize our own weaknesses so that we can get the expert help we need. In this case, all stakeholders would be better served by John calling in an independent consultant, an individual with the expertise to analyze FOI's particular technology needs and determine which system would be the best, most cost-effective match.

HUMILITY

Virtues are character traits that result in habitual good behavior. We identified several of the virtues in Chapter 2. Wisdom, courage, temperance, justice, honesty, generosity, thoughtfulness, tolerance, faith, hope, and charity or love are among the virtues commonly found on most lists. **Ethics** are the principles or rules of right and wrong. If we follow all the rules of right and wrong until they become habit, this generally makes us virtuous people. To have **humility** is to be humble, which is characterized by thinking and behaving without excessive pride and/or arrogance. Virtues and ethics can only emerge from a state of humility.

Humility requires us to honestly identify our strengths and weaknesses. It is a lie, rather than humility, to argue that our accomplishments are without merit. Humility requires us, however, to recognize the help and privileges we may have received that make our accomplishments possible. **Arrogance,** where we behave as though we think we are better than others (even if we are!) interferes with our effectiveness. The people we deal with may fail to receive the message we intend and react instead to our overbearing and offensive attitude.

There are superior people. There are people who have gifts of high intelligence, musical or artistic talents, or unusual abilities in any number of fields. There are people who are driven to achieve, and, against all odds, succeed. When we are the recipient of one or more of these gifts, it is necessary to understand that we received the gift not due to anything we did, but, rather, by the chance of our birth. That our gift might have been recognized and nurtured by a parent or other significant person is a further gift that we must be grateful for. Again, what did we do as children to deserve or warrant any of these gifts? Is one baby more deserving than another? We must admit that life is inequitable and that we are so fortunate.

Those of us who are successful at something generally work hard for our success. We may have to force ourselves to study, put in the extra effort at work, or practice our sport or music. We cannot succeed without effort and growth in our field of choice. That we have the strength, the stamina, the will power, the desire, and even the knowledge that success is possible with hard work, is a profoundly important gift. To acknowledge this gift is the difference between arrogance and humility.

Excessive **pride** is taking undeserved or deserved credit while failing to acknowledge the help and gifts that made the achievement possible. Pride is considered to be a serious vice by all the major religions of the world, because it refuses to recognize the sovereignty of God. We take a certain amount of pleasure in taking prideful people "down a peg or two," seeing them come off their "pedestals" or their "high horses." Many of us have found that "pride comes before the fall." We may have noticed that as soon as we are feeling cocky about our achievements, something happens to **humiliate** us, where we are publicly shamed or embarrassed. These humbling experiences are common to all of us.

As children, most of us were taught to share our toys with others. To be selfish meant we ended up playing by ourselves. We tend to think better of celebrities and wealthy people who practice **philanthropy** by sharing some of their money and talents for the benefit of needy people. We think less of those who keep it all for themselves. Politicians who use their political power for the greater good rather than for amassing personal profit are respected and honored by the population they serve. How we choose to use our gifts is indicative of our level of personal enlightenment.

If we are cognizant of and grateful for the gifts we have received, we can be more open to recognizing other peoples' gifts without jealousy or envy. If we are able to honor our own gifts, we are better able to honor others' gifts. In management, when we honor our employees' individual gifts without feeling threatened, we enable them to be their very best, which makes us more successful managers. We remember Lao Tzu (see Chapter 1) who said, "As for the best leaders: the people do not know of their existence."

To be truly humble we must recognize both our strengths and weaknesses, and then live them honestly without pretending to have strengths we do not possess. This honesty spares us the energy it takes to live a lie. We do not have to defend ourselves, worry about making mistakes, or worry about harming our reputations. We have the freedom to be who we are without conflict. This allows and gives others the courage to recognize their own strengths and weaknesses and to live them honestly.

When we live without illusions we are better able to accept and enjoy reality. Humble people are realistic, confident, have a good sense of self-esteem, and are often filled with joy. They take pleasure in personally doing good work and in the good work of others. Humility is based in equality and gives us the strength to stand up for ourselves and others. Abraham Maslow's highest level of motivation is "self actualization" and goes hand-in-hand with humility.

People like us better and our employees respond with more enthusiasm when we are humble. Humility makes relationships work better. We are more apt to get our own needs met in relationships when we are able to clearly state what they are. Our humility allows us to be attuned to the needs of the other person. Thus the relationship will be more equally beneficial for both parties.

BECOMING HUMBLE

If we do not voluntarily become humble, life will most likely force us to. The consequences of humility are far more pleasant than those of pride and arrogance. Humble people experience more contentment and long-term joy, so it behooves all of us to take steps to practice humility until it becomes a habitual way of thinking and acting. If we do not, we can be assured that life's lessons will be unrelenting and painful.

The first step in fostering a humble mindset is to honestly appraise our strengths and weaknesses. We must see ourselves as we really are—not better, not worse. We might want to ask a trusted friend to do the same for us, and then compare the results. Do both perceptions match? We all have been given gifts. We must identify our own particular gifts. Perhaps we have the gift of making other people comfortable, the gift of listening, the gift of organization, or the gift of patience. Whatever our gift is, it is valuable and must be recognized and appreciated by us.

Another step in fostering a humble mind is paying attention to other people, recognizing their individual gifts and affording their gifts proper value and appreciation. If we all had the same gifts, they would not be gifts, and they would not be special. It takes all of our gifts combined to make the synergistic whole. We can identify others' weaknesses too, because we all have weaknesses and it makes us more equal. It is a false humility to believe that others are perfect or have perfect lives.

We gain in humility when we admit our mistakes and take full responsibility, learning from them. We do not dwell on past mistakes, but, rather, we move on, grateful that we have had the opportunity to improve ourselves for the next time. We give the present moment the attention it deserves. It takes discipline to pay attention, taking advantage of all lessons, opportunities, and simple pleasures. We cannot be virtuous without humility. It is not a virtue to be excessively proud that we are wise, or generous, or thoughtful. Pride negates the virtue and leaves us only arrogant instead of virtuous.

We all face adversity at different times in our lives. Whether we bear affliction with acceptance and dignity or with anger and self-pity are choices we make. Our behavior in times of hardship or pain is not contingent on the conditions we find ourselves in, but rather on how we decide to act. We are accountable for our behavior regardless of the situation. The habit of humility helps us to honestly and objectively view our options so we can make wise choices.

Becoming humble requires that we obey the rules because we do not feel that we are exempt or above them. "Do as I say, not as I do" smacks of arrogance and is not an effective management strategy. We can graciously submit ourselves to the same conditions everyone else is expected to endure. Whining and complaining are useless and do more to aggravate negative situations. We must practice treating everyone and everything with the respect due them because they exist. Someone once said that if we are not part of the solution, we are part of the problem.

Moderation in all things, combined with simple living, simple dress, and simple speech, often become the style of people who choose humility as a way of life. As we practice being humble, it is very helpful to choose our friends wisely so that humility is modeled for us and we can trust our friends to be honest with us. We have very little control over much of life. We do, however, have control over the way we think and behave. Humility works much better than arrogance. If we wish to be successful people in our relationships on and off the job, the choice to practice humility will help us to realize our desire.

ETHICS AND HUMILITY

Humility is the foundation for the ten Ethical Principles for Hospitality Managers. Arrogance violates all ten of the principles. We cannot look at ourselves or others *honestly* without humility. Humility allows us to identify both our strengths and weaknesses, admit to them, and endeavor to live accordingly. *Integrity* means we do what is right under all circumstances. Without humility we may be unable to discern the truth that makes it possible for us to do what is right. To be *trustworthy* we must be whole. That is, our behavior must match our words, and our insides must match our outward persona, otherwise our behavior is unpredictable and we cannot be trusted.

Arrogance can be a barrier to *loyalty* because we may not be able to subordinate selfish interests for the good of the company or other party. If we believe we are better than others and fail to recognize and value their contributions and gifts, our behavior may feel and appear to them as *unfair*. The consequences for failing to hold and show *concern and respect for others* is that others may feel unappreciated, offended, and in turn, they may not like us. They may become less cooperative and might choose to leave our employ, our family, or our friendship.

To be successful managers we must do excellent work at all times. Our *commitment to excellence* requires that we identify our faults and correct them so that they do not interfere with the quality of our work. An attitude of humility is more effective with employees we are attempting to manage, so, even if we do not want to be humble, it is our responsibility to behave in ways that are good for our companies. We must be humble if we are to be excellent managers. Our employees will only follow managers they trust. Our *leadership* is enhanced when we are not too full of ourselves, and our employees recognize that our motives are without hidden agendas.

If we are known as arrogant, our *reputation* will precede us and hinder our ability to communicate our message. It is difficult to recognize others' attributes when we have little or no humility. The *morale* of our staff may deteriorate if they are not treated with the respect and appreciation due them. We are *accountable* for our own behavior, the behavior of our staff, and the success of our operation. No amount of knowledge and skill will make up for poor treatment of staff. It is through our humility that our staff will be able to respect and honor our knowledge and skill and then trust us enough to lead them in success.

CONCLUSION

John Fallin, General Manager of the Freshwater Oasis Inn, is basically a good man. For the most part he abides by the Ethical Principles for Hospitality Managers. Both situations from the case study presented in this chapter force John to make decisions. In *You Reap What You Sow,* the bookkeeper asks John to sell FOI's customer database to a direct-marketing broker. The bookkeeper sees nothing wrong with this option. Our analysis brought us to the conclusion that, although the consequences were not grave and far-reaching, it would be unethical to sell the database. Because John is the general manager, it is not enough for John to do the right and ethical thing. He must also take it upon himself to instruct the bookkeeper in the appropriate ways of conducting business at FOI.

A pattern is emerging where John, although generally making the correct ethical decisions himself, feels frustrated and overwhelmed by the overall inability of his staff to make good decisions. John has yet to recognize that he has a management problem. So far he has failed to ask what he might be doing or not doing that could be contributing to his staff's decision-making inadequacy. When things are not going well, we must first honestly assess our role to determine our responsibility in the problem. That requires humility, and through humility we can identify the root of the problem, which allows us to formulate possible solutions.

In *Lex Luther* John is supposed to give the go-ahead to purchase a new technology system. This is an important decision that could result in huge losses and problems if he takes the wrong route. To be able to make a good technology decision, John must admit that he does not have the necessary expertise and get some outside help. None of us are strong in all areas. If we are lacking in humility, we may find it difficult to admit to our weaknesses. We may not have adequate self-esteem (based in the reality of our strengths) to have the courage to admit to a gap in our knowledge. It is necessary to have humility to make ethical decisions and behave in an ethical manner. Honestly identifying our strengths and weaknesses, and recognizing and appreciating the individual gifts that have been given to all people, helps us to fulfill our leadership role successfully.

KEY WORDS

Property Management System	Ethics
Point-of-Sale System	Arrogance
Humility	Pride
RFP	Humiliate
Virtue	Philanthropy

CHAPTER THOUGHT QUESTIONS

1. Describe an instance where you used work technology (such as copy machines or computers) to do personal tasks. [If you have never done this, describe an instance where someone you know used work technology for personal purposes.] Identify any of the ethical principles that were violated by your use of work technology, and then give an explanation why you chose to use it. Would you choose differently the next time? Why or why not? If you were the manager, how would you feel about one of your employees doing what you or someone you know did?

2. Describe the amount and type of junk mail, phone solicitors, and spam you receive. How do you feel about it? Does sending any of these unwanted messages violate any of the ethical principles? Which ones? Describe how you would feel if a company you did business with sold your personal information to a direct-marketing broker.

3. How adept and comfortable are you with some of the new technologies? Were you ever uncomfortable with having to learn a new computer program or some new way of doing business such as online banking or using a debit card? Describe your feelings at the time and the process you went through until you became comfortable with the new technology. Do you have older relatives or friends who are afraid or wary of technology? Describe their discomfort. Will it ever change? Does it need to change? Why or why not?

4. Describe a time and situation where you had to purchase something expensive that you did not know much about (such as a car or a computer). How did you go about deciding what to buy? Did you get help? From whom? Did you end up making the right decision? Could you have done something different that might have worked out better? Discuss.

5. Try to think of a time when you did not know something, asked someone for help, and were treated with disdain, sarcasm, mockery, cruelty, or with any other negative response. How did it make you feel? What did you think of the person who mistreated you? Why do you think he or she was abusive? Identify any ethical principles that were violated by that person's response to your question. Write the exact response he or she should have given you. Compare the consequences of both responses.

6. Discuss why it is important to get employee input before making any significant changes that will affect employees. Include in your discussion any positive or negative examples of changes that you have been involved with on the job (or in your personal life) where your input was or should have been considered.

7. Discuss the relationship between virtues, ethics, and humility. Define each and discuss in terms of management behavior.

8. Define arrogance and discuss why it is not an appealing and effective management strategy. Describe someone you know who you think is arrogant. What is he or she like? How does he or she behave? What do you think of this person? How might he or she improve?

9. In writing, analyze your own strengths and weaknesses. Then identify any gifts you have been given. Describe your attitude about your gift(s) and how you use them. How do these gifts make you feel compared to others who do not have your same gifts? Has your attitude changed over time? How and why?

10. Describe someone you know who has true humility. What is this person like? How does this person think and behave? What do you think about this person? Is this person financially successful? Does it matter to you if this person is or is not financially successful? Does it matter to the person? Compare yourself to this person. What level of humility do you have? What changes might you make to be more humble? Why would this be necessary and how would it affect your behavior?

REFERENCES

Collins, G. R., & Malik, T. (1999). *Hospitality information technology.* Des Moines, IA: Kendall/Hunt.

Frankl, V.E. (1959). *Man's search for meaning.* New York: Pocket Books.

Gensler, H. J. (1998). *Ethics: A contemporary introduction.* New York: Routledge.

Hall, S. S. J. (ed.). (1992). *Ethics in hospitality management.* MI: Educational Institute.

Myers, D. G. (1999). *Exploring psychology* (4th ed.). New York: Worth.

Smart, N. (1989). *The world's religions.* Australia: Cambridge University Press.

Van Hoof, H. B., McDonald, M. E., Yu, L., & Vallen, G. K. (1996). *A host of opportunities: An introduction to hospitality management.* Chicago: Irwin.

Chapter 13

Ethics and Cost Control

Consider this simple pie chart of a restaurant's total sales. One-third might be food cost, another third might be labor, and another large slice of the pie might be other costs such as rent, utilities, supplies, and so forth. Observe how the remaining tiny slice is profit. It gets worse too. If food goes bad in storage and must be thrown out, if too much scrap is going in the garbage during preparation, or if food is stolen or given away, the slice of food cost will enlarge while the tiny profit slice will get smaller still. If employees are not productive enough, if employees are hurt on the job and have to be replaced, or if employees make too many mistakes, the slice of labor cost will enlarge while the tiny profit slice will get smaller. Any additional costs due to waste, theft, or whatever reason, come out of the tiny profit slice.

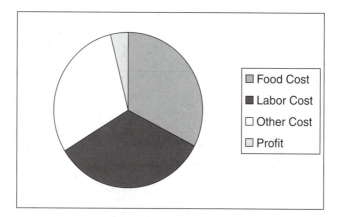

The purpose of **cost control** is to maximize profits by minimizing unnecessary costs. We identify **critical control points** where control measures can be implemented to avoid loss or waste. Critical control points are identified by collecting data that is comprised of numbers we can compare to standards. When our numbers are higher than the standards, we are alerted that there is a problem. When our numbers are lower than the standards, we are alerted that something good is going on and we then will want to figure out what it is and how to do it again. For example, if we compare food cost percentages from week to week and the percentage goes up, that means that our profit for that period will go down. We can then figure out why the percentage went up. Could it be increased supplier cost, food going bad, or theft?

If we do not take the measure and compare it with a standard, we will not be aware that anything is wrong and will not know to fix it. The tiny profit slice of the pie will get even smaller, and, in some cases, disappear altogether. In the worst-case scenario, we could actually end up owing money after all is said and done. It is easy to get into the restaurant business but very difficult to be profitable. The key is to have a product our target market wants and then to produce it without waste, utilizing our resources as efficiently as possible.

Foodservice cost control monitors costs in the various components of the foodservice operating system. Purchasing, receiving, storing, prepping, cooking, and serving are all areas where waste, theft, and spending errors can occur. The large amount of money involved in the area of purchasing opens both buyers and sellers to temptations for misconduct and **collusion** (a secret agreement between buyer and seller) and is in particular need of control measures. (A purchasing ethical dilemma was addressed in Chapter 8.) Cash handling, bank deposits, and accounts payable are other areas of foodservice where cost control measures must be in place to ensure that the right amount of money is going to the right place.

COST CONTROL AT FRESHWATER OASIS INN

Gilded Marinade (see the segment of the case study in the back of the book) provides for us a dilemma that cuts across two departments, the bar and the foodservice. Mike Scales, the bar manager, became irate when he discovered that Dardina Traylor, the sous chef, had been taking expensive wine from the liquor room for the past 6 months without signing it out. Mike had spent the last half-year worrying about his department's high liquor costs and trying to find the cause, finally enlisting a spotter company to identify who perhaps might be a thief amongst his staff.

Mike confronted Dardina's supervisor, Chef Eric Altman, and words were exchanged, which escalated into a shoving match. John, the general manager, eventually had to step in to settle the matter. Some of the previous situations we have analyzed had obvious decision options. Many ethical dilemmas, however, are not so obvious or clear-cut. We know what happened between Eric, Mike, and Dardina, but now the general manager must decide what to do in this situation. Through analysis we will try to determine the best option for John and all the stakeholders. We will enter *What should be done in this situation?* on an Ethics Analysis Form, along with the stakeholders who may be affected by John's decision; *Mike, Eric, Dardina, other employees, John,* and *FOI.* A completed form follows this discussion.

ANALYSIS OF POSSIBLE CONSEQUENCES
FOR MIKE SCALES

Mike Scales is responsible and accountable for the bar inventory. If the loss continues each month, Mike could lose his job as bar manager. He has been very worried about the high liquor costs. John, gave Mike the manager position in spite of Heidi's reservations (about checks and balances), and Mike does not want to let John down. He went so far as to hire spotters to see if a member of his crew was stealing. He trusts everyone on his staff except Floyd, the new guy, and felt bad doing this.

We must identify the responsible party in this situation. Who is responsible for the expensive cabernet being taken from the bar inventory without documentation? Mike rightfully holds Eric responsible for Dardina's actions, but Mike is responsible for the controls in his bar inventory. For 6 months he was unable to figure out where the loss was. He was a bartender promoted to bar manager and probably did not have the necessary inventory control skills. It is management's responsibility to put controls in place to keep unauthorized personnel from removing stock from the inventory without proper documentation.

Mike was taking responsibility for all of his employees in trying to find the culprit through hiring spotters, an action that would not prove successful, because it was not his employee who was taking the wine. Dardina's actions were hurting him and his department and gave him good reason to be angry. However, Mike's behavior toward Eric was unprofessional and ineffective. His anger got in the way of his message, and Eric reacted with his own anger. His future working relationship with Eric could be damaged, which could cause tension between the two departments and the personnel of each, unless he makes an effort to restore the relationship.

Mike's unprofessional behavior and lack of management and communication skills have been problems in the past. Mike cares about his job but needs additional training in order to be effective. That is the responsibility of the person who put Mike in the bar manager position to begin with. That, of course, is John Fallin.

ANALYSIS OF POSSIBLE CONSEQUENCES
FOR ERIC ALTMAN

The numerous bottles of $38 cabernet had not been calculated into Eric's food cost over the past 6 months. Eric must go back and redo the numbers. Mike will also have to go back and redo his bar costs. What was once Mike's problem will now be Eric's. Mike would then not show a loss while Eric's food cost would be too high because an expensive product was substituted for an inexpensive one.

If Eric trained Dardina properly but she did not follow directions, Eric would have to discipline Dardina and ensure that others on his staff did follow procedures. If it was Eric's fault that Dardina did not know the correct procedure for selecting wine for their marinades, he could face disciplinary action himself and his reputation as a manager would be damaged. Either way, when it comes to Dardina, he is ultimately responsible for her actions.

Eric responded to Mike's anger with his own, and they got into a physical confrontation and had to be restrained. This is *not* professional behavior. Although it is natural to respond to anger and aggression with similar behavior, it is never appropriate in a business setting. Mike's bad behavior does not excuse Eric's. The executive chef could have stayed calm, discovered the facts, and responded in a more reasonable way, which would have avoided a fistfight. John would not have been called in if they had not gotten in a fight, and Mike and Eric could have worked this out between themselves without their superior drawn in. Eric is responsible for his own inappropriate behavior and must do something to restore his and Mike's working relationship.

ANALYSIS OF POSSIBLE CONSEQUENCES FOR DARDINA TRAYLOR

Dardina did not seem to be aware that she was doing anything wrong. There are two possibilities here: (1) either she was never shown or told what wine to use for the marinade and the correct procedure for signing out the wine, or (2) she was shown but was not following the correct procedure. If Dardina was never shown the correct procedure and did not know which wine to select, it would not be fair to hold her accountable for her actions. Dardina could resent Chef Eric for not training her and lose respect for him.

Chef Eric was responsible for training and supervising her. If she had been shown and was either too lazy or forgetful, or just did not do it, she should be disciplined by Chef Eric. Failures to follow recipes and procedures can change the outcome of the recipe and incur additional expenses. It is the manager's responsibility to make sure all recipes and procedures are followed. Dardina could lose her job for refusing to follow procedures.

ANALYSIS OF POSSIBLE CONSEQUENCES FOR OTHER EMPLOYEES

If Chef Eric did not properly train Dardina, and then disciplined her for not following procedures she was not taught in the first place, other kitchen staff could think Chef Eric was unfair to Dardina and could lose trust and respect for him. Their morale and cooperation could decrease, and turnover could increase.

Kitchen employees were holding Mike and Eric apart after they came to blows. While employees might relate to the fighting, employees expect managers to be professional. Eric and Mike could lose the respect of their staff. What would Mike and Eric do if two of their employees (like a bartender and a cook) got in a fist fight? Both parties would most likely be disciplined. They could even lose their jobs for such behavior.

Department heads are to model correct behavior. Managers must never do things that employees would get in trouble for. Employees would get the wrong message about what behavior is acceptable and would feel abused if, at a later date, they were punished for doing the same thing managers do.

ANALYSIS OF POSSIBLE CONSEQUENCES FOR JOHN

John delegates responsibility to managers to run their departments, but is ultimately responsible for everything they do. Two of his department heads just got in a fist fight and he has been called to intervene. What he does will affect Eric, Mike, and their employees.

How department heads and/or managers work together is John's responsibility. If they do not work together well, teamwork, morale, turnover, guest satisfaction, and so forth, could all suffer, and this could have a negative effect on John's success as general manager of the inn.

John is also responsible for the management practices and procedures each of his department heads employ. Mike has had ongoing problems with communication and management strategies and needs some help in these areas. Mike may not have the management experience to know how to put all the appropriate controls in place, and John must do something to help Mike be more effective in this area.

ANALYSIS OF POSSIBLE CONSEQUENCES FOR THE FRESHWATER OASIS INN

When there are problems between the staff, between staff and management, or between management and management, these problems can negatively affect employee satisfaction, which can negatively affect guest service and satisfaction. FOI could lose business and employees.

ETHICAL PRINCIPLES INVOLVED IN JOHN'S DECISION

Fairness is an issue when it comes to John dealing with the two fighting managers. Employees could see it as unfair if the managers were not disciplined for something the employees would most certainly be disciplined for. *Fairness* is also an issue in that Eric benefits from low food cost and got it at Mike's expense (even though he most likely was not aware that Dardina was taking Mike's best cabernet without signing it out). It would be unfair to Mike if an adjustment was not made to the inventory numbers for the past 6 months.

Neither Eric nor Mike acted with *concern and respect* for each other. Their behavior was unprofessional, and they both were poor role models for their subordinates. *Commitment to excellence* was lacking in either Dardina not doing as she had been trained to do, or in Eric not training her properly. One of them was not doing the best job, and Eric is the responsible party between the two of them.

Leadership was not demonstrated by Mike or Eric. John, however, has the chance to demonstrate *leadership* by handling the dispute *fairly* and with *integrity,* and *concern and respect* for all parties involved. The *reputation* of FOI as a good place to work and *morale* of the employees and managers could be damaged if this dispute is not handled well by John. *Accountability* is the prime issue here. Mike is accountable for his inventory controls. Chef Eric is accountable for his employees. Dardina is accountable for her performance. John is accountable for everything.

THE DECISION

This analysis was conducted to determine what John should do. The entire situation could have been avoided if Mike had tighter controls over access to the bar inventory and/or if Chef Eric had closer watch over Dardina. To correct this situation, John can either personally help Mike set up some tighter bar controls or direct him to another manager, a class, or a book that can help him. John could also instruct Heidi to keep a closer watch on Mike.

Eric will most likely pay closer attention to what his employees are doing—Dardina in particular. He may need to design or redesign training in areas that could be problematic in the future in order to avoid other such occurrences.

Both Eric and Mike should in some way be disciplined for fighting, just as any regular employees would be. John should counsel them in appropriate professional behavior, and act as mediator to reestablish a good working relationship between the two managers. Both managers should be guided to acknowledge their unmet responsibilities that caused this situation (tighter bar inventory controls/better supervision of Dardina). John must follow up to ensure that the controls and training/supervision are in place and implemented.

Eric should handle his own department by disciplining or retraining Dardina. John should confer with both Eric and Mike to make sure they know how to appropriately speak of the dispute and its resolution with their own staffs. John delegates the responsibility to his department heads to run their departments, but John is accountable for what they do and must have controls in place to monitor and ensure everyone is doing what they are supposed to.

Ethical Analysis Form

Gilded Marinade

Decision Option: What should be done in this situation?

Stakeholders	Principles	Consequences
Mike (Bar Manager)		• Mike could lose his job if high liquor costs continue
		• Mike could not find the loss on his own and subsequently hired spotters. He does not have the inventory control skills necessary for his position.

(continued)

Stakeholders	Principles	Consequences
Mike (Bar Manager)		• His angry confrontation with Eric was unprofessional, ineffective, and could damage their working relationship. This could negatively affect their personnel. He needs to apologize for his unprofessional behavior.
Eric (Chef)		• Eric's food costs these past 6 months did not account for the $38 cabernet. Therefore, his calculations would have to be refigured and the numbers would go up. • Eric is responsible for the actions of his staff. His employee's misbehavior hurt Mike. He would either have to discipline Dardina, or, if it was his failure to train her, then he should face discipline himself. He would appear less competent. • Eric is responsible for his unprofessional response to Mike's behavior and must do something to restore their working relationship.
Dardina (Sous Chef)		• Dardina could lose respect for Chef Eric if he did not train her to properly get the correct wine from the liquor room. • If Dardina is disciplined but was never originally trained, she could feel Chef Eric was unfair to her. • Dardina could be disciplined or lose her job if she was trained but failed to follow procedures.
Other Employees		• Morale and cooperation could decrease if employees felt Dardina was treated unfairly. Turnover could increase. • Employees expect managers to behave professionally and could lose respect for them when they do not. • Employees would be punished for doing what Mike and Eric did. They would find that unfair if there had been no disciplinary measure taken against these managers.
John (General Manager) [Decision-Maker]	Integrity Fairness Concern and Respect for Others Commitment to Excellence Leadership Reputation and Morale Accountablity	• John was called to intervene in the fistfight. How he handles the aftermath affects Mike, Eric, and their employees. • If John's department heads do not work well together, his leadership position will be jeopardized. • John is responsible for the policies and procedures his department heads employ. Mike needs to be taught and shown how to be a more effective manager and how to better control his inventory.
Freshwater Oasis Inn		• Problems between the staff and/or management can negatively affect employee satisfaction, which can negatively affect guest service and satisfaction. FOI could lose business and employees.

This was a difficult situation to analyze because we were not analyzing a particular decision option, but, rather, we were trying to determine what the decision option should be. It was through the analysis process that we eventually were able to see how the situation should be resolved and how to avoid another situation of this sort.

There are times when we must make snap decisions. Most management situations, however, are best handled after careful deliberation. The Ethics Analysis Form is a very useful tool to help us in the deliberation process, enabling us to design the best course of action.

DINNER AT MARTHA'S

Eddie, one of the bartenders at FOI, and Kelly, one of the servers, had become good friends at work. (See *Dinner at Martha's* in case study at end of text.) Although Eddie did not think it was a good idea to date coworkers, he liked her just the same and agreed one night to have dinner at her apartment. He was distressed when he saw that all of Kelly's linens, china, silverware, and crystal were from FOI. Eddie knows that theft is wrong, and now has to decide whether or not to report Kelly's theft to management.

This is unlike the ethical dilemmas we are used to seeing thus far in the text. It is more about the relationships we enter within the context of performing our jobs in an often frenetic environment. Friendships are made that are sometimes tested when the conduct of one person affects the others' standing at work. Eddie is not a manager, so what is his responsibility in this situation? Where should his loyalties lie—with a fellow worker, or with his employer? We can enter: *Whether to tell management that Kelly has been stealing from FOI*, and the stakeholders, *Eddie, Kelly, other employees*, and *FOI*, on an Ethics Analysis Form to determine what Eddie should do.

ANALYSIS OF POSSIBLE CONSEQUENCES FOR EDDIE

We have to determine whether Eddie's loyalties should lie with Kelly or FOI. We can accomplish this by asking questions such as: How will Eddie feel if he tells on Kelly, and, how will Kelly and his relationship with her be affected? Or, if he does not tell on Kelly, how will Eddie feel, and what affect will this have on their relationship? Also, how could this affect his reaction to other employee misbehavior? Could Kelly ever get caught even if Eddie does not tell? Could it ever be discovered that he knew about Kelly stealing and neglected to say anything? Could Eddie get in trouble? Is it possible that FOI might suspect Kelly of stealing and ask Eddie to keep an eye on her? What would he do then? (Answers to these questions are on the completed Ethics Analysis Form following the discussion.)

ANALYSIS OF POSSIBLE CONSEQUENCES FOR KELLY

There is nothing that Kelly can do about the situation at this point. It all depends on Eddie's reaction to his discovery of her theft. Mainly their future relationship is at issue here. If Eddie keeps quiet about the theft (to her and management), how might she interpret his silence? How might their relationship change by Eddie's discovery of her theft? How might Kelly feel about this? What would most likely happen to Kelly if Eddie tells on her? How would Kelly react to this?

ANALYSIS OF POSSIBLE CONSEQUENCES FOR FOI

How does employee theft affect the profits of FOI or any business? If we reconsider the pie chart at the beginning of this chapter, we can conclude that the theft of dining room service materials will come directly from the tiny profit slice the inn is expecting to garner. Although the pilfering of a few place settings might seem inconsequential, these instances all add up and affect the bottom line. Employee theft can devastate a business.

Management is responsible for putting controls in place that discourage and limit the temptation to steal. If employees are allowed to get away with theft, how could this affect FOI in terms of reputation, turnover, and quality of service? What costs could changes in these areas incur?

ANALYSIS OF POSSIBLE CONSEQUENCES FOR OTHER EMPLOYEES

If Kelly gets away with theft, would other employees be aware of what Kelly is doing? What might they think about what Kelly is doing? How could it affect their behavior? Not all employees can be tempted to steal. There may be some who could be very disturbed by Kelly's behavior. How might they feel? Will they be more comfortable telling on Kelly—or keeping quiet? What are the consequences for either option? How will employees feel about management if management either does not find out about the theft or finds out and does nothing? How could this affect employees' attitudes and performance?

ETHICAL PRINCIPLES VIOLATED BY EDDIE'S DECISION

Kelly's theft of FOI property violates many of the ethical principles such as *honesty, integrity, trustworthiness, loyalty, fairness, commitment to excellence, reputation and morale,* and *accountability.* Kelly put Eddie in a very difficult and uncomfortable position, which violates *concern and respect for others.* Perhaps she does not think she did anything wrong or assumes that everyone steals. However, she did steal and her unethical, illegal action has caused this dilemma to begin with.

If Eddie does not tell on Kelly, all of the same ethical principles are violated. He would be keeping important information from management that harms FOI, and he becomes a party to the theft. *Honesty, integrity, trustworthiness, loyalty, fairness, commitment to excellence, reputation and morale,* and *accountability* are violated by his silence. Furthermore, he would be uncomfortable with the knowledge that she steals FOI property, and the relationship will cool. Their relationship is over either way. There is an old saying, "Two wrongs don't make a right." Old sayings are still around because they are often true. On the other hand, we know that if Eddie tells on Kelly, she will most likely lose her job, blame Eddie, and feel betrayed. He might have to endure the wrath of other employees (friends of Kelly's) who feel that Eddie's informing on her was inappropriate.

Being human, Eddie should be concerned that Kelly could lose her job, be unhappy, and feel betrayed if he tells on her. This is a difficult situation. If Eddie was a manager at FOI it would be a simple decision. His loyalty would be with the company, and his management position would determine his action. Because Eddie is not in management, however, this situation is similar to one student telling on another student for cheating.

Being a tattletale or a snitch has very negative connotations in our society. Most students will not tell on cheating students, but often feel annoyed that the teacher is unaware of or ignoring the cheating. It is a question of responsibility. Students generally feel it is the teacher's responsibility to make it very difficult to cheat and to catch the students who try. This situation is the same. It is management's responsibility to make it very difficult to steal FOI property and to catch those who somehow do steal. So, does that mean that we do not have to tell on fellow workers or fellow students when they are breaking the rules, even though to stay silent violates many of the ethical principles?

Let us consider ethical violations for the decision to tell on Kelly. Eddie would lose Kelly's *trust* if he told on her. Eddie has to choose between having Kelly's trust and management's trust. If Eddie had encouraged Kelly to steal FOI's linens, silver, crystal, and china, and then told on her, she would rightfully feel betrayed. He was not a party to her decision, however, so he is not responsible for it. Management would certainly want Eddie to tell them Kelly is stealing FOI property.

To tell on Kelly would violate *concern and respect* for Kelly, but we must question where Eddie's concern and respect should be. Obviously the act of theft does not deserve respect. Employee theft hurts the company, harms the *reputation and morale* of the staff, and destroys *trust*. Eddie has to choose between having concern and respect for Kelly or for FOI, management, and all his fellow employees.

The decision to tell on Kelly violates none of the ethical principles. Eddie was not given a say in her decision to steal FOI property. It is not his responsibility to stand by Kelly when she is squarely in the wrong. Wives and husbands do not have to testify against one another in courts of law. Eddie and Kelly are not married. They are coworkers. Eddie knew it was not a good idea to date a coworker. If Kelly had not invited Eddie to her home, or if Eddie had followed his better judgment, Eddie never would have known she stole FOI property.

Ethical Analysis Form

Dinner at Martha's

Decision Option: Whether to tell management that Kelly has been stealing from FOI

Stakeholders	Principles	Consequences
Eddie (Bartender) [Decision-Maker]	Honesty Integrity Trustworthiness Loyalty Concern and Respect for Others Excellence Reputation and Morale Accountability	• Should Eddie be loyal to Kelly or to FOI? He could feel uncomfortable whether he tells on Kelly or not. • To not tell on Kelly will make him realize his loyalty is not with the company, so it could be easier to make questionable decisions in the future. • His relationship with Kelly will be strained because her theft has put him in a difficult situation. If he says nothing it comes across to Kelly (and others) as approval of her theft. • It is possible that Kelly could get caught stealing, get fired, and then mention that Eddie knew she had the stolen goods. His loyalty and trustworthiness would be called into question, and he might even face disciplinary action. • If FOI suspects Kelly of stealing, Eddie could be asked to keep an eye on her at the bar. • His hidden knowledge of her guilt makes him a party to the theft.
Kelly (Server)		• Kelly may interpret Eddie's silence as approval and/or assume he steals FOI property as well. • Eddie's feelings for Kelly might cool because of the uncomfortable position she has put him in. She may feel betrayed or hurt by this. • If Eddie does tell on her, she will most likely be terminated and blame him.
Freshwater Oasis Inn		• Employee theft increases costs, which reduces profits. • If Kelly is stealing place settings from the dining room, perhaps she is stealing other items as well. • If Kelly is caught stealing, hiring and training costs will incur. • The reputation of FOI as a good place to work could be damaged if employees are allowed to get away with theft. Turnover could increase. Quality of service could diminish.
Other Employees		• If other employees know Kelly is stealing FOI property, they may be tempted to steal as well. • If some employees are aware of other employees getting away with theft, respect and moral could deteriorate, which can harm the working environment for everyone.

(continued)

Stakeholders	Principles	Consequences
Other Employees		• Management could lose the respect of employees, which could lead to decreased productivity, less cooperation, and/or other management problems. • If other employees discovered what Kelly did, should they say something and to whom should they say it? One ethical dilemma leads to another and another.

MAKING THE DECISION

We can compare the ethical principles that are violated by each decision option and determine which principles take precedence and which decision option causes the least negative consequences to the fewest stakeholders. The decision to tell on Kelly has the least negative consequences to the fewest stakeholders and violates no ethical principles. Eddie is still stuck with the offensiveness of telling on a fellow worker. To keep his silence hurts FOI, but his relationship with Kelly appears to be over regardless of what he decides. To tell on her directly hurts Kelly but is good for FOI and everyone else.

As always, doing the right thing—the ethical thing—is easier and much less painful. Perhaps Kelly should have thought of the consequences of stealing FOI property before she took it. Perhaps she should have thought of the consequences of letting other people know she stole FOI property before she invited them to her house. Eddie should have followed his initial instincts and not dated a coworker. As managers we are responsible for putting controls in place that limit access and temptation for theft. We are responsible for clearly stating the rules of appropriate behavior, and the consequences for failing to follow these rules. It is also our responsibility to be constantly aware of our employees' behavior.

Here is another old saying: "One bad apple can spoil the barrel." It is our responsibility to make sure we do not hire bad apples, do not enable anyone to become a bad apple, and get rid of any bad apples that we discover. Bad apples cause trouble. Kelly is a bad apple or at least is behaving like a bad apple. At the very least, her behavior can lead others to theft, decreases profits, and creates management and morale problems.

ETHICS AND CONTROLS

Management's **control** goal is to keep everyone doing exactly what they are supposed to be doing. It is preventative in nature, rather than about catching employees who have already broken rules. When we are designing and implementing control tools or procedures, we must keep the more positively stated goal in mind. A control tool that helps keep our employees on track is good for our employees. It allows them to be better workers within the legitimate system. Management

IN THE TRENCHES

Jason Pesch, 19, Northbrook, IL

"My second job was for a large gourmet coffee establishment. I went ready to work. What I didn't know was that I was working at the worst one in the area. I soon discovered that my manager was a drug addict who wanted to teach us how to steal without the corporate headquarters being able to tell. The manager also told us that she would 'cover our asses.' That's bad ethics, eh?"

must not in any way tempt, encourage, or allow employees to break any of the rules.

Several segments of the case study have mentioned the use of "spotters" as a means of ferreting out employee wrongdoing. **Spotters** or **secret shoppers** are people who have been hired by the facility to evaluate the service while acting as customers. Upon completion of their visit, they file a report identifying their positive and negative findings. If we were trying to catch employees doing things wrong, we would not inform them that spotters might be among their customers. If we are more interested in making sure that all customers are being properly served, then we would let our employees know that they can expect some of their customers to be spotters. We could offer incentives for good spotter reports.

If an employee has stolen from us in the past but stops because of a control procedure or tool we have implemented, our theft problem no longer exists. The goal of control procedures is to maximize profits by reducing loss, waste, and unnecessary expenses. Our goal should not be retaliation and punishment. The ethical use of controls means that we are *honest* in their use. Our employees can *trust* that we will not try to tempt them into wrongdoing so we can catch and punish them. Our employees will feel *loyalty* for us and the company because we are *fair* to them and show *concern and respect* for them. Our *commitment to excellence* requires us to design and implement effective controls that are ultimately good for the operation and the employees being controlled. *Reputation and morale* rise as employees respond to our ethical *leadership.*

Some managers have taken it upon themselves to "test" the honesty of their employees by putting them in situations where they must make a choice whether or not to do the right thing. A manager who accomplishes this by slipping an additional $50 into a bartender's bank (please see *A Date With Kate* segment of the case study at the back of the text) violates every ethical principle. If Kate the bartender pockets the $50, she will be guilty of theft, but would Kate have stolen the money if the manager had not placed it in her cash drawer? She has an exemplary employment record. The manager, Heidi Bell, tempted the employee to do something she might not have otherwise done. See the following analysis of this decision.

Ethics Analysis Form

A Date with Kate

Decision Option: To test an employee's honesty by putting an additional $50 in her drawer

Stakeholders	Principles	Consequences
Kate (Bartender)		• Kate works only day shifts and makes considerably less than other bartenders. The extra $50 pays for a lot of groceries. She could be very tempted to take it if she thinks it is free money.
		• Being caught stealing could ruin her otherwise good employment record. She will most likely feel humiliated, betrayed, and angry.
		• She will probably no longer enjoy her job. She may look for another job and leave, if she was not already fired for stealing.
		• The manager's act tempted her to steal and then to bear the consequences for theft. This was not a positive control procedure and hurt both the bartender and the operation because they may lose what had been an otherwise good employee.
Other Employees		• The bartender would tell other employees what the manager did to her and they would most likely think it was cruel, mean, and unfair.
		• They would no longer trust the manager. Their attitudes could deteriorate, service levels could fall, and turnover could increase.
		• Employees would be very unlikely to ever pocket any overage in their drawers.
Manager [Decision-Maker]	Honesty Integrity Trustworthiness Loyalty Fairness Concern and Respect for Others	• Employees' attitudes could deteriorate, and they could be less cooperative.
		• The manager might have to deal with increased turnover and employee problems.
		• The working atmosphere would become more suspicious and less conducive to excelling.

(continued)

Stakeholders	Principles	Consequences
Manager [Decision-Maker]	Commitment to Excellence Leadership Reputation and Morale Accountability	• The manager could be accused of entrapment.
The Operation		• If employees become dissatisfied, service levels could decrease, turnover increase, and business suffer as a result.

OTHER DECISION OPTIONS

For the purpose of analysis we have assumed that the bartender in this situation did indeed steal the $50, which is of course unethical and illegal. The decision to test the bartender with the good employment record, rather than employees already under suspicion, violated every ethical principle. The test was not done in response to suspected thievery, but, rather, to see what she would do. She was set up and then punished.

This is similar to the idea of a professor testing a student's honesty when the student's honesty was never in question. The professor calls the student into her office and tells the student she will be back in 10 minutes. She leaves the key to the final on her desk in the student's full view. She is able to tell that the student's answers were copied from the "test" final key, so she gives the student an "F" and puts "cheating" on his or her permanent record. Yes, the student cheated, but would he or she have broken into the professor's office and stolen the final key? Probably not. The student was set up by the professor and hurt by the tactic.

The student's attitude toward school and professors will be damaged. He or she will most likely tell other students, which will negatively affect the reputation of the professor and the program. The tactic will make students leery of attempting to cheat, but will also have a detrimental effect on the education experience and the department itself. Not a good strategy. Nor is the unnecessary testing of the bartender's honesty.

CONCLUSION

We must have controls in place to know how we are doing and to identify problem areas. Designing and/or implementing controls is one of management's responsibilities. Controls make it easier for our employees to do the right thing. We must clearly explain the control procedures and then monitor their use and effectiveness, making any necessary changes to them.

This chapter focused on cost control. *Gilded Marinade* described the effect of ineffective control procedures utilized in the liquor room at FOI. *Dinner at Martha's* dealt with an employee theft situation. Most any theft control systems we put in place will be vulnerable, but good ones can cut down on theft and make tracking thieves easier. The control methods we choose, however, must be well thought out. We must consider the consequences of the control methods and determine whether they are truly in line with our initial objectives. Unethical control systems or methods generally have negative consequences for all stakeholders.

KEY WORDS

Controls   Collusion
Cost Control   Spotters/Secret Shoppers
Critical Control Points

CHAPTER THOUGHT QUESTIONS

1. You understand the relationship between food, labor, and other costs and profit. List and describe several unnecessary costs in a foodservice operation that could reduce profit. How could these costs be avoided?

2. List and describe various cost control techniques that are utilized where you work or have in the past. What was their purpose? Were they effective? Why or why not? What might have been more effective?

3. How did the cost control techniques or methods in question No. 2 make you feel? Were you offended by them? Why or why not?

4. Discuss the importance of effective cost controls and why we need them. Discuss why their design and/or implementation are the responsibility of management.

5. Think about life situations where you might feel compelled to tell on an individual doing something wrong. What would those situations be? How would you feel about telling on the person? Define when it is appropriate and not appropriate to tell on someone.

6. Describe management's responsibility in monitoring employees' behavior and adherence to the rules of the operation. As a manager, how will you feel about enforcing the rules? Discuss any differences or similarities between management and employee responsibility when it comes to enforcing and following the rules. Try to use personal experiences in your discussion.

7. Have you ever taken anything from work for use at home? Have you seen other people do this? What did you and/or they take for their personal use? Is it ever okay to take company property for personal use? When? Why? Do you think the owner of your company would agree with you? Why or why not?

8. Think about all the jobs you have had. Were there ever any fellow employees that could be classified as "bad apples" like Kelly in *Dinner at Martha's*?

What did they do that made them so? How did they affect the other workers? How did they affect you? What did the other workers think of them? What did you think of them? What happened to the employee in question?

9. Compare and contrast control methods that are preventative with those that are primarily designed to catch wrongdoers. Describe what they are, how they work, and their ultimate effectiveness. Which is better? Why?

10. Discuss the relationship between trust and cost control systems. If we employ controls, does it mean we do not trust our employees? Why might control systems be good for employees? Use personal examples to support your answer.

REFERENCES

DeFranco, A. L., & Noriega, P. B. M. (2000). *Cost control in the hospitality industry.* Upper Saddle River, NJ: Prentice Hall.

Keiser, J., DeMicco, F. J., & Grimes, R. N. (2000). *Contemporary management theory: Controlling and analyzing costs in foodservice operations* (4th ed.). Upper Saddle River, NJ: Prentice Hall.

Pavesic, D. V. (1998). *Fundamental principles of restaurant cost control.* Upper Saddle River, NJ: Prentice Hall.

Sanders, E. E., & Hill, R. H. (2001). *Foodservice profitability: A control approach* (2nd ed.). Upper Saddle River, NJ: Prentice Hall.

Schmidgall, R. S. (1992). Hotel managers' responses to ethical dilemmas. *FIU Hospitality Review, 10*(1), 11–18.

Chapter 14

Developing Codes of Ethics and Ethics Programs

John Fallin, general manager of FOI, is tired and overwhelmed with the cavalcade of one problem after another. (Please see the *Frank Eyes Everyone Over* and the *Conclusion* of the Case Study in the back of the book.) He no longer enjoys his work and wants to quit. John is suffering from job **burnout.** He is not alone. Hotel managers experience higher levels of burnout than managers in other industries. Research has found that only about 20% of hotel managers are not emotionally exhausted. The other 80% suffer varying degrees of emotional exhaustion with many choosing to leave hospitality management for less stressful careers.

Professional management requires that we have the ability to see our operations conceptually. That is, we are able to see the whole and all its related parts. We are able to see and understand how all the components work together. They function properly because we design and implement policies and procedures and control measures. This ensures that everyone is doing what he or she is supposed to be doing, when, and how he or she is supposed to be doing it. When we have management controls in place, we are able to oversee the entire operation and actually enjoy ourselves. Management can be fun when we know what we are doing.

In many segments of the case study we have seen problems stop at "John's desk." He is a manager that is much in demand. Many of these problems could have been alleviated by better management control, but, in its absence, John feels as though he is holding untold loose ends together—and if he lets go, FOI will disintegrate. John *is*, essentially, holding FOI together, and that kind of pressure will put any of us into a burnout state as it has done to John.

MANAGEMENT DEFICIENCIES AT FRESHWATER OASIS INN

Several of FOI's department heads have made poor decisions or decisions that are not in line with John's vision of how the inn should operate. The problem is that they do not know what John's vision is because they are not mind readers.

AND IT'S GOT THESE TWO BIG FINGERS...

They have not been socialized into John's preferred culture, because the culture is in John's head rather than a reality. The general manager's task is to identify and create the culture. He or she does this by designing policies and procedures that support the culture. The general manager hires people who are at home in the culture and teaches them how to nurture the culture. Unfortunately, John does not know how to do this.

This is an ethics textbook. Ethics, however, do not and cannot stand alone. They must be part of every aspect of management and of life in general. We have discovered through numerous analyses that unethical decisions result in painful consequences. Hopefully, we are in agreement that it is best to make ethical decisions. In order to accomplish this, we must have a culture of ethics and teach our people how to behave in line with the culture. We are doing our best work when we are making ethical decisions and behaving ethically. We are honest, trustworthy, and loyal. We care about our fellow workers and guests alike.

John needs to clarify what each of his department heads are supposed to be doing and how they are to be doing it. He needs to communicate this information to his people, along with some specific training on how to do what he wants. He must follow up by keeping apprised of what his management team is doing, when, and how. He must give immediate corrective feedback and make sure they are doing what is expected of them. Up until now, he has let his department heads basically do whatever they wanted to do, and, then, after the fact, he had to deal with the problems their decisions caused. This might be seen as *delegation* run amok. John needs to rein in his managers and establish some ground rules. The direction must come from John so that his department heads are all on the same page and it is the page that John, as general manager, has determined.

John made some hiring mistakes. Bill Gardner, Kathy Lawhorn, and perhaps Heidi Bell may not have been good matches for the positions they were hired to fill. John made Mike Scales bar manager without helping him to attain the management skills enabling him to do his job effectively. Kathy and Heidi both made hiring mistakes of their own that caused problems. John must design human resource management policies and procedures, and then they must be communicated to his department heads. They must be trained in how to follow the policies and use the procedures, and John must check that they are indeed doing so. Ethics are incorporated into the human resource management policies and procedures.

If everyone followed all the ethical rules (even without consistent policies and procedures in human resources, sales and marketing, cost control, and the various operational areas of the inn), nothing too awful could happen. Our department heads would be making ethical decisions daily that would be honest, create trust, be fair, and so forth. We do not, however, have to reinvent the wheel every time we make a decision. There are management theories, strategies, methods, and systems of operation that are already proven to work effectively. This is what students learn in university hospitality programs. Successful managers utilize this information and apply it to their operations.

John does not have consistent human resources policies and procedures that all of his department heads are to follow. He does not have adequate control over what his department heads are doing. He does not communicate to them what he wants, and he does not check to see that they are following through with his directives. He must devise systems of operation for all functions of the inn that will ensure administration and utilization of consistent policies and procedures throughout. He can be assisted in this endeavor by consultants who are experts in hospitality management and/or by studying some of the many hospitality management books available.

Good management is possible because it is steeped in ethical principles. The results of good management are beneficial for all the stakeholders: customers, employees, managers, the company, and the surrounding community. Good management is taught in university hospitality management programs. Consistent integrated ethics instruction, however, is missing in most of these programs. While many professors touch on ethics, it is not taught throughout the curriculum in a way that prepares students to incorporate ethics into management systems.

This text is designed to enable students to understand how ethics play into every aspect of hospitality management. The purpose of this chapter is to show students and managers how to develop codes of ethics and how to put together ethics programs that can result in consistent and integrated ethical behavior

---

IN THE TRENCHES

Laurel Ashland, 25, Jacksonville, OR

"Working at a pizza restaurant during my senior year of high school, the only thing on my mind was saving money for college. Four of my girlfriends worked there as well, and every night we would go home complaining about the same problem: our managers were chauvinist pigs. We were permitted to wear denim shorts (standing near a pizza oven can feel like 230 degrees at times) and a work shirt. It was hard taking orders and preparing pizzas with our managers literally watching our behinds. Sometimes they'd show us their appreciation for a job well done by slapping them, much like a coach would an athlete being called into the game. Feeling so uncomfortable at work made me more timid. Knowing what I know now could have prevented the humiliation and loss of self-esteem. I wonder how they got away with it for so long. I know we weren't the first group of girls to experience this treatment. Where was the general manager? Obviously not worried about his managers' actions, or maybe he was the same way. Thankfully we were strong enough to deal with it, but this kind of action should not occur in any establishment. But it did, and I learned from it."

---

in any operation. John, at FOI, must develop structured management procedures where he will be able to communicate desired behaviors and results to department heads—and then the means of monitoring these behaviors and results. We will use the remainder of this chapter to describe the design process for developing an ethics code and ethics program for all employees at FOI. The management policies and procedures that John must design for FOI must support and adhere to all of the ethical principles in the FOI ethics code.

ETHICS CODES

The goal of any ethics code is to create an environment conducive to ethical behavior, because it is through ethical behavior that guests' needs will be met or exceeded, and the organization will profit. Making ethical decisions requires the ability to recognize ethical issues and analyze them in terms of appropriate ethical principles. Individual ethical values are not always the same, so organizations must establish common values that everyone can be comfortable with. Organizations need shared value systems in order to maintain consistency within their operations. A written code of shared values can serve as a guideline for dealing with ethical dilemmas, and also as a framework for employees' behavior.

Organizations prefer having trustworthy employees—ethical employees—and, because traditional values have become less prevalent, written codes of ethics may be necessary. An ethics code must match the beliefs of the organization, and all levels of the organization must be committed to its success.

Perceptions of unfairness, favoritism, and inconsistency in employee selection, supervision, promotion, and performance may be the result of miscommunication. For ethical awareness programs to be successful, communication must be open and honest and the standards must be specific, communicated in clear language and understood by all. Adherence to ethics codes must be backed by the power of rewards and punishment, or else they are often ineffective.

To successfully implement an ethics code it is necessary to introduce it and foster an awareness of ethical situations with the entire staff. Management and workers can be taught the four-step method of problem solving by (1) identifying the ethical dilemma in a case study, (2) identifying the stakeholders, (3) determining possible solutions, and (4) implementing the solution. Realistic case studies can help employees to match appropriate decisions and behaviors to various situations.

DEVELOPING ETHICS CODES

Developing ethics codes begins with identifying the ethical principles that are relevant for our particular operation. Then we must write the principles in a simple, clear format that relates directly to the organization. It can be useful to look at other organization's ethics codes to get an idea what they look like. We can use one that appeals to us and personalize and modify it for our own use. There are many examples of ethics codes available, and many organizations are happy to give us permission to use theirs.

We have included several codes of ethics developed by various organizations. In Chapter 6 we included the "Principles of Professionalism" from Meeting Professionals International. In Chapter 8 we included "Principles and Standards of Ethical Supply Management Conduct" from the Institute for Supply Management with the accompanying guidelines in the appendices. Also included in the appendices are the American Society of Association Executives Standards of Conduct and Marriott Corporate Policy 1, *Ethical Conduct.*

The Center for the Study of Ethics in the Professions at Illinois Institute of Technology has a Web page with numerous examples of ethics codes that can be accessed at http://www.iit.edu/departments/csep/PublicWWW/codes/codes.html. And, of course, we have the Ethical Principles for Hospitality Managers we have been utilizing throughout this text. You may feel free to modify it in any way that is useful for your particular organizations.

Ethics codes are not all alike, but they are similar. We are, after all, trying to make everyone honest, trustworthy, loyal, caring, accountable, and so forth. The actual code may be less important than the process of devising the code, introducing it to the entire organization, training and talking about the code, and yearly evaluations of how the code is working and whether any changes are necessary to make the code more effective. It is through the ethics code process that our managers and employees will become aware of what the various principles in the code mean in their daily business lives.

Large organizations may want to assemble a committee including top management to draft an ethics code they believe is in keeping with the organization's identified values. They can do this by individually studying ethics codes that have been effective in various other organizations. Then the group can discuss which items they liked and which items they did not think were pertinent. They can perhaps add new items, sort and organize the agreed-upon items, and put together a first draft of the ethics code.

Copies of the first draft can be given to other managers and representative employees to critique and give input. A revised draft can then go to a larger circle for continued review and revision until a relevant, agreed-upon ethics code emerges from the process. The ethics code does not have to be original. We are allowed to build on the work of others, as long as we give them credit. The final ethics code should be written in the clearest terms possible. It should be simple, specific, and brief. Everyone must be able to understand it.

Small organizations such as FOI can use the same design process, including all the department heads with the general manager, in producing a first draft. There are some benefits to including managers in the process. They may accept the concept of an ethics code better if they have been part of determining which values should be on it. It can be an ethical awareness building exercise for those managers who may be somewhat ethically challenged. It will be the managers' responsibility to enforce the ethics code within their departments. Working through their own skepticism, under the positive guidance of the general manager, may help them to understand their employees' possible lack of enthusiasm and will enable them to sell the new ethics program more effectively.

On the other hand, the general manager may draft an ethics code without the help of a committee. It would be a very good idea, however, to share the draft with the department heads and provide an explanation of the purpose, have them review the draft, and then meet later to discuss any additions or changes they would like to see. Discussion would be encouraged where input on how best to implement the ethics code might be received.

Department heads can review their relevant policies and procedures, identifying any inconsistencies between their department documents and the ethics code. They can then alter any policies and procedures so that they are in compliance with the ethics code and support the intent of the code. This process should be done in partnership with top management. It provides an opportunity for top management (where the whole ethics effort must originate) to offer direction and emotional support for the endeavor.

FRESHWATER OASIS INN ETHICS CODE

John Fallin, general manager of FOI, has identified communication as one of the biggest problems at the inn. He will begin having weekly department head meetings where they discuss the week's happenings at FOI and share issues they are dealing with in their particular departments. Each weekly meeting will have a training session either presented by John or an expert on a variety of topics such as interviewing and selection, supervision, employee appraisal, and ethics. All of the training sessions will be made specific to FOI policies and procedures. New policies and procedures will be introduced at the department head meetings as they are developed, and training will accompany each change or addition.

John will begin meeting with individual department heads regularly, discussing departmental problems and goals and devising strategies for solving problems and reaching goals. He will make sure that any department head skill gaps are closed through specific supplemental training. In all the discussions he will incorporate ethical analysis and guidance, helping the department head to understand what is important at FOI and how to obtain it. John will give positive corrective feedback and recognize good work and effort.

John needed an ethics code in place in order to design management systems that incorporate ethics in all the new policies and procedures. John simply modified the Ethical Principles for Hospitality Managers for FOI managers and staff. This working draft of an FOI Ethics Code is adequate for his use. It can later be presented to the department heads for their input and any necessary revisions.

Freshwater Oasis Inn Code of Conduct for Managers and Staff

Honesty: FOI managers and staff are honest and truthful. They do not mislead or deceive others by misrepresentations.

Integrity: FOI managers and staff demonstrate the courage of their convictions by doing what they know is right even when there is pressure to do otherwise.

Trustworthiness: FOI managers and staff are trustworthy and candid in supplying information and in correcting misapprehensions of fact. They do not create justifications for escaping their promises and commitments.

Loyalty: FOI managers and staff demonstrate loyalty to the Freshwater Oasis Inn in devotion to duty and loyalty to colleagues by friendship in adversity. They avoid conflicts of interest; do not use or disclose confidential information; and, should they accept other employment, they respect the proprietary information of FOI.

Fairness: FOI managers and staff are fair and equitable in all dealings; they do not abuse power arbitrarily nor take undue advantage of another's mistakes or difficulties. They treat all individuals with equality, with tolerance for and acceptance of diversity and with an open mind.

Concern and Respect for Others: FOI managers and staff are concerned, respectful, compassionate, and kind. They are sensitive to the personal concerns of their colleagues and live the "Golden Rule." They respect the rights and interests of all those who have a stake in their decisions.

Commitment to Excellence: FOI managers and staff pursue excellence in performing their duties and are willing to put more into their job than they can get out of it.

Leadership: FOI managers are conscious of the responsibility and opportunities of their position of leadership. They realize that the best way to instill ethical principles and ethical awareness in their organizations is by example. They walk their talk!

Reputation and Morale: FOI managers seek to protect and build Freshwater Oasis Inn's reputation and the morale of its employees by engaging in conduct that builds respect and by taking whatever actions are necessary to correct or prevent inappropriate conduct of others.

Accountability: FOI managers are personally accountable for the ethical quality of their decisions as well as those of their subordinates.

DEVELOPING AN ETHICS PROGRAM

Operations that have management control systems and policies and procedures already in place can develop ethics programs to encompass all the existing systems. FOI's situation is more like a start-up where all systems must be developed and implemented at once. It is most effective to teach ethics to employees within the context of the policies and procedures of the job. So, we begin with an ethics code. We then either analyze our existing policies and procedures, ensuring they are compatible with the ethics code and making any necessary changes, or we develop new ethical policies and procedures.

Once we have ethical policies and procedures we can develop the ethics program. An **ethics program** consists of ongoing activities and training designed to promote ethical awareness and the reinforcement of expected ethical behavior. It is based on the organization's ethics code. This textbook and the accompanying materials (the curriculum/teacher's manual) is an ethics program for hospitality students. It includes content (the textbook), lectures, activities, and tests. Developing the ethics code is easy. Designing an ethics program is a little more involved.

There are many ethics programs available; search online under "Ethics Training Programs" and related headings. We can modify existing programs to make them specific for our own operations, we can have a consultant design an ethics program for our operation, or we can design them ourselves. Designing the instruction is time-consuming but a lot less expensive than hiring a consultant. We have to balance time, money, and expertise while deciding which option is best for our particular situation. We will go through the step-by-step design process so students/managers have the expertise to design ethics programs themselves if they choose to do so.

DESIGNING AN ETHICS PROGRAM FOR FRESHWATER OASIS INN

John Fallin decided it would be better to hire a consultant to design FOI's ethics program while he was working on management policies and procedures. The consultant will design introductory materials for the ethics code, training

Honors

Honesty

and

Honor

materials, ongoing activities, and evaluation procedures all specific to FOI's operation. For the purposes of this text, we, the authors, will act as design consultant and explain and demonstrate the design process used to develop the FOI ethics program.

We will be using a standard training design model because we are essentially designing ethics training. That is what the FOI Ethics Program is—ethics training for everyone at FOI.

Training Design Model

Step #1	#2	#3	#4	#5	#6	#7
Needs Assessment	Training Plan	Lesson Plans	Trainer Training	Training Implementation	Training Evaluation	Coaching and Counseling

Needs Assessment

The first step in any design project is to conduct a **needs assessment** where we determine the specific training needs. In several interviews with the FOI general manager, we determined that an ethics training program was necessary because, while most everyone at FOI tries to do "good" work, there is no agreement on what the term means. John has not communicated his professional code of ethics to his staff, and has been disappointed when they have made work decisions that are not in keeping with his code. John has since modified the Ethical Principles for Hospitality Managers into a written code for FOI that mirrors his personal professional code of ethics.

John has been developing formal systems of operation in the areas of human resources management, cost control, sales and marketing, and so forth. We reviewed his documents, along with all existing documents such as job descriptions, evaluation instruments, and various written policies and procedures, to determine whether or not they adhere to the Freshwater Oasis Inn Code of Conduct for Managers and Staff.

We identified the ethical needs of the organization, the ethical needs of the various positions, and the ethical needs of the individuals employed by FOI. This was accomplished by reviewing the mission and company philosophy, reviewing job specifications and job descriptions, and by interviewing John Fallen, all department heads, and a representative number of employees. We found that most everyone knows the difference between right and wrong, but they do not know how to differentiate between right and wrong on the job. They do not have a clear, consistent sense of what is expected of them.

We are not trying to teach everyone at FOI how to do their jobs (they already know how to do that), but, rather, how to live the ethics code while doing their jobs. We need to understand where the ethics code applies in the tasks of each position in order to design ethics training. We get this information from employees in the various positions and by watching them do their jobs.

We clarified with John what he thought the scope and purpose of the FOI Ethics Program should be, how much time and money they were prepared to make available for the program, what he thought it should look like, and how willing he was to support the program. If top management does not take an active positive role, program success is unlikely. We toured the facility and were shown where training sessions could be held. We reviewed employee schedules to determine when it would be convenient to conduct training sessions.

Training Plan

The next step in the design process is to develop a **training plan,** which includes a list of all the training topics and a schedule of when, where, and by whom they will be presented. The training plan also identifies the trainees, the broad training objectives, and selects the trainers. Stated behaviorally, the broad training objective of the FOI Ethics Program is: Upon completion of the FOI Ethics Program, all FOI employees will adhere to the ethics standards listed on the FOI Code of Conduct for Managers and Staff.

Behavioral objectives, where we state what the trainees will be able to do upon completion of the training, are always used in training design. We are concerned with outcomes in training. Knowing or understanding something may be nice, but does not necessarily mean that the trainee will be able to actually do it. Stating what we expect the trainee to be able to do upon completion of the training helps to keep our focus on that goal and to design appropriate instruction and appropriate instruments to test whether or not the trainee can do what he or she is expected to do at the end of the training.

If our behavioral objective for training servers is that servers should be able to take dinner orders upon completion of the training, it would be necessary to teach server trainees about the menu so they could accurately describe menu items and answer guest questions. We could use some sort of classroom instruction to familiarize the trainees with the menu, but most likely we would choose demonstrations and simulations where trainees would actually be answering guest questions and taking orders. The test at the end of the training would be to take orders, because passing a written test about taking guest orders would not ensure that trainees could actually take guest orders after completing the training.

The information collected in the needs assessment phase of design was analyzed in conjunction with the FOI Code of Conduct and resulted in the following training topics:

1. Introduction of the FOI Code of Conduct for Managers and Staff, why it is important, and the consequences for failing to adhere to it.
2. How to identify ethical dilemmas.
3. How to determine the ethical solution or action when in doubt.

In training design we do **task analysis,** which is where we break down a task into all of the minute steps it takes to complete the task. It is expensive and time-consuming to design training. If we do not bother to do task analysis, we could design training that misses a step or that does not quite work. Our training would be less effective, and we would be subjecting the trainee and trainer to frustration. Designing training is not difficult; it is tedious!

The first training topic (Introduction of the FOI Code of Conduct for Managers and Staff, why it is important, and consequences for failing to adhere to it) is not the usual behavioral training topic. We cannot do task analysis on something that is not a task. Instead, we write out exactly what the code is, all the reasons why it is important to everyone, and the consequences for not following rules. We then write a behavioral objective for the first topic, which is: *Upon completion of the training, FOI employees will be able to list and define the ten (or seven for nonmanagers) ethical principles on the FOI Code of Conduct, discuss why the code and each principle is important, and state the consequences for failing to adhere to the code.*

The information in this topic is the same for every FOI employee and can be presented at an employee meeting. We might need to schedule a couple different sessions so that everyone can attend one or the other. FOI is a 24/7 operation, so some employees will always be working.

Topics 2 and 3 are behavioral. We are teaching our employees to do something. In this case, how to identify ethical dilemmas and determine the ethical solution or action when in doubt. The combined behavioral objective will be: *Upon completion of training, the trainee will be able to identify ethical dilemmas and determine the ethical solution or action.* We can do task analysis on these items, although it is not as straightforward and obvious as identifying the steps in setting a table or making a quiche. (A recipe for quiche is basically a task analysis.)

Task analysis for Topic 3: determining the ethical solution or action.

1. Identify the problem.
2. Identify possible decision options and enter them on an Ethics Analysis Form.
3. Identify stakeholders and enter them on the Ethics Analysis Form.
4. Ask questions to determine any possible consequences for each of the stakeholders for each decision option and enter them on the Ethics Analysis Form.
5. Go down the list of ethical principles to determine if any are violated by any of the decision options, then enter them on the Ethics Analysis Form.
6. Choose the decision option that has the least number of negative consequences for the fewest number of stakeholders and that violates the fewest ethical principles.

The results of task analysis form the basis for the content of instruction. We will further break down each of these items. In step 1 of the task analysis, *identify the problem* is broken down by determining how we do so. The solution is put in writing and we move on down the list.

Topics 2 and 3 have general and specific meanings for FOI in various positions. We can do some general instruction at a large employee meeting, but then we will also need to do specific instruction for the particular position. There are myriad situations that will arise in the different departments, and, if all employees are going to be able to identify dilemmas and choose ethical solutions and actions, we will have to make the instruction specific to those situations.

Define the Trainees

For instruction to be effective it needs to be geared to the particular trainees' learning styles and backgrounds. It is not discriminatory to describe the typical worker in housekeeping as middle-age, Spanish-speaking, female, and minimally educated—if that is, indeed, the case. It is, however, discriminatory to say that we will only hire workers who fit that description. If most of our workers fit that description, the training must be presented in Spanish and avoid teaching methods such as lectures with written tests.

Training differs from education in that students are responsible for their coursework and can flunk if they do not achieve the standard. A grade of "D" is not very good but passes the course. In training, everyone must get an "A," and it is the trainer's responsibility to make sure that everyone does. An "A" in training means that the standard has been reached. Everyone must reach the standard. If a cook gets a "C" in training, that would mean that perhaps 30% of the time he or she might burn the steak or ruin the recipe. Or, 30% of a "C" server's customer encounters might be unsatisfactory. Clearly, average grades in training are unacceptable in the hospitality industry. If 30% of our customers leave dissatisfied, we will soon be out of business.

Our responsibility as trainers is to ensure that the trainees meet the objective of the training—that they will be able to do what is expected of them when training is complete. So we must design training that they will be able to relate to, understand, and be comfortable with. Just as our service product is not one size fits all, neither is training. The FOI employees are diverse. There are college-educated professionals, skilled and unskilled laborers, Spanish-speaking skilled and unskilled laborers, young adults, older adults, minimally educated and some employees with little or no formal education at all.

When we define the trainees, we become aware that scheduling several big employee meetings (to present Topic 1 and parts of Topics 2 and 3) is not going to work. It may make sense to have a training session for all the department heads and then training sessions in both English and Spanish for the rest of the employees. There is a variance from department to department in the typical ethical situations that employees might encounter. For that reason, we will have to plan on individual department training for those parts of Topics 2 and 3. This means that we have to add a Topic 4: Train the managers to train their employees.

Training Methods

There are numerous methods that can be utilized to train employees. We want to choose the ones most suitable, resulting in trainees obtaining the objective.

Lectures, demonstrations, simulations, role plays, self-instruction activities, classroom methods, and on-the-job training are some of the methods we can use to train. The method has to match the objective. That is why we write the training objective first. In the hospitality industry, we have often experienced the "shadow" method. This is where a new employee follows around an experienced employee for a shift or two, and then is expected to be able to do the job. With high rates of turnover, this could mean that a relatively inexperienced employee is training new employees. The shadow method results in inconsistent, and oftentimes low-quality, training.

The behavioral objective for the first topic is: *Upon completion of training, FOI employees will be able to list and define the ten (or seven for nonmanagers) ethical principles on the FOI Code of Conduct, discuss why the code and each principle is important, and state the consequences for failing to adhere to the code.* This objective has several parts. To select appropriate training methods, we first must consider how each part will need to be taught. We will break the objective into the following sections.

Upon completion of training, the trainees will be able to:

1. Describe the Code of Conduct and discuss why it is important
2. List and define the individual ethical principles
3. State the consequences for not adhering to the Code of Conduct.

We then select appropriate methods to use in training each of the items in the above objective for Topic 1. All three items could be taught using lecture with discussion. We might choose to use some additional worksheet/analysis activities for item 2. We go through the same process for Topics 2 and 3.

Select the Trainer

Just like not everyone can be a good teacher or wants to teach, not everyone has the ability or desire to be a good trainer. We have to select trainers who want to train, are capable of training, and then we must train them in how to do so effectively. Potential trainers must be flexible, understanding, attuned to the people they are instructing, and it might also be useful to have a sense of humor. They must be taught how to effectively present instruction utilizing all of the adult learning principles.

The Principles of Adult Learning

- Trainees prefer an informal atmosphere for training sessions where they are treated as professionals rather than students.
- Trainees need encouragement and positive feedback as to their progress.
- Trainees should not compete with each other.
- Trainees learn at different speeds and may need individual attention and training.
- Trainees must understand why the material is necessary and want to learn it.

- Trainees must be told what they are to do and then shown the sequential steps to do it.
- The training should be related to trainees' life experiences.
- Trainees need real and tangible examples.
- Trainees learn better by doing.
- Trainees should learn to do the activity correctly, then build up speed.
- Training should be conducted in numerous shorter sessions.
- Repetition and practice result in better retention.
- Keep lag time short between the time of training and the job.
- Use a combination of training methods.
- Make the training interesting and relevant.
- The trainer should be well prepared.
- The trainer must create a positive learning environment.
- The trainer must exhibit enthusiasm.

The FOI Ethics Program is essentially a training plan and emerges as we work through the topics. Our initial idea of the big meeting was scrapped, and we have determined that we should design ethics training specifically for FOI managers. Included in their training is a segment on training them to train. We can design the instruction that they can use to teach their own department staff members about the FOI Code of Conduct. We will use this same process and devise a training plan for training nonmanagement staff later.

We will be training nine members of the management team. FOI has a small conference room that will be perfect for the type of training we will be doing. We will present all the instruction to the management team as well as train them how to use the specific materials we will be designing to train departmental employees. We went ahead and broke down the other topics, determined training methods, and entered them on the following training schedule.

FOI Ethics Training Program Schedule for Management

(General Mgr., Asst. General Mgr., Bookkeeper, Bar Mgr., Dining Room Mgr., Front Desk Mgr., Exec. Housekeeper, Chief Engineer, Exec. Chef)

5-Week Training Program, Tues. and Thurs. 2–3:30 PM

Training Topic	Training Method	Trainer	Time and Place
1. Introduction of the FOI Code of Conduct for managers and staff, why it is important, and the consequences for failing to adhere to it	Lecture with discussion	John Fallin and Consultant	Tues. Sm. Conf. Rm.

(continued)

Training Topic	Training Method	Trainer	Time and Place
2. How to identify ethical dilemmas (Week 1) (Topics 2 and 3 are taught together)	Lecture with discussion and case study practice activities	Consultant	Thurs. Sm. Conf. Rm.
3. How to determine the ethical solution when in doubt (Weeks 2 and 3)	Lecture with discussion and case study practice activities	Consultant	Thurs. and T/Th, T/Th, Sm. Conf. Rm.
4. Train-the-trainer (Weeks 4 and 5)	Lecture, demonstration, simulations, instructional activities	Consultant	T/Th, T/Th Sm. Conf. Rm.

We have our initial training plan for the management of FOI. We will, of course, have to do another training plan for training nonmanagement employees. Our training plan must remain flexible, however, because through the design process we often realize that changes will be necessary to improve our initial plan. Chapter 15 will address the next step, which is to design the lesson plans for instruction of the topics on this training plan.

CONCLUSION

John Fallin is an ethical man. He has not, however, formally shared his ethics with his staff. Subsequently he has been disappointed when they have acted in ways that are not in keeping with his sense of right and wrong. An ethics program will go a long way in helping his employees to make good decisions when they are in doubt. John has also neglected to provide his employees with adequate policies and procedures that are consistent with his ethical principles. His burnout is a result of his own failure to guide and supervise his management team. He has finally begun to develop the written policies and procedures that he will put in place, introduce to his managers, and monitor through ongoing communication in meetings with his management team as a whole and individually.

John determined that he personally did not have the time or the expertise sufficient to design the ethics program so obviously needed at FOI. He established an ethics code by modifying the Ethical Principles for Hospitality Managers to accommodate his own ethics (and FOI's), and then hired a hospitality training design consultant to design the program. Acting as consultant, we went through the process using a training design model that resulted in a plan for training the management team about the ethics code, how to make ethical decisions, and to train them to train their own department personnel in the ethics code and its use. The next chapter will continue with lesson plan design for the training topics outlined in the training plan.

It is very important for us to be able to make ethical decisions. Our employees will notice that we always do what is right. We will gain their trust and respect, which allows us to lead them in ways that are good for the organization, good for employees, and good for us. Our example is powerful, but, if we want them to also be able to make ethical decisions and behave ethically, we need to do more than just model ethical behavior. We need to teach them how to be ethical on the job.

Training design is not difficult, although it is certainly tedious. Entire degree programs are available in the discipline of instructional design. Parts of two chapters in an ethics textbook are hardly adequate for providing you with the skill necessary to design training. You are, however, being exposed to the design process and can attempt it yourself, learning through trial and error or by studying the process further through a course or a training design textbook. (Our hospitality training design textbook is listed in the References at the end of this chapter and may be useful.)

We do not all have the same idea of what right and wrong is. Some of our employees may have *no* idea of right and wrong. To operate successfully today, our customers and our workers must trust us or else they will leave us. They must be able to get their needs met through our service product or our employ—and this requires our commitment to excellence. This commitment to excellence is realized through ethical business practices that must be taught. We are learning them here and can apply them later to our management positions. We can then teach our employees so that we are all operating according to the ethical rules that make long-term success possible.

KEY WORDS

Burnout	Training Plan
Ethics Program	Behavioral Objectives
Needs Assessment	Task Analysis

CHAPTER THOUGHT QUESTIONS

1. Have you ever suffered burnout? Describe the situation, what you felt, why you felt it, what you did about it, and the final result of the ordeal. In retrospect, could you have avoided burnout? How?

2. Discuss the management responsibilities of the general manager position. Include in your discussion why general managers are responsible for what everyone in the operation does. What do you think about this? How can general managers handle this responsibility without suffering emotional exhaustion or burnout? How will you do it?

3. Describe the relationship between ethics codes and management policies and procedures. Can either of them stand alone? What is the best relationship between ethics codes and management policies and procedures? Why?

4. Think of jobs you have held. Did the general manager or person in charge communicate his or her ethical beliefs to you and the staff? How? If not, why? What effect did the communication or lack of communication have on you and the staff?

5. Think of jobs you have held. Did the person in charge communicate what and how he or she wanted you and/or the staff to do? How? If not, why? What effect did the communication or lack of communication have on you and the staff?

6. Describe ethics codes and discuss why they are necessary. Use personal examples when ethics codes were or were not in place. Support your discussion.

7. Why do we have to teach our employees about the ethics code and what it all means? Discuss why we cannot just assume they will do the right thing in most situations.

8. What is a needs assessment, why is it important, and what are the possible negative consequences for skipping this step in a training design project? Think of a personal situation where you did or should have done something similar to a needs assessment. Describe the situation and the effect the needs assessment had or could have had on the outcome.

9. What is a behavioral objective? Why do we use behavioral objectives in training design? What is their purpose and what could happen if we did not start with stating a behavioral objective?

10. Discuss the difference between defining the trainees and discrimination. Why do we need to define the trainees we are designing training for? Think about classes you have been in. Describe the "target audience" or typical student in the class. Were there any students that did not match the target audience profile? Did the teacher design instruction to match the needs of the target audience, and how did this affect any students who did not fit the profile?

REFERENCES

Coughlan, R. (2001). An analysis of professional codes of ethics in the hospitality industry. *International Journal of Hospitality Management, 20*(2), 147–162.

Cullen, N. C. (2001). *Team power: Managing human resources in the hospitality industry.* Upper Saddle River, NJ: Prentice Hall.

Jaszay, C. (2002). *An integrated research review of ethics articles in hospitality journals 1990–2000.* Paper presented at the Council on Hotel, Restaurant, and Institutional Education. Conference, Orlando, FL.

Jaszay, C. (2003). Review of hospitality ethics research in 2000 and 2001. *Isbell Hospitality Ethics Web Page:* www.nau.edu/hrm/ahrrc/isbellcenter.html.

Jaszay, C., & Dunk, P. (2003). *Training design for the hospitality industry.* New York: Delmar.

Van Hoof, H. B., McDonald, M. E., Yu, L., & Vallen, G. K. (1996). *A host of opportunities: An introduction to hospitality management.* Chicago: Irwin.

Woods, R. H. (1997). *Managing hospitality human resources* (2nd ed.). MI: Educational Institute.

Chapter 15

Training Management and Employees in Ethics

Our job as managers is to ensure that employees are doing what they are supposed to be doing, in the correct way, and at the right time. This will only happen if we hire people who are willing and capable of doing what we require of them. They must then be trained so they know how they are supposed to be doing it. Willingness, capability, and training all go together, and all three must be present if an employee is to be successful at his or her position.

Training, like education, is not all the same. Some training is more effective than others. Much of the training in hospitality operations is the "follow around another employee" variety. This informal shadow method is often chosen because managers have never experienced formal training themselves. They have not been taught what formal training actually is, and, subsequently, they do not know how to design it themselves. Basically, they enlist shadowing techniques because they do not know any better. This style of training often results in inconsistent and less than satisfactory outcomes.

Some of the larger chains have instructional designers at the corporate level who provide structured **formal training** for all units of the company. Trainers are selected and trained to train using the corporate-designed materials so that each employee trained for a specific position receives the same comprehensive, consistent, high-quality training. Formally trained employees are better prepared to do the job when they first encounter customers, alleviating the need for a new employee to ever tell a customer, "Please bear with me; this is my first day on the job."

Service levels suffer with informal training, but willing and able employees can eventually catch on and excel at their jobs. Many, however, get frustrated, and more new employees quit in the first month of employment than at any other time. Employers must then find and "train" other new employees. Formal training has been found to cut down on new employee frustration and/or turnover and results in better-trained employees faster than less effective informal methods.

If managers and long-term employees are all behaving ethically, a culture of ethics may pervade the operation. New employees will most likely be socialized into the desired behavior or end up leaving. Conducting ethics training speeds up the assimilation process and eliminates some of the painful experiential learning. The shadow method can sometimes work well for **psychomotor** activities such as showing someone how to set a table, but it is totally ineffective for teaching ethics.

Ethics is **attitudinal** rather than psychomotor and requires a less straightforward, more influential type of instruction. An attitude is an inclination to make certain choices in particular circumstances. A health-conscious person may tend to choose grilled chicken breast over deep-fried pork rinds because eating healthy is an attitude he or she holds. In ethics training we are trying to change employees' attitudes so that they will tend to make ethical choices.

In the last chapter we began the training design process from the perspective of a consultant that John Fallin, general manager, hired to develop the FOI Ethics Program. Through needs assessment we determined it would be necessary to train management personnel in ethics and then teach them how to train their own department personnel. We devised an FOI Ethics Training Program Schedule for Management (see Chapter 14), and in this chapter we will explain and show how to design instruction for the four topics deemed necessary.

IN THE TRENCHES

Amanda Messick, 22, Show Low, AZ

"I'm a server at a downtown restaurant. I noticed some time back that my tips were drastically decreasing. For about a year they averaged between $60–$80 on Friday or Saturday nights, then suddenly dipped to $40–$50. This just didn't seem right. I knew the other server wasn't stealing my tips because we are good friends and she had been experiencing the same thing with her tips. Then one night I saw the owner/manager walk over to one of her tables and steal her tip off it, putting it in his pocket! He would also cheat us at the end of the night when we cashed out our credit card tips. He would say, 'Here is $10,' when I knew I'd made at least $20–$30. When we finally confronted the owner he got all sheepish and made excuses and it was ugly. I hate working there as a result, and as soon as I find another job I will quit. My friend, on the other hand, was so upset that she began stealing from the restaurant. Instead of cashing out guest checks, she would just keep the money for herself. So the owner created a bad situation, and then it got worse."

LESSON PLANNING FOR THE FOI ETHICS PROGRAM

The **lesson plan** is a document we prepare that consists of subject matter for the training topic, all the learning activities and materials, and the trainer directions and script for presenting the instruction. Lesson planning is the third step in the Training Design Model.

Training Design Model

Step #1	#2	#3	#4	#5	#6	#7
Needs Assessment	Training Plan	Lesson Plans	Trainer Training	Training Implementation	Training Evaluation	Coaching and Counseling

Our design task is to prepare lesson plans for the four training topics identified in step No.2 of the Training Design Model. The lessons are to be designed to match the learning needs of the trainees (general manager, assistant general manager, bookkeeper, bar manager, dining room manager, front desk manager, executive housekeeper, chief engineer, and the executive chef). The training sessions will be held in the small conference room every Tuesday and Thursday afternoon from 2:00 to 3:30 for 5 weeks. The training consultant will deliver the instruction.

Training Topics with Methods

1. Introduction of the FOI Code of Conduct for Managers and Staff, why it is important, and the consequences for failing to adhere to it. (Lecture with discussion)
2. How to identify ethical dilemmas. [Topics 2 and 3 are taught together] (Lecture with discussion and case study practice activities)
3. How to determine the ethical solution when in doubt. (Lecture with discussion and case study practice activities)
4. Train the managers to train their employees (Lecture, demonstration, simulations, instructional activities)

Because most of the training in the hospitality industry is for psychomotor skills, the subject matter or content for the lesson ordinarily comes from the task analysis. Topic 1 is not a psychomotor skill, so the subject matter cannot come from task analysis. Instead, we have to assemble and write the subject matter we will be teaching. The behavioral objective for Topic 1 serves as the guide for our lesson plan development, helping us to determine what information needs to be included in the subject matter or content of the lesson plan.

Behavioral Objective: *Upon completion of training, FOI managers will be able to list and define the ten ethical principles on the FOI Code of Conduct, discuss why the code and each principle is important, and state the consequences for failing to adhere to the code.*

Obtaining the Subject Matter

The first part of the behavioral objective states that the trainee will be able to list and define the ten ethical principles of the FOI Code of Conduct. We obtain a copy of the FOI Code of Conduct for Managers and Staff and note that each principle is already defined on the code. Our instruction will have to be designed in a way that will result in the managers being able to list and define each of the principles.

The second part of the behavioral objective says that the managers will have to discuss why the code and each of the principles on the code are important. We do not have this information and will have to write it. We can use a variety of sources to help us to do this. We will be using the information from Chapter 1 that discussed the ten principles. The third part of the behavioral objective requires a copy of the policy that states the consequences for not adhering to the principles on the ethics code. If a policy does not exist, one will have to be written. In training, we include only the information and activities necessary for the trainee to meet the objective.

Defining the Trainees

The nine members of the management team all have years of hospitality experience, are intelligent, speak English as a first language, have high school and/or college/graduate school education, and range in age from about 24 to 53. We will use discussion, examples, and activities that are appropriate for this group.

The Lesson Plan

The lesson plan is the actual instruction. It is the guideline that the trainer will follow when delivering instruction. It includes the topic, the behavioral objective, the time and place of the meeting, the length of time the lesson should take, the materials needed, and any prep work or setup that might be necessary. A good lesson plan may be followed by anyone who can read and has some familiarity with the subject matter. The quality of the presentation will vary depending on the preparation and experience of the trainer, but the information and activities will be identical regardless of who presents the lesson. It is time-consuming to develop lesson plans, but, once they are written, they can be reused and everyone is assured to receive the same excellent training.

The way to begin writing the lesson plan is just to get started. It evolves as we go. We can return to the beginning and fill in parts of the lesson plan that we did not know until later, or we make any changes that came about while we were designing. We will use a standard format. Any format can be used so long as it is clear and easy to follow. All of the lesson plans for a particular operation should, however, be in the same format. We will begin writing the lesson plan for the first training session. We state the behavioral objective (this is from the training plan) and then break it into the steps we think will be required to achieve the objective. Again, the steps may need to be modified as we go because instructional design is a creative process. The steps are then entered on the lesson plan form with the corresponding script and directions. Experienced trainers may choose not to use a script, opting instead for detailed outlines. Below is the lesson plan for Topic 1 for the first ethics training session for FOI management. Lesson plans contain all copies of any handouts, overheads, and so on. They will not be included here, however, for lack of space.

Lesson Plan

Introduction of the FOI Code of Conduct for Managers and Staff
Trainees: Nine members of the FOI Management team
Day and time: Tuesday, 2:00–3:30 PM
Place: Small Conference Room
Trainer: Training design consultant with an introduction by John Fallin, general manager
Training method: Lecture and discussion

Materials needed:

- (9) 3-ring notebooks with blank paper, pens, and handout packet
- Overhead projector
- Wet-erase pen for writing on transparencies
- Dry-erase pens for writing on the dry-erase board in the Conference Room
- Transparency of the FOI Code of Conduct
- 12 blank Ethics Analysis Form transparencies

Objective: Upon completion of training, FOI managers will be able to:

1. List and define the ten ethical principles on the FOI Code of Conduct.
2. Discuss why the code and each principle is important.
3. State the consequences for failing to adhere to the code.

Training steps to meet the objectives:

1. Introduce the FOI Code of Conduct and discuss why it is important.
2. Present the FOI Code of Conduct.
3. Go over the individual principles using real-life examples and discuss why each is important.
4. State the consequences for failing to adhere to the code.
5. Assignment/quiz.

Step	Procedure	Trainer's Directions [trainer instruction in brackets]
1	Introduce the FOI Code of Conduct	*[The general manager, John Fallin, stands at the head of the table in the conference room (by the overhead projector). He greets the other eight members of the management team as they enter, inviting them to take their seats. The training design consultant should take the seat at the other end of the table. At each place should be a handout notebook with paper and pen. John introduces the FOI Ethics Program and the training design consultant who then delivers the instruction.]* **John:** Good afternoon, everyone. Thanks for coming. I'm aware that for some of you today's actually Saturday or Sunday, your day off—so know that I appreciate you're making the time. I scheduled this meeting because I want to go over some changes I think are needed with regards to the way we run FOI. What I'm talking about is establishing a new code of conduct for management and staff. An *ethics* code, if you will. . . . I think our customers are pretty well satisfied with us; we do a good job—*you* do a good job. But, from a management perspective at least, we have been experiencing one avoidable problem after another. As general manager I'm spending all my time officiating in squabbles, and that's got to change.
2	Discuss why it is important	It's my fault—I know that now. I've come to the realization that I have failed to give you any solid guidelines for managing your departments. The result of this failure is that each of you deal with things that come up in the way you think is best. Unfortunately, our nine separate ideas of what is best aren't always the same . . . and, sometimes, frankly, they are quite counterproductive. Then I wind up having to deal with another headache. I want all of us to be on the same page here. And since none of you are mind readers, it occurred to me that I need to tell you what page that is. I want to be really clear about this; the failure is mine, not yours. I have not adequately communicated what I expect you to be doing, nor have I told you how to do it. I am in the process of writing out management policies and procedures so that we're all doing things the same way. We will be meeting together once a week so that communication is regular and open between all of us, and I will also be meeting with you individually. What I think we need, more than anything, is a shared sense of what is right and wrong for FOI—a shared sense of how we all ought to be behaving in every situation we find ourselves in here at the inn. I have written a code of conduct so that we all know precisely what is expected of us. I am using this code of conduct as the foundation for the policies and procedures I am developing—making sure that all of our management practices are in line with the principles on the code.

(continued)

Step	Procedure	Trainer's Directions [trainer instruction in brackets]

I hired a Hospitality Training Design consultant to create an FOI Ethics Program for us . . . and to design formal training for all of our employees. None of us have the time or the expertise to do this. The consultant will teach the nine of us all about our new FOI Code of Conduct . . . and then she will teach us how to use the training materials that were designed so that you can train all of the employees in your own departments.

Having this ethics program in place is going to make all of our work lives better—easier, less complicated, with fewer problems. It will enable us, and our employees, to handle situations that invariably come up in this industry. We'll be able to do it with greater confidence and ease, and with far fewer problems. We are all so different, but this program will allow us to operate according to the same rules that will provide us with the direction we have been lacking.

Remember, folks, we are in this together. So now I would like for us to welcome our training design consultant! Let's give her our full cooperation and attention. Thank you.

[The training design consultant comes to the head of the table and switches places with John.]

Consultant: Hello, everyone. I'm very happy to be here. This is my first visit to FOI, and John gave me the grand tour earlier. I was quite impressed with the facilities, décor, cleanliness, and we had a wonderful lunch in the Oasis Lounge. The Southwest chicken special was wonderful, by the way, Eric. Excellent service! I believe the waiter's name was Lisa? At any rate, I can tell you that I was definitely impressed with what I saw here this afternoon. As far as I could tell, you all seem to be pretty much on top of things here at the inn. John did not hire me to tell you how to do your jobs. You obviously know how, and you do your jobs beautifully if my experience is any indication.

John is right, though. Without consistent policies and procedures in place, management is too difficult and too wrought with problems. What we are going to do here is help you to systemize management, which will eradicate a lot of the guesswork and unnecessary problems.

Most of us are not too keen on change, particularly when it comes from someone outside the organization. But, to remain competitive, which safeguards your positions and futures, it is necessary to enable managers and staff to make decisions and behave in ways that reduce problems and promote the future success of FOI.

This will not happen on its own. A program with training is needed, but, as John already indicated, no one here has the time to develop the program and design the training. So, that's why I'm here.

(continued)

Step	Procedure	Trainer's Directions [trainer instruction in brackets]
	Present the FOI Code of Conduct	You each have a notebook in front of you. Everything that I am going to put up on the overhead, you have copies of in your notebooks. We're going to be meeting twice a week for the next 5 weeks and you will need to bring these notebooks with you to each session. For those of you who didn't particularly enjoy school, I don't think you'll mind this. We'll be talking about what we do, why we do it, how well it works, and what might be better. And all of it will be directly related to your positions here at FOI. I'll be going over this stuff with you, and then you will go over it with your own employees. I will show you how to do that effectively. When you've got good materials and are well prepared, it's actually kind of fun. You'll see. *[Put up the transparency of the FOI Code of Conduct.]* This is the FOI Code of Conduct. You have your own copy on page 1 in your notebook. John put this together using a generic hospitality ethics code, and I think it's comprehensive and as good as any others that are available. Toward the end of our training, however, we will review the FOI Code of Conduct and make any changes we feel will make it a better fit for FOI. John will, of course, be going through this whole training with us. As managers, our behavior has the most influence on the behavior of our employees. Our employees will believe what they see over anything we say. That's why it is so important for us to follow our own rules and procedures. You are going to be held responsible for your employees adhering to this Code of Conduct. They won't do it if you don't do it. That's human nature. So, you need to know the FOI Code of Conduct backwards and forwards, because you need to be living it so that your employees will take it and you seriously.
3	Go over the individual principles and discuss why each is important	Let's start the familiarization process by reading the Code of Conduct out loud. Who will read the first principle out loud while the rest of us follow along? [Have volunteers read the ten principles until all of them have been read.] When we look over the ten ethical principles, I think most of us would agree that they are good. Most of us think honesty is good, dishonesty bad, that it's good to have integrity, good to be trustworthy, and so forth. I have heard people say that the rules are nice but that in business you can't always afford to be ethical. The truth is, however, we can't afford to *not* be ethical. The hospitality industry is so very competitive. If our customers aren't satisfied they'll go elsewhere. If our employees aren't happy, they'll go elsewhere too. How we treat our customers and our employees will determine how successful we are as managers. If FOI loses its competitive edge, management and line positions become less desirable and less secure.

(continued)

Step	Procedure	Trainer's Directions [trainer instruction in brackets]
	Go over the individual principles and discuss why each is important	*[While pointing at Honesty on the transparency say:]* **Honesty:** FOI managers and staff are honest and truthful. They do not mislead or deceive others by misrepresentations. A friend told me about staying at a motel one time that had one of those paper things over the toilet seat assuring him that the toilet was completely clean and sanitized. He said there were gross spots all over the seat. Was that toilet completely clean and sanitized? *[Acknowledge responses.]* They misrepresented that toilet as clean when it wasn't. That sounds like dishonesty to me. Who does this misrepresentation affect? Who are the stakeholders here? *[Guide answers to the stakeholders: customer, employee, other employees, manager, the motel. Put up a blank transparency of an Ethics Analysis Form and write the stakeholders and consequences on the form using the wet-erase pen.]* You have a bunch of copies of this Ethics Analysis Form in your notebooks. You should write down all these examples on your blank forms because it will be helpful when you are doing the assignment you will get for next time. What are the consequences of that misrepresentation to each of these stakeholders? *[Let them think of all the possible consequences, and list them next to each of the stakeholders on the form. The list should include things like customer dissatisfaction, no repeat business, call to the front desk complaining, bad word of mouth, reduced business, manager held accountable for employee not doing his or her job, housekeeper gets in trouble, other employees think they can cut corners, and so forth.]* Take a couple minutes and jot down some examples of dishonesty in your own departments and then we'll discuss them. *[Make sure they understand what you mean. Are they writing? You may need to give some more examples like making a reservation for someone when you are overbooked.]* Who has one they'd like to start with? *[Wait for a volunteer or cajole someone into starting. Be very careful not to offend or embarrass anyone. Ask the following questions to get the discussion going and to familiarize the trainees with the analysis process. Write the stakeholders on the dry-erase board and jot down the possible consequences to each as you go through the following questions.]* Why is this an honesty issue? *[This helps them to review and better understand the principle of honesty.]* Who are the people who may be affected by this—the stakeholders? What are the consequences to each? *[Ask for another example of honesty from their personal FOI management experience. Have*

(continued)

Step	Procedure	Trainer's Directions [trainer instruction in brackets]
	Go over the individual principles and discuss why each is important	*everyone identify the stakeholders and the consequences and write them on the board. Be sure everyone is giving answers.]* Why is honesty important in our FOI management? What are the possible negative consequences if we are dishonest? With our employees? Customers? Colleagues? Top management? *[Illicit specific reasons and consequences from the trainees.]* *[Point to Integrity on the overhead of the Code of Conduct.]* **Integrity:** FOI managers and staff demonstrate the courage of their convictions by doing what they know is right even when there is pressure to do otherwise. John, will you tell everyone about the Sam Riley pool problem you experienced and what you did? *[John had agreed to this in advance—Riley asked for a bribe to issue the building permit. John refused even though no one would have known, and it caused considerable problems for FOI.]* This is definitely an integrity issue. John did the right thing when it would have been easier and less costly to go ahead and pay the bribe. Who are the stakeholders here? *[Riley, city government, community, FOI, John, other employees, customers]* What is Riley doing now, John? Each of you take a couple minutes and jot down an example of an integrity situation you have experienced in managing your departments. *[Go through the same procedure, have everyone read their examples, identify the stakeholders and the possible consequences for each stakeholder for each example. Be sure everyone is involved. It may be necessary to ask some questions to get their input.]* Why is integrity important in our FOI management? What are the possible negative consequences if we don't do what we know to be right? With our employees? Customers? Colleagues? Top management? *[Illicit specific reasons and consequences from the trainees.]* *[Point at Trustworthiness on the overhead transparency and read:]* **Trustworthiness:** FOI managers and staff are trustworthy and candid in supplying information and in correcting misapprehensions of fact. They do not create justifications for escaping their promises and commitments. Our employees can't trust us if we're not honest. Trustworthiness means that we're reliable; they can usually predict what we will do or what our response will be. And at FOI we want to make sure that what we do or how we respond is in keeping with the FOI Code of Conduct. A server gave a customer regular coffee instead of decaf because she didn't feel like making a fresh pot for one person. Stakeholders? Consequences?

(continued)

Step	Procedure	Trainer's Directions [trainer instruction in brackets]
	Go over the individual principles and discuss why each is important	*[Have everyone write down an example from their departments where trustworthiness was violated. Go over each example, having them identify the stakeholders and consequences. Write the answers on the board.]*

Why is it important to be trustworthy in our FOI management? What are the possible negative consequences if we are not trustworthy? With our employees? Customers? Colleagues? Top management?

[Illicit specific reasons and consequences from the trainees.]

[Go through the same steps for every principle on the FOI Code of Conduct: (1) state the principle, (2) give an example of the principle, (3) have everyone write down a personal example from their departments, (4) have them identify stakeholders and consequences, (5) have them state why the principle is important and the possible negative consequences for not adhering to it.]

Loyalty: FOI managers and staff demonstrate loyalty to the Freshwater Oasis Inn in devotion to duty and loyalty to colleagues by friendship in adversity. They avoid conflicts of interest; do not use or disclose confidential information; and, should they accept other employment, they respect the proprietary information of FOI.

When we are loyal we are trusting that the organization (or our boss) has our best interests at heart. If we don't trust the organization, our loyalty will most likely dissipate, and, along with it, the sense of belonging that makes us care about what we do. Trustworthiness inspires loyalty, and loyalty is the bond that holds organizations together so they can meet their goals. As managers, to be loyal to FOI means that we put the best interests of FOI ahead of our own selfish interests.

To be loyal to the company means that I wouldn't take a kickback from a supplier. My company can trust me to spend their money in the best way possible for the benefit of the company. Who are the stakeholders and the possible consequences to this example?

[Go through everyone's examples identifying stakeholders and consequences.]

Why is loyalty important in our FOI management? What are the possible negative consequences if we aren't loyal? With our employees? Customers? Colleagues? Top management? Why is it important for our employees to be loyal to us? To FOI? What makes an employee loyal?

[Illicit specific reasons and consequences from the trainees.]

Fairness: FOI managers and staff are fair and equitable in all dealings; they do not abuse power arbitrarily nor take undue advantage of another person's mistakes or difficulties. They treat all individuals with equality, with tolerance for and acceptance of diversity, and with an open mind.

(continued)

Step	Procedure	Trainer's Directions [trainer instruction in brackets]
	Go over the individual principles and discuss why each is important	How many times in our lives have we said, "That's not fair!" I think we all have a pretty good handle on the concept of fairness. Go ahead and write down departmental examples of fair/unfair and we'll go over them just like we have gone over the other principles on the Code of Conduct.

Concern and Respect for Others: FOI managers and staff are concerned, respectful, compassionate, and kind. They are sensitive to the personal concerns of their colleagues and live the "Golden Rule." They respect the rights and interest of all those who have a stake in their decisions.

What is the Golden Rule? *[Do unto others as you would have others do unto you.]* Are we getting into some kind of religion thing here? Why should this apply in business? Let's think of experiences we've had at FOI that might violate this principle. Go ahead and jot examples down and we'll go over them like the others.

Why is having concern and respect for others important in our FOI management? What are the possible negative consequences if we don't? With our employees? Customers? Colleagues? Top management? *[Illicit specific reasons and consequences from the trainees.]*

Commitment to Excellence: FOI managers and staff pursue excellence in performing their duties and are willing to put more into their job than they can get out of it.

We've all heard things like, "go the extra mile." In good organizations—ethical organizations—if we in management go the extra mile, we will get something out of it. What will we get? *[Promotion, pay raises, respect, more autonomy, other job options, etc.]* What will our own employees get from us if they go the extra mile?

Most of us have had bad job experiences where we've worked for a manager who didn't seem to appreciate our efforts, and, in fact, seemed to be threatened. Unless we were totally enlightened at the time and did our best work because we like to do our best work all the time, we may have felt resentful about not being appreciated. We may have wondered, "Why bother?"

Think about commitment to excellence and your experiences here at FOI. Write down anything that applies to this principle and we'll discuss your examples like we did for the other principles.

Why is having a commitment to excellence important in our FOI management? What are the possible negative consequences if we don't? With our employees? Customers? Colleagues? Top management? *[Illicit specific reasons and consequences from the trainees.]*

Leadership: FOI managers are conscious of the responsibility and opportunities of their position of leadership. They realize that the best way to instill ethical principles and ethical awareness in their organizations is by example. They walk their talk!

(continued)

Step	Procedure	Trainer's Directions [trainer instruction in brackets]
	Go over the individual principles and discuss why each is important	Our success as leaders depends on whether or not our employees will follow us! If they don't trust us, they won't follow us. If we don't do what we expect our employees to do, then they will see whatever it is as unimportant. Please jot down some examples of your leadership in your respective departments. Then we will go over all the examples and identify the stakeholders and possible negative consequences if you had not done what you did.
		Why is leadership important in our FOI management? What are the possible negative consequences if our employees don't trust our leadership? With our employees? Customers? Colleagues? Top management?
		[Illicit specific reasons and consequences from the trainees.]
		Reputation and Morale: FOI managers seek to protect and build Freshwater Oasis Inn's reputation and the morale of its employees by engaging in conduct that builds respect and by taking whatever actions are necessary to correct or prevent inappropriate conduct of others.
		What difference does it make to each of us what people think about FOI? Do you care? How does the reputation of FOI affect each of us? What about our employees? What about our ability to attract good employees? To retain them?
		What do you think your reputation is with your own employees? Don't worry, I'm not going to go around the group and make you tell! But think about it. Are you happy with what you think your reputation is? Why or why not? How does our reputation affect us with ourselves? People we meet? Colleagues? Our employees? Our boss?
		Write down personal work examples of reputation and morale problems. Then we will go through them all, identifying stakeholders and possible consequences.
		Why are reputation and morale important in our FOI management? What are the possible negative consequences if we have a bad reputation or morale is low? With our employees? Customers? Colleagues? Top management?
		[Illicit specific reasons and consequences from the trainees.]
		Accountability: FOI managers are personally accountable for the ethical quality of their decisions as well as those of their subordinates.
		John has started this whole ethics program because he understands that he is accountable for this entire operation and for what all of us do. In management we are responsible for everything that goes on in our departments and for how our departments relate to the other departments. I think we all want to be successful and to do good work. We take pride in what we do and how we do it, and it feels

(continued)

Step	Procedure	Trainer's Directions [trainer instruction in brackets]
	Go over the individual principles and discuss why each is important	good. It doesn't feel so good when we aren't doing real good work, when we are frustrated and constantly dealing with problems we may not know how to solve. Yet, we're still accountable.
4	State the consequences for failing to adhere to the code.	That's what this whole ethics program and the FOI Code of Conduct is about. John is taking responsibility for the actions of all of his employees and putting in place a program that will ensure that all of his employees know what is expected of them and how to do what is expected of them. John will be holding all of you accountable for your end of this program. If John cannot successfully manage FOI, he will ultimately quit or lose his job. And the same goes for all of us. If I do not design and present effective training, word will get around, and I will not be able to do this work anymore. Ethical decisions and behavior are now required at FOI. Unethical behavior is unacceptable. We are providing you with the knowledge and tools you will need to be able to meet this requirement. Through this program, John is ensuring that you will be better able to effectively run your departments, which makes your positions more secure and enjoyable.
5	Assignment and Quiz	We've covered a lot of material today, and I think you have a pretty good handle on the principles of the FOI Code of Conduct. As I said before, you need to know this code backwards and forwards because you have to lead your employees in it and will be held accountable for their behavior. Eric, how did you learn to cook so wonderfully? *[Eric will say something about school and practice.]* Most everything we do well takes lots of practice to get it to that level. And the same goes with this Code of Conduct. Folks, your assignment for next session can be found after all of the blank Ethics Analysis Forms in your notebook, is *[Wait till everyone is done gasping.]* For each of the 40 situations on the assignment, you are to determine which of the principles from the Code of Conduct are violated. There may be several for some of the situations. I want you to do your own work. Cheating on ethics homework is a most egregious sin! At any rate, when we get back together on Thursday, we'll go over all 40 of the situations and see if we agreed and why or why not. Your quiz will be in 2 weeks. You will be required to write out all ten principles and definitions on the FOI Code of Conduct. Yes, you have to memorize them! There are blank copies of the quiz in your notebooks so you can practice writing them out. As I said, you have to know these backwards and forwards.

(continued)

Step	Procedure	Trainer's Directions [trainer instruction in brackets]
	Assignment and Quiz	You will also have to discuss why the FOI Code of Conduct and the individual principles making up the code are important, and you should be aware of the consequences for not adhering to the Code.
Conclusion		Most of us are never too thrilled to be handed a list of rules we're supposed to follow. However, having the rules actually makes life a little easier. We don't have to ponder what to do every time. We can just follow the rules. Following the rules on the FOI Code of Conduct will result in better outcomes than not following the rules. We have looked at possible negative consequences and can avoid them by following the rules.
		John's goal with the FOI Ethics Program is for every FOI employee to follow all the rules on the FOI Code of Conduct. If we are all honest and trustworthy, concerned for each other and our guests, if we are all fair and loyal and doing our best work, won't this be a lovely place to work?
		I've enjoyed getting to know you today and look forward to Thursday. I'll be working in the main office here, so feel free to drop by and talk ethics with me! Thank you. John?
Closing		**John:** We have our work cut out for us, don't we? I can hardly wait to start memorizing these principles! I think this Code of Conduct can make a huge difference for all of us—make it better for all of us here at FOI. I am proud of the good work you do, and I want us to be able to grow personally and professionally, because it's good for each of us, and it's good for FOI. Thanks for your participation today, and we'll meet again on Thursday.

This completed lesson plan would be put in a three-ring binder along with the transparencies of the FOI Code of Conduct, a blank Ethics Analysis Form, the assignment key, and the contents of the handout notebook (which includes the FOI Code of Conduct, Blank Ethical Analysis Forms, the assignment, and several copies of the quiz). It would be necessary to develop the assignment and key. We have not included the materials in this lesson plan due to space limitations.

We go back to the objectives and note that all three have been addressed in the lesson plan. We will not know if the objectives have been met, however, until after the instruction has been delivered. We will do a trial run of the lesson to time it and make any necessary adjustments to the instruction. Once we have the lesson plans written we can implement the training, that is, the trainers can deliver the instruction to the trainees.

Training Evaluation

The purpose of **evaluation** is to improve the training and the training instruction. Evaluation (Step No. 6 in the Training Design Model) is as important as needs assessment. In *needs assessment* we figure out what the problem is and what training is required to solve it. In *evaluation* we figure out if the training we designed actually solved the problem. We design ways to determine how well the trainees liked the training, whether the trainees met the objectives of the training, and whether the training solved the original problem, which in the case of FOI was the lack of a shared sense of right and wrong behavior for FOI employees. Once we do the evaluation, we can then go back and correct any problems or disparities we found in the training as it was delivered to trainees.

Coaching and Counseling

Coaching and Counseling are the activities that make up supervision and are forms of ongoing training. In **coaching** we monitor the performance of our employees on the job and offer praise and/or give immediate corrective feedback to ensure that employees maintain the standards achieved in the original training. In **counseling** we meet with individual employees to help them seek solutions to problems that are interfering with their ability to maintain standards they achieved in the original training. It is beyond the scope of this text to sufficiently discuss implementation, evaluation, and coaching and counseling. (Students may be directed to our training design text listed in the References at the end of this chapter for a thorough discussion of these topics.)

CONCLUSION

Most of us know that training is important, but very few of us actually know how to design it. Some of us may still be relying on the mostly ineffective shadow method, which is definitely not a good method choice for teaching our employees to behave ethically. The behavior we as managers model is, of course, very influential, but it is more efficient to design ethics training than to rely on a natural socialization process.

In Chapter 14, we determined the training topics through needs assessment and put together a preliminary training plan. In this chapter, we developed a lesson plan for the first training topic: Introduction of the FOI Code of Conduct for Managers and Staff, why it is important, and the consequences for failing to adhere to it. This is not a training design textbook, so the treatment we have given the design process in these two chapters is superficial. It merely points students in the proper design direction.

Training topics 2 and 3 (how to identify ethical dilemmas and determine solutions) would be developed using the same training design model. We would also have to design training for the managers to train them how to train their own employees. Designing training is not particularly difficult; it is, however, tedious and very time-consuming. Professional managers reduce risks and leave little to chance. Well-designed formal ethics training can give our employees the tools enabling them to make ethical decisions on the job. This is good for the operation, the managers, the employees, and our guests.

KEY WORDS

Formal Training	Evaluation
Psychomotor	Coaching
Attitudinal	Counseling
Lesson Plan	

CHAPTER THOUGHT QUESTIONS

1. Compare and contrast formal and informal training. Why is formal training usually better than informal training? Which type of training have you experienced in jobs you have held? Could the training you received have been improved? How?

2. Most of the training we do in the hospitality industry is for psychomotor skills. Explain how training in ethics is different. Discuss the importance of managers modeling ethical behavior and explain why it is also necessary to have ethics training.

3. What are lesson plans, why are they important, and how and why are they used in training?

4. Discuss why most managers do not know how to design formal training. What effect can this management skill gap have on hospitality operations? How can this gap be closed?

5. In Chapter 14 we included a list of Adult Learning Principles. Go through the lesson plan for Topic 1 (Introduction of the FOI Code of Conduct for

Managers and Staff) and identify where particular Adult Learning Principles are addressed throughout the lesson plan.

6. Itemize and discuss how the objective for training Topic 1 was utilized and addressed in the lesson plan.

7. In all your college experience, have you been aware of lesson plans being used by your instructors? Do you think they use them? Why would it be beneficial for your instructors to use lesson plans? Why might they not use them? What are possible negative consequences for instructors and students if instructors do not use lesson plans?

8. What three outcomes do we evaluate when we evaluate training? Why are these three outcomes important, and how might you evaluate them?

9. What is the purpose of training evaluation and why is it important? What can happen if we do not bother to evaluate the training?

10. Describe the supervision you have experienced on jobs you have held. Discuss coaching and counseling, what they are, why they are important, and if and how managers you have worked for utilized them.

REFERENCES

Jaszay, C. (2002). Teaching ethics in hospitality programs. *Journal of Hospitality and Tourism Education, 14*(3), 58–63.

Jaszay, C., & Dunk, P. (2003). *Training design for the hospitality industry.* New York: Delmar.

Conclusion

Civilized people follow ethical rules. Less attention has been given to teaching the rules in many homes and schools. As the ethical rules fall by the wayside, our society becomes less civilized. We cannot trust that those we deal with will not hurt us in some way. We become less cooperative, and life becomes more difficult. When everyone else is "looking out for number one," we are somewhat forced into that same mentality in order to survive in a "dog-eat-dog" world.

We all have the same basic needs to survive—food, water, shelter, and so forth. Unfortunately, these necessities are not equally accessible to everyone. While we can fight for our share, none of us are individually strong enough to prevail if others band together in an effort to take more than what is rightfully theirs. Thus, we are left without. While some kind souls might share with us, counting on such generosity may be risky.

In a utopian world, life should get easier and not more difficult as a society advances. If individuals decide to organize and cooperate, they can agree to work together to produce enough goods and then distribute them equitably without harm to each other. In this way, societies are formed where everyone is better off. Enforceable rules are agreed upon that allow us to live together cooperatively. These rules revolve around the application of ethics to life's situations.

We instinctually seek security in order to survive. While the sentiments of self-defense and revenge are very strong, we as human beings are capable of sympathy and understanding the benefit of being part of a larger community. Within this larger community, individuals have rights that must be agreed upon and protected by society in order to provide the security we all find essential. Because we do not always agree on these standards, the only way to decide may be by simply determining what is best for the most people.

We agree to give up what may be personally desirable for the general welfare of the larger community, because it is ultimately individually better to live in a safe society where rights are protected equally and impartially. If there is a conflict between the individual and society, we agree in advance to opt for the greatest good for the most people.

Ethics, then, are rules that control or guide how we are to treat one another. They are mutually beneficial rules we agree to accept and follow. At times, the application of ethics in the decision-making process requires that we opt in favor of others over ourselves, but this process ultimately results in a civilized society where we are safe and can live and grow beyond mere survival.

It is not in our best interest as individuals, or as leaders in the hospitality industry, to work outside of or against the community to get ahead.

Those of us who are older may have learned many lessons the hard way. Painful consequences of decisions we made in the past may have taught us to make better decisions in the present. As young people we sometimes do not realize the long-term ramifications of our seemingly unimportant actions. Our elders perhaps taught us some system of ethical rules, but, when asked why we should follow them, maybe their answer was, "Because I said so." On looking back we know that we would have been much better off had we just followed them. Most of us, however, are less apt to respond to orders and insist on learning the hard way, which is why we have tried to provide students with a more persuasive reason for following the rules.

We presented the Ethical Principles for Hospitality Managers and applied them to numerous situations that occur in the hospitality industry. We analyzed situation after situation, discovering that the consequences for following the rules were almost always the least painful for the most stakeholders. We have shown again and again that honesty is the best policy, that right makes might, and that it is better to follow the rules than to not follow the rules.

We have provided students practice with a tool they can utilize to analyze decision options and their possible outcomes, all with an eye toward making decisions resulting in the best outcomes for the most parties. If we can know, accept, and agree to the rules up front, it is easier to just follow them, saving the analysis for less obvious situations. Our purpose with this text was to alleviate the painful learning curve, which has a detrimental effect on the health of our industry and our country overall. We have shown through the analysis process that following the rules results in better outcomes for all parties involved.

Ethics are probably best taught to children by parents through their actions and words. We have lost the shared ethics of a couple generations ago, however, and many of today's parents simply do not know the rules, have learned through adversity to fudge the rules, or they are just too overworked and tired to share these rules with their children. So, we may not have been taught to be ethical when we were children. In time, most of us will parent our own children. How are we to teach them things we may not know ourselves?

This textbook is a means of incorporating realistic, practical ethics education into university hospitality programs. For those of us who were not adequately schooled by our parents in ethics, or who may have been beaten into a survival mode by life, analysis of the dilemmas in the case study allow us to discover or rediscover the personal and corporate benefits of following the ethical rules. We are provided examples of situations we may find ourselves in when we are managers. We are given the opportunity to think through the possible decision options in advance so that we are prepared and not surprised when we are one of the players and it is real life.

To successfully follow the ethical rules in management requires that we have the social and behavioral skills that make such an endeavor possible. We must be able to know and understand ourselves and others, be able to communicate effectively with them, and we must take good care of ourselves so that we can be at our best. Ethics do not work by themselves. In management, arrogance or social ineptness do not mix with the successful application of ethics, and that is why we addressed topics such as civility, courtesy, humility, and diversity.

As managers, we need not only to be ethical ourselves, but we must also effectively communicate our ethical expectations to employees. We must train them how to meet our expectations in every situation that they may encounter while doing their jobs. With management comes many responsibilities, and hospitality graduates must be prepared to meet these responsibilities. Chapters 14 and 15 dealt with developing ethics programs and training for our employees that gives us the tools to make our ethical expectations reality in our workplaces.

While some of us may not follow the ethical rules ourselves, we certainly like for everyone else to follow ethical rules. We want to be able to trust the people and companies we do business with, our neighbors, our teachers, the government, and so forth. Unless we make the first move and do something different, though, nothing will change—and our society is in dire need of change.

We cannot wait for society to change and become ethical before we do so ourselves. It will most likely not occur unless someone takes the first step. We must become ethical and then teach our children to be ethical. As managers in the hospitality industry, we must also teach our workers to be ethical. They probably have or will have children too. It sounds overly simplistic, but in this way we can and will change society. We are the biggest industry in the country. There are over 500 university hospitality programs in the United States. Each semester thousands of hospitality graduates go into hospitality management. We can have a profound effect on all of the people working in our industry, and all of the people who support our industry by their patronage. Hospitality managers today must be leaders.

REFERENCES

Dosick, W. (1995). *Golden rules: The ten ethical values parents need to teach their children.* New York: HarperCollins.

Mill, J. S. (1979). *Utilitarianism.* Indianapolis, IN: Hackett.

Rachels, J. (1999). *The elements of moral philosophy.* Boston: McGraw-Hill.

Case Study

Freshwater Oasis Inn

By Paul Dunk

Case Study Contents

The Freshwater Oasis Inn (FOI) is a fictitious 100-room, full-service hotel. Our target market is upper-middle-class professionals who expect excellent service within a quiet, safe, and attractive setting.

FOI is located in Copper Hills, Arizona, just 20 minutes from Phoenix International Airport. Despite being newly constructed, great pains were taken to give the hotel an Old Southwest kind of feel while incorporating the best that modern technology has to offer. Professionally landscaped gardens overlook the rugged desert from most vantage points on the premises. The *Lobby* is spacious with white painted adobe walls and vaulted ceilings. Highly polished sandstone covers the lobby floor and is continued on the surface of the Front Desk. Nearby, the *Sitting Room* welcomes guests with comfortable overstuffed chairs and a large stone fireplace. Guests and visitors feel at home in this relaxed atmosphere. The *Oasis Lounge* is adjacent to the Sitting Room and provides beautiful garden views while offering a wide range of liquid refreshments, including our own private-label draft beers. An abbreviated menu is available from which guests can order appetizers or sandwiches while the kitchen is open.

A breakfast buffet featuring fresh fruits and home-baked pastries, along with cooked-to-order eggs, is served each morning in the *Garden Vista*. Weather permitting, a wall of Spanish-style arched doors can be opened ushering in the soothing sounds of nature: water fountains, birds, and softly rustling leaves. Lunch is served either inside or on the patio where wrought-iron tables and chairs surround a meandering pool stocked with goldfish. Chef Eric prepares healthful, eye-catching dishes selected to delight our guests' palates and please their sensibilities. In the evening, the Garden Vista is filled with fresh flowers while small antique candelabras are lit on each table to set the mood. There are separate lunch and dinner menus, as well as daily specials with a Southwestern flare.

FOI has state-of-the-art audio/visual equipment and conference facilities perfect for small- to medium-size groups. The patio is enchanting for weddings or special events. Weather permitting, there is a large in-ground pool for guests, with a lifeguard on duty. Amenities provided in each room include a TV, small refrigerator with mini-bar, hair dryer, BOSE radio, and Internet access. There is a safe in each room for guests' valuables, and, for a small charge, housekeeping will take care of their dry-cleaning needs. FOI provides agreeable accommodations for business travel or just an appealing time-out from the day's routine.

ORGANIZATIONAL CHART

General Manager: John Fallin, 41, was hired 6 years ago to open and manage FOI. He has a master's degree in business and for 10 years was food and beverage manager for a large, successful hotel in Los Angeles. His experience, combined with a refreshing vision for the inn, convinced owner Frank Stratten that John could make his business a success. As part of his contract, John has the opportunity to make a year-end bonus based on job performance and occupancy rates.

John compensated for his lack of comprehensive experience by hiring excellent people in top management positions. His emphasis is on FOI as a team. He allows them a certain amount of autonomy but provides guidance to ensure that the needs of the target market are met. His mantra is that managers be courteous, caring, and professional.

Assistant General Manager: Heidi Bell, 32, has been with John since opening. She has worked nearly every job in the hotel business over the past 14 years. Her last position was front desk manager at the elegant Bennett Arms downtown. Heidi felt her lack of formal education, however, was limiting her career and believed that FOI offered more responsibility, autonomy, and potential.

Front Desk Manager: Gabe Deflores, 26, has a degree in sociology but grew restless after 3 years in urban social services. He worked the front desk at two major hotels before coming to FOI. He supervises the AM and PM front desk employees and the night auditor.

Dining Room Manager: Tony Marziano, 31, began waiting tables at FOI 5 years ago. He has been supervising waitstaff the past 2 years. In addition to scheduling servers, he is also in charge of the host/hostesses and splits time between both positions.

Bar Manager: Mike Scales, 24, opened FOI as a server and moved behind the bar a year later. He was promoted 2 years ago and manages a staff of four along with his duties of inventory and ordering.

Bookkeeper: Edna Duncan, 57, is a close friend of Frank's who worked as a CPA at a major firm 25 years before embracing semi-retirement. Her limited duties at FOI amount to roughly 20 hours a week.

Executive Chef: Eric Altman, 39, received training at the Culinary Institute of Chicago and has worked some of the country's top hotels and restaurants. He wanted stability and less stress in a smaller operation and has been content at FOI these past 5 years. Similar to John's contract with Frank, Paul is also eligible for a year-end bonus based on performance and restaurant sales. He is responsible for all foodservice activities and supervises cooks and dishwashers on the day shift.

Sous Chef: Dardina Traylor, 22, was hired by Chef Eric 4 years ago to wash dishes. She began helping him with prep and soon moved into that position full time. She has been in formal training under Chef Eric these past 2 years and was recently promoted to Sous Chef. Part of her responsibilities is to supervise cooks and dishwashers in the evening shift.

Executive Housekeeper: Kathy Lawhorn, 26, completed her hospitality degree and worked 3 years at a large hotel chain before coming to FOI. Kathy supervises housekeeping and the in-house laundry/dry-cleaning staff.

Chief Engineer: Bill Gardner, 53, worked 15 years as an assistant engineer at a high-rise apartment building in Phoenix. After completing union school and getting his license, Bill came to work for FOI at the hotel's opening. In addition to supervising a maintenance staff of four, he is also responsible for maintaining the in-ground pool and scheduling lifeguards.

STAFF DIRECTORY

Owner: Frank Stratten

General Manager: John Fallin

Assistant General Manager: Heidi Bell

Business Manager: Lex Lilly
Bookkeeper: Edna Duncan/Sheri Eggmeyer

Building Engineer: Bill Gardner
Maintenance Employees: Donny and Milt

Executive Housekeeper: Kathy Lawhorn
Housekeeping Staff: Maria, Trini, Claudia, and Lucy

Front Desk Manager: Gabe DeFlores
Front Desk Staff: Rod, Jim, Ellen, and Molly
Bellboy: Kip

Executive Chef: Eric Altman
Kitchen Employee: (Sous Chef) Dardina Traylor

Headwaiter: Tony Marziano
Dining Room Staff: (Servers) Kelly and Raul, (Busser) Jimmy, (Host) Tony

Head Bartender: Mike Scales
Bar Staff: Eddie, Floyd, Chip, Billy, and Kate

INTRODUCTION

It wasn't so much the building. No, it was the bodies, ghosts and otherwise, that filtered through it. Six years is ample time for a hotel that size, 100 rooms, to store up memories. People coming and going all the while. The American Southwest, a city called Copper Hills, just 20 minutes from the airport in Phoenix. Frank Stratten owned every stick of it, put together by artisans known in the immediate vicinity and some even around the world. Like the architect who designed the structure itself, 8 years back, when all that existed of *Freshwater Oasis Inn* was desert and cacti and rattlesnakes. That same man was responsible for the new *Hotel Salzburg* in, well, Salzburg.

That's Austria.

He was floating around there somewhere. Jan Lesniak. The famous architect. Inside the adobe walls and skittering across a smoothly polished sandstone lobby floor. The vaulted ceilings and arched doorways Jan molded into a subtle nuance of the Southwest of yore in his mind. Though that was mainly a teepee, of course, even *he* knew that, but nobody pays to spend the night in a bison-hide funnel. People need things like Internet access, BOSE radios, and small fridges with mini-bars now. Dry-cleaning service and round-the-clock maintenance and lifeguards watching the in-ground pool in case guests drink too much and can't float anymore. People are needy, and Jan designed the guts of the thing that'd serve them. How many others had passed through during the mere 6 years of the inn's existence? Lots of bodies—customers, employees. Thousands of people, each with their individual quirks and needs and wants. After all, people are in essence needy. Players need certain things and workers are there to serve.

Lots of employees are required to staff a hotel that size. Some stay awhile, some go. The most difficult task of a general manager is just to keep the card house standing. John Fallin was one of Frank's first hires, and the most important. He was 35 years old back then and had received his master's degree from the business program at Stanford. School seemed so long ago now. Back when Ronald Reagan was touting the miracle of trickle-down economics and tattoos were some faded blue nonsense you saw occasionally on the arms of ancient sailors. A different time, indeed. He'd paid tuition those days by working nights in the service industry, then decided he liked it and worked his way up to food & beverage manager for a large, successful hotel in Los Angeles. Stayed there 10 years. That experience, combined with a refreshing vision for the inn, convinced Frank that John could make his business a success.

Before construction was even completed, before the first plant had been situated in what would become the famous Freshwater Oasis Inn gardens, before any of this tinsel was even in place, John Fallin was putting in long hours staffing the rest of the joint.

John stood in the lobby now, 6 years later, and took it all in. There was his first hire, Heidi Bell, breezing in for the evening shift. John always tried to be present there in the lobby for the changing of the guard as it were. Good ol' Heidi. He'd stolen her from the Bennett Arms over on Interstate 17. He'd stayed there while the hotel was under construction. Left the towels, but took the front desk manager. Promised Heidi the assistant general manager position and she blossomed in it. Saved his butt more than once.

It hadn't really been that much of a gamble hiring someone like Heidi. She'd started out in the industry as a server before she could even sell booze legally. Working at an American Legion doing the Friday Fish Fry at the age of 14. She'd done just about every position there was, and what she didn't know about management John figured he could teach her in the months preceding opening day. It'd been a smart move.

Gabe Deflores. Heidi's the one who found him, three years ago at a seminar in Tucson. He was managing the front desk at a Hilton out by the airport. Sat next to Heidi during this tedious lecture on ethics. The speaker, some diminutive troll in a cheap brown suit. Gabe kept rolling his eyes and finally turned to her, said in her ear, "Y'know, I'd take this guy a lot more seriously if he didn't look like George Costanza, y'know, the fat bald guy used to be on *Seinfeld?* Feel like he's tryin' to sell me some bad chicken." They talked in the bar afterwards and hit it off. FOI had tried three different bodies in the position before Gabe came on board, but none of them stuck. Finding Gabe was a godsend. Kind of silly, though, at times. Wasn't necessarily a drawback. Could always count on Gabe for a chuckle when things looked bleak.

Had a degree in Sociology. Taught teenagers about childrearing before switching careers. Told John during the interview that he quit one day when it dawned on him that children shouldn't be having children, and that he really didn't even care for them in the first place. Pretty amusing fellow, that Gabe Deflores. It was almost quitting time. One of the things John liked about his job was the fact that many of his duties involved merely being *waited on.* Quality control. How does one check the quality of a restaurant? It's easy. You sit on a comfy chair in the dining room. Sure, things could get dicey at times, and he was essentially just a babysitter, but sitting down to a free dinner and calling it "work" was, well, it was a powerful lot better than snaking sewer drains.

Snaking sewer drains. Thank God for college.

He crossed the sandstone and headed for the Garden Vista. Saw Tony Marziano by the podium getting the special menus together for that night's shift meeting. He was the head waiter. Tony Baloney's what Heidi referred to him as. Killer waiter, though. Also worked the podium on weekends and did all the scheduling for the hosts. A man of many hats. Standing there with Chef Eric getting the lowdown on roast duck. There'd been a time John waited tables, years ago. Couldn't say he missed it much. Always felt like a moron approaching a new table. As if he were more likely there to measure the stiffs for coffins than serve them dinner. Or like that butler on the Adams Family: *You rang?* Just didn't look the part. But Tony Baloney, he was a natural.

Eric saw John and nodded. Wasn't any baloney about Eric Altman. Trained at the Culinary Institute of Chicago. Was like some kind of Macgyver in reverse. You could give him a block of C4 and he'd whip it into pate in 18 seconds. Dude was a wizard. Worked at the Four Seasons there in Chicago but didn't care for the pressure anymore, or the winters for that matter, and lucky for FOI. Frank took care of him, though. Had the same year-end bonus deal as John did. Head Chef was a key position for a hotel like FOI. You couldn't just hire some boob off the street. Clichés applied. Like the one says you get what you pay for. It was true.

John went out on the deserted patio and took a seat by the pool. Goldfish swam around and a fountain stirred shadows on the water's surface. The sun was about to drop in it too, all gold and afire in a bizarre purple and red Southwestern sky. The duck sounded good. Soon as Eric gave his spiel to the assembled servers he'd bring a plate out for him. Always ate the specials. Every day.

Life was good.

SWIM-UP POOL FRANK

It was just after the Maricopa County sewer system processed the last residue of digested turkeys, late November something or other, a Tuesday, and Frank Stratten was in the building. Least that's what Gabe hipped him onto—well, not really *in* the building—more accurately, he was out by the pool in a steady drizzle. Least that's what Kathy told Gabe. She'd seen him out there with hands on hips, just staring at the south end of the pool. Thought he'd gone nuts.

As John got closer to the doors, the ones in the rear that led onto the pool deck, he began to wonder if maybe Gabe was playing a joke on him or something. Which wasn't a good idea the way he felt that morning. So dreary outside, *again*. Frank was supposed to be in Huatulco, Mexico, getting a tan. Got a postcard last week from Cozumel where the yacht'd docked for a couple days, taking on supplies. All it said on it was: *"How's the weather? I'm in my SWIM-SUIT right now, drinking a MAI TAI! See ya NEXT MONTH! HA HA HA! ADIOS!!!"*

Thanks, Frank.

How's the weather? Well, it sucked, and that's why it wasn't a good idea for Gabe to be playing jokes on him. Frank must've been reading the weather reports in *USA Today*. Five days since last they'd seen the sun. Forty-five degrees, tops. This was the busy season, and business was tanked. He came to the doors and two of the maintenance guys were standing just inside, intently watching something on the deck.

John inquired, "Hey, guys? What's goin' on here?"

Milt, the one nearest, with the stutter: "It's F-F-F-F-F-F-Frank! He's by the pool! T-T-T-T-T-T-T-Talkin' to Bill."

By the third 'T' on *talking*, John could see for himself.

"Well, go figure," he said.

Frank *was* out there, and Bill Gardner was there with him. Kind of comical. Frank, oblivious to the rain, all golden brown, gesticulating wildly, and lanky ol' Bill Gardner next to him in his gray outfit with an arm raised shielding Navy-issue glasses from the bizarre chilly drizzle. Nodding every once in a while. Like a cat some kid was splashing, wanting to be anywhere else but there.

"What're they doin'?"

"Got me," admitted Donny, the other maintenance guy.

"It's r-r-r-r-r-r-rainin'."

John patted Milt on the back. "Yeah," he said, opening the door and stepping into it, "Don't I know it."

John ran out there in his $800 black suit and hoped whatever bug'd crawled up Frank's butt, y'know, back on the Yucatan coast, would crawl back out of it before long and the jacket soaked through to the silk shirt, etc., etc., etc., and then he'd hafta walk around the next hour or so drying off.

"Jeez, Frank," he hollered. "What're you nuts doin' out here?"

Winter was their best time of year. Sure, it got down at night, but days were usually 70 or so degrees. Something weird with that global warming business, John figured, making everything *colder*. Huh? Didn't make sense. Golfers sitting around the lounge all day, looking sullen. Ordering Long Islands. Needed parkas on a day like this. Insulated. Keeping the icy drizzle out. Like John's expensive coat, but made to withstand it. Frank didn't hear the question, yet turned when he heard John's Italian loafers pattering across the sandstone deck.

Frank roared, "Johnny, me-boy! Glad you could join the party!"

John got over there and shook Frank's outstretched hand.

"Welcome home, Frank. What're ya doin' back so soon? Thought you were gonna be in Huatulco till the end of the month."

Bill Gardner was in the background and rolled his eyes at John, like as if to explain, the rain all beaded up on his lenses: *The big cheese has lost his mind, boss. That's what it is. That's why.*

"I'm goin' back soon as I get the ball rollin' here, Johnny."

John felt silk clinging to his shoulders.

"What ball, Frank?"

Frank crossed arms and rocked back on his heels. Sandals, actually. Flat. Had on a Hawaiian shirt over khaki shorts, like he'd just stepped off the pineapple boat. Paused for a long drizzly moment. Unawares of the rain. There was a crack of thunder and it picked up. Wasn't drizzle anymore—it was a storm. Started pouring. Sheets.

Good grief. What happened to the drought?

Bill Gardner moved back further behind Frank and made the loony sign, by his left ear, twirling a finger.

Frank finally said, "Ever been to a *swim-up . . . pool bar?*"

"What?"

Frank turned to Bill real quick then and almost caught him making the international this-guy's-a-nut sign. Bill pretended he was unplugging his ear, though, and Frank boomed, "Show the man what I'm talkin' about, Señor Gardner."

Bill's heart wasn't in this at all.

"It's a ground-level bar attached to the pool," he droned. The engineer started moving around in the downpour, pointing here and there as he talked. He was soaked to the bone. "Well, it's actually below ground level, y'know, if ya wanna get technical. We could excavate here and build the fixtures and stuff, then install some stools there in the pool—"

John made a face and turned to Frank.

"I know what a swim-up pool bar is, Frank. Can we talk about this inside?"

It was a week later and the ball was rolling. Actually wasn't a bad idea when considered out of the rain. In dry clothes. Apparently Frank'd stayed at a hotel in Huatulco that had a swim-up pool bar. Fell in love with it. Sitting on a stool in water up to his belly. Drinking shots of tequila and chatting with Juan the bartender.

"And he's dry," Frank had laughed. *"Just standing there, tending bar! Like it's just another day. And you're in the pool, Johnny!"*

He'd felt at the time like he *was* in the pool.

Frank was a character. Always had been, always would. It'd gotten worse over the years, though. Left his wife a couple Augusts ago. Married 25 years. Kids in college or done with it. Was going through some sort of midlife crisis, Frank was. Got a tattoo on his right arm looked like a bar code. Swipe it at the checkout line and it rings up a meatball. Jeez. John hoped it didn't happen to him one day. Couldn't afford it like Frank could. The pool idea was pretty good, though, regardless of Frank's ex-wife feeling used up and thrown away. Poor woman. John'd spent a lot of time with the couple socially before the sudden breakup. Anna. Felt bad for her. Pool idea was killer, though. If they could just get the stupid building permit.

He sat across from Sam Riley in the Oasis Lounge. He was an inspector from the city. In charge of, well, *inspecting*. John still couldn't figure out just exactly what it was Mr. Riley actually did. He'd gone downtown and applied for the permit, and three days later this guy shows up. Inspecting. They'd been out back by the pool, John showing him around, but now the party'd moved indoors and the man was making a big show of analyzing blueprints for the in-ground bar. Looked like he didn't know a blueprint from an arrow to the men's bathroom.

"I dunno, Mr. Fallin. This could be a problem."

Tony Marziano came up with their lunch orders. Riley'd gotten the 16 oz. T-bone, and John was having just a spinach salad.

John said, "Huh?"

"Ah," mused Riley, sniffing the charbroiled beef as the waiter set a platter in front of him. "Looks good enough to eat, son! Tony, right?"

The waiter smiled at him, but John could tell right off the bat that Sam Riley wasn't Tony Marziano's cup of tea.

"Yes, sir. Enjoy."

The man raised his empty rocks glass and rattled the ice around. "Another V.O., *Tone.*"

Tony took the glass, nodded, and went away toward the bar. For the fifth time. Fuming in his soul.

John persisted, not caring much for spinach anyway.

"What problem?"

"Be patient, John. Let's not spoil the meal with business talk. There'll be plenty of time for that later."

He winked and dug in on the T-bone.

"I couldn't believe it," John hissed, through clenched teeth. He had a pencil in his hand and was rapping the eraser end on top of his desk. "The scumbag!"

He was in the office with Heidi who'd just arrived for the night shift.

"What're we gonna do?" she asked. "What *can* we do?"

Tap tap tap tap tap tap tap.

"The audacity!"

They'd just wrapped up lunch earlier when that city inspector, Sam Riley, walked with him toward the revolving lobby doors, put an arm around John, and laid it all out on the line.

"We can get around these snaggles with the permits, John. I've done it before. Plenty-a times. But these permits, John, they can get bogged down in paperwork for months. I seen it happen. Just need a little grease to get things movin'."

"Uh-huh?"

"Like my oldest daughter. Thirteen next week. Needs braces, John. I don't make that kind-a dough workin' for the city, not like you fancy-pants newcomers. Hell, look at this place. What's that, marble?"

"What're you getting at, Mr. Riley?"

"Five hundred dollars, John. Have it on my desk Monday morning. You'll be breakin' ground by Tuesday. Man, whadaya think about this weather? It's like

stinkin' Chicago! Went there once when I was in the Navy, '67. You ever serve in the military, John?"

Heidi sat with John in the office and looked at the man's business card. Had the official seal printed on top and then the name and his title and all that jazz underneath.

"Says he's a 'Building Inspector.' Hmmmm: Sam Riley. What's the guy look like?"

John peered up from the desk. Made a face.

"Who cares what he looks like? He looks like a wood tick. Jeez, Heidi. Who gives a damn what he looks like?"

Heidi shook her head and set the card down.

After a couple seconds, she said, "Well, what're we gonna do?"

TONY MARZIANO AND THE INFAMOUS DOUBLE TIP

Tony had a nine-top in the Garden Vista room on a Thursday, his best night for waiting tables. Bunch-a mopes from some backwater in the desert or something. He couldn't remember exactly where it was they came from. Probably some adobe huts next to one of those big cacti. Nice mopes, though, for the most part.

Visiting the inn for some conference he couldn't remember either. They'd told him about it when he'd approached first thing and got their drink orders. He was weird that way. Names were a mystery. People and places. Could remember their faces and cocktails and their entrée preferences—and whether or not they liked sour cream on their baked potatoes—5 years later, y'know, but ask him what their names were and it's all a blank. Probably some kind of psychological problem, he figured.

Never got enough love as a child.

It'd been dreadfully slow that night. Eight-thirty already and he'd only had three tables. Two of them ordered iced tea despite Tony's lonely heart screaming for Dom. This nine-top was a godsend. All of them, drinkers. Top-shelf cocktails before and wine later with the meal. Steaks and fish. Dessert. Coffee. His kind-a people.

They weren't mopes at all. What'd he been thinking?

They were Christ and his eight dinner guests. Tony's *last supper* for the night. The difference between walking with $40 bucks and well over a c-note. He almost wanted to kiss them when he brought the check afterwards as Jimmy the busboy refilled their coffee cups. The bill came to over $700 and parties over eight meant an automatic 18% tip, plus anything on top of that if they were pleased with the service. Which they were. Tony was good and he knew it.

"You folks sure I can't get ya anything else?" he asked, smiling, cradling the leatherette check folder in his hands. "Maybe an aperitif? A cactus frond?"

They all laughed. Tony had them in his hands. The one who'd obviously been the big cheese held his mitt out for the bill.

"No, Tony," he smiled. "I think we've had quite enough. Early day to-morrow, y'know. You've been great though."

Tony returned the smile.

"Well, thank you very much, sir."

He turned to leave as the man rooted in the breast pocket of his jacket for a wallet. Looked like cashmere, the jacket that is.

"I'll be back for this in a minute."

Tony felt bad about not remembering the guy's name as he tidied up some plates and ramekins in the bus station. Jimmy'd not gotten around to transferring them to the tub under the counter. He looked over and the kid was busy clearing plates from one of Kelly's tables. He was turning 21 next month and angling for a promotion to server, concentrating a little more than he should on things like pouring coffee and chatting up the customers. He made a mental note to talk to the kid about it later. Reminded Tony of himself at that age. Couldn't blame him, really.

Tony liked the added responsibility of his position but sometimes resented the fact he lost out on weekend shifts. That's where the big money was, and working the host podium those nights took a big bite from what he was used to making. It was all about the future, though. That all-important resumé.

He wiped his hands on a towel and glanced at the table where Mr. Big had situated his credit card out the top of the check holder. Tony walked over and smiled, picking it up.

"I'll be right back, sir."

He went to the service bar and had Mike run the charge, then returned it to El Queso Grande with a pen. He noted one of the ladies in the party had finished her coffee and asked if she'd like a refill, or if anybody else needed anything. She declined, as did the rest, and the party seemed completely satisfied.

"Well, okay, then," he said to The Man, and, then, in his best Arnold Whatshisname voice: "I'll be back."

More laughter. God, he was good.

Tony saw Heidi, the assistant general manager, standing by the podium and went over and talked a minute about the covers they'd done thus far. It was a weird time of the year for the service industry, the month and a half going from just before Thanksgiving to the second week of January. Hard to gauge, really. Some days people stayed at home and roosted. Other days they engorged themselves with holiday cheer. It encompassed the time before credit card bills started trickling in, and the time immediately after. On this day, however, it had appeared to Tony that the "roosting" phenomenon was occurring, and—Tony had no control over things like that—but, for what business they had, Tony was confident they'd done a bang-up job. He'd gotten that impression from every customer he'd observed in the restaurant. No complaints. Just smiles. Everybody laughing and carrying on.

He'd developed a refined peripheral vision in his years as waiter and detected the credit card voucher'd been filled out. He excused himself and went over and collected it, thanking all and inviting them back to FOI for a repeat performance. They were very happy as he left.

Back at the bus station, Tony opened the check holder and saw a figure of $80 written on the voucher's tip line. There was a smiley face next to it and the wheels began to spin in his head. The tip was always included for parties of eight or more—it was clearly stated on the menu. He never mentioned it when approaching a table because it was *that* obvious, and talking about his tip was rather presumptuous. Big, bold letters on the menu's bottom. Eighteen percent; two percent less than the norm. He always hoped for additional tippage if customers felt they'd been treated well, but *eighty bucks?* On the other hand, if that was the tip it wasn't even 10 percent! Were they mopes after all? Could he have been *that* wrong?

The smiley face, though: was the eighty bucks *extra?*

It leered at him.

$80 TAKES ON A LIFE OF ITS OWN

The smiley face. It was quarter of nine and he'd probably not be getting another seating by the looks of things. Tony glanced up from the tip folder and Jimmy the busboy'd dropped some dirty dishes into the bus tub and was making for the coffeepot on the hot plate.

"What're *you* doin'?" Tony asked him.

Jimmy looked confused.

He went, "Huh?"

The dining room manager smiled.

"Listen, Jimmy. I appreciate your help with the coffee and all—when we're *busy*—but when I'm standin' around twiddlin' my thumbs, y'know, things like pouring coffee are *my* responsibilities. You just worry about clearing tables and keeping the bus station clean. Comprendo?"

"But the lady needs a refill. I just thought—"

"*What* lady?"

"On your nine-top; Kathryn."

Kathryn? Who on earth was Kathryn? The kid was on a first-name basis with his customers. Tony could hardly even remember his own name, much less anybody else's.

Tony smirked, "Oh, *Kathryn*, ya say."

"Yeah."

Tony grabbed the coffeepot and started over, then turned back to address his busboy.

"Listen, you let me take care of *Kathryn*. That's why I make the big bucks. You just clear the plates, Laddy."

The busboy watched him walk off and seethed. *You just clear the plates, Laddy.* What a jerk. Jimmy knew he could be a better waiter than that guy. All he needed was a chance. In a month he'd be 21. Tony was glad-handing the nine-top. *Dining room manager. Hah. Tony was nothin' but a waiter who sat people on the weekends.* Jimmy saw the check folder lying open on the station counter and peeked at the completed charge. He saw the smiley face and the $80 tip.

"Well, well," he mused. "What do we have here?"

He knew all about the automatic tip on parties of eight or more. Seemed like Tony-baloney was up to his ears in deceit. Fleecing those rubes from Prescott. He noticed that the charge hadn't been closed out yet and busied himself with cleaning the station till the waiter finished pouring coffee and came back and picked it up. He watched him heading for the service bar and smiled. The guy was a thief. Ripping those people off. Cashing out the $80 with good ol' Mike who was obviously in on it too.

Couple minutes later he was standing in the bus station when Tony came back whistling and went about making an iced tea for himself. Jimmy folded his arms.

"Well, Tony, my man. That was a mighty nice tip there on that nine-top. Eighty bucks, plus the 18%. Sure beats a stick in the eye."

Tony gave him a sideways look as he stirred eight sugar packets into his tea with a long soda spoon.

"Sure does," he said, grabbing a lemon wedge.

Then Jimmy winked at him and went, "Hey, so next month I'm 21. Who'll be trainin' me?"

The wink. What was that about?

"Excuse me?" Tony said. "Trainin' you for *what?*"

"Waitin' tables."

"Who said you were getting promoted? We're overstaffed, Jimmy. We don't have enough shifts to go around as it is. And what's with the *winking?* You got somethin' in your eye?"

Jimmy nodded at the pocket of Tony's apron where he knew the waiter kept his cash tips and charge slips.

"Don't worry," he said, kind of coyly. "Y'know, about the double tip. I won't tell."

Tony screwed up his eyebrows and stared at the kid.

He went, "You have *got* to be kidding."

THE TIP THAT KEEPS ON GIVING

Tony was at the bar with Heidi, the assistant general manager, whose job it was to assist him with tabulating final numbers for the dining room after the kitchen closed. He was irate.

"I can't work with him anymore," Tony stated.

"Are you sure about this?"

"He *winked* at me, Heidi."

She almost started laughing.

"But I thought you said he was so good. Didn't you just tell me he gets the first server opening?"

Tony felt a migraine coming on. He leaned on the bar and started massaging his temples, the basis for his current dilemma between elbows leering up at him. Mister Smiley Face. He wished he'd never even met the guy. He'd spoken with the man whose charge card it was—and clarified that the tip'd already been included—but the guy assured him that he knew that and the eighty bucks was *extra*. He'd closed the charge out afterwards with Mike at the bar, and when he came back to the bus station that Jimmy punk was suddenly acting all weird. He'd been over this eight times with Heidi already.

"That's what upsets me so much about this," he admitted. "I don't know how I could've misjudged the kid's character so badly."

Heidi detached herself from some numbers and suggested, "So, why don't you have a beer or something?" She gestured to Mike who was breaking down one of the wells. "Hey, Mike!"

Mike came over.

"Yeah," he said. "What's happenin'?"

"Tony wants a beer."

Mike looked at him and raised a brow.

"I'll have a Bass Ale," he sighed.

Mike said, "Man, you look like you're gonna start cryin' or somethin'."

Tony laughed.

Heidi said, "Mike—please."

Mike shrugged and went after the beer. Heidi continued.

"These are serious allegations, Tony. Are you sure you didn't just read something into it that wasn't there?"

Tony gave her a look.

"Listen, Heidi, I know when I'm being blackmailed."

Now it was her turn to sigh. She hated it when employees came to her with garbage like this. When they couldn't deal with things in their own departments and had to involve other people. It made things ugly. Messed with morale. She was being asked to fire this busboy on the word of a trusted employee who'd been with the company for years. There was the question of the double tip, though, and it was essentially one guy's word against another's. Do they call the customer at home and get him involved too? It was a quagmire and she didn't appreciate being sucked into it. Not at all.

Busboys blackmailing waiters. She'd never heard of such a thing. Mike showed up with the beer. Heidi looked at her watch and the shift'd been over for 10 minutes. Why was she still working?

"Mike," she said, "I'll have one too."

THE BEST-LAID PLANS

Eric and Dardina had just cut two dozen 4 pound beef tenderloins into filet portions. It was Friday afternoon and the special for Saturday was grilled filet mignon. It was from Tate Brothers, their regular meat supplier. They'd been running a special on whole tenderloins that Thursday. Had to order over 50 pounds, though, to get the bargain rate—so this special'd probably last all weekend depending on how business was. Trick was pricing it accordingly so that it'd move. Spoilage was a dirty word.

He'd had a discussion earlier with John and decided a price of $17 would ensure a sellout. Dardina made a quick phone check around town on what their closest competitors charged for one-pound filets. They came in at least a buck less than everybody. John always had a bargain basement entree with the specials, though usually it was a pasta or similar-caliber dish with less pricey ingredients. This was a one-time deal, though, according to the delivery guy. Middle-aged dude named Mack with the weirdest nose he'd ever seen on a body wasn't eating ants. Really long and reddish in color. Looked like an aardvark.

That's what they called him in the kitchen when he wasn't around. The Aardvark. *Did you confirm that delivery time yet with the Aardvark?* Or, *Has the Aardvark stopped by?* Real nice guy, though. Said there'd been a snafu at the office where somebody typed an extra zero on the order form. Four hundred pounds of tenderloin.

He wanted to send the guy a Christmas card or something.

In the restaurant business there was a very thin profit margin. One of the biggest responsibilities Eric had as kitchen manager was cutting corners—and the best way to do that was by adapting his menu to reflect seasonal changes in produce and meat availability. Accordingly, items on the specials menu were usually the most profitable.

"If I look at another dead steer," said Dardina, applying a dry spice rub to a tray of 24 filets, "I'm gonna hurl."

Eric smiled.

"Yeah? Just don't do it on the steaks."

"Not to worry," she laughed.

Eric had a large silver mixing bowl they'd been using to store end-cuttings from the tenderloins. There were a couple packages of 6 inch bamboo skewers soaking in a pan of water they planned to use for making shish kebobs. There wasn't much you could do with the tapered ends of tenderloins. Same excellent meat, of course—and just as costly—but it didn't work for too many dishes that didn't involve bamboo skewers. The filets needed to marinate overnight in the walk-in, but these kebobs'd move tonight as appetizers on the specials menu. A little red wine and garlic/ancho pepper marinade, and there ya go.

You might think that 96 pounds of steak worked out to 96 one-pound tenderloins, but that's not the way it worked. Not by a long shot. Not everybody wanted to eat a pound of beef, so there were the petite portions (8 oz.), and then irregularities in shape made the waste larger than one might assume. In the end, 96 pounds of tenderloin worked out to more along the lines of 88. Yes, there'd be shish kebobs the whole weekend long; priced to move, brother.

He put the marinade together and set the dish aside for a couple minutes till the skewers were soaked enough. Without soaking they'd burn up on the grill. Then he washed his hands and went into his small office in back to make some calls. Dardina was almost finished with the spice rub. He kicked back with his feet up on the desk and dialed Bob Hinton's number over at McCauley's. Another supplier Eric dealt with, but for dry goods like cleaning supplies and paper products. Couple minutes later he was talking with Bob about toilet paper when Dardina walked by with three trays of filets. There were ramekins on the corners of each so they could stack without bruising the meat, and a couple damp towels were draped over the top. He watched his sous chef walk by, ordered three cases of White Fluff, and a couple seconds later heard a loud crash by the walk-in.

Then, Dardina: "Oh, no."

He dropped the phone and burst outside the office. Dardina was standing over 88 pounds of beef tenderloin, tears welling up in her eyes. Ramekins were still spinning on the tile, most of them broken. She looked up at him in despair.

"It slipped," she blubbered. "I can pick 'em up! They're okay! You'll see!"

Eric said, "Oh, my God."

TO THE RESCUE OF JIM DANDY

Eddie Bates was tending bar on a Saturday. It was late. Things were winding down. He was 34 but felt like 50. Back of his calves hurt as if lined with steel plates just under the skin. Kelly'd informed him at the service bar earlier that they were called "shin splints."

He'd been whining about how much his *calves* hurt.

"Those are *shin splints*," she said, toddling off with the margaritas.

He started breaking down the second well and still didn't know what on earth was wrong with his calves. *Shin splints, my eye.* Sounded like something little girls did on the balance beam in Greece. Whatever. Mike'd gone home at 8:00 because it was slow and tonight was his turn to split early. Which was fine with Eddie except the part about how he now had to break down two wells instead of one. Mike'd offered to kill it before he left—but, y'know, it was still too early then. That's all he needed was for it to get busy or something. What with his shin sprints or whatever they were called.

"Hey, Eddie!"

He looked up from the well. It was one of the regulars, Jim Lansing, a pretty nice guy when he wasn't loaded. He'd been trying not to look at him the past half-hour or so. Didn't want to serve him anymore. Guy was getting hammered. Showed up a couple hours ago with some employees from his car dealership. They'd at least had the sense to call it a night. Not Jim, though. Dude was a high roller. Commercials on late-night TV with the bonehead always calling himself "Jim Dandy."

Wasn't so dandy now.

"Yeah, Jim—what's up?"

"C'mon down here," he said, directing him with a hand like he was maneuvering new cars off one of those big truck thingamajigs. "I ain't gonna shout!"

Aw, man.

Eddie dropped a steel champagne bucket he'd been using to remove the ice and dried his hands on a bar towel as he moseyed over to where Jim slouched all dandified. Twenty minutes till last call. Just Jim left and a couple tourists sipping coffee on the end. Why didn't ol' Jimbo have a cup? Yeah, that's the ticket: a little cup-a Joe.

"Jim Dandy," he mused, stopping in front of the man, shaking his head with mock sadness.

"What?" went Jim, suddenly defensive.

It was like he could sense there was trouble in the air. That maybe a river'd run dry somewhere. The guy's check was just under $150. Biggest tip of the night if Eddie didn't screw things up now. His calves hurt like no tomorrow. Why didn't Jim Dandy just finish his bourbon/rocks and go home?

"Whadaya want, Mr. Dandy?"

Jim's eyes were sort of crossed.

His car was out in the parking lot.

He smiled.

"Just one more drink, buddy!"

Aw, hell . . . .

EDNA BUMPKIN

John entered his office Monday morning and sat with resignation at his desk. As general manager he made his own schedule and liked Saturdays and Sundays off. Working 7 days a week the first 3 years after opening FOI, well, he felt he'd earned it. Whatever. Heidi was a capable assistant and he trusted her to handle the weekends by herself.

The nuts and bolts of daily operation mirrored the Monday through Friday grind anyway, regardless of the fact weekends were busiest. Outside of emergencies, vendors and the like as a rule didn't work weekends either. He had an entire list of rationalizations excusing him from duty on Saturdays when he rented a cart and golfed 18 holes, 12 pack on the back, and especially Sundays when he conducted his ritual of padding out to the stoop for his fat newspaper . . . and then reading it. Slowly. All day long. The big magazine crossword puzzle. Sports. Business. Everything.

If John got out of his big terry cloth robe and those Eddie Bauer slippers on Sundays, well, there was something wrong with the world.

John looked at his desk and the mat was buried deep with paper, as usual. Notes from department heads, files and printouts, etc., etc., etc. A computer that never got shut off and never shut up either. Oh, well. He liked to get in early on Mondays so he could wade through the flotsam with a minimum of disturbances. It was 6:30. Right on top was an incident report from Heidi describing a problem between the head waiter and one of the busboys. He read it and shook his head.

"Good Lord," he muttered. "I'm on *Falcon Crest.*"

Under "plan of action" he read that she was scheduling a meeting between herself and both parties, with a preliminary leaning toward letting the busboy go if relations between the two could not be restored. She was not going to involve the customer for verification that the tip was extra, citing the fact that it was well under the 18% automatic. He nodded his head in agreement.

Onto the next one—this big printout from the bar, the monthly inventory, with a *Post-It* note from Mike that read: "MONTHLY INVENTORY/ NOVEMBER/MIKE SCALES, BAR MANAGER."

John murmured, "Yeah, no kidding, Mike."

He flipped through to the only numbers that mattered, those being the bottom-line figures. Liquor costs were way too high and had been so for the past 6 months. Especially the wine. Something would have to be done. The wine. It was going out the back door or who knows what. Maybe someone was stealing. He'd spoken with Mike about it several times, and Mike had vouched for his staff . . . but, the numbers didn't lie. If there was one thing he trusted in this world, *really* trusted, it was numbers. Numbers didn't lie, people did.

By 8:00 he was finished and'd written notes to himself in his daily planner. Things he had to see to. People he had to speak with. Delegations of his own authority. He filed the incident report in Tony Marziano's folder and shook his head at the thought of a grown man not being able to deal with busboys on his own. Bringing his dirty laundry to Heidi. Ridiculous. Maybe they'd made a mistake promoting him. Time would tell. He wrote one final note to Heidi that said: "HEIDI, LOOK INTO HIRING SPOTTERS FOR THE BAR. LIQUOR COSTS **OUT OF CONTROL.**" Then he sat back and yawned and peered over at Edna Duncan's vacant desk, wishing she were sitting at it doing some work. Printouts were spilling over onto the floor. Ledgers stacked up like junkyard tires.

Edna Duncan. She'd been there 6 months. The wife of Frank's best friend who'd passed away last year. Worked 25 years as a CPA before retiring some time back. Their regular accountant had moved on last December, though, and Frank brought Edna in thinking it might take her mind off the loss of her husband. Now, John was all for helping people out—but a part-timer was not what they needed. What was he supposed to say to Frank, though?

"Hey, Frank. Get rid-a the widow."

No, that would not do.

He'd have to come up with something quick, though, before the floor collapsed from under that woman's weighty desk. She was due in at 9:00. Perhaps she'd get something done today. Like, hey, maybe some *accounting.*

He grabbed his radio and left the office, calling for Bill Gardner as he walked out to the lobby. Bill was chief engineer for the property, knew every inch of it. John suddenly got this horrific image of Bill Gardner moving on and Frank bringing in his nephew whose dog just got run over or something. *"Hey, Johnny. My nephew's gonna be workin' for ya. He got an 'A' in shop class. Whatever ya do, though, don't say nothin' about dogs."* He shivered at the thought.

"Yeah, John. This is Bill. Read ya loud an' clear."

"What's your 20?"

Bill: "I'm in room 605 fixing the pipes. Got a leak up here. Maybe another half hour."

"Vacant?"

"Yeah."

"All right, Bill. I'm coming up there right now. I got a work order for ya."

"Ten-four."

All requests for maintenance were routed through the front desk. Employees would fill out a three-copy work order form and leave it in a box underneath marked "maintenance." Bill or one of his crew checked this box intermittently throughout the day. If it was an emergency, of course, they were notified immediately on the radio. What John had, though, was a request for some work in the prep kitchen that kept getting routed to the front desk and never completed. Every Monday he sat down at his desk and there was a note from Chef Eric saying, "WHERE ARE MY #?&!% NO-SKID STRIPS?!!"

There was a break in the chain somewhere and John felt that the personal touch might be needed in this instance. Apparently Eric's cooks were sliding all over the place down there. Dropping product. Chancing injury. Wanted Bill to apply that sandpaper-like tape on the prep kitchen floor by the walk-in. How difficult could it be for Bill? Never got done, though. What was the problem? Half of what John did was babysitting. He'd known that for years.

Two hours later he was back in the office and Edna Duncan still hadn't shown up. John figured she was probably out mowing the grass around her husband's plot. Positioning lilies by the headstone. He felt bad about being so uncaring, but there was a business to run here and he just didn't have the time. Twelve noon rolled around and she still wasn't there. He decided to give Lex Lilly a dingle and discuss the problem. She was Frank's CPA/business manager and could maybe enlighten him on the perils that loomed if they didn't get someone in here who was serious about bookkeeping. Was just about to call her Phoenix office when in walked Edna carrying a box of donuts.

Brushing off the fact she was 3 hours late, she merely smiled and said, "Mornin', John."

"Hello, Edna."

"Is there coffee made yet?" she asked. "I got donuts. *Krispy Kremes.*"

Oh, goody gumdrops. She couldn't see him rolling his eyes.

"No, hon. I been dealing with some problems in the kitchen. Just sat down a minute ago."

"Okay, I'll put a pot on."

Coffee. It was lunchtime. The phone rang and he picked it up. Spent the next 45 minutes dealing with the president of the Phoenix Philatelist Club. Guy wanted to rent out 25 rooms for a weekend next June. Close off the Garden Vista one night for a party. John was trying to steer the guy from the first of the month to the middle when the heat was worse and they had more vacancies. Tendered what the guy probably thought was a good deal and rang off with the booking. Large groups were always given a 10% discount, but John'd held off with that till crunch time when the man was wavering about the dates.

Finally he had put the hammer down: *"Tell ya what . . . if ya book for mid-month I can get you a discount. Ten percent. How's that sound?"*

Sold. He pictured all those stamp collectors sweating in the middle of June, 120 degrees, with their little perforated squares sticking to fingers. John leaned back in the chair and felt like he'd been there for 8 hours already—but it wasn't even 1:00 yet. He rubbed his eyes and wondered what kind of headway Edna'd made on that pile of printouts. He swiveled around.

There she was, staring into the monitor of her computer.

Weeping.

Good grief.

"Edna? Are you okay?"

She burst out in despair, "Oh, John, I'm sorry! I hafta go!"

WILY RILEY

John watched his sometimes bookkeeper, Edna Duncan, scramble to get her things and split. He tried to console her but she was inconsolable, weeping about her not-all-that-recently deceased husband . . . yet, oddly enough, still pausing for a Krispy Kreme on the way out. The door closed behind her and he was alone.

"Great googily-moogily," he sighed.

He'd not had time for lunch, though, and could hear the hollows of his stomach crying out for a donut. He went over to Edna's desk and reached in for one of those Krispy Kremes that everyone'd been talking about for so long. He'd never eaten one before. Picked the thing up and it looked like a regular old donut. Glazed. Hole in the middle. Like, *big deal.* Took a bite, though, and it was heaven.

"Oh, my . . ."

So he was standing there at Edna's desk, thinking that this little bit of dough with glaze on it and a hole in the middle—might just be the best damn donut he'd ever had in his life, bar none, the best stinkin' donut he'd ever eaten in all his days, and that's when he gazed up at Edna's monitor and noticed she was still logged onto the Internet. She'd been so beside herself with grief that she'd forgotten to sign out. John ate the last morsel of his Krispy Kreme and sank down in Edna's chair.

"That's the best donut I ever had in my life," he swore, getting grease all over her mouse. He looked at the monitor, though, and could not believe his eyes. It was a chat room. The heading read: "FRIENDS, COPING WITH GRIEF." Edna'd been online with a bunch of other grieving sorts, widows or widowers, parents of drowned children, etc., etc., etc., and meanwhile he'd been going about his own business earlier, assuming, quite naturally, that she was maybe doing some *accounting*. Like she'd been hired to do, y'know, on company time, but instead she was online with a bunch of survivors chatting about death. That greasy little donut began mixing with acid in his stomach and he felt sort of queasy.

The phone rang on his desk.

RING!

Went over there and picked it up.

"Good afternoon, this is John Fallen."

"Hah," grunted a voice, even with just the one syllable conveying contempt, and, then, silence.

"Hello?"

"*Mister* Fallen . . . . Johnny Johnny Johnny. You been a bad boy."

The voice sounded sort of familiar.

"Who is this?"

"Riley. Sam Riley."

That crook from the permit department. Krispy Kreme bubbled up from his innards and emerged, far less tasty than it'd been before. That's all John needed now was Sam Riley. Some sleazy two-bit cretin from who-knows-where. Shaking people down. Or, rather, *trying* to shake people down.

"What do you want, Mr. Riley?"

There was a pause as the city guy drew in a breath and then cleared his throat.

"So, I come in here today . . . bright and early . . . expecting to find an envelope from you here on my desk. . . . But there's not an envelope, *Johnny-boy*. No, there's not an envelope here on my desk at all."

"Listen, Mr. Riley, I don't have time for this. I'm very busy and . . . "

Riley cut him off.

"You're very busy, is that right? I don't find an envelope on my desk because you didn't put an envelope on my desk, *Johnny-boy!*"

"Mr. Riley . . . "

"But, do you know what I did find on my desk? Do you know what I found?"

"I couldn't possibly imagine."

"I found a memo, *Johnny-boy*. From my supervisor. Apparently he wants a word with me. D'ya know anything about this memo, *Johnny-boy?*"

John almost started laughing. He'd spoken with Riley's boss last Tuesday and told him at great length about what crimes and misdemeanors his underling was perpetrating under the auspices of city government. He'd been assured that whatever permits they needed to proceed with construction of the swim-up pool bar would be "provided immediately," and they had in fact followed through with that. Riley's superior had also assured John that crooks like Sam

Riley would not be tolerated during "his watch," and, furthermore, they would "swiftly be dealt with" in the most serious possible fashion, thank you very much.

So, why was Sam Riley still on the streets?

"Well, *Sammy-boy*, to tell you the truth—I got my own memos to deal with here. Yours are not a concern of mine."

"Yours are not a concern of mine," parroted the wily one. "Well, aren't you the fancy boy! You city slickers come into town an' think ya own everything. Well, let me tell *you* somethin', *Johnny-boy*. If I find out you been talkin' to the *Soup* about our little arrangement here . . . "

Now it was John's turn to interrupt.

"Aw, shut your pie-hole," he said. "Have a nice day."

FALCON CRUST

Heidi hated garbage like this. It was a half-hour before the dinner shift began on Monday. She was sitting at a table in the sparsely populated Oasis Lounge with the dining room manager, Tony, and Jimmy, the busboy. Both of them had their arms crossed like children. Heidi rolled her eyes and stirred sugar into her coffee.

"I've thought this over, guys, and I'm comfortable with the opinion that the tip in question was quite obviously over and above the automatic 18 percent. The customer was merely rewarding Tony for his excellent service."

She addressed Jimmy who uncrossed his arms and began fidgeting with a napkin.

"Tony seems to think you were trying to blackmail him into promoting you to a server position . . . by threatening to turn him in for stealing . . . which, as I said, I don't believe occurred in the first place."

"I was just jokin'," said Jimmy. "Guy's nuts or somethin'."

"You were *not* joking," declared Tony. "And I don't appreciate being talked to that way."

Heidi almost started laughing. Tony *was* sort of nuts. Well, at least *anal*. More she got to know him, more anal he showed himself to be. The kid was out of line, though.

"Enough," said Heidi, holding up a hand. She took a sip from her coffee and looked from one to the other. "I can't have these kinds of rifts amongst my staff."

Jimmy interrupted, "He's the one with the problem."

Tony snorted. Shook his head.

"Tony," she said, "I'm gonna talk to Jimmy in private. Thanks for coming in."

He got up to leave. Heidi noted that the guy looked skinnier than usual. Almost sickly.

"Sorry about this, Heidi," he said. "It was out-a my hands."

Heidi nodded as Tony grabbed his apron and left. Jimmy was smoldering.

"So, what's up? Am I gonna get fired for this?"

"Jimmy," she said, leaning across the table, "What on earth were you thinking? This is the most ridiculous nonsense I ever heard of . . . in all my years. I'm not pleased with either of you, frankly, but *especially* you. Understand, though, that's it's not really the blackmail part that chips me off. Though that's pretty bad. It's the fact that you didn't come to me in the first place. If you felt that Tony was stealing—you should've come to me about it and I would've dealt with it."

Jimmy looked away.

"So, am I fired?"

Heidi took a form from her folder and placed it across the table in front of the busboy. It was a write-up sheet with the incident described and a place for the employee to sign at the bottom. It occurred to Jimmy that for whatever "meeting" had just taken place, any decision with regards to right and wrong, or punishment for the guilty party, had already been determined. This little write-up form'd been filled out long ago over coffee and scones in the managers' office. So, what was the point?

Far as Jimmy was concerned, the whole thing stunk.

"I'm suspending you for a week. I'll sit down with John and decide if your position is going to be terminated. This is a write-up. I want you to read it over and sign at the bottom."

"What if I *don't* sign it?"

This kid was bad news. She looked into his eyes and decided right then and there not to even bother John with him.

"Well," she said, "then you'll be terminated immediately."

"Whatever," he smirked, standing. "You were gonna fire me no matter what. Why'd ya even waste my time? Now I gotta pay again to take the bus home. Thanks for nothin'."

Bad news. All the way around.

LEX LUTHER

Lex Lilly was Frank's CPA/business manager, and John's quasi-boss in terms of hierarchy within the overall chaos of what Frank jokingly referred to as his "empire." She couldn't fire him, but she had Frank's ear and what Lex wanted Lex pretty much got. John had called her about the problem with FOI's part-time bookkeeper, Edna Duncan, the problem being that she was, well, *part time.* They needed more hours out of Edna, but she did not have them to give.

He liked her enough, but the job for Edna was merely something she did to distract her from the none-too-recent death of her husband. Pushing all sentimentality aside, John felt the welfare of the business was at stake, and Edna's not-enough bookkeeping was to blame. That and the grief chat room nonsense. He'd had quite enough of Edna Duncan. So John sat in his office on a sunny

Monday, on hold, waiting for Lex Lilly's secretary to transfer him. Seconds passed into minutes and John was doodling on a legal pad when Lilly's breathless voice came on the line.

"John, I'm soooooo sorry for keeping you waiting! It's a madhouse around here! There's just not enough hours in the day!"

John'd been to her office in Phoenix a couple times and tried to imagine just how mad that house could possibly be. He suspected this "not enough time" business was something peculiar to the accounting profession, as if their wall clocks were sped up by God's divine hand.

"No problem, Lex," he lied, jamming the pencil in a smiley face cup on his desk.

"I was just going to call you, in fact. How funny!"

That kind of threw him. *Funny? What was funny?*

He could've used a laugh right about now. He lit a smoke and said, "Oh, yeah?"

"Yes!" she gushed.

Everything with Lex was exclamation points. She could be describing the eggshell-colored paint on the wall, and by the time she finished you'd think Van Gogh'd applied it with his toes. John figured that's why Frank liked her so much. She was nuts. Sharp as a tack, but certifiable.

"Hand-held wireless."

That's all she said. Just kind of left it hanging there.

"What?"

"Technology, John."

He laughed.

"What are you talkin' about?"

"You know I also do some work for Hank Winston over at *Sun-Micro Systems*—y'know, handle his personal finances?"

John rubbed his jaw. "Well, no," he admitted, "I didn't know that. Winston? Like the cigarettes?"

"Don't be silly, John! *Hank* Winston. A pioneer in micro technology, one of the richest men in the Southwest."

"Okay. What about him?"

There was a rustling of papers on Lilly's end.

"Well, they've developed this new micro system. I have it here . . . somewhere . . . the literature. . . . aha! There you are! It's called, 'Point-of-Order Micros.'"

John dragged off his smoke and leaned back in the swivel chair. He was in for the long haul. Put his feet up on the desk. Forgot about Edna Duncan and exhaled at the ceiling.

"Hello? John?"

"Yeah, Lex. Point-of-Order Micros. Winston tastes good like a cigarette should. What about it?"

"I'm thinking for Freshwater. It's perfect, John, cutting edge, and Hank positively *adores* me . . . and that equates to a BIG **BIG** discount."

John still didn't know what she was talking about. Whatever it was, though, it was a bargain.

"I've already got the go-ahead with Frank," she informed him. "He just wanted me to run it by you, y'know, get your feelings."

John took his feet off the desk and sat up, alarm bells clanging in his head.

"Whoa! Wait a minute here, Lex. What're you talkin' about? What is this Point-of-Order stuff?"

"It's technology, silly!" she laughed, like he was a rube. "You know the basic setup for restaurants and bars, John. You got your point-of-sale terminals and your waiters running around with pens and those quaint little guest checks. All that's a thing of the past, dear!"

Oh, God. . . .

"Hand-held wireless," he repeated, kneading his right temple where a migraine was suddenly making its presence known. "I hope you're not talking about what I think you're talking about."

"It's the future, John, and Freshwater's gonna be there first. Hank's giving us a KILLER deal. Fifty thou and we get seven wireless hand-helds, the menu system, plus they throw in setup for free. A wireless network throughout the bar, the dining room, patio, the pool deck; *everywhere,* John!"

John could picture one crammed down his throat.

"No, no, Lex! C'mon, that system don't work!"

"Whadaya mean?" she blurted, taken aback. "Of course it works!"

She was referring to a system where servers punched orders into a handheld device, which in turn transmitted them directly to the appropriate site, be it kitchen or service bar, etc., thereby cutting out the need for on-floor terminals and the redundant act of servers having to reenter the orders. In theory, the technology was fantastic.

"We tried wireless at the last place I worked. It was a fiasco, Lex. System kept crashing, every other week. Waiters couldn't read the screens when the sun was out, y'know, like on the patio. Took too long to find the menu items. It was useless, Lex!"

There was a pause.

Then, Lex: "How long ago was that, John?"

"Excuse me?"

"You've been at Freshwater 6 years, am I right?"

He snuffed the cigarette out, said, "Yeah?"

She gave him that you're-a-rube tone again. "Six years is a long time, John. The technology has improved substantially since then. Hank assures me it's top of the line now. All the bugs've been worked out. System is impregnable."

John chewed on the word *impregnable,* two seconds, then spit it in the ashtray alongside the still-smoldering butt. Acid started bubbling in his stomach and he lit another. *I'd rather fight than switch.*

"If it ain't broke, don't fix it," he recited, like it was a mantra. "Our system has been in place just 6 years. It's fine, Lex. No problems whatsoever."

"We *lease* our present system, John," she pointed out, sounding annoyed. "It's not cost-effective. The wireless will pay for itself in 5 years. No rental fees, greater efficiency; the list goes on and on."

John closed his eyes and breathed. Lex Lilly'd never worked in a restaurant her whole life. She gave orders, never took them. Good ol' Lex. He didn't understand why people couldn't just leave well enough alone. People were always busy. Fixing things. It didn't make sense. Busy, busy, busy.

He sighed.

"And you've talked with Frank about this, huh?"

"Yes, John. I already told you."

"And he likes it, huh?"

"Yes, John."

He could picture Lex there in her Phoenix office. Queen of the madhouse.

"Well," he mused. "Isn't that just dandy."

It wasn't a question.

"By the way," she said, changing the subject, "what was it you called for?"

Good grief. He couldn't remember. He kept picturing his staff running into each other or hiding away in the bus stations playing Super Mario Brothers on their ridiculous hand-helds. Good grief.

Oh, yeah—that was it! *Grief!*

DINNER AT MARTHA'S

Eddie showed up at Kelly's place about 7:00. They'd worked together at FOI the last couple years; him as bartender and her as a server. They'd always gotten along and had pretty much the same shifts. Though Eddie knew it was a mistake dating coworkers, they'd increasingly flirted with each other at the service bar. It was only a matter of time, he knew, before this cardinal rule was broken.

So it wasn't any surprise last Saturday after work when they were at the local hangout, Mulligan's—drinking with a group of FOI employees—and Kelly started talking about what a great cook she was and how fun it'd be if maybe Eddie came over for dinner on Thursday. They both had Thursdays off, and, well, she wasn't doing anything, and, um—

"Dinner?" he prodded.

"Yeah," she smiled. "Just dinner."

So he agreed and showed up in her lobby about 5 minutes late, great trepidation and a bottle of Cabernet in his hands. The doorman had this cheap blue blazer on and looked like he'd be more comfortable doing crowd control at a traveling freak show, so long as nobody attended. He was reading *Field & Stream,* his lips struggling with every word.

"Hey, how're ya doin'?" Eddie smiled. "I'm here for Kelly Linquist in apartment 1027."

The guy finished the sentence he was on and gazed upward.

"Huh?"

Oh, one-a these.

"What part did ya miss?"

"Why don't you start from the top?"

Eddie repeated what he'd said and the guy picked up the house phone and wet his fingertips with saliva to facilitate his movement through the directory. Smelled like a cross between Ten High Whiskey, cinnamon Tic Tacs, and boll weevil posterior. Sorta reminded him of his own doorman. Perhaps it was a cologne brand the union boys passed out with the polka-dotted ties. A fringe benefit. Eddie rolled his eyes and turned to gaze through large windows that made up the facade of 925 South Oak Street. He could hear the moron babbling into the phone and pretty soon the door buzzed.

Eddie went through and headed for the elevators.

This was probably a big mistake, he fretted. He waited for the elevator to arrive, then got in and pressed 10.

Whoosh.

"Yep," he murmured to himself. "Big mistake."

The 10th floor. Only elevator building in Copper Hills, and Kelly had the penthouse. Eddie stepped out and looked both ways for the 27 unit. Apparently lots of people had the penthouse. She'd said it was on the end, left side of the cars, but there were elevators on both sides of the hall. So it really depended on which way you were facing. Left was right, or left was wrong. *A mystery.* Long hallway. There were at least 30 families with penthouses in Copper Hills. Deciphered the number scheme and walked down Kelly-ways like it was a green mile and knocked. The door flew open. It was her, smiling.

"Hello, you," she said.

"What's up, honey?"

"C'mon in! Don't just stand there."

Eddie did what he was told and his coworker shut the door behind him.

"I brought some red," he declared, lamely.

"Fantastic," she said. "Come with me to the kitchen and you can open it. I'm right in the middle of preparing veggies. Dinner's gonna be real good."

"Sounds good to me," he babbled, wincing at what a dork he sounded like.

Kelly was bustling about, rifling through drawers trying to locate the corkscrew. He just kind of stood there feeling like an idiot. Wishing he had a corkscrew to busy himself with. Had to admit, though, whatever she was cooking smelled great.

"God, somethin' sure smells great."

Doh!

He'd done it again.

"Oh, here it is," she announced, triumphant. "There's wine glasses through there on the dining room table. Be a dear, would ya?"

She handed him the implement.

"No problemo," Eddie said, glad to be escaping somewhere. Anywhere. A place where maybe he could regroup and stop sounding like such a dork. *No problemo.* He walked into the dining room and realized he was just nervous because of the situation. Or maybe it was the altitude. She was probably feeling the same way and dealt with it by hiding herself in the broccoli or whatever it was she called *veggies.*

Veggies. He was sweating bullets. Eddie wiped his brow and that's when he noticed the table. White linen with matching napkins. Stoneware plates with a thin blue line around the outer edge. Thick beveled glass water goblets. Thinner yet matching wine glasses. Stainless place settings with the FOI monogram on the handles. He'd been here before. It was the dining room at work. He took a closer look at the corkscrew and that had the monogram on it too.

He turned back toward the kitchen where Kelly was and half-expected Chef Eric to emerge holding a platter of FOI canapés.

"Aw, man," he muttered. "Never date your coworkers."

"What?" shouted Kelly from the kitchen. "Did you say somethin'?"

ONE-MINUTE EGGMEYER

It was another Monday and lots'd happened this past week, but lots always happened in a week, leastways how John saw it. Edna Duncan was gone, vamoosed, and that was the long and short of it. He felt bad but had the will to get over it. Good ol' Lex Lilly'd swooped down on poor Edna like a hawk. John had been dreading the prospect of letting Edna go, but he knew it was a dreary thing they'd have to do or everybody'd be in the drink. The books were a shambles because of Edna's unintentional neglect, yet the books were what this whole house of cards rested on. Little columns of numbers at FOI, making it possible for John to get those duel 300 outboards for his Bayliner docked at Lake Pleasant. Or send Frank jetting off to Rio for Carnival next winter or whenever it was. Everybody depended on those little columns of numbers that Edna just didn't have time for, so wracked was she with grief for her dear departed husband.

John gazed across the room to where Edna's desk had once been drowning in neglected printouts and myriad flotsam, and he smiled. The desk was still there, of course, but the nameplate read: "Sheri Eggmeyer." Gone were the stacks of manila files and printouts and Krispy Kreme two-for-one coupons. In their place was order.

WITHOUT ORDER, THERE IS CHAOS.

He looked at his watch and it was just before 9:00 in the morning, the hour Sheri was scheduled to start another day. She'd burned through Edna's backlog of work in the first 4 days of employment with FOI. It'd been unbelievable. The girl was a human dynamo, even better than the bookkeeper they'd had before Edna came on board, and that one'd been a real terror with numbers. This Eggmeyer woman was something else, though. Interned for Lex up in Phoenix a couple years back when she was still in college getting her degree. She wasn't a youngster, not even then, and her job app said she was now 43. The woman was rather close-lipped about her personal life, but Lex'd filled him in that she was a single mother gone back to school in order to get that degree and make something of herself. Two kids—a girl and a boy—somewhere in their teens. No, she wasn't any spring chicken, but, man, she could crunch the numbers.

John lit a smoke and contentedly blew a plume up toward the ceiling. There'd be hell to pay for Lex's handling of the Edna situation, like having to get on board for the hand-held wireless system Lex'd been pushing, but, for the time being, it was worth it. For months John'd had this creeping sensation whenever he came into that office and beheld Edna's desk. The piles of pressing accounting business, pages squeezed together till they formed a stratified rock you could count the months by. That matters of such grave importance should be relegated to someone quite obviously unconcerned about things of this work-a-day world. John sat there and he was quite alone, but he said to himself, "C'mon, Edna," as if her ghost were still there weeping, "he's been dead a year now. I mean, gimmie a break."

That didn't make him feel any better about unleashing Lex on her.

"It had to be done," he resolved, quietly, to nobody. "Poor Edna. Big bad John."

It did a body no good to fret over decisions that had to be made. Painful decisions, the ones affecting another human being's livelihood. But that's what she'd been doing, really, when he thought about it. Affecting their very livelihoods with her shoddy work. Jeopardizing the entire operation while she blew ledgers off to lay wreathes by her husband's tombstone, or type tears into a coping-with-grief chat room as columns of numbers dropped dead by the wayside. Tell me about grief. No, John wasn't going to lose any sleep over Edna's departure. If she hadn't been a personal friend of Frank's, well, he'd have sent her packing a long time ago. Some people had different performance standards they had to aspire to, as if lameness were somehow an accepted birthright. That was one of the problems with working outside the corporate structure. You had owners to deal with, and they could sometimes be a real trial. Frank was cool, but he'd had others in the past . . .

Anyway, Edna was gone, and that's all that mattered. He snuffed out his smoke in the ashtray and tried to make sense of a note left on his desk by Bill Gardner, the building engineer. It looked like this:

Googily-Moogily

John just couldn't make it out. Hmmm. He supposed it was the way Edna just up and disappeared. He'd spoken with Lex last week about the grief chat room business, and the fact she wasn't doing her job, etc., etc., and how he didn't know how to proceed, y'know—being that she was the widow of one of Frank's best friends—and, blah, blah, blah, that apparently was all Lex needed.

Lex'd said to him, "Don't you worry about Edna, honey. I got just the ticket for you! She'll be there tomorrow morning! The woman is positively egg-cellent! You just sit tight and think about how you're gonna incorporate those new handhelds! I'm meeting with Hank Winston again this afternoon! Wait'll you see this new system in action!"

John was confused: "Did you just say egg-cellent?"

Anyway, John supposed in the back of his mind he felt sort of impotent, or, perhaps, like he didn't have much of a spine to speak of. Poor Edna just up and disappeared all of a sudden. That very next day, in fact. Just stopped coming in to work. Now ya see me, now ya don't. Lex'd called her up maybe on the phone and told her to get lost. Maybe the same thing could happen to him? Live by the sword, die by the sword? Jeez. And now the hand-helds. What part did Frank play in this? Who knows? John didn't know, and maybe that was the rub. He'd just let someone else do his dirty work and now was sitting around fat and happy and, well, that must be her now —

"Good morning, Mr. Fallin," she chirped, all cheerful like a bird, breezing through the door. "Gosh, I was almost late. Traffic's all snarled out there!"

"How're ya doin', Miss Eggmeyer? You're right on time. Minute early, actually."

What a peach.

Now, what on earth did Bill Gardner want?

NO IFS, ANDS, OR BUTTS

Gabe was two-thirds into his shift on Wednesday, which was really his *Monday*—the weekend, as it were, occurring for him on Monday and Tuesday. Saturday was Thursday and Sunday was Friday. His mother in Sioux City never understood when the topic turned to days. *I'll call you on Sunday.* Everybody in the hospitality industry knew that Saturday and Sunday were not weekend days. *Which Sunday? Yours or mine?* Gabe always had to work. Busiest days of the week. Family'd get mad at him when he couldn't attend functions. Whatever.

His week. Monday and Tuesday was the weekend. Or sometimes Tuesday and Wednesday.

Wednesday was Gabe's Monday this week. It was just after 6:30 and things were pretty quiet. Ellen was checking two middle-aged couples in from Ohio. Looked like they were in town for an Ugly convention. As front desk manager, Gabe scheduled himself from 1:00 to 9:00 so he'd be on hand for shift change—maintaining continuity, so to speak. Touching base with all his people. Thirty more minutes, though, and he could leave things in Ellen's capable hands and get some paperwork done. It'd been piling up in the back like dormant locusts, and would soon emerge to devour his real weekend . . . which was still 5 days away . . . and which he'd planned to spend camping at Lake Pleasant.

Ahhhh. The in-house phone.

After the second ring he picked it up.

"Freshwater Oasis Inn. This is the front desk. Gabe DeFlores."

It was an old lady's voice. Irritated.

"Hello. This is Meta Adams in room 710. They're having a party next door! I can't sleep! I can't even hear myself think!"

Gabe double-checked his watch.

Yep: 6:30.

"A party, ma'am?"

"Yes! A party!"

Gabe tried to imagine which was more bizarre; somebody throwing a party at 6:30 in the evening, or someone being kept awake by it. He figured both possibilities didn't really exist in the world he and his mother lived in, despite the confusion about weekends. The old bag was probably senile. People next to her dropped a comb in the bathroom, knocked her off the bed. He tried to sound sympathetic.

"Oh, no," he went, rolling his eyes. "I'm sorry, ma'am. Can you hear loud music? Or, um, talking?"

"They're havin' a party!"

Gabe couldn't hear anything in the background. Just the lonely echoes of Alzheimer's.

"You're in 710, Miss Adams. Would that be the room across the hall? Or, um, is it the—"

She cut him off.

"708," she said.

He punched numbers into his computer and the guest's name came up: Seymore Butts. *How clever.* He remembered the guy checking in the other day. A rock star whose band was playing at the stadium. Didn't know him from a hole in the ground. Signed in under a pseudonym so fans wouldn't bother him. Sort of obnoxious. Reminded him of the troubled teens he'd spent 3 years counseling for DCFS, but this guy wasn't even remotely cute anymore.

Probably *was* having a party.

Gabe went, "Oh, I see: 708. I'll call up there immediately, Miss Adams. Sorry for the disturbance."

"Make it snappy," she snapped, dispensing the phone before the Y was even out her mouth. It was amazing how rude people sometimes were. Like it was him up there in the next room popping champagne corks at the wall. Keeping her from that all-important beauty sleep. He tried to put the voice with a face he might've seen checking in, but kept conjuring prunes in a fright wig. Probably attending that Ugly convention with those people from Columbus.

Called up to the infamous Mr. Butts's room. It rang four times before a man answered.

"Rock and roll," said the voice.

He could hear music in the background. People talking. Not much for 6:30, though.

"Hello. Front desk calling. Is this Mr. Butts?"

There was silence.

"What?"

Gabe felt stupid just saying it.

"Mr. Seymore Butts. This is the front desk."

Laughter.

"Oh, yeah. I'm Mr. Butts. Whadaya want?"

More laughter, this time in the background. Some female voices. Another guy.

"Mr. Butts, we're getting complaints here at the front desk about noise coming from your room."

"What?! You gotta be kidding! It's 6:30, man!"

It really wasn't all that loud. The old lady was a prune. Hated to see anybody else having fun. Gabe knew the type. Sat around wishing everybody else was older than her. More incontinent.

"Well, I'm sorry, Mr. Butts. There's some elderly guests on your floor and they're sensitive to the noise. Just turn your radio down a bit and you won't have to talk over it."

"It's 6:30, man!"

"Mr. Butts—"

"All right," he said. "Whatever, dude."

Click. . . .

Dude. Gabe couldn't wait to get started on that paperwork. He looked over and Ellen had finished with the uglies and was now fiddling with the printer. Thing kept jamming. They'd tried everything they could think of, but it kept jamming. Probably have to call someone. Gabe knew computers but he didn't know how to *fix* them. He suspected that The Man programmed bugs in software, ensuring that The Little Guy would forever be kept in the dark.

"Ellen, I'm gonna go do some work in back. You okay here?"

"Yeah," she said. "Sure."

The phone rang. Ellen grabbed it.

"Freshwater Oasis. This is the front desk."

Gabe was heading for the back room.

"Room 710? Uh-huh? You spoke with Mr. Deflores?"

It was like in a dream when a monster was chasing him and his feet were mired in quicksand. He turned around to face it. Put his hand out.

"I'll take it," he said.

Ellen went, "Uh, Miss Adams? Mr. Deflores is here. Hold on a sec."

She handed the phone over.

Gabe: "Hello, Miss Adams?"

He could hear music in the background this time. The old lady was frantic. She started whining but he cut her off.

"Miss Adams? I'm coming up there right now. Okay? Just relax. I'll be there in a minute."

Gabe hung the phone up. Ellen looked at him.

"What was that about?"

"Mr. Seymore Butts apparently is having a party. She called a minute ago. I gotta go up there and talk to him."

"The rock star? Why don't ya just call him?"

"Already did, Ellen. Seems Mr. Butts is being a hard-ass. Get it?"

Ellen laughed as he ducked out and headed for the elevators. Gabe hated having to act on noise complaints. Especially domestic stuff. A guy and his wife screaming at each other. Him knocking on the door with a master key-card for protection. This wasn't gonna be a big deal, though. Seymore Butts, the rock star. A hundred and forty pounds of snarl, and 10 of it hair.

He caught the elevator and went to seven. Walked out and could hear the music. The jerk'd actually turned it up since his last call. Seymore Butts, the rebel rock star. Probably didn't know one iota about heartache, or two cents about revolution, yet most likely he sang about both subjects as if they were his lovers. Whatever, dude. Gabe knocked on his door several times but the music was too loud. He was inserting his master key when the door was flung open from within.

The rock star. Hair all over the place. Couple leather-clad women in the background and another long-haired guy playing air guitar. Yeah, plenty of heartache. Revolution galore. The BOSE radio at full blast.

"Mr. Butts," Gabe scolded, feeling like the guy's mother, "you turned your radio up. You need to turn your radio back *down,* right *now.*"

"Hey, listen, buddy," he protested, "it's 6:30 in the bloomin' day. I never heard-a nobody complainin' about noise at 6:30."

Now he recognized him. This turd was from Pittsburgh! He'd watched a story about his band on *Entertainment Tonight* nearly 2 months ago. Bloomin' Pittsburgh! Gabe just wanted to do paperwork.

"Turn your radio down, Mr. Butts."

One of the ladies started laughing while the other made for the air-guitar idiot, groping at his shirt buttons.

Seymore reached into his pocket.

"I get it," he said, pulling out a crumpled bill. "Tell ya what. I give you this hondo and we forget about it. We're havin' a little party, y'know?"

It was Wednesday but it was Gabe's Monday. Gonna be a long week. *Hondo* was a hundred-dollar bill. He looked at Mr. Butts and wished it was Sunday, which was Friday, but Sunday just the same.

Seymore Butts: "Well . . . whadaya say, mate?"

FIRST YA SEYMORE, THEN YA DON'T

Maria Espanosa got the bad duty cleaning up room 708. It was her floor and Señor DeFlores'd insisted she get to it right away while the mess was still fresh. *Still fresh? What is fresh?* She only spoke so much English, but Maria gathered from the front desk manager that the guest was some kind of famous rock star. Said he was kicked out for making too much noise. Gabe led her into the room and shrugged his shoulders.

"Lo siento," he said, then split.

"Aye yi yi," she muttered, looking around.

Furniture was all turned over and the sheets were a mess as if a hurricane'd drifted over slow and hung around awhile. Like Hurricane Gilbert when she'd lived in the Yucatan back in the '80s. She stood there a full minute taking it in. The cart was still down the hall where she'd been going about her usual routine till Gabe showed up with news about Señor Butts.

There was a leather cocktail dress balled up in the bathtub, looked like it was coated with egg whites. She'd never heard of any Señor Butts.

"Aye yi yi," she said again.

Executive housekeeper Kathy Lawhorn arrived for work at 6:30 the next morning with a headache and slight nausea. She'd felt herself coming down with something yesterday and went to bed early to fend it off—but that didn't work, obviously. Maybe it was the flu. One of her maids'd been wandering around all last week like the dead till finally she called in sick on Tuesday. It was Thursday now and there was a light blinking the presence of two messages on her answering machine.

She hit the Play button.

"Kathy, this is Gabe. We had this jerk last night in room 708. Had to kick him out. Some kind-a rock star calls himself 'Seymore Butts.' I know, very clever. Before he left, though, the guy made a mess of the room. You should see what he left in the tub! (laughter) Anyway, I had Maria take care of it. So, if she didn't get to her normal stuff—that's why. Thanks."

"Oh, great," sighed Kathy. "Seymore Butts."

The next message:

"Hi . . . Kathy? This is Claudia. I ain't gonna make it in again today. I got the flu or somethin'. I'll try to be there tomorrow. Sorry. Bye."

"Yeah, an' thanks for givin' it to me, Claudia," Kathy moaned, hitting Stop on the machine. She felt a sensation in the back of her throat then and thought she might get sick. She stood and staggered to the bathroom and hovered over the toilet.

"Oh, God . . ."

The feeling passed after a minute and she moved to the sink to splash her face with some cold water. There was something in it, though. Some kind of leather garment in a plastic bag. She picked it up and wondered where it came from. Sort of slimy. She tossed it in the corner and washed her face under cold water. Fixed her hair in the mirror and trudged back out to her desk and sat down. Couldn't afford to be sick today. Too much work. Had to tough it out. Saw a note on the desk in Maria's handwriting.

"Señora Lawhorn—dress in bathroom sink, 708. Found in bathtub. All messy. Señor Butts. No bueno!"

Kathy stared at the note a second and then her hands. Face got all scrunched up with disgust. She retched. Ran back to the toilet.

Trini came in early after her boss called, all deathly ill sounding. She wasn't happy about it, but what could Trini do? It was the boss. Had to work on Thursday, her Saturday. Break the news to her boyfriend, Mark, that she couldn't come over and play. He was mad but what was *she* supposed to do about it? *The jerk.*

At least Trini didn't have to actually do anything, really. Just sit in the office all day and answer phones and man the radio. One of her normal jobs was checking the mini-bars in all the guestrooms, but this was her day off and someone else was assigned the duty. She didn't know who it was and didn't care much either. Trini was going to do as little as possible today. Whatever. Sounded kind of fun telling other people what to do for a change. Lucy was there when she walked into the office and looked only too glad to get back to cleaning rooms. Couldn't speak much English. That's why Trini always had to sub for Kathy. Only employee could speak both Spanish and English, aside from the boss who said she was bilingual but really only knew enough to order a taco at Pepe's. Kat was always stretching the truth when it came to her own capabilities, least it seemed that way to Trini.

Español. Kat Lawhorn comprende nada. Lucy brought her up to speed on the day's events and went back to the 4th floor where she'd been working when Kathy had her take over the office. Trini leaned back in Kathy's chair and put her feet up on the desk. She sighed.

"Ahhh. This is the life."

The phone rang and she almost had a heart attack. Like it was Kathy Lawhorn and she'd been watching her through a peephole or something.

She snatched it off the desk.

"Housekeeping! Good morning! This is Trini!"

"Yeah," said a woman's voice, kind of rude. "Front desk transferred me to your department. My name's Sheena Williams. I was stayin' in your lousy hotel and think I left a leather dress in the room. Did the maid find it? It's real expensive and I want it back."

"Okay," said Trini, grabbing a pencil. "What room were you staying in? Was it under your name?"

"No, it was under Tommy's name. We were on the 7th floor. I don't remember what room it was exactly."

Trini rolled her eyes and went over to the Lost & Found basket where they kept things from the guestrooms. There was a belt there with a scrap of paper taped to it and the number 1205 on it.

No leather dress.

"Oh, yeah," said the woman. "I just remembered! Tommy registered under another name! It was *Seymore Butts!*"

Then she started laughing.

Trini went, "Excuse me?"

"No, for real! I'm serious. That's the name he registered under. You got Lost & Found down there or somethin'?"

Trini wondered if someone was messing with her. Like that Gabe doofus who worked the front desk. Maybe he'd put someone up to it. Guy was always fooling around.

"Who is this?" Trini asked, not in the playing mood. It was her Saturday, after all. The woman was laughing again. She started to hang up.

"No, wait a minute," implored the voice. "I'm not kidding. The dress was real expensive."

"Uh-huh," doubted Trini.

"Where do the maids bring stuff they find in the rooms?"

"Right here," Trini answered, picturing Gabe listening on an extension, "but there ain't any leather dresses in Lost & Found. Maybe *Seymore Butts* has it."

The woman laughed.

"Well, listen," she said, "I'm gonna give you my cell phone number. If it turns up, give me a call, okay?"

"Yeah, sure," said Trini.

She took down the number, feeling like a fool. Hung up the cordless and shook her head. That Gabe jerk. She was sure it was him. Messing with her. All these managers did was sit around and think-a ways to make their employees' lives more difficult. She went into the bathroom for a tissue and there was a black leather dress balled up in plastic in the corner. She picked it up and dumped it from the plastic bag into the sink.

"Wow," she said, truly amazed that the caller was for real. She looked at the thing and there was some kind of goo all over it. Looked like her size, though. She picked it up by the shoulder straps and shook it out. Yeah, it was her size. She ran it under the water a bit and washed some of the stuff off. Thought about that cell number sitting on Kathy's desk. Nice dress. Real leather; not the fake stuff. Looked like just her size. The woman'd probably never call back again. Nobody'd ever hafta know.

There was a label at the back said it was a size 8. A perfect fit for Trini. She looked around and wondered what'd happen if she just took it home. That phone number sitting on Kathy's desk. Probably never call back. Tom'd really love this leather dress.

Hmmmmm.

It was just her size.

LOCKED UP OR TIGHT?

Bill Gardner liked it a lot better now that locks didn't use keys no more. Something went wrong with the card keys—well, *call the man*. It ain't my problem. Sure, he'd have to install new card readers if the unit was broke, but that was a piece-a cake. Had enough to do what with every hairbrain manager in the joint thinkin' he was their personal Bob Villa.

Man, he hated that Bob Villa guy. Bill Gardner knew more on his pinky finger than Bob Villa knew in his whole body about fixin' things up. Well, except for computer stuff like those card reader things. Yeah, Bill figured Bob Villa was just the type of guy that knows a lot about computers. Prob'ly spends half the dang day online or whatever they call it. Going to those *Playboy* sites or somethin' while Bill was scrunched over a toilet tryin' to hacksaw a stinkin' flange bolt off.

Cripes, Bob Villa didn't know nothin'!

Bill was thinking about Bob Villa because there was a half-page ad from Sears in the paper he was reading . . . and Bob Villa was on it big as life. Some kind-a fancypants tool for unscrewing stripped or rusted bolts. Bill guffawed as he sat in the maintenance office hunched over Bob Villa's mug, a cup of coffee next to him on the long foldup table.

"Yeah, that ain't gonna work! Hah! You see this, Milt?"

Milt was at the other end repairing the guts to a toilet tank from one of the guest suites. A tank they'd simply replaced with a new one yesterday, but Bill never threw anything out and always had his crew tinkering and whatnot when there wasn't a big job to be working on. The shelves around them were filled with broke things that weren't broke anymore and could be used to replace broke things in the rooms, y'know, in a pinch. Milt looked over at his boss and felt his tongue get all tied up and twisted like the metal part that connected the tank floater to the thingamajig.

"Wh-wh-wh-wh-wha . . . huh?"

"This garbage here," Bill spat, turning the paper around so Milt could see it. "Some kind-a fancypants wrench looks like it'll fall apart first time ya use it! Hah! Bob Villa don't know diddle about *home improvement!*"

He said "home improvement" with disdain like it was something to be scoffed at. Milt didn't even want to get his boss started on Tim Allen, so he just nodded his head emphatically and grunted.

"Hmmph," he said.

Just then something caught Bill's eye from the front page of the local newspaper. It was the headline: "COPPER HILLS SLASHER STRIKES AGAIN."

"Whoo-ee," he said, then whistled low. "Man, there been another attack, Milt. This guy's one sick puppy."

There'd been a maniac going around town raping women and slashing them afterwards with a knife. For the last month or so. Nine different instances, all along the main drag there in Copper Hills. Mostly he'd break into ground-floor hotel rooms and attack women who were staying alone. Real bad character. From hospital beds, some of the victims described him as either Hispanic or white, late 20s or early 30's, about 5'9" or thereabouts. Most were too traumatized to really remember much. Like every third man in the valley was fitting that description, Bill figured.

He squinted to read the small print and noted that the new attack was at the Copper Hills Vista Inn, just down the block a mile or so. The guy'd jimmied a window on a ground-floor room and just went in and did his business. A woman in her late 50s, they didn't know if she was gonna make it or not. Was in town for a conference on school reform, or some such gobbily-gook. Bill figured the gal was wishing she'd just skipped it. Stayed home and baked some cookies for the old man.

"I tell ya, Milt. It's gettin' so a body ain't safe goin' to bed at night."

Milt had been reading about this nut for the past month and was frankly sort of concerned. He wondered if they, meaning Bill and him and Donny, should maybe be doing something about securing the windows in their own ground-floor units. FOI was standing in the path of this moron and they weren't doing anything about security. Like they needed to put bars up on all those windows. They wouldn't be pretty, he knew that, but there didn't seem to be much of a choice. He tried to put it into words.

"W-w-w-we ain't safe, Bill. Need to secure those windows on the ground floor. Put up security b-b-b-b . . . bars. On the windows, y'know?"

Bill knew what he was referring to. Those black iron things they bolted onto windows in the ghetto. But this was Copper Hills, not New York City or Los Angeles. And those security bars'd eat up his budget for the next year and a half. He stared over the paper at Milt and made a face.

"Like what, Milt? You want me to pull these security bars out-a my ear or somethin'? You kiddin'?"

Milt tried to formulate a response but could not. Eventually he looked back down at the toilet tank guts and sighed. He wished to God he could speak up for himself and what he believed in. But it was so awful hard.

GILDED MARINADE

Liquor costs'd been high the last 6 months. Mike was finishing up with inventory in the liquor room where they kept backup bottles. Costs compared to sales just didn't jive. The wine was all off, which didn't make any sense at all. Draft beer was usually where a thief got ya, and those numbers were pretty reasonable. It was a small staff and he trusted everyone but the new guy, Floyd.

Some waiter who'd been promoted to his staff because he was so good, and then suddenly became bad, and now he was stuck with him.

The guy was probably putting together a wine cellar underneath his trailer. Mike laughed at the thought, despite how dark things looked. There'd been some reservations on the part of management when the responsibility for doing inventory was relegated to him. Something about checks and balances and how it didn't sit right with Heidi that a manager who still had bartending shifts should be cracking the numbers. Heidi was sometimes kind of anal, but John was cool and trusted him. That was the problem, of course. Mike felt like he was letting John down every time those figures came in.

And it was happening again. Somebody was stealing. Mike sat on a case of *Zing Zang Bloody Mary* mix and counted the bottom shelf where the silly booze was. Stuff like crème de menthe white and green and crème de cocoa light and dark and blah, blah, blah, every month the same. No way was it Eddie. He'd have to be Houdini to be stealing. They worked together all the time and he'd not seen one thing to make him think otherwise. Now, Floyd—that was another matter. And Kate who worked days had the opportunity, but she just didn't seem the type.

Mike hated the idea of hiring spotters to watch his people, but quite frankly was running out of options. Most of all, though, he wanted to solve this problem on his own without involving Heidi. That's all he needed was Heidi getting a little more ammo on him. That woman wanted to run everything. His job. Tony's job. Everybody's job.

Just then Dardina peeked in.

"Oh, it's you," she said. "How're ya doin', Mike?"

"I'm just peachy," he lied, looking up at her. It was 9:00 A.M. on his day off and he was counting maraschino cherries. "Whadaya need?"

She came in and scooted around him and grabbed two bottles of $38 cabernet.

"Oh, just some red for marinade. What're you doin' here so early?"

Mike stared at her.

"Inventory," he said.

Dardina laughed.

"I know what *that's* like," she said, heading back out. "Keep the faith."

There was a sign-out sheet on a clipboard nailed to the wall. She didn't even bother writing the wine up.

"Dardina," he said, about ready to explode, his voice even as he could manage. "Come back here, please."

She turned around.

"Yeah. What's up?"

"You know you're supposed to sign that wine out on the sheet, don't ya?"

She looked blank as the sheet.

"Huh? What sheet?"

Mike felt one of those Zing Zangs going up his butt. He tried to control his temper, but it was difficult. Started twirling his pencil.

"So, how long ya been doin' marinades with my cab?"

"I dunno," she said, suddenly defensive. "Since I made sous chef, I guess. What's the problem?"

Six months.

What's the problem.

"Put the cabernet down, Dardina."

"What?"

"Right now. Put it down!"

Eric and Mike almost came to blows in the back kitchen office, Mike all irate about his $38 cabernet being used to soak beef in. He'd come in there fuming as it was, and Eric being on the phone with suppliers didn't help much. By the time he rang off, though, Mike was leaning over the desk in his face, his white knuckles planted firmly on the oak top.

"What's yer problem, Mike?"

Mike started yelling, and then Eric responded in kind, and that set Mike off even more—and push came to shove—and that's when the prep cooks had to come in and separate the two. Dardina was off in the corner crying hysterically, feeling she'd been to blame for the episode. So, when John arrived on the scene, that's how it looked, and it was ugly.

"What's goin' on here?" he yelled. "You guys are friends! What're ya doin'?"

Eric shouted, "The guy's nuts, John! Comes into my office yellin' about his cabernet or some such nonsense. I don't even know what he's talkin' about!"

This caused Mike to start straining against his prep cooks and then Eric started straining against his prep cooks, and Dardina cried all the more till John himself had to get in the action and separate the two warring factions. He felt like Moe on the *Three Stooges*.

"Stop it! *Now!*"

It was later and things'd calmed down, least to the point where all parties understood the other side's beef. John's first task had been to get Dardina out of the room as soon as possible, as her hysterical sobbing was putting everyone on edge. Kate had come in from setting up the bar and John had her take Dardina off somewhere to get herself together. Once that cacophony was isolated, he kicked everybody out of Eric's office but Mike.

"Jeez, Mike! What just happened in here?"

"That idiot! She's been usin' $38 cabernet for her stinkin' marinades! Six months, John!"

"What?"

"Dardina! I'm doin' inventory and she comes in there and grabs two bottles, doesn't even sign 'em out! Just waltzes off with 'em! Says she been usin' my cab since Eric trained her for sous chef! Six months, John! I couldn't believe it! Been sweatin' inventory all this time, thinkin' my staff is stealin', and it's this idiot all the while!"

"Mike, just calm down and stop with the *idiot* business. I'm sure it was an honest mistake."

"Honest mistake? I buy Chilean red for the kitchen to use. By the case. Cost-a three bucks a pop! An' she's usin' my $38 cab! There's no excuse for it! I been catchin' hell, John! We got spotters breathin' down our necks because-a her!"

John sighed and leaned back in the kitchen manager's chair.

"Okay, fine, but what's the beef with Eric?"

"He *trained* her, man! I go back there an' he's on the phone an' then has some smart-ass reply when I ask him what's what. I been sweatin' my people for months now about the wine costs. Like I'm calling them thieves, John. My own people. Because-a Eric's slipshod training!"

John laughed when he heard Mike's use of the word *slipshod*, and then Mike laughed at it too and the tension eased a bit.

"Aw, man," Mike groaned, putting elbows on his knees and running fingers through his hair. "God, I should-a known."

"Should-a known what?"

Mike looked up.

"The table wine. The Chilean red. They weren't goin' through it, y'know? It didn't even occur to me that they were using my good stuff. I been countin' the same 60 bottles-a cheap red for months. Didn't even think of it."

John crossed his arms and considered the situation. Chef Eric was technically his subordinate, but he was indispensable to the organization and needed to be handled carefully. He was responsible for Dardina, though, and Mike was bar manager and justified in being upset (though not *that* upset, y'know, to the point of violence). Regardless, Mike was responsible for inventory irregularities that were not his fault or the fault of his people. Good grief. Lots of big toes around here to be stepped on. A career in management was sometimes like treading through a minefield. Someone had to answer for that marinade, though. Question was *who*.

THE INK IS GRAY

After Dardina got written up for that wine fiasco, she was irate. The sous chef figured she'd been unfairly signaled out because she was the lone woman, see, and, more to the point, the lone *black* woman in the mix, and wasn't that just typical of men? And though she knew it wasn't right to go over Chef Eric's head and all, she assumed naturally that another woman, the assistant general manager, Heidi, would be more sympathetic to her cause. Like, one write-up wasn't that much of a big deal, but she'd been written up last year for tardiness—and now this meant that she had *two* write-ups. . . . And one more meant that she got the ax. It just wasn't fair! So when she entered the manager's office to complain rather loudly about it, she was lucky that John and Heidi weren't there.

Sheri Eggmeyer looked up from a bagel and didn't know her from a hole in the middle.

"Yes? Can I help you?"

"Where's Heidi?"

Heidi was still at home reading the newspaper. John was out back on the pool deck watching workmen prep the south end for Frank's swim-up pool bar. Bill Gardner was there too for the groundbreaking as it were, in that his capacity as building engineer somehow required his presence, of course, because, well, nothing really got done around this joint if he didn't see to it himself. Or, so he thought.

"I dunno, boss. Still think we should-a went with my cousin on this one. These fellas look like they don't know what they doin'."

Bill's cousin was this fat guy who operated a "construction" company out of his claptrap garage. His name was Bill too, go figure. John couldn't imagine how a close-knit family such as the Gardners would independently, and, presumably of sound mind and body, perpetuate the gaffe that was naming two boys of nearabouts the same age, well, the same name, that being "William," of course, each born within 3 months of the other, naming them both *Bill*. Good grief. John tried to picture what it was like at Gardner family get-togethers, out in the sticks, with two Bills running around playing horseshoes or something.

One fat, one skinny.

Jeesh. Go figure.

"Know what I mean?"

John looked sideways at his engineer and raised a skeptical brow.

"Please, Bill," he droned, drawing the two words out like molten black taffy.

Bill removed a toothpick from his shirt pocket and stuck it in his craw.

"Hate to say I told ya so, that's all."

"Yes, Bill. Uh-huh. I've been warned."

Bill shrugged and meandered over to the work site for closer inspection. A gander, as it were. Good ol' Bill Gardner. The Arizona hardtack Gardner clan. It'd been about a year ago when John first came in contact with Bill's cousin Bill. He'd given his building engineer some latitude in choosing a contractor for some work they couldn't manage in-house. Namely, construction of a gazebo on the north lawn. Yeah, he'd told Bill Gardner to manage the project himself, initiate bids from local companies and so on and so forth, and blah, blah, blah, and he was ultimately supposed to select the most able contractor with the lowest bid. Pretty simple stuff, of course, least till John drove in for work one day and saw fat Bill out there on the grass nailing two-by-fours together. Good grief. Was like a three-ring circus: eight weeks of Bill's cousin Bill, the fat one, nailing boards together and staring at project plans like they were written in Swahili.

That was the last time he'd given Bill Gardner any latitude.

Heidi rolled the newspaper up and crammed it back inside the plastic bag it came in, then discarded the whole nightmare in a dumpster on the way to her burgundy Dodge Neon. Time to make the donuts. She got in and started the engine and split. Fifteen minutes later she was tooling past Cousin Bill's "gazebo" and it dawned on her that it resembled the leaning tower of Pisa, y'know, if it had perchance been fashioned out of rotten shantytown boards.

She made a mental note to tell John about her revelation when they met for the shift change. That "gazebo" was a constant source of agony for poor John, every time he looked upon it. Time to make the donuts. Parked in the usual spot and went in with her briefcase. Dardina was waiting for her at the front desk outside the manager's office. She looked peeved.

"You're just the person I'm lookin' for," the sous chef announced.

Huh? What's this?

It was a couple days later and John and Heidi were in the Oasis Room huddled over a table in the corner with Chef Eric. He looked like he'd swallowed a woodpecker.

"Listen," he said, "I don't give a rat's ass if she's black. She was black when I hired her, she was black when I promoted her, and she was black when I wrote her up. The whole race issue is ridiculous. She could be green and I'd still want to fire her. Race? You gotta be kidding. It's besides the point, John. She's got two write-ups, and now *this*."

John kneaded his temples.

"We have to be careful here, Eric," Heidi said, filling the void. "I just think maybe you're overreacting in this situation, y'know? Maybe we just need to step back for a minute and consider things."

"Consider things? C'mon, Heidi! She went over my head. How'd you like it if one of your subordinates went and complained to me about some action you'd taken? Like maybe if Tony Baloney said you were a lousy manager. How'd you like that, Heidi?"

"Well," she began to reply, hoping another word would attach itself to that one.

The wheels spun.

John saved her the trouble. "I'll tell ya what, Eric," he said. "We got a situation here. It ain't gonna go away. I understand what you're dealing with. Believe me, *I feel your pain*."

Eric snorted and Heidi burst into laughter.

"You feel my pain," Eric repeated. "Well, isn't that special."

John smiled. He'd been relieved a couple days ago after this whole thing started and Eric told him he'd deal with the problem himself. Saved him the trouble, didn't it? Nah, but he'd been worrying about stepping on Eric's toes, meddling in his department and all, so when Eric said he'd deal with it John just figured the best thing to do was butt out. So, that's exactly what he did.

Now he was paying for it.

ENTER THE POTTY PLANNER

John left his office and walked behind the front desk where Gabe DeFlores was registering a middle-aged obese couple on the east terminal. He went over to the west and punched in dates for when Bob Grobbins's family would be staying at FOI. The man was an event planner for the Association of Funeral Home Operators of the greater Phoenix area. Mr. Grobbins was getting his rooms comped for the weekend, with the hopes he'd direct business their way in the future. John was looking ahead to July when AFHO had their yearly seminar.

They'd stayed at *The Abbey at Copper Hills* last year, and John knew from spies that it'd been quite lucrative for them. June through August was a black hole in Arizona's hotel business, and any time you could book two-thirds of your rooms in July, that was sweet.

Gabe finished with the fat couple and came over.

"They're from Liechtenstein," he said. "That little country in Europe?"

John chuckled.

"*That* couple? Jeez. Wouldn't think there'd be room to move around. Y'know?"

Gabe smiled.

"Yep," he said. "That's just what I was thinkin'. Like if they have dinner guests, y'know, their elbows are spillin' over into Switzerland. So, what're ya doin' there, Chief-a-reeno?"

John explained to him about Bob Grobbins and the seminar. Said he couldn't find adjoining rooms for the couple and their two children next weekend for the comp stay. Gabe took over at the terminal and brought up the screen listing vacancies by floor. Their 5 and 6 units had doors that could be unlocked to create a more suite-like accommodation. The 6 units were smaller and had two double beds, while the 5 was larger and had a king-sized bed. Perfect for the Grobbins clan. Problem was, on such short notice most floors were booked for either one or the other. Gabe remembered one of the people who he'd personally set up in a 5 unit just yesterday, which was Wednesday, and this guy was a single businessman with no specifications other than a king bed. He took this man and moved him from the ninth floor to the second floor 3 unit that met that need. Consequently, this freed up the ninth floor 5 and 6 units for the Grobbins.

"Somebody, stop me," he gloated.

"You da man," said John, patting him on the back. "Say, you're on next weekend when the guy comes in. Man's in his 50s. Wife, two teen-aged kids. I want the red carpet for this family. Call housekeeping and make sure there's a fruit basket in the king room, wine and cheese tray. The works."

"Will do," Gabe assured him, making a note. "Kathy's back on the job since yesterday. I'll talk to her personally and make sure the rooms are spotless and so on. Fruit, wine and cheese baskets. Razzle-dazzle. You want anything in the twin room?"

"Just make sure it's clean. They're teen-agers, Gabe. Give 'em a bar of soap and some mouthwash."

Gabe chuckled.

"Nice to have Kathy back," he said. "Looked like she was gonna die last week. You see her walkin' out-a here?"

"No. Heard about it, though. Everybody was passin' that flu around. Just glad I didn't get it."

At that point, one of the housekeeping employees, Trini, came by on the way out from the morning shift and said hello in passing. She was wearing a short black leather dress with matching stiletto heels. There was a duffel bag over her shoulder that most likely had her work clothes inside.

"Good gracious," John exclaimed at the sight of her. "You got a date tonight?"

"Yeah," she blushed. "My boyfriend's pickin' me up. We're goin' dancing."

Gabe coughed and covered his mouth.

"Well, don't hurt anyone," said John.

Trini smiled and headed out the revolving door. They watched as she got inside a black Mustang that was waiting in the drive-thru, waved, and sped away. When all that was left was a trail of exhaust, Gabe let out a guffaw and doubled over with laughter. John looked at his front desk manager and wondered if he'd gone mad.

"You all right there, Gabe?"

When the man finally stopped laughing enough to catch his breath, John saw there were tears in his eyes and handed him a tissue from under the counter. Unfortunately, this caused him to laugh even harder. People were starting to look over from the Oasis Lounge where the pre-dinner crowd had begun to form.

"Oh, God," sputtered Gabe, leaning against the register for support. "Seymore Butts!"

"Seymore Butts?" John repeated, raising a brow. "The rock star? What about him?"

Gabe laughed some more.

"That's the dress!"

"Huh? What dress?"

"Y'know . . ."

Then, it clicked, and John started laughing. In his position as general manager of FOI, he shouldn't have, but he did.

THE GHOST OF SAM RILEY

It was 11:30 and last call wasn't for another hour. Eddie felt like he'd been dragged behind a wagon full of hay and frolicking drunk idiots. Singing songs about counting down a zillion bottles of beer. Him having to bend over each time and yank fresh ones from the cooler.

"That'll be $4 please," he said to this woman who looked to be about 29. She'd just ordered a Becks Dark, and if his back didn't hurt so much he might've been more enthusiastic about her. Blonde, nice makeup. That's the thing he always noticed about women. Their makeup. Nothing worse than a woman who didn't know how to apply it. Like his Aunt Cecilia who looked like one of those tin soldiers in *The Nutcracker,* what with those big red blotches on her cheekbones.

No, this woman knew what she was doing. He took a ten from her and trudged over to the register and rang it up. God, his back hurt. Least it made him forget about the shin splints. Almost. He was just making change out of the drawer, though, when he sensed movement directly behind him and turned to find a skinny gray suit standing there.

"I'll be with you in a sec," said Eddie, sort of smiling.

The guy pulled a leather billfold from his inside jacket pocket and there was a sheriff's badge attached to it.

"No," he snapped. "You'll be with me right now."

Eddie stopped what he was doing and felt a sort of dread.

"What's the problem, officer?"

The guy nodded toward the female to whom he'd just served a Becks Dark. "You card that little girl?"

Huh? Little girl? Eddie looked over at her and she winked.

Heidi was at a floor terminal voiding a couple items from one of Manuel's checks when she saw the commotion at the bar. Her bartender, Eddie, being placed in handcuffs by some guy in a gray suit and waiters and customers all sort of lingering around watching. She stopped what she was doing immediately and went over to see what the trouble was.

"Oh, God," she groaned. "What now?"

Tony was watching from the podium as she passed: "Uh-oh!" he said, "Eddie got busted!"

Heidi got there just as Eddie was being led out from behind the bar. He saw her and rolled his eyes.

"This is a joke, Heidi," he said, disgusted. "I been set up."

Heidi approached.

"Excuse me, sir. What's going on here?"

The man in the suit let go of Eddie and addressed her.

"Are you the manager on duty?"

"Yes," Heidi admitted. "I'm the assistant general manager, Heidi Bell. Who are you and what are you doing with my employee?"

The guy smirked and withdrew his badge again, along with another set of cuffs, which he proceeded to dangle in front of her.

"You're just the person I was looking for. As his boss you are also subject to arrest for serving a minor at this here place of business. Now, ma'am, if you'll turn around, please . . ."

Heidi looked at the badge, then over at Eddie who was standing there with his eyes closed in complete disgust, and then she gazed at the cuffs and the guy in a gray suit who was now grabbing her by the shoulder and attempting to turn her around.

"You're under arrest, ma'am."

Heidi looked sideways at Eddie as the man clicked one then the other cuff around her wrists.

"Eddie," she said, "What did you do?"

He'd opened his eyes back up by now, and gestured with a nod over to where the "minor" in question sat at the bar filling out forms and looking very major.

"That's the chick over there. I served her a beer, Heidi, and I didn't card her 'cause she looks like she's stinkin' 30!" Then he addressed the sheriff: "Man, you gotta be kidding! This is entrapment!"

"Tell it to the judge, son."

It wasn't really funny, per se, but Gabe DeFlores still had to bite the insides of his cheeks to keep from grinning as he watched the sheriff lead Heidi and that red-headed bartender out through the lobby in cuffs. Tony, the dining room manager, was running along behind them in his hostess outfit assuring the assistant general manager about how he would "hold the fort down" till she got back.

She shouted to Gabe: "Call John at home! They say Eddie served a minor at the bar!"

He replied, "Will do, Heidi!"

Now he could laugh. But without the visual props, well, it wasn't even remotely funny anymore. Had it ever been funny? If not, then why was it so hard to keep from laughing just a second or two ago? Only God knew. Gabe grabbed the phone and speed-dialed John. He figured the general manager wouldn't think it was funny at all, y'know, being roused from sleep to go bail out a couple employees from jail. No, John wouldn't have any trouble at all keeping the grin off his face.

It rang three times before a groggy John Fallin answered the phone.

"Yeah?"

"This is Gabe. We got trouble, Chief."

"Gabe? Where *are* you?"

"Where ya think? I'm at work."

There was a pause.

"It's almost midnight. What're you doin' at work?"

"Oh, yeah," Gabe said, the truth finally dawning on him as to why he'd found it so amusing watching Heidi get led out through the lobby in cuffs. "The night auditor called off so I gotta do a double. It's that flu business, apparently. Real pain in the butt."

John was fully awake now.

"Why am I talking to you, Gabe?"

"Oh, sorry," he said, matter-of-factly. "Heidi's been arrested—"

"What?!"

"Yeah, some business about that red-headed bartender serving minors. Took both of 'em out through the lobby in cuffs. You should-a been here."

"Aw, man?"

"Yep. A sight to behold. But, not to worry, Tony Macaroni is in charge."

"Who?"

"The head waiter."

There was silence for a long moment, after which Gabe added, "But, y'know—just the same, Chief, I think you better get on down to the station and bail 'em out."

There was a loud click that actually made Gabe wince.

"Ouchy-poo," he said, removing the phone from his ear.

Nope. Not funny at all. Someone's head was gonna roll, and most likely it was the red one.

MORE OR LESS BLACK LEATHER DRESS

"C'mon, Trini, let's get real here," said Kathy Lawhorn, head of housekeeping. "We've had several calls about that dress."

"Yeah? What dress? I dunno what yer talkin' about."

It was 8:30 in the morning. The general manager had sent a memo about Trini sporting that finery the previous afternoon and she'd heard similar tales from a couple other employees. What a meatball! Punishment for stealing that black dress had already been meted, though. Just by her walking around in it like a big dummy the past week. Good Lord. Kathy just wanted to gauge her reaction, though, to the accusation, and see what kind of implications it had toward her future responsibilities with FOI. Like, could Trini still be trusted? Should they let her go? Frankly, that was something Kathy did not want to do. After all, you didn't need Mother Teresa for cleaning a hotel room, and, a bilingual white girl was not something you just tossed out over the side.

Over a party dress.

"You didn't hear about Seymore Butts?"

Trini laughed nervously.

"What's that? A porno?"

Now it was Kathy's turn to laugh.

Afterwards, "Yeah, well—sort of."

Trini sat there and twisted. What was with this woman? She'd taken that black leather dress, but, y'know, big deal. Nobody'd ever called *Kathy Lawhorn* about it. What'd Kat care so much for? It wasn't like she was making a million dollars a year. *Lighten up, sister.* Seemed like it was a big joke or something, though. A joke Trini wasn't in on.

She tried to piece it all together. On one hand, Kat'd sat her down for a talk . . . but, then again, she was just sort-a meandering around the subject. Tiptoeing. It was weird. Like it was a test, yet her job somehow depended on it.

"What's this about?" Trini asked.

Kathy laughed some more.

Trini folded her arms, utterly chapped.

The boss finally got control of herself, then went, "You took the dress home, didn't you? Don't lie to me. The leather one? The mini-skirt?"

Trini had a revelation: if Kat was laughing about it so much, then it must not be such a big deal. At first she'd been worried about her job and all, but after a while it seemed like the whole leather dress thing was a joke. She made a decision right then and there about coming clean with the fact she'd brought home that dress.

"Yeah," she admitted. "So what?"

Trini's world careened a bit.

Kathy laughed a little more and then sobered and popped a stick of Dentine in her mouth. Felt much better afterwards, like she'd just brushed her teeth.

"Want a stick?"

Trini looked at the little rectangle in her boss's hand.

"Nah," she said. "No, thanks, Kat."

Kathy hated this part of her job.

"Listen," she said, chewing, getting all I-can't-speak-Spanish serious. "You ever take anything from the lost-and-found again . . . and you're fired on the spot. Comprendo?"

Trini blurted, "Excuse me?"

"You heard me," said Kathy Lawhorn.

She'd heard her, all right. Still didn't know what was so funny about her taking that dress, though. Trini got up to leave.

"Okay," she said. "I didn't think it was a big deal, Kat."

"Yeah, whatever."

Kathy watched her leave and tried to remember where she'd put that *Passport to Spanish* book. Somewhere in her shelves at home. She'd look for it later. That's for certain. If it was the last thing she ever did. She'd find that stupid book.

LOYALTY SCHMOYALTY

It was Friday morning and Mike was at the bar dealing with the building engineer, Bill Gardner, who was supposed to repair a leak under the triple sink about a month ago. Work orders had been sent through proper channels, messages had been left on his office phone's answering machine, and Mike'd even gone to the trouble of tacking notes on his superfluous bulletin board. But Bill Gardner never fixed the leaky pipe thing, and Mike'd begun to wonder just exactly what it was that maintenance actually did during the day. Y'know, when he was sleeping. Which he should've been doing right now, but wasn't, and that was because he'd come down in person to light a fire under where he imagined Bill Gardner kept his to-do list.

He was leaning down behind it when some joker in a shiny blue suit came in and sat at the far end of the bar.

"Jeez, Bill. Maybe you could requisition a belt or a length a rope or somethin'. I can almost see your tonsils."

Bill grunted, "Huh?"

It was hard for Bill to hear, of course, being that he was wedged so tightly under the sink.

"Nothin'," said Mike, yawning. "I gotta go see what this guy wants. I'll be right back."

"Huh?"

Mike walked down to the man at the bar who'd opened his briefcase and was spilling papers and whatnot all over the place. He figured it was maybe another one of those crooks from the city who kept hassling them every 5 minutes. It'd been crazy lately. Three times they'd had liquor inspectors testing the alcohol content in bottles behind the bar. Then poor Eddie getting busted for serving that minor who looked like she qualified for the AARP discount. He'd talked to John about it because liquor costs'd been out of whack lately too—and he'd honestly begun to fear for his own job.

John was cool, though. Told him not to worry about Eddie and that FOI would represent him in court and pay the $500 fine if need be. Apparently there'd been some dude from the permits department who'd solicited them for a bribe. Some business about the new swim-up pool bar construction, but John'd turned the guy in and that's why all the problems started in the first place.

Five hundred bucks was what the guy asked for. Well, Mike appreciated his general manager standing behind Eddie and all, but $500 was no big deal compared to all the nonsense that'd taken place just because John got all self-righteous and stood up for his principles. Everybody else had to suffer. Man, even Chef Eric was getting inspected by these dudes. At least twice they'd gone through his kitchen and gave it the white-glove treatment. Not too many kitchens could stand up under that kind of scrutiny, but Eric's did.

At any rate, he'd thought the torment was over because he heard John got Frank the owner involved—and that dude was supposedly real heavily connected downtown. Didn't look that way now, though, what with this sharkskin pencil pusher getting all set up on his bar.

"Sorry, sir," he said, dreading what was most surely to come. "The bar's not open till 10:00. We're just in here doing some maintenance. Y'know what they say: got time to lean, got time to clean."

"No problem," said the guy, extending his hand. "I'm Vaughn Harding, from Bettis Incorporated. I was hoping to speak with the bar manager."

"That'd be me," Mike replied, shaking the man's hand. "Name's Mike."

"Oh, great! I'm in luck!"

Luck, thought Mike. *I'll be lucky if I'm back in bed having nightmares about Gardner's to-do list. Lucky-schmucky.*

"Bettis Incorporated? What's that?"

"Liquor distributors, new to Arizona but we've been operating in California and Nevada since '87. If you can spare a couple minutes, I'd like to introduce you to our line of product."

"Uh-huh," Mike said. "We've been using the local guys pretty much since opening; happy with 'em, I guess . . . but, I dunno. Suppose I got a minute or so. What kind of deals you folks able to offer?"

"We can go 3 percent lower than you're getting from Raleigh on the premiums, and a whole 5 on the well. Plus we got quantity freebies."

"Quantity freebies," Mike mused, rubbing his jaw. The guy had a printout in front of him with what looked like the exact numbers FOI was paying Raleigh for booze. "I see . . . . And so we're supposed to just blow these guys off, huh?"

The dude in the flashy suit nodded, hopeful.

Just then Bill Gardner crawled out from under the sink and hiked his pants back up: "Hey, Mikey," he announced, "Pipe's all fixed."

In the best of all possible worlds, Mike thought, *there'd be nothing flashy about plumbers.*

He testified, "You da man!"

SHRINKAGE

Tony came in for his host shift on Friday and the waitstaff was all in a tizzy. He was hanging his coat up in back when Kelly appeared with hands on her hips and an eyebrow raised.

"Ex-squeeze me?" he said.

"The new stations."

"Huh? What're you talkin' about? What new stations?"

Kelly folded her arms and smirked at him.

"Don't play dumb. The new stations. They've shrunk everybody's stations!"

Tony hadn't even been out on the floor yet. He'd worked last night and nothing was amiss. Another waiter, Raul, saw them back there and came up.

"What's goin' on here?" he asked. "I got three five-tops and a deuce. This is ridiculous."

Tony looked at Raul. He didn't know what they were talking about.

"I just got here," he said, all defensive. "If they changed the stations, Heidi didn't tell me about it."

"Well, they're all about one or two tables smaller," Kelly sniffed. "I got one large round, a four-top and two deuces. How'm I gonna pay rent on that kind-a business?"

Tony held his hands up in surrender.

"Let me go to the podium an' check this out. Take a look at the seating chart. If Heidi's switched things around, I'll go talk to her an' see what's up. I work here too, y'know."

"Okay," conceded Raul, but Kelly just stared at him.

"This is stupid," she said.

He walked out and headed for the podium. Two other waiters tried to way-lay him but Tony waved them off, indicating he already knew what they wanted. It was like he had a mass revolt on his hands. Suzanne, the day hostess, was there at the podium looking besieged.

"Everybody's mad," she said, giving him a look.

"I don't blame 'em. What *is* this nonsense?" he asked, unearthing the seating chart from under some menus. "Heidi didn't say a word to me about changing the stations."

"I guess there were a couple bad spotters' reports last week."

He stared at her. "Spotters' reports? Since when do we have spotters at FOI?"

She shrugged her shoulders.

"Since last week, I guess."

Tony looked at the chart and everything'd shrunk.

"You've gotta be kidding," he gasped, dropping his jaw. "No way. No way, baby. Nobody is gonna wanna work here. Station six has four deuces! Oh, my God."

Suzanne nudged him.

"Here she comes now."

It was Heidi, entering the dining room. Tony was incensed. Not merely about the changes, or the hiring of spotters, but Tony was outraged that all this'd been done without even consulting him. He was dining room manager, after all. What kind of insult was this? His whole staff looked at him now like some kind of impotent stooge. He yanked the seating chart up, which'd been taped on the podium, and met the assistant general manager halfway across the dining room floor.

"Heidi," he snapped, pointing at it. "This will not do."
She folded her arms and said, "What?"

FRANK WILL BE FRANK

They saw a lot more of Frank Stratten after the pool bar opened about midway through the month. Frank actually went so far as to adopt the swim-up pool bar as his de facto office, though Frank didn't really do anything much resembling work at FOI. Unless you considered working on his tan some kind of gainful occupation. Mainly, Frank just held court there, drank pina coladas, and chewed the fat with Jorgé the bartender. Except one Friday afternoon all bright and early (for Frank) when John passed the doors leading to the pool deck and saw him sitting there all buddy/buddy, stool-to-stool with that rat, Sam Riley.

John stopped in his tracks, uttering, "What the . . .?"

Yep, it was Sam Riley. John couldn't believe it! Talking business? He almost stormed out there to see what was what, but held back at the last moment. Stood there chewing the left side of his cheek. What was going on here?

He'd just dined on Chef Eric's wiener schnitzel and could feel it suddenly roiling in his stomach. The cucumbers and red onions marinated overnight in sugary white vinegar and then drained and coated with sour cream, served on the side, especially nasty now, and the parsley/boiled new potatoes simmered in butter, *oh, God*. John thought he'd seen the last of Sam Riley, yet he was out there right now snorting fu-fu drinks with the owner, Frank Stratten.

Looked like a strawberry daiquiri.

He stormed back toward the lobby with his mind racing. If this is what Frank meant when he said he'd "take care of it," *it* being the problem with Riley and his buddies in the city inspector's office, well, forget it! He could've just paid the rat off himself and avoided this whole mess! Why'd they have to go through all this nonsense if Frank was just gonna pay him off anyway? John could've paid him off! But he'd taken the high road, and now the owner was knuckling under!

He was in a cold sweat by the time he got to the front desk and leaned on it, both elbows, with his fingers massaging temples in the middle of which a migraine had lodged itself. It was 1:30 in the afternoon. Gabe must have just started work and was over on the far terminal dealing with this rotund man, about 40 years old, who had his black hair all slicked back and sounded like he was from New Jersey. The guy didn't just talk real loud, he *boomed*, as if everyone within 20 yards should hear just what be-jabbers he had to say. Which didn't help John's headache much, y'know.

The guy: "So, it's like—ba-da-bing/ba-da-bang/ba-da-boom! Next ting I knowed it was snowin' all over da place an' I'm goin', *I'm out-a here!* But you know they ain't flyin' no planes! Sose I gotta wait 24 hours for da next flight! I got a tab at the hotel bar three-fitty 'fore I knows what's what!"

John closed his eyes and tried to block the man's ramblings out, but it was impossible. What's worse was the entire conversation was one-sided because Gabe's part was a reasonable volume and didn't carry all the way over, so it was just a murmur really, and then the fat man'd start blustering again and blah, blah, blah. Like listening to some moron on the subway shouting into a cell phone. A full 5 minutes before Gabe finished checking him in and the blowhard waddled away behind Kip the bellboy. At last there was blessed silence.

Gabe came over.

"Somebody, kill me," he groaned.

John asked, "Who was that idiot?"

"Oh, him? Why, that's Johnny Haagen-Dazs. He's in from the Big Apple."

John laughed, despite himself.

"Good grief," he said.

"No, he's some guy here for a *salt and pepper shakers* convention. John Schmedley's the name, salt 'n pepper's the game. No kidding. In Scottsdale, believe it or not. Apparently every year tens of thousands of collectors converge on a lucky town somewhere and they set up booths and sell antique salt and pepper shakers. It's real lucrative, according to Johnny Haagen-Dazs."

John laughed again. Gabe had a real knack for coming up with just the perfect nicknames for people, he supposed because in his job he came across so many types and learned to peg them right off the bat. And this one was better than most, but then John remembered about Wily Riley out drinking in the pool with Frank.

"Hey," he said, getting all serious: "What's that guy from the city doing here? Sam Riley. He's drinking at the pool bar with Frank."

Gabe knew who Sam Riley was and had been instructed by John never to let him inside the premises again. Gabe held his hands up as if to demonstrate how he had no control over this particular situation.

"No, no, no, no, no. The guy said he had an appointment with Frank. In his 'office,' no less. I knew he was tellin' the truth 'cause he was standing there in a *swimsuit*. What was I supposed to do?"

John shook his head. Frank's *office*.

This place was becoming a three-ring circus. John suddenly wanted to take a nap. Dream about, well, nothing. But just then Sam Riley came gliding over the lobby tiles like he was the King of Southwestern Rhode Island. He saw John standing there and came straight for him. He was drying the back of his head with a towel from the pool area, real brisk-like, and smiling in that conspiratorial rat way these guys from the inspector's office were becoming famous for. When he arrived at the desk, he deposited the damp terry in front of Gabe like he'd know just what to do with it, then offered his hand out to John for a shake.

The way John looked at Riley's hand was exactly the way Gabe was considering his lousy towel. Both were disgusted.

Riley: "No hard feelin's, John. I had a nice talk with yer boss 'n everything's worked out."

John still didn't say anything, and certainly wasn't going to shake the rat's hand, so eventually the rodent got self-conscious and let it drop to his side.

"Listen," he said. "You're mad. I can understand that. I just wanted to apologize for any misunderstandings, y'know, 'n let you know there won't be any more interference from the city."

Gabe meanwhile'd taken a pencil and was skewering the wet towel with the eraser end, and he was attempting to maneuver it over into a plastic garbage can that was under the front desk. He had this expression on his face that implied: *This is not a towel. It is a buffalo chip.*

Sam Riley caught that and sighed. John just stood there saying nothing.

"Well," Riley concluded. "I'm sorry, anyway. So Frank's got my card. If there's any trouble in the future—with permits, or inspections, or *anything*—well, you just give me a call."

John wanted to hurl wiener schnitzel on the rat.

"So, bye now," said the guy, after which he turned and walked purposefully out across the tiles and exited through the revolving door.

What had Frank done?

HEIDI HIGH, HEIDI LOW

Gabe was on his break Friday evening and had gone to the lounge for a plate of Chef Eric's wiener schnitzel that John'd been whining about earlier. Everybody was always running around like chickens with their heads cut off. They all needed to chill out. Not take everything so seriously. Especially John. Like with that creep from the permits department or whatever. Poor guy was gonna die of a heart attack if he didn't get his shorts unbunched. They could all learn a thing or two from Gabe. It was yoga, actually. Three mornings a week he went to yoga class at the gym. That's how Gabe managed to keep everything in perspective. The mind and the body were inseparable.

They were one.

Chef Eric brought the plates out himself. It was the end of his day and he'd finally get to try the schnitzel he'd been making over and over for 8 hours. Gabe couldn't imagine making wiener schnitzel all day and then eating it. You'd think it'd get kind of sickening after about the 400th plate. At any rate, Chef Eric came over with the righteous vittles and sat down across from him at the table usually set aside for employees. Gabe looked up and smiled. Not so much at Eric but more so at the prospect of eating that wonderful pounded veal. It smelled fantastic! The mind and the body were one with yoga, and both needed Eric's special breading to prosper.

He contemplated the plate in front of him and fanned the aroma into his nostrils. He hadn't eaten since that morning before work. He was ravenous.

"Oh, my!" he exclaimed. "That smells *vundiba!* Thanks for the weiner schnitzel!"

"Yeah, no problem," Eric grumbled, "but don't call me schnitzel."

"What?"

Just then Gabe's radio crackled and it was Ellen at the front desk.

"Gabe! Come in, please!"

Gabe rolled his eyes. He complained to the schnitzel: "Aw, man! I should never take this stupid radio when I'm going for dinner!"

Eric sliced a triangle of schnitzel and forked it into his mouth. Nice texture, pleasant, unassuming flavor. He'd gotten the recipe from his grandfather on his mother's side. Grandpa Laszlo, from Hungary. Guy was crazy as a loon and had swore he'd seen two-headed space aliens on at least three occasions while boating on Lake Powell, but he sure knew how to make schnitzel.

"You gonna answer that?" he inquired of Gabe, pointing at the radio with his now empty fork.

Gabe picked up the offensive black troll. He closed his eyes briefly and tried to picture his body and mind as one, oblivious to the siren's call of schnitzel.

"Yeah, Ellen. I copy. What's up?"

"Gabe, you need to come back to the desk. We have a problem."

Yoga. Schnitzel.

"I'm eating dinner. Can't it wait?"

"It's that promotion thing Heidi sent out. The one for the weekend rates? You gotta see it, Gabe. I got a guest trying to make reservations on the phone right now. I've got them on hold."

Gabe looked at the schnitzel and could sense it getting cold.

"I don't get it, Ellen. Just take the stinkin' reservation. You want me to hold your hand or somethin'?"

"No, you don't understand. There was some kind of printing error. This guy called and said he wanted to book a room for that weekend, y'know, and I quoted him the price . . . and he said it was wrong. It's seventy-five a night, y'know, and he said it was seven-fifty. So, I'm thinkin' he's crazy, y'know, but I go take a look at one of our copies of the promo, and . . ."

The transmission got kind of choppy all of a sudden like maybe Ellen was crying. Gabe had been meaning to talk to her lately about that yoga and how it might be something that she could benefit from. Ellen was always getting emotional about one thing or another. She just needed to chill out. Take an aspirin or something.

"Just calm down, Ellen. What's wrong with Heidi's promo?"

"He's right! They must've misplaced a decimal point or something! It says $7.50 a night for the weekend! The suites! What're we gonna do?"

Gabe's stomach twisted up in a knot and his eyes almost popped out of his head. That Heidi! The moron'd messed up! Not seventy-five dollars a night, not seven hundred and fifty dollars a night. *Seven dollars and fifty cents* a night for the weekend, in the suites no less, printed out and sent to every customer on their mailing list!? Oh, my God! Eight hundred and ninety-some-odd copies mailed out to every blooming customer on their mailing list!?

WHAT IN GOD'S NAME ARE WE GONNA DO?!!

A ROMP THROUGH COMP

Floyd was annoyed. The guy just parked his keister right in front of the register and sat there drinking a Coke like he did this every Friday night. Uh-huh. Went out to the local hotel bar and drank sody-pop? Yeah, right. Wasn't fooling anybody. Sipping his beverage and watching every move Floyd made. Like, how obvious can you get?

The dude was a stinkin' SPOTTER.

They'd brought them in over at the last joint he worked when liquor costs went up and management thought everyone was stealing. That was real nice coming in to work and seeing these stiffs planted there on the bar stools, taking furtive notes every once in a while. Like some stupid stuff about your shirt not being tucked in or you didn't say *thank you* when some tightwad left you a buck on twenty worth of drinks. Taking up valuable space at the bar. Like a constant reminder that management doesn't trust you, and, in fact, is so sure that you're stealing that they've committed funds to try and catch you in the act. What a joke. And now they were doing it here at FOI.

Great.

Whatever. The thing that really killed Floyd was that these SPOTTERS didn't know squat about bartending or waiting tables. You could be drinking straight vodka and robbing the store blind, and all they'd do was submit a big report to management about how there was dirt under the nail of your left index finger. Management would sit you down and go, "Listen, buster, we need those nails clean . . . stat!"

It was funny, actually. These guys didn't know the first thing about working in a restaurant. Floyd knew all the angles. He'd been around. Floyd could've become a SPOTTER and nailed every bartender in the valley for stealing, well, if he could find it in himself to sink so low. Not likely, amigo. There was a certain honor amongst thieves, and no self-respecting bar gangster would turn on his brothers. Like—the way drug dealers felt about NARCS—that's how bartenders looked at SPOTTERS. No, Floyd'd never do *that* job.

"How're ya doing here, sir? You ready for a refill?"

The SPOTTER didn't smile or anything, just sat there all noncommittal. Waiting for Floyd to engage him or who-knows-what.

"No, thanks," he said, and then: "So what's the menu like here?"

Yeah, there it was. Now the guy'd be rating his knowledge of the menu and his spunk and blah, blah, blah. Get him jumping through hoops. The SPOTTER didn't really care what the menu was like here; he just wanted to make life difficult for Floyd T. McElwain. But Floyd'd been a waiter here at FOI just about a month ago before being promoted to the bar, so he knew more about the menu than all the other bartenders at FOI put together. So Floyd T. McElwain set about to bedazzle the SPOTTER for a full 5 minutes, and, when it was over, that stiff knew more about FOI's breakfast, lunch, and dinner menus than even John Fallin the general manager did.

Finally: "So, did you want to order something from the kitchen, sir? We have a great selection of entrees and appetizers on the bar menu, but it's slow enough tonight where I could probably manage anything off the regular menu too. Whadaya think?"

"Oh, no," said the SPOTTER. "No, thanks."

Uh-huh. Right. Floyd smiled at the guy and nodded.

"Well, let me know if you change your mind, sir. My name's Floyd, F-L-O-Y-D, and I'm here if you need me."

An older couple had just sat down on the other end, so Floyd bebopped over all spunky and whatnot and imagined Godzilla crashing through the ceiling and plucking that SPOTTER'S head clean off. The new stiffs looked like they'd been out in the sun too long for the past 50 years. Native Arizonans. Floyd was from the East Coast originally and referred to these leathery sorts as "hard-tackers," which was a wafer of unleavened bread the western settlers and mountain men used to eat up like it was truffles.

"Hi, folks! How're ya doin' tonight? Can I get you somethin' to drink?"

And so the night progressed, Floyd gallivanting in front of the SPOTTER looking as gung-ho as he could possibly manage, every once in a while asking SPOTTER if maybe he'd like another refill. *Or, maybe you've had second thoughts about not wanting to order something off the menu, sir?* It was hard making money here at FOI when you were the new guy and a SPOTTER was sitting right in front of your register. They didn't give new bartenders comp checks till they'd been on the job a couple months—and if you couldn't buy customers a drink every once in a while, well, you just weren't gonna make any dough. So Floyd charged everybody for every drink until about 9:30 when the SPOTTER headed for the little boys' room to drain out some of that sody-pop.

It was quite fortuitous at the time, really, in that he'd been waiting on this group of suits who ordered various brown drinks (i.e. scotch/soda, bourbon/water, CC/rocks, etc.). So, SPOTTER got up and toddled off to the toilet just as he was charging the suits for their round.

Said Floyd: "That'll be $19, guys."

The group's biggest cheese pulled out a twenty from his billfold and handed it over.

"Keep it," he said.

Floyd T. McElwain looked over and the SPOTTER was off tinkling.

He thought to himself, *Hmmmmmmmm.*

CAN YOU SPELL SNAFU?

John sat in the office Saturday morning with Heidi and that Eggmeyer woman who he really didn't care for much, despite the fact she was so efficient at her bookkeeping. He couldn't say egg-zactly why, but he just didn't trust her. He liked to hire his own people, and he felt like this bookkeeper'd been shoved down his throat. He almost missed Edna Duncan. He was sure that Eggmeyer woman was nothing more than a spy for Lex Lilly.

That's how it happens, he thought to himself. First you experience paranoia. Next you hear voices.

Then, it's the loony bin.

"I assure you, Mr. Fallin, the text for the promotion was just a file when I e-mailed it to Delphagraphics. I had no idea whatsoever what was contained therein, and was merely doing what Heidi instructed."

"Well, that was very egg-spedient of you, Ms. Eggmeyer."

Sheri Eggmeyer could not stand John Fallin. The guy thought he was very clever with the egg jokes all the time, like she was so dense that she couldn't tell he was making fun of her name, no, not likely, John Fallin just *thought* he was clever. But he wasn't clever. And neither was that Heidi Bell who'd probably made the mistake in her promo ad and was just now trying to blame it on the printers. Seven dollars and fifty cents a night for the suites. Hah! Wait till Lex hears about this one!

John swiveled in his chair and gazed at Heidi through fingers that were kneading the painful space between his eyebrows. He felt like his head was gonna explode. The weekend before Christmas they had three bookings already for suites at $7.50 a night. There was nothing they could do. Almost 900 of the ads had been sent out already, and if the customer wanted to be a hard-ass about it, they had no other choice but to rent them the rooms at the advertised price: SEVEN DOLLARS AND FIFTY CENTS.

"John, I swear," said Heidi, "I checked that copy a hundred times! I don't care what they said; it was them that messed it up. You think I'm gonna make that kind of mistake? No way!"

John had called Hal over at Delphagraphics earlier and the man swore up and down that he too was blameless. He said he merely prints the copy that clients submit. *If you want to pay me to do your ads, John, then I'll stand behind the content. Otherwise, you got a problem with the color or somethin', well, you feel free to lemmie know about it.*

Good grief.

Heidi was really messing up, big time. First the thing with the server stations being changed without the dining room manager knowing about it. The entire staff up in arms all week. Now this. What a mess!

"Well," he said, "I think the letter's a good idea. Make sure that Ms. Eggmeyer proofreads it afterwards, though, so there isn't any egg-strainious verbiage contained therein."

John had spoken with Frank's lawyer for the hotel and was advised that a disclaimer should be sent out to each name on the list as soon as possible. Until sufficient time went by where it could be assumed that each guest on the list had received their disclaimer, well, they had no choice but to honor the weekend rate of $7.50 per room if the customer insisted. A lot of the people responding to the ad were understanding about the mix-up, but some were not. Gabe had been pulling his hair out the past two days. What a piece of work.

John figured that poor guy was gonna die young if he didn't learn to control his emotions.

He asked Heidi, "So, where are we at right now?"

Heidi was bent over a legal pad composing the disclaimer. It'd been a very long night for her yesterday, and now coming in early this morning was shaping this day into another very long night. She just wanted to dunk her head in a giant vodka martini and call it a day. She simply could not think straight anymore.

"The last graph—say, that looks wrong. How do you spell 'snafu'?"

Eggmeyer looked up from some printouts.

"What are you working on?" she inquired, "Your resumé?"

"Very funny," said Heidi, clearly annoyed.

THE EAGLE HAS LANDED

The vibrator went off on John's cell phone while he dined in the Garden Vista at lunchtime. He was having a private meeting with his assistant general manager, Heidi Bell, about a recent snafu where waiter station sizes were changed in the restaurant—without the dining room manager's knowledge—thereby bringing into question his leadership role amongst the staff. Heidi could see the mistake she'd made, and the two of them had met to devise a way of backing out of the problem without ruffling any more feathers. It was all about saving face. For Tony Marziano, obviously, but if placating him meant undermining Heidi's authority, well, that too was a problem.

John plucked the phone off his belt and read the text message.

THE EAGLE HAS LANDED.

It was from Gabe DeFlores, his front desk manager, a man whose sense of humor he sometimes appreciated, but not today. Because this was an actual Saturday, and John never worked the working stiff's Saturdays, and, furthermore, he didn't appreciate having to don suit and tie so that he could deal with the various mini-crisis that other people should've managed on their own. That's what they were getting paid for, after all. By design, his job should've always gone smoothly, without a hitch, but that depended on his subordinates' jobs running just as well. There was always a fly in the ointment.

It was just a half-day, though, and Gabe's silly text message signified the end of it. That party planner from Phoenix, Bob Grobbins, had arrived with his wife and two kids. John had wanted to be there to make sure everything went smoothly. It's not that he didn't trust his employees, he just didn't trust them when it came to a possible block of July room rentals. Worst part was, though, that not only was half his Saturday blown, but he'd have to repeat the process on Sunday as well.

John Fallin was booked for brunch with the Grobbins family on Sunday, the working stiff's Sunday, the day he never got out of his slippers and robe.

"It's Gabe," he explained to Heidi. "The big cheese is here. Him and his brood."
Heidi nodded.

"Sure'd be nice if we could land that booking, though. July's pretty lean."

"You know it," John sighed, clipping the phone back on his belt. He pushed the mostly eaten plate of shrimp linguini away and dropped his napkin over it. He asked her, "Are we clear on this station thing?"

"Yeah," she confirmed. "We run the new station charts for one more Saturday, then revert back to the old one. I think that's the best way. Frankly, John, I can't blame Tony for being upset about the whole thing—but, at the same time, I really don't appreciate his snippy attitude."

John looked at Heidi, but was really picturing his fat Sunday paper sitting on the stoop tomorrow while he ate flapjacks with Bob Grobbins and company.

"Heidi, it's that very snippiness that makes him a good dining room manager."

Heidi laughed as John pushed his chair back and stood to leave.

"I s'pose," she said, reaching for her teacup.

"One more week," John reiterated. "Talk to Tony today and let him know. Everything'll be back to normal in 7 days. I gotta go deal with these Grobbins."

"All right," she smiled. "Go get 'em."

Heidi watched her boss head out the restaurant and finished her lunch. She wasn't happy about having to knuckle under to Tony and the servers about the station size change, but she supposed it was a painful lesson she'd have to learn and take in stride. There were chains of command and they must be observed. Without which, there was chaos.

They'd just have to deal with the spotter company, though. Least till the dead wood was gone.

MEET BLOB GROBBINS

John walked from the restaurant and saw Gabe across the lobby checking in the Grobbins family at the front desk. Kip the bellboy was stacking their bags on the luggage cart. Nice enough sort, but the kid had gotten his hair buzzed recently and looked like an escaped Russian mental patient. John made a decision right then to order hats for all the bellboys, like the ones the Shriners wore when they were driving around in those little go-carts, y'know, in parades. He'd seen them in the catalog 6 years ago when he ordered the original uniforms, and they matched, but nobody on his staff back then looked like an escaped Russian mental patient . . . so he passed on them. A big mistake. At any rate, the Grobbins: two sets of golf clubs and lots of suitcases like maybe they were staying for a week. The two teenagers meanwhile playing tag or something, scuffing up the floor.

Wasn't that special.

He kept thinking about that possible solid block of bookings come July. Hundred and ten degrees outside. That's what it was all about. Bookings. Covers in the dining room. Christmas bonuses from Frank at year's end. Everything looked great. Bill Gardner from maintenance had overseen the refurbishing of the floor's surface last night when lobby traffic died down. From midnight till four that morning. FOI was a well-oiled machine. Housekeeping had gone over the ninth floor 5 and 6 units the Grobbins would be staying in with a fine-toothed comb, and John had inspected their efforts personally with Kathy Lawhorn a couple hours ago. Chef Eric, though, had really outdone himself with the specials menu for Saturday and Sunday. John might've been upset with having to work that weekend, but nobody else had it off either. Even Tony Marziano'd been yanked from his host shift and put back on the floor as waiter, because he was without a doubt the best. Every time the Grobbins clan sat down to eat, it'd be good ol' snippy Tony taking their orders.

John smiled thinking about it. Poor Tony whining about the new smaller stations, and all weekend he had just one little four-top. He was taking one for the team, unofficially doling out the three other tables in his section to other waiters, looking like a prince. That'd been John's idea. A way to placate the servers till next week when the stations expanded back to normal, and a way also to drill into Tony the idea that he should try to be less snippy in his dealings with Heidi.

A master stroke of management, John pronounced inwardly, even if he did say so himself.

"Hello, Mr. and Mrs. Grobbins."

The couple was standing at the desk while Gabe finished up with their check-in. Mid-fifties, the wife maybe a little younger. The man, Bob, was large like Orson Welles in those early noir films. Hairline receding, going eventually bald. Sort of gray like the oily spit from a couple sharpening stones had grazed both sides of his head. The wife was dyed blond and better looking, but, as John smiled from him to her, he noted with horror that she had tattoos where her eyebrows should've been. Little evil ones. Like blond blow darts or something. His stomach did a quick turn.

"I'm John Fallin, General Manager of Freshwater Oasis. Welcome to you both."

Bob Grobbins took John's offered hand and shook it vigorously.

"John," he chuckled. "Nice-ta mee-cha! Slick operation so far! Place looks beautiful! I'd like ya-ta meet my wife here, Barbara!"

John shook her hand as well.

"The pleasure's mine," he said, avoiding those weird eyebrows.

"Hi-ya!"

He smiled and addressed them both.

"Drive up was all right, I assume?"

"Yeah, a breeze," went Bob, turning back to Gabe who was waiting there with the key cards and a perfunctory smile. John knew Gabe pretty well and could tell that the Grobbins were just the kind of people Gabe detested. While Gabe explained to Bob about the key cards and the mini-bar and so on, John made small talk with the fake eyebrows and pretended that her obnoxious children weren't playing tag in the lobby, something that the woman did without even breaking a sweat, which was a good thing, John figured, seeing as she didn't have any eyebrows.

They finished with the check-in and John sent Kip up with the luggage cart and the master key he'd provided the kid with earlier. The Grobbins introduced Bob Junior (Robbie) and Kathryn, the girl, and mercifully sent them along with Kip to show him in which room the respective bags went. As John led them away for a tour of the facilities, he could see Gabe behind them doing this Groucho Marx thing with his eyebrows for John's benefit. More of that unappreciated humor, he acknowledged, figuring he might have a talk with his front desk manager on the way back.

Bob and Barb were quite impressed overall with the premises by the time they'd finished the tour and were waiting for the elevator to come down. John tried to imagine Bob operating a funeral home, though, but couldn't. That's what the January seminar was for: the Greater Phoenix Association of Funeral Home Operators. He'd expected someone a bit more solemn, really. Not this garrulous Orson Welles sort with the equally loud wife. It just didn't fit. On the other hand, maybe that's why he'd been chosen to arrange the function. He certainly wasn't a professional party planner. No, not by a long shot. This guy was a funeral home putz. John'd discerned that much just by listening to him talk.

"Yes," said Bob, taking a stubby cigar from his pocket and unwrapping it slowly, "you run a tight ship here, John. We'll see, but right off the bat I can tell ya *The Abbey* ain't got nothin' on you."

"Well, thanks, Bob. We're all here to make sure our guests enjoy their stay. Freshwater Oasis Inn is state-of-the-art. I think you'll find our facilities quite conducive to getting things accomplished during your seminar."

"What about golf?"

John looked at him, momentarily confused.

"Golf?" he repeated. "There's several excellent courses in the area. I go often as I can, which ain't nearly enough."

The elevator came and they stepped inside and John pressed the button for the 9th floor.

Bob Grobbins: "Can you get me an' the wife in at *Timberlanes?* Y'know, this weekend? Comped?"

Timberlanes was the most exclusive of Copper Hills's three professionally designed courses. It cost $118 just to put your golf shoes on in the parking lot. Nine holes'd run you another $300. John had been there just once in the last 6 years since coming to FOI. It was far too rich for his blood.

"We really don't have any kind of arrangement with Timberlanes, Bob. Now, any of the others . . ."

Bob widened both eyes in mock disbelief.

"No arrangement with Timberlanes? Jeez, The Abbey does. What's goin' on here, John?"

Then the guy lit his cigar. Right there in the elevator.

BOBBIN' GLOB GROBBINS

John came back down in the elevator after showing Bob and Barb Grobbins their adjoined rooms on the 9th floor. He'd told the man politely as possible about FOI's policy of no smoking in public areas, especially the elevators, to which Bob sort of snorted—adding onto his growing mental list, another great injustice dealt out by his host. Which'd be John, of course.

He trudged across the lobby and tried to picture the place teeming with like-minded slobs from the funeral home industry, all of them lighting up stogies and moaning about how much the greens fees are at Timberlanes.

"Jeez, The Abbey does."

Kept going through his mind.

Went over to the front desk where Gabe was fiddling with the computer. Leaned exhausted against the counter and sighed. Gabe looked up and did that thing with his eyebrows again. John remembered about that lecture he was going to give regarding inappropriate comic routines, but the sight of Gabe fluttering those eyebrows prompted him to laugh instead. Alas, there was a place for comedy at FOI after all.

"You don't even wanna know," groaned John.

Gabe, in fact, wanted to know.

"What?" he asked, smiling with anticipation of further evidence that the Grobbins were idiots. "What's with the eyebrows? Who *does* that anymore?"

John shook his head. "I dunno," he said. "Brunettes tired of dying their eyebrows blond, I guess."

Gabe laughed, then leaned closer for the *real* scoop.

"So, tell me. What happened?"

John filled him in on Bob's blatant grab for comps at Timberlane, his stogie-smoking in the elevator, and the obnoxious teenage antics of Junior and Whatshername in the adjoining room. Aside from the tattooed eyebrows, they concurred after a while, the fake blond so far was the most palatable of the bunch. Which, of course, was hard to imagine.

John said, "I'm through for today. You see Heidi, tell her to call me at home. I'll be there in about 20 minutes."

"You got it, Chief."

Again, the fluttering eyebrows. Gabe was nuts. John walked out, got in his car, and drove home. He needed to let Heidi know what kind of people they were dealing with here, but he wasn't going to spend another minute of his day off at work. Forty-five minutes later, though, the phone rang. He'd just changed into his Saturday comfies and was reclined and sipping off a frosty beer mug on the couch.

He grabbed the cordless.

"Hello?"

It was Heidi.

First words out of her mouth: "I don't believe these people!"

"What?"

"These *Grobbins*. They're impossible!"

She said the name like it was a skin malady that'd materialized on her foot. He sat up.

"What'd they do? Man, I just left. They weren't even unpacked yet."

"Those little monsters broke the TV in their room!"

"What?!!"

"The father calls down to Gabe all upset because the screen's cracked in his kids' room. Says it's *faulty!* No way, John! I was up there myself this morning! It was those obnoxious brats of theirs!"

John felt a migraine coming on and pinched the bridge of his nose with the first two fingers of his free hand. He sighed. Heidi continued.

"An' get this: I go up there and that Bob jerk has the gall to say *this kind-a nonsense wouldn't happen at The Abbey!* That's what he said! *This kind-a nonsense wouldn't happen at The Abbey!*"

She was doing Bob's voice with an annoying Midwestern twang, which was uncannily accurate, and all the more impressive considering Heidi was a member of the opposite sex. John sighed again, wishing he'd never even heard of the Association of Funeral Home Operators for the greater Phoenix area. Bob Grobbins. The "party" planner.

"What're we gonna do, John? That TV's 300 bucks!"

"Oh, God," he moaned.

It was Saturday. *His day off.*

A DATE WITH KATE

Kate worked days, just days, of which Saturday was her most profitable and Sunday came in a close second. She had a 4-year-old girl in daycare, Molly, so the morning gig worked out well as she could expect. The father had split a couple months before she was born, some creep named Rick, and so he wasn't around to help watch her or pay so much as a dime of the expenses incurred in the raising of a child. Lucky for Kate that her mother lived close and could watch her for the 3 hours that lagged between when daycare got out and she did. There was the insurance, of course, and just enough money to keep her nose above ground while paying that shyster she'd hired to track down good ol' Rick. Yeah, and so the day gig was okay.

It was on a Saturday, though, just after the lunch rush, and Kate was tidying up the back bar when Heidi appeared with a new cash drawer and came through the hatch. Went straight over to her register and put the key in, opening it up. Kate walked over and wondered what the assistant general manager was doing. Kate was responsible for her $500 bank and didn't like anybody toying with it, regardless of whether or not they were on managers' salary.

"Hey, Heidi. What's up?"

"Don't worry," Heidi assured her. "New thing—sorry. We'll be doing it periodically with all the bar staff."

"Doing *what?*"

Heidi had removed her drawer and was sticking the new one in its place. Very businesslike. Cool as a cucumber.

"Do you have any open checks?"

Kate balled fists on hips and looked over the bar. The last people had left 20 minutes ago. She could feel her stomach tying up in a knot. This was some kind of inquisition here and she did not like it one bit.

"You see anybody, Heidi? What's going on here?"

"Just relax, Kate. We have to count the banks mid-shift. We're doing it with everyone, you just happen to be the first. Nothing to worry about. We just run the numbers and count the bank, then compare the total with the ring. You have no checks open?"

Kate was suddenly so mad that she thought she was going to cry.

"Well, yeah," she said, "I got the manager's comp. That's it."

Heidi saw the chit rolled up in a rocks glass and grabbed it.

"This it?"

"Yeah, Heidi. That's it."

The assistant general manager punched the check number into the terminal and closed it out, then ran the report.

"You have a fresh bank of $500. Just ring off that till shift change and we'll do the numbers again. It's just policy, Kate. Everybody's under the same microscope. There's been some problems with liquor costs and we're trying to get a handle on it. Don't take it personal."

"Yeah, well, I've never heard of this before. Why me? You think *I'm* stealing?"

Heidi rolled her eyes and looked at Kate.

"Listen," she said. "We gotta start somewhere. Don't get all freaked out on me."

Kate huffed.

Heidi continued: "Just count your bank and verify that there's $500 in it. I'll be in the counting room, so call me and let me know if there's a problem."

"Sure thing," said Kate, popping the No Sale key and opening the new drawer. She was hyperventilating, that's how mad she was. Picked up the 20s and began to count.

"You sure you can trust me with this on my own? Maybe you should stay here and watch?"

Heidi shook her head and made for the hatch.

"Just call me if the bank's off," she said. "I'll be in the counting room."

Kate watched her go. God, was she mad. As if her life wasn't hard enough, now she had to put up with this nonsense. The tears started flowing and she could hardly see the bills through them as she counted, so, when the first count added up to $550, well, Kate thought she'd made a mistake. She counted them two times more.

Five hundred and fifty dollars.

Five hundred and *fifty* dollars.

Kate glared off toward the counting room. The jerk! It'd serve her right if she just kept it!

IN GOOD HANDS WITH MY HANDS

Bill Gardner walked into room 906 with Donny and figured there was gonna be a big mess they'd hafta clean up. That's why he brought Donny along. One of the few perks of his job made it possible for him to "oversee" somebody else doing the heavy lifting, or the doggie doo scooping, or what-have-you, and that suited him just fine and dandy. John'd said the TV was broke, and so it didn't take too long to locate the objective of his quest and designate.

"Yep," he said, "It's broke all right."

Donny concurred.

"Uh-huh."

"Well, get it disposed of."

It was Monday morning and the place'd been vacant since Saturday afternoon when John supposedly kicked out a couple undertakers for breakin' that TV set. Yeah, an' it sure was broke good. Them undertakers really knew how to bust up a place. Stinkin' rock stars, they thought they was.

"Whoo-ee! Will ya look at that, Donny! Thing's in a million pieces!"

"Yeah, boss," Donny agreed, leaning over the shattered glass and maneuvering his dustpan and a little whisk broom, just so he could transfer the hodgepodge into a box'd been cut off short. "Sure is."

Bill stood there a while taking it all in. He'd been up late the night before with his brother-in-law drinking on the stoop. Felt like there was a squirrel up somewhere in his brain and it was gnawing on fresh meat. It was that stupid imported beer James always brought over like he was the Generalissimo of Mexico. Airs. Thought he was man-of-the-world because he growed up in Phoenix, but he'd growed up before that in Prescott and that was before Prescott was anything more than a pin on some tourist's map. Some fancypants Midwestern ding dong that wanted to see nothin', y'know, up real close and personal. That's where everyone was from these days: Chicago.

Bill wanted to send them all back packing.

Backpacking. He'd made a joke. Thought about telling Donny but all that'd do was interrupt him from his work. Didn't wanna do that. No, sir. Leave the boy alone.

Stinkin' *Coroni,* or somethin' like that. Mex beer. Gave him a damn headache eatin' all those pansy lime wedges. Like, what's with these people? Lime wedges in their beer? All they're trying to do is hide something. Like maybe the hangover you get the next day after sucking three gallons of citrus. Didn't tell ya about that in the commercials. He took a free sample bottle of Bufferin out of his shirt pocket, removed two more tabs, and started chewing on them. Different strokes for different folks. And what in God was that on the carpet? Looked like a cigarette burn or somethin', but worse. Right off the edge of the dresser the TV sat on. Bill walked in close for a look-see and sure enough there was a corresponding smoke burn on the dresser itself, y'know, like some mo-ron'd laid a cigarette there and forgot about it . . . and then the thing toppled over and put a big trench in his carpet.

"Whoo-ee!" he exclaimed. "Damn your eyes. You get a load-a this?"

Donny had filled the box pretty much to the top and was wondering where he'd go with the rest of it. The TV parts, that is. There was a trash chute at the end of the hall that'd make things a lot easier on him, but he knew ol' Bill Gardner wouldn't go for that. Dropping heavy TV bits down nine floors in the early morning, waking all the beauty-sleeping guests. *Rattle rattle clatter clatter boom boom bang!* Hell, that's what he'd really like to do with this TV set. Perform a little gravity test on it. Like that Newton guy or whatever his name was. The guy that did those gravity experiments in 1600 or whenever.

Fig Newton.

"What'd you say, Bill?"

"Look at this," his boss clarified, getting testy. "Some bonehead burned a hole in my carpet! It's a mile long! I don't *believe* it!"

Just then the radio hissed and crackled and John Fallin's voice came over loud and clear.

"Bill, do you copy?"

To Donny: "Aw, it's God callin' again. This guy never lets up."

"I hear ya," Donny confirmed.

Bill took the radio off his belt and pressed the Send button.

"Yeah, John. What's up?"

"You're in the six unit, right?"

"Yep, an' it's a mess."

"Well, I need you to document all the damages so we can make an in-surance claim. The TV's broken, isn't it?"

"Yeah, it sure is. An' they put a big cigarette burn in the carpet too. Right by the dresser."

There was silence for a sec, then John's voice.

"Cigarette burn? No, Bill, there was just kids in that room. The father smoked but he was in the five unit. They weren't there long enough to commingle."

"Commingle? What's that?"

"Forget it, buddy. Don't worry about the cigarette burn. Is there any damage to the carpet aside from that? Like, y'know, any rips where the thing fell?"

Bill eyed the area and there wasn't any damage to the carpet except for the cigarette burn. But that was plenty.

"Naw, John. There ain't nothin' but the TV broke. I can make it look like the burn's a result-a the fall, though. A little knife work's all it takes. We're makin' an insurance claim anyway, so why not go for broke?"

"What?"

Bill clarified: "A smart man makes lemonade out-a lemons, boss."

YOU REAP WHAT YOU SOW

Makes lemonade out of lemons? Good grief. John slammed the radio down and massaged his temples there in the office. It seemed at times like the whole world was coming down on his head. Please. He could not be held accountable for everything. Sure, he'd been the one that hired Bill Gardner, but he'd been entrusted with the weighty task of hiring *everybody* at the time. And Bill wasn't all that bad, really, if you didn't rate people too much on brains. Oh, God. He'd been the one that hired Bill and then Bill put his considerable intellect to the task of fleshing out the maintenance staff. John didn't know these guys much personally, but it didn't take Einstein to see that the one was a certifiable idiot, and the other just plain couldn't talk. Like they were stooges set up to make Bill look good.

In his dreams, John Fallin saw his desk as a place where the buck did not always stop. Yet, in his waking world, that's where it always was. Every day. Sitting there waiting for him. The buck.

"Hey, Sheri," he said. "You got a gun?"

He was talking to Sheri Eggmeyer who was the new bookkeeper and was sitting at her desk being ever so efficient, as always.

She let out a nervous laugh. Smiled, "No, I don't think so."

"Well," John said, "If ya did have a gun, I'd take the thing and beat myself over the head with it till I was dead. How ya like them apples?"

Sheri thought about them apples and didn't know what to say. Sheri wondered if Lex Lilly knew what an idiot she'd entrusted with running this operation. Beat himself over the head? The guy was absolutely nothing. Good-looking, but she'd seen his type before: all flash, no cash. Sheri Eggmeyer believed in her heart that all men were scoundrels, and the ones that didn't appear to be so were just more adept at being crafty. Yes, if she had a gun, Sheri Eggmeyer would've most certainly supplied it to Mr. John Fallin. That and then some.

"Well," she offered, "I've maybe got some good news for you."

"You're a peach," he declared. "I'm all ears."

"I got a call on Friday, late, just before I was going home . . ."

"Yeah?"

". . . this company out of New Jersey that specializes in direct mail advertising, not really in direct mail advertising, but more like a broker so-to-speak. To make a long story short, though . . ."

"Honey, it's too late for that. Could you get to the point? I've gotta go blow my brains out."

Sheri gave him a look but then composed herself.

"Anyway," she said, "they've offered FOI a very lucrative sum for its customer database: i.e., names and numbers, e-mail addresses, home phone numbers, and so on. We're sitting on a gold mine."

John felt like he was sitting on something, but it wasn't a gold mine. It was a pickax. He inquired: "And you think this would be a *good* thing?"

Sheri looked at him and couldn't gauge his eyes. She got kind of nervous.

"Well," she stammered, "I dunno. Money is money. What's not to like about it? Who are these people to you?"

John rifled through the possibilities.

STAR-TENDER

It was 7:30 on a Saturday night and the bar was slammed with people waiting for tables. The bar itself was an elongated oval shape and pretty easy to work with the right crew. Eddie had service bar because of his speed and the fact he got along with the waitstaff pretty good. They were required to tip out 10% and Eddie's charm sometimes garnered more. Floyd, the new guy, was working the east side and Mike had the rest. Nothing was set in stone so far as turf, but there were three wells and three registers—east, west, and south—and it just made sense to divide things that way. It was expected, though, of course, that a bartender would rove to wherever he was needed. Like a fort beset by hostiles, you shot where the hatchets were.

Mike was at the service bar helping Eddie with the server checks. Waiters wrote their drink orders on the back of them and categorized them according to type. Frozen drinks were top left, mixed drinks in the middle, and beer and wine on the bottom right. They did this because it was easier to read big red grease pencil lettering than the check itself, what with the dimmed bar lights and whatnot. Mike'd gone through the tickets and was grabbing the bottled and tap beers for Eddie. He came back and set them on a couple upside-down drink trays they used at the service bar. Kelly the waitress was there and Mike could sense some tension between her and Eddie, which was odd, Mike thought, because they were usually flirting like a couple school kids.

Eddie'd just set a Gran Marnier down and Kelly put it on her tray with a couple drafts and a cosmopolitan. She started to leave.

Eddie said, "Hey, Kelly."

She looked back, annoyed.

"What?"

"Now, we need that snifter back. Okay? Don't forget."

"Drop dead, Ed," she said, storming off.

Eddie laughed.

"Jeez," went Mike. "What was *that* about?"

"Aw, nothin'," said Eddie, ladling strawberries into the blender.

Someone went, "Yo!"

"God, I *hate* that," Mike sighed, walking over to the jerk. "Can I help you?"

"Four Buds and a scotch/soda and that red martini."

"You mean a cosmopolitan?"

"Yeah," said the guy. "I guess. It's for a chick."

No kidding.

The night went on like that and Mike never seemed to get out of the weeds. Every time he found himself on Floyd's side the dude was yukking it up with customers. One party was a raucous group of middle-age businessmen up near the point, and the other was two 20-something couples by his well. A great desert existed between in which ordinary citizens thirsted for service. Mike'd have to nudge the guy aside sometimes in order to get at the ice.

Floyd was a waiter recently transferred into the bar. He'd taken the server job in the beginning with the understanding he'd be given consideration should a bartender position become open. Mike'd always liked him as a waiter. Tipped out big time at the service bar—and appeared to make good money—but Mike was beginning to have reservations about this new bartender. It was all about teamwork, especially behind the bar. They pooled tips, so if someone wasn't making money they were in essence taking money away from the others. That wasn't the problem with Floyd, of course. He did very well. It was the other teamwork things wherein he was lacking.

Like doing his share of the work, maybe.

"Yo, bartender!"

It was a brown suit in the middle. Mike looked over and Floyd was telling a joke or something to his businessmen buddies. He had a stainless steel champagne bucket over his head. *Gee. Maybe that's why he can't see the suit.* Mike seethed. He picked up a soda spoon and approached the ex-waiter.

Calvin Templeton was watching the whole thing. He worked for Private Eyes Security Services as what was commonly referred to in the hospitality industry as a "spotter." Calvin didn't much care for that title, though, and when asked what it was he did for a living, he usually described himself as a "private security associate." To wit, he had recently been talking to a woman who had asked just such a question, and, when she requested further explanation, he said to her, *"Well, sorry, but I'm really not at liberty to discuss the specifics of my job. What is it that **you** do?"*

If truth be told, Calvin was really just a junior college history teacher by day, and he did this Private Eyes gig 3 nights a week for a little extra money. A friend of his had told him it was a great way to meet chicks, and—why not get paid for it? But Calvin took the job seriously and found that it was difficult to hit on ladies when he was drinking bottled water and watching bartenders or waiters all night long. So he had been watching these three clowns and was watching them still when the big guy, Moe, went up to Larry from behind and hit him on the head with a soda spoon. Lucky for Larry he was wearing a champagne bucket at the time, so it probably didn't hurt all that much, but it sure was loud. A big clang! Jeez! The third guy, Curly, started laughing so hard that he knocked his blender over and red slushy stuff spilled all down his leg. *Very* unprofessional.

Calvin shook his head and commenced to scribbling in a little blue notebook.

"Clowns," he muttered.

WINK FLOYD

Mike and Floyd were working the bar one Thursday night. Floyd was on service so Mike could keep an eye on his tendency for glad-handing. Liquor costs were still a little high and Mike suspected there was some correlation between the two. Liquor costs and Floyd's glad-handing.

Somebody signaled Mike at the point and he went over.

"Hi, there. What can I get for ya?"

"I'd like a cosmopolitan, chilled. Do you have those big martini glasses?" Mike smiled.

"Sure do," he said.

"Great. And can I also see a menu for apps?"

Apps = appetizers. Holy guacamole. Mike figured she was either a waitress or simply didn't have time to say the whole word. If that was the case, though, he wondered why she didn't shorten "cosmopolitan" as well. Hmmmm. Either way, he disliked her strongly. She had this plastic smile like maybe she'd attended the same charm school as Floyd.

Mike handed her a menu and started in on the C. That's what he decided he'd refer to it as when he brought it over. *Okay, Miss. Here's your C.* Mike needed a vacation. He poured the vodka and other nonsense in the shaker and tried to remember the last time he'd been out of town. Shook it for about 20 seconds and poured it into a 10 oz. martini glass he'd been chilling with ice water. Been about a year, he figured. Went camping at Mesa Verde. One lousy weekend, dodging rattlers.

Wasn't really even a vacation.

He squeezed a twist in the stupid drink and set it on a bev-nap in front of her. Decided against that zinger about the C.

"The special sounds wonderful," she smiled, again with the injection-molded lips. Set her menu down on the bar.

"The marinated tenderloin kebobs?" he confirmed.

"Yes. With the dipping sauces."

She sipped off her drink. Mike took the menu back. There weren't any dipping sauces.

He repeated, "Dipping sauces?"

She sighed with delight and set the big glass down.

"Mmmmm. You make a fantastic cosmo," she gushed.

Whoops, there it is: Cosmo.

"Thanks," he said, opening the menu back to that night's specials. "There aren't any dipping sauces with the kebobs, though."

"Huh?" she blurted, leaning in so she could read the menu too. "I could've sworn I saw *dipping sauces.*"

He pointed it out to her.

"Nope. It's marinated tenderloin. I could get ya some catsup."

She gave him this look like he was a smart ass and she didn't really appreciate it.

"You can keep the catsup. Plain'll be fine. Thanks."

He nodded and went to his register and started a tab, muttering low: *I could've sworn I saw dipping sauces!*

Meanwhile, Floyd was leaning over the service bar talking to Kelly, the waitress. She was telling him about this table of high-rollers she had and how they were gonna tip big time. Could Floyd maybe swing them a round? She'd take care of him at the end of the night. Mike was coming around the side laughing about his catsup joke just then and caught the end of Floyd's wink. What was *that* about? Kelly walked off and Floyd made six drinks, notching the ticket afterwards with a red grease pencil.

Floyd pointed out to him, "Hey, Mike, this is like watchin' paint dry."

"No kiddin," Mike agreed. "Hell, it's like watchin' someone else watch paint dry. Why-n't you go have a smoke or somethin'. I'll go when ya get back. I got some food comin' up."

"Sounds good," said Floyd, grabbing his pack from the back bar. "I'll be back in a minute."

"Cool."

Mike watched him scamper off toward the locker room and picked up Kelly's check. Just as he expected: no ringy-dingy on the drinky-winkies. He set it back in the plastic holder thingamajig and leaned against the counter. Looked at the six prepared drinks there and there wasn't a one rung up. Hmmm. Good ol' Floyd. Kelly swung by after a while and smiled as she scooped up her drinks.

"Sure is dead tonight," she said.

Mike went, "Uh-huh."

PALMAS NO COCONUTUS

In Frank Stratten's office, the only thing his "in" box usually held was pina coladas. But there was a new love in his life: banana daiquiris. Frank was on his sixth and either the sun or the booze was starting to get to him. Jorgé, the pool bartender, figured it was both.

"Say, Jorgé," Frank babbled, "I been meanin' to ask ya—whas wi-this *Jorgé* business? I mean, it's spelled with a J, is it not?"

Jorgé was in the middle of tying up the plastic liner inside a garbage can he'd needed to haul out and empty into the dumpster. Like, 10 minutes ago. It was overflowing with banana peels and whatnot. The pool bar'd been busier than usual that day, and, though they had a cocktail waitress, Judy, business was never such that management felt they needed to assign a busboy or bar-back to the area. So it was Jorgé who had to run back and forth to the dumpster, or the liquor room, or the kitchen in search of ever more stinking bananas—for Frank and every sunbird that saw him smacking his lips over banana daiquiris and thought that maybe they too would like to try one. So every third person was ordering bananas this and bananas that, and now Frank was loaded again and about to needle him over the pronunciation of his name. He stopped what he was doing and leaned on the bar.

"Yes, Frank," he said, for the 10th time in a week. "J-O-R-G-É. Jorgé."

"So, what? Thas Pig Latin, right?"

Very funny. Frank was trying to get a rise out of him, but Jorgé merely rolled his eyes and turned his attention back to the overflowing garbage can. He figured nuts with tying a knot in the plastic and just lugged it up the stairs. He could hear Frank chuckling as he dragged it over the pool deck out toward the dumpsters. He liked Frank well enough, when he was sober, and he didn't mind so much that he was parked there most every day, taking up one of his eight bar stools, and stiffing him all the time, but, what he really didn't appreciate was *anybody* making fun of his Mexican heritage. It wasn't like his family had just swam over the Rio Grande or something. His old man fought in Vietnam! He knew what Pig Latin was, and he knew that Jorgé was the word "whore." It just wasn't funny; that's all.

Not funny one bit.

Meanwhile, Frank sipped off his sixth banana daiquiri and then tilted his head back to soak up the sun. It was almost perfect out today. About eighty-five, he guessed. Not a cloud in the sky. The pool area was beautiful. He was glad he'd spent the extra money 6 years or so ago when they asked if he wanted the pool heated or not. His reasoning then was that winter was their best time of the year, but it still got cold at night. So any outdoor pool'd be too cold to swim in, regardless of whether or not it was 85 degrees in the day, and Frank Stratten was just tickled pink that he'd gone the extra nine yards. And those palm trees were coming in nicely too! But, but—where were the coconuts?

Right then Judy the cocktail waitress flitted up with a drink ticket for Jorgé to fill.

"Hey, Frank," she said, smiling. "Nice day, huh?"

Frank liked that girl. Real cutie. Reminded him of his ex-wife, Anna, before she had the first of three kids and got all serious on him. *That was the thing about havin' little ones,* Frank theorized on more than one occasion, *ya gotta be serious all of a sudden.* It'd happened to him too, but, thank God, he was better now. He was cured.

"Judy, Judy, Judy," Frank blathered, doing what he thought was a passable Cary Grant. "Say, you know why there ain't no coconuts in these palm trees?"

She thought he was telling a joke.

"No," she smiled, getting ready for the punch line. "Why?"

He was just as confused.

He blinked. Said, "No, darlin'. I'm wonderin' why there ain't no coconuts—aw, forget it."

Frank grabbed his cell phone and called the front desk. That brainiac Gabe would know why there weren't no coconuts on these palm trees. The phone rang three times before he picked it up.

"Freshwater Oasis Inn. This is the—"

Frank cut him off.

"Yeah, yeah, yeah," he blurted. "This is Frank."

"Oh, hello, Mr. Stratten. How're you doin' this fine—"

Frank cut him off again.

"Listen," he said, cutting right to the chase. "I'm in the office. I'm lookin' around me at these palm trees. There ain't no coconuts on 'em."

There was silence a sec while that sunk in.

Frank inquired: "Why is that?"

Gabe stood there at the desk and wondered if Frank had finally lost his mind. He could picture him waist deep in daiquiris.

"Well, Mr. Stratten, good question. There aren't any coconuts on the palm trees surrounding the pool deck because that genus of palm does not produce fruit. It is the genus most commonly referred to as, 'Palmas No Coconutus.'"

There was silence a sec while that sunk in.

Frank blustered, "Listen, Gabe! I don't care what genius planted these palm trees! I want 'em cut down and I want some palm trees planted—ASAP! And they better have coconuts on 'em! You unnerstand?"

Gabe started to sweat.

"Well, uh—"

Frank: "You get Bill Gardner on the horn 'n tell him to get his butt over here! We're gonna move on this; DO YOU READ ME?"

"Yes, sir, Mr. Stratten! I'll send him right over!"

Click.

Gabe set the phone down slowly and wondered what on earth he was supposed to do. This was crazy. Coconuts? What was the big deal about coconuts? The man was the owner, though, and his decrees were like the word of God. What should he do? John was at court today with Eddie for that underage drinking business, so he couldn't just drop it in John's lap. What on earth . . .? Well, he'd do what he was told. Gabe grabbed the radio and called out for Bill.

"Hey, Bill! Front desk here. Do you read?"

A couple secs later: *"I copy,"* droned the building engineer, sounding like he'd been sleeping. *"Whadaya need?"*

"It's not me, Bill. Frank Stratten wants you out by the pool—ASAP! Bring a saw!"

There was silence a sec while that sunk in.

"Come again?"

Jorgé returned with the empty garbage can and was inserting a fresh bag just as Frank was finishing up a call on his cell phone. The *queso grande* sounded upset.

"I tell ya, Jorgé," he said, "sometimes it seems like you're the only one does their job around here. Hey, make me another-a those banana things when ya get a minute. Nobody does it like you, amigo."

Judy came back from where she'd been doing some busywork, trying to get away from Frank most likely, and Jorgé saw she had a ticket sitting there for who knows how long. He got Frank's bananas going first, though, and knocked her drinks off before the daiquiri was even done blending.

Judy marveled at his speed and dexterity.

"Wow, Jorgé! You're the fastest bartender I've ever seen! Where'd you learn how to do that?"

"He's the greatest!" Frank declared.

Jorgé basked in the afterglow a few secs while Judy shook her head with admiration. But then she took off with her tray full of drinks and the moment was gone. He was just jamming a straw in Frank's banana daiquiri, though, placing it on a fresh bevnap in front of him, when there was a loud *crash-boom-bang* and the accompanying clatter of a woman screaming in agony.

It was Judy!

Jorgé bounded up the stairs and over to where she laid writhing on the pool deck.

Judy: "Oh, God! Oh, God! Oh, God! Ouch, ouch, ow-wee! Oh, God! Jorgé! Help, it's my back! Oh, God! It hurts! Oh, God!"

"It's all right, Judy! Don't move! I'm gonna call an ambulance!"

A crowd'd formed around them, and there was an old lady pointing to a banana peel—partially mashed into the tiles—a couple feet from where Judy was in extreme pain, yet trying to keep still as possible, like a trooper, just like Jorgé'd told her.

"My goodness," gasped the old lady. "Look at that! She slipped on a *banana peel!* I don't believe it! Poor girl! Oh, my goodness!"

"Everybody spread out," boomed an authoritative voice. "Let's give 'em some room here!"

It was Frank. He had his cell phone and was dripping water from the pool where he'd been only moments ago.

"Yes, emergency!" he dictated into the phone. "Possible back injury. Freshwater Oasis Inn, over on 35th and Paley Avenue! We're in the pool area. There's a side entrance off the south parking lot where you can get a stretcher through, y'know, so ya don't hafta bother with the lobby!"

Meanwhile, Bill Gardner'd moseyed up with a hacksaw. He stood there next to Frank a minute while the man answered a few questions from whoever it was he was talking to on the phone. Bill figured the phone call had something to do with the cocktail waitress whimpering there on the pool deck, but what'd they want with him? The saw? ASAP? What's he s'posed to do with the saw?

When Frank clicked off on the cell phone there was a break in the action, so Bill Gardner got his attention.

"S'cuse me, Mr. Stratten, but what you want I should do with this here saw?"

Frank glared at the maintenance man a sec, sizing him up and down. What was he doing with that hacksaw? Shifting his beady little eyes from Frank to poor Judy, that little girl who reminded him of his ex-wife before she had all those brats, and the guy was just standing there with a hacksaw! Like a *moron!*

"What're you doin', Gardner? Can't you see we're in the middle of an emergency here?"

"She slipped on a banana peel," added the old lady.

NEW KID ON THE BLOCK

Heidi had been too quick about hiring Nancy to take Kelly's place on the floor. It was a spur of the moment thing, of course, dictated by the woeful circumstances that'd arisen last Thursday. That being the day both Kelly the waitress and Floyd from the bar got fired on the spot for stealing. Heidi had been shocked to say the least. She thought back to that Floyd guy working the floor, at large, 2 years before his promotion to the bar, and Kelly waitressing for a year and a half . . . and she just about boiled. How long had they been stealing?

Only the shadows knew.

And Kelly's firing begot Nancy. Like a snowball rolling down the mountain, getting bigger and bigger, one problem leading to another. Nancy was a mistake-hire made out of Heidi's desperation, due to her being flustered, and the fact that a busy week was coming up right on the rabid dog's heals. So it was that Heidi was sitting at the bar doing paperwork when Nancy came in for her first training shift on Monday afternoon. Good grief. Nancy looked different in the uniform. It was a white, nursey-looking thing, that when adorning a reasonably slender body was actually quite fetching. In fact, most waitresses raised the hem a bit from the way it came, increasing their tips exponentially—but this one, this Nancy girl, had simply left it the way it was.

Slightly below the knee.

Worse, though, she'd apparently gained about 20 pounds since the interview. Heidi gazed slack-jawed as Nancy walked into the employee area—and Tony, the head waiter/dining room manager, trainer of new-hires, man about town, mirrored her expression from the podium where he'd been checking the station setup.

He looked over at Heidi and held his hands up like the door of his Impala'd just fallen off and broke three of his toes.

Heidi went, "Oh, my God," under her breath, "what have I done?"

Nancy exited the employee locker room and headed for the bar lounge where waiters congregated before their shift. It was there they sampled menu specials and tasted any new wines the bar might be featuring. Only Marian was present this early, though, reading a potboiler paperback, and Tony because he was to train the new girl. Nancy picked up that evening's menu off a stack on the table nearest, but then saw Heidi at the bar and walked over smiling. The creases in her spanking new uniform could be seen from Mesa.

"Hi, there! Today's the big day!"

Yes, it certainly was, Heidi thought. *Extremely big.* She returned the smile. "Hey, Nance. Welcome aboard."

Tony came over and extended his hand.

"Hi, you Nancy?"

They shook hands.

"Yeah. Are you the trainer?"

"Dining room manager, but I'll be training you today. Name's Tony."

"Nice to mee-cha!"

"Likewise," he said, leading her off to a four-top in the corner. "Let's go over here an' we'll get ya started. Where else you worked?"

Heidi watched them walk away and shook her head. The girl looked utterly ridiculous. She'd worn her hair up during the interview, but now it flowed straight and listlessly down her back. She resembled a Viking woman, should've been holding a battle-ax and not Chef Eric's upscale menu. She retrieved the girl's original application from a manila folder she'd brought along with the other stuff and looked it over. Nancy was apparently from Deluth, some town in Minnesota. Probably got real cold there in the winter. She'd worked several middle-of-the-road restaurants as a waitress. Nothing all that fancy, but adequate. One year at a small hotel she'd never heard of in Glendale. Waiting tables. Growing hair.

This just wasn't going to work, Heidi realized. That hair. And the rest. They'd have to do something. Get rid of her somehow.

As if on the same wavelength, Tony left Nancy reading the employee handbook and sidled up to the bar. He leaned over with an elbow on the brass and smirked.

"You gotta be kidding," he said. "What am I supposed to do with this one? I mean, great googily-moogily! That stupid white dress! You could show a movie on her rear end."

Heidi started laughing and doubled over, resting her forehead on Tony's shoulder.

"I'm so sorry," she gasped. "She was sitting down during the interview! I didn't see it!"

Tony got to laughing too, then went into an impersonation of Dr. McKoy from *Star Trek.*

"I'm just a doctor, Jim! I'm not God!"

Heidi lost it some more, eventually burying her head in arms that were folded atop the paperwork like she was giggling through a nap in kindergarten. Tony broke down on top of her and they both laughed till even Marian looked up from her silly book.

Nancy was watching too. She'd heard the guffawing and peered over from the handbook where that Tony guy was in hysterics with the assistant general manager, Heidi. Were they laughing about *her*? Tony seemed like sort of a jerk. Kind of rolled his eyes when she'd gave him a brief rundown of the places she'd worked in Deluth and then out here in Glendale. Heidi seemed pretty cool, though. She was probably just being paranoid, first day on the job and all, but what was so funny?

She bit her bottom lip and nervously rearranged her hair. They were still laughing like a couple crazy people. That other waitress, the brunette, the one that'd been reading the book, got up and hustled over to participate in the merriment. Tony said something to her and pretty soon she was laughing too, stealing a glimpse over to where Nancy was sitting. *Oh, my God! They were laughing at her! All three of them! In hysterics!*

Time passed. It was Nancy's first shift after completing her weeklong training program with Tony. Felt like she'd been through a meat grinder. A Wednesday, lunch. She'd stood around doing sidework the first hour and a half before finally getting sat with a deuce. Her station was what they called "The Nines," and consisted of a four-top and two deuces by the kitchen. For the life of her, Nancy couldn't figure out why it wasn't called *The Eights*, y'know, as there were just eight seats, and not nine, y'know, so why not call it what it is? Whatever. She didn't care anymore. Nancy hated her new job already. Everybody was rude to her, if they even acknowledged her presence at all. Like she'd been wondering if the hostess even knew she was there. All the other waiters had several turns by this time, and when Nancy finally got sat it was just because there weren't any other tables where that skinny host girl could put people. Even so, she'd had to storm up there anyway and ask her what's the problem.

"Is there some reason why I'm not getting any tables?" she'd asked the girl earlier.

Her name-tag read, "Cynthia."

Cynthia went, "Excuse me?" She was plainly antagonistic, putting balled fists on her slender hips. "We got a problem here, girl?"

"No," lied Nancy, trying to sound reasonable. "It's just that I've been standing around all day and I'm still not getting any tables. I need to make a living, Cynthia, y'know?"

The hostess went, "You'll get a table when I give you a table."

So it was 1:30 before she got the deuce. Two guys who looked like they sold gum for a living. Not that sugarless gum, mind you. Something along the lines of *Bubble-Yum*. Watermelon-flavored or grape. The kind you find on the soul of your gym shoe. Lots-a sugar.

It'd rotted half their teeth out.

"Welcome to Freshwater Oasis, gentlemen," she exaggerated, arriving promptly at their table. "Can I get you something from the bar?"

But they were from Tennessee and they sold heavy machinery, not gum. One of them leered at her.

Ho hum. Just another day shift.

Eddie was training a new guy and saw that Nancy girl waddle across the floor toward the service bar. Her dress looked long and stupid, and she had a bun of hair on top her head that swirled down into a ponytail that was still a good foot and a half long. He'd heard about her from one of the waiters, but seeing her in person was a real experience. The woman was pushing 180, he guessed. That white dress never looked so, well, *bad*. Like a cloud or something. His trainee, this nice kid named Chip, kind of stared at her too like he was wondering what sort of joint he'd just started working at. Eddie sensed the kid's apprehension. You could tell when a place was going downhill by the attractiveness of its servers. Frankly, this Nancy girl looked like they should maybe all start seeking employment elsewhere.

He edged the new guy aside and met her at the service bar.

"Hello," she said, smiling, setting her ticket in the tray. "I need a 7/7 and a Moosehead."

Eddie grabbed the ticket and looked on the front to make sure she'd rung everything up.

"Baby," he said, "you already got a Moosehead."

The Chip started laughing.

"Just give me the drinks, please," choked Nancy, fighting back tears.

What a jerk. She didn't understand these people. Seemed like all of them were jerks. Nancy just wanted to get this day over with and go home. Hang out with her dog, Chow. He didn't have any problems with her. Didn't judge. Didn't say cruel things to her.

Good ol' Chow the dog.

Couple days later, Tony plopped down in the blue plastic chair next to Heidi's desk in the office and yawned. His jaws opened wide and Heidi, who'd been perusing a Macy's ad in the *Arizona Republic*, got a glimpse of the metal tucked there in his molars. Apparently he'd liked candy as a kid, she figured. Or that weird green gum that everybody called "watermelon" but tasted like sugar and clever chemicals.

"Good grief," she blurted.

"What?"

Aw, nothin'. Heidi folded the paper away and swiveled her chair around to address that Eggmeyer bookkeeper. The woman was getting her usual torrent of work done, ever so egg-speditiously, and Heidi ever so hated to disrupt her, but she'd scheduled the meeting with her dining room manager 2 days before and had to deal with it. After all, it was Tony's day off and that was that.

"Excuse me, Ms. Eggmeyer?"

Sheri peeled herself from a pile of printouts on her desk.

"Yes, Heidi?"

"Ms. Eggmeyer, I need a couple minutes alone here with Tony. Think maybe you could take a break or something? Maybe get a bite to eat in the lounge? We'll just need about 10 minutes or so."

They'd met for a discussion about what on earth to do with the new waitress, Nancy. It was Tony's idea, actually.

Sheri glanced over at Tony and nodded.

"Mmmm-hmmm. No problem," she said, raising a brow. Then, to Heidi: "I was just wrapping things up for the day anyway. I'll be out of your hair in 2 seconds."

Could life be so wonderful, Heidi thought.

She turned to Tony and rolled her eyes. Not that he knew the attitude they'd been getting lately from that woman. The "Egg Lady," they'd taken to calling her when she wasn't around. Which was hardly ever. *They,* of course, being her and John.

Tony made a big show out of twiddling his fingers as Sheri scooped up a couple printouts and squeezed them into her large black purse. She stood and grabbed her coat off a hook on the wall and folded it over an arm.

"I'll be back Tuesday, about noon," she said, grimacing from the weight of the bag slung over her shoulders, heading dutifully for the door and whatever it was that freedom brought with it.

It was just Friday.

"Tuesday?" Heidi repeated, utterly mystified. "What happened to Monday? You're not coming in on Monday?"

Sheri stopped in the door frame and looked back at Heidi as if the entire world was in her bag and it weighed heavily upon her.

"You know Monday's when I visit my sister. I never come in on Mondays. You know that."

Heidi didn't know that. She said, "Oh, sorry . . . well, I guess we'll see ya then . . . then."

The Egg Lady nodded, blinked, and split.

"Jeez. Visits her sister on Mondays?" asked Tony, after her retreating heels were out of earshot. There was a half-smile on his lips and he looked slightly hung over.

Heidi couldn't remember anything about Monday being Sister Day or Groundhog Day or whatever. Seemed like every day was Mess-with-the-AGM Day, least so far as Heidi was concerned when it got around to the Egg Lady.

"Ms. Eggmeyer is very egg-centric," she informed him, sighing. "And she has a sister, apparently."

Tony sort of snorted and covered his mouth like it'd been a cough.

"Excuse me," he said, and then cleared his throat. "Jeez, sorry to hear about it."

No, you're not. Heidi was getting a headache and took a bottle of Advil from the middle drawer of her desk. She fished a couple tabs out and chased them with a swig from a container of lukewarm Evian. Whenever Heidi drank bottled water she could picture it zooming along a factory conveyor belt toward the municipal water spigot, and then the label machine, and then the price tag stamper, ad nauseam.

Tony could sense a story in here somewhere.

"What's this? She goes and visits her sister? Every Monday?"

"Egg-zactly," Heidi said with finality, not wanting to talk about it anymore. "So, how's our Nancy doing?"

Tony crossed his legs and slowly made a pistol out of his right hand, then shot himself squarely in the temple.

Heidi: "That bad?"

"Well," he explained, uncrossing his legs and then crossing them the other way, "she's not so bad as a waitress, but . . . I mean, did you get a good look at that chick? The hair? I dunno, man, she looks like Thor's wife or somethin'. Like she should be carryin' around a sledgehammer and a shield. Plundering villages, y'know?"

Heidi knew. She'd had similar thoughts, but what was with Tony? She hadn't really noticed when he came in and sat, but the guy looked like he was losing weight. Like, a *lot* of weight.

"Wow, Tony, have you lost some weight?"

Tony nodded in the affirmative.

"Yeah," he said, contemplating his bony left knee. "I'm wasting away. Twenty pounds in the past 5 weeks."

Tony'd been thin already.

"Why?" she asked, then stated the obvious: "You didn't need to lose any weight."

Suddenly it dawned on her that maybe Tony was ill. Heidi never pried into the personal affairs of employees, like their sexual orientation per se, but nevertheless it'd always been the assumption that Tony was gay. So, looking at him now all thin and whatnot, it hit her like a ton of bricks that perhaps Tony had AIDS.

Oh, God . . . .

Heidi: "Are you okay?"

"Well, yes and no," Tony hedged. "I went to the doctor last week 'cause I'd been losing all this weight . . . and I started worrying about it, y'know, like maybe I had AIDS or somethin', and I didn't feel so hot . . ."

Heidi couldn't stand the suspense.

"Yeah?"

" . . . so the doctor did all these tests . . . and you're not gonna believe what he found."

"Uh-huh?"

Tony uncrossed his legs and leaned closer to Heidi.

"A tapeworm," he said, almost whispering.

"What?"

"Yep. Don't tell anyone. Just thinkin' about it makes me sick to my stomach. I got a tapeworm inside of me about a yard long."

"A tapeworm? You're kidding!"

"No, I'm not, Heidi. The doc said he could extract the thing through my nose, y'know, and I was like, *No way, José!* And so he prescribed this liquid stuff I gotta take every day with lunch that's supposed to kill the thing . . . "

Heidi's face was all scrunched with the thought of a tapeworm maybe slithering around inside her own stomach. Chewing on an Advil or something.

"My God. You've gotta be kidding!"

"Nope; it's sickening beyond belief."

They sat there a while contemplating the worm.

Heidi wondered, could you catch a tapeworm from another human being? *Nah.* She shook it out of her head.

Tony recrossed his legs and went, "So, anywho, what're we gonna do about Helga the Horrible?"

Heidi was glad to get off the subject, even if it meant getting back on the Nancy chuckwagon. She took another swig off the Evian and pictured Nancy let loose on the floor with her white creases and that tapeworm-long mouse-brown ponytail. There was probably nothing they could do about her, though. It was far too late.

"Well," she said, twisting the cap back on the water bottle, "I'm at a loss, Tony. Short of getting Nancy a tapeworm of her own, I don't know what we *can* do."

Despite himself, Tony laughed, and they were both in hysterics when John walked in. It was 3:30 and his day was drawing to a close.

He went, "What's so funny?"

LOUIS THE WHAT?

Yeah, so Chip stood there and he was the new bartender on his first shift alone and blah, blah, blah. Whatever. Stinkin' day shift. Like, what a joke. How was he supposed to make money when nobody's drinkin'? Sure, the bar'd filled up by noon and he was busy for awhile, but it was mostly people waiting for their tables to open up. Sipping tea or lemonade: *that'll be two dollars and fifty cents, please, Mr. Stiff.* Oh, and then all the mopes drinkin' Bloody Marys on the floor. Man, he should've applied for a waiter position. At least those guys were makin' money. All he was doin' for 3 hours was makin' Bloody Marys.

And then they all split.

Now he was doin' nothin'. He'd stood there the last 3 hours and nothing but a couple pairs came up and drank blah, blah, blah. Like, what's the point? Thanks for nothin', honey.

Nut'n Honey. That was a cereal brand, wasn't it? Yeah, it was a cereal brand that came in boxes for the stiffs. What-the-whocares-ever. Oh, and now two more stiffs meandering up to the bar. A husband and wife team out of nowhere in search of a tan. On vacation. Tourists.

Chip wanted to scream.

"What can I get you?" he inquired.

The woman: "You got iced tea back there?"

The man: *waiting for the answer.*

"Well," answered Chip, "I'm fresh out."

There was silence awhile as they chewed on that lie.

Whatever, stiffs.

Chip had worked at a lobster place before this, and, though he'd been a waiter, the customers drank so much that he felt like more of a bartender, actually, and, well, y'know, when he applied at FOI, well, he'd just fudged a little on the application. Whatever. They were lucky to have him. Who else were they gonna get for three lousy day shifts and one lousy night? A Monday, no less. Who goes out drinking on a Monday night?

"You got any lemonade?" asked the broad.

Whatever. He couldn't win. Chip got the broad some lemonade and the man a Lite beer. Buck tip and some change, if the dude didn't pick it up. Then he could retire. See ya later. What a joke this whole place was.

The phone rang. He walked over and picked it up.

Ho hum.

"Hello, Freshwater Oasis Inn. This is Chip."

"Chip? Like, like chocolate chip?"

Oh, a comedian. Chip was really impressed with mopes who made big funny jokes about his name. Chocolate chip. Hah, hah, hah. A regular ol' chip-off-the-block, eh? Hah, hah, hah. Ahoy, Chip! Hah, hah, hah. Whatever.

"Wow," he said. "That's really funny. I've never heard that one before. Can I help you?"

"Well, actually, I'm lookin' for Floyd. Is he there?"

"No, he's not working today."

"But he works every Thursday. Is he all right?"

Chip exhaled through his nose and decided that he was gonna quit. Soon as this shift was over. Maybe sooner. Two hours was a long time.

"Yeah," he said, "Floyd's fine. He's on a hot-air balloon ride today. He's probably floating over Scottsdale even as we speak."

"Hot-air balloon ride? You gotta be kiddin'!"

"Nope."

Chip picked up a matchbook from the back bar and started flossing around his canine tooth where he'd felt a bit of lunch earlier, like, well, he couldn't imagine what it was. He'd eaten hot dogs from a stand outside the Home Depot where he'd stopped off before work. Had to buy some fluorescent tubes for his bathroom overhead. Relish maybe? A piece of onion?

"Well, okay. You know when his next shift is? I got some friends in town and wanted to come see him."

Oh, gross! It's like some kind-a meat from the hot dog!

"Hello?"

"Yeah, I'm sorry. What was the question?"

"When's his next shift?"

The dude was getting testy. Had a chip on his shoulder. Hah, hah, hah. Chip almost laughed.

"Um, I think . . . uh . . . Friday! Yeah, he works Friday night."

"Okay, thanks a ton, Chippy."

Click. . . .

Chip smirked and hung the phone up. Like, who cares? Hot-air balloon ride. Hah! Who was Floyd anyway? Never met the guy. Never would. Oh, and here comes that Heidi chick with a couple more stiffs in tow. Time to look busy! Busy-buzz-buzz. Whistle while you work. Got time to lean, got time to clean. He'd worked at this one joint a couple years ago, place called Johnny Rocket's, and they served $8 hamburgers and loud rock music on the sound system. Anyway, one day he was starting his shift and the manager had them all in the back hall-way for the usual pre-shift pep talk and here's-the-specials nonsense. So this man-ager dork was talking about how messy the restaurant had been lately, and how we all needed to work together, y'know, and he announced, "There's no I in team-work." *Oh, please.* Before Chip could even think about it, he blurted, "Yeah, an' there's no U in cool." God, was that a scream! Everybody laughed their guts out!

Dork didn't think it was too funny though. That was pretty much the end of the line for ol' Chip and Johnny Rockets. Like, who cares anyway? There's an I in Unemployment Insurance, thank you very much.

"Hey, Heidi. How's it goin'?"

"Ahoy, Chip," she said, and then announced the two cheeseballs that were with her. "Chip, honey, this is Dr. Katz and Mr. Garagiola. They're staying with us the next couple days."

Katz and Garagiola? Sounded like a bowel ailment. And, what was with this "Ahoy, Chip"? Huh? Heidi think she was funny or somethin'? She'd see how funny it was when he didn't show up tomorrow and she was makin' Bloody Marys and lemonade and iced stinkin' tea. Yeah, and then she'd have a real hah hah.

"Hey, guys. How're ya doin'?"

Nods and pleasantries all around.

"Chip, I'd like you to take care of these gentlemen. First couple rounds are on the house. Whatever they want, just put it on the manager's comp check and I'll sign for it later."

"No, problem, Heidi-ho. Will do."

She looked at him kind-a weird and then nods and pleasantries all around as she split.

When they were alone, "Hey, nice place," said the doctor. "You got Louis the tres here?"

Louis the tres? What's that?

"What's that?"

"Louis the thirteenth," sniffed his buddy, like Chip was a moron. "It's cognac."

Oh, that stuff. Louis the tres. Like, French. . . .

Wow.

Couple hours later his shift was done so Heidi came back behind the bar to sign that comp check. It was just under $800 and her jaw dropped.

"What in God's name is this?"

"Louis the tres," answered Chip, all helpful and informed. "Some kind-a cognac. French. Couldn't believe how much that stuff cost. God. . . . Anyway, so we get an automatic tip on this manager's comp, don't we? Y'know, I really don't wanna be paying taxes on $800 bucks without getting the tip. Like, that's a whole lotta money, y'know?"

She just looked at him.

DO YOU COPY, ROGER?

It was a Friday morning before the lunch rush when Lex's friend, Hank Winston, showed up. He had in tow a couple gung-ho reps for a demonstration on the new point-of-order micro system. John was not in the mood. He'd just learned of this little twirp behind the bar yesterday who'd put four shots of Louis XIII on the managers' comp, then had the audacity to ask for the automatic tip. It would've been almost funny if it weren't for the $800 hit. Apparently his assistant general manager, Heidi, had okayed the comp for a couple jerks in for some convention or what-have-you, and she'd instructed the little twirp to give them "whatever they want." Well, what idiot's gonna take that literally and pour four snifters of Louis XIII?

His name was Chip.

Chip off the ol' blockhead.

So, Heidi fired the kid on the spot. Filed a report and left it on his desk like a cat turd. He was still digesting this morsel when the three of them bounded into the Oasis Lounge with the entrée: *technology!*

"You must be John Fallin!" said the bald guy, holding out his hand. John shook it and the beige head continued talking: "I'm Hank Winston with Sun-Micro Systems, and these are my assistants, Jim and Julie."

Jim and Julie. John wanted to puke.

"Nice to mee-cha," he said instead.

"Lex told me a lot about you," said the knucklehead. "All *good* things, though. Don't worry! That Lex—she's a character, is she not?"

"Yeah," John agreed, "she's a regular riot."

The guy cleared his throat.

"Well," he said, "I think you're going to be very impressed with the new, improved version of micros. Lex tells me you had a bad experience with the technology a few years back. Six years back, was it not?"

Jim and Julie got busy setting up some easels in the corner by the big picture window. They worked in tandem, like they'd done it a thousand times before. And, of course, they had. Julie reminded John of a saleswoman he'd bought a used car off a few years back. Same flat posterior, was it not? As a rule, John tried not to be a chauvinist pig when appraising women, but this car turned out to be a real lemon and flat ass pretended she didn't know him when he drove up the next week with the back axle rattling. She'd been so positively the opposite before, what with her fake blue contact lenses and that big capped smile, but, y'know, she showed her real side when he returned with the lemon—and it was flat.

And, y'know, that's what this Julie woman's can looked like.

"I'm sorry?"

Baldy: "You worked with the old version of this system, am I right?"

Is she not? Was it not? Am I right? What was wrong with this moron? Like, who's gonna pour four snifters of Louis XIII and think that's what management meant when they said, *"Get them whatever they want and just put it on the comp check. I'll sign for it later."* This Chip kid was either the biggest dummy in the world, or he was trying to screw the company over. What was Mike thinking when he hired the twirp? Did he ever check these peoples' references? Sure, he'd not been responsible for that Floyd guy, the thief, but this one was *his* mistake, *his* screw-up, *his* bone-headed move. How did these people get up in the morning and put their pants on? What was wrong with everybody? Was everybody stupid?

Yeah, John was sure of it.

Just then Chef Eric came out from the kitchen with his new sous chef, this guy named Bobby, fresh from the Culinary Institute of Phoenix. The new guy was holding a platter of something or other. They started making their way over to where John was standing with the bald guy named after cigarettes. John thought that he might indeed like a cigarette himself, so he reached in his shirt pocket and pulled out a pack of Camel Lights.

He held the pack out for Baldy and said, "Camel, Winston?"

The guy laughed, sort of.

"I get that all the time," he said. "No, thanks, though—I don't smoke. Never have, never will."

"Sorry," John replied, taking one out and feeling for the Zippo in his pants' pocket. "Well," he said, "I worked with a similar system back a few years, but, frankly, I was not very impressed. I realize that things change, of course, improvements and what-have-you . . ."

"Exactly!" stressed Baldy, seizing on the moment, unsnapping a brown briefcase that'd materialized out of nowhere. "It takes time to work the bugs out! Does it not?"

Was that rich Corinthian leather? John lit the Camel and sat down in one of eight chairs surrounding what they called a "large round." He indicated one of the opposing chairs to Baldy but he wasn't interested. Instead, Baldy waved John off and extracted a couple gadgets that looked like Game Boys.

"You're going to positively *love* this, John. I guarantee it."

Yeah, if it's a Game Boy. Whatever. John doubted there'd be any romantic sparks flying between him and the hand-held micros. He remembered back in L.A. 6 years ago when the hotel he was managing switched to this technology they were touting as the "wave of the future." This whole *wave of the future* business had always made him wary. Like, if it wasn't a *wave* till the future came, then, what good was it *now?* John was more interested in a *wave of the present.* At least that he could use. Not like those stupid hand-helds in L.A. The waitstaff all frantic and running around every time the system crashed, which was at least once a day for the week-long trial period. Or all frantic and running around because they couldn't read the stupid thing out on the street-side dining area. All frantic and running around, all stupid week long.

Eric and the platter walked up and the new guy set it in the center of the large round. John could tell he was quite proud of the concoction, which, on closer inspection, resembled pigs in a blanket sans pig. Sure smelled good though.

"Mmmm, what's that?"

"Try it," answered Eric, who then folded his arms and stared at the bald guy.

"Oh, I'm sorry," John said. "Mr. Winston, this is my executive chef, Eric Altman. And his sous chef, Bobby . . . uh . . ."

"Lezack," supplied the new guy.

They all started shaking hands while John explained.

"Mr. Winston is President of Sun-Micro Systems, and he's here today to give us a little demonstration on their new point-of-order micros."

"Oooh, the *president*," joked Eric. "Smokin'."

There was an uncomfortable moment as John tried to keep from laughing and Eric went back to standing there with his arms folded. He looked over at the platter and nodded at John.

"Well, ya gonna try that or what?"

John grabbed one of the appetizers off the platter and sniffed it.

"God, that smells *terrific.*"

Meanwhile, the new guy Bobby had picked up one of Baldy's micros and started punching commands into it like he'd done so a thousand times before.

"Wow," he said. "These things are great, man. That's all we used at the institute. Wow, bro . . . you're *the* Hank Winston?"

John looked up from his pigless blanket.

VE HAF VAYS TO MAKE YOU VALK

Mike and Eddie were working the bar. It was the Friday after the Winter Olympics and they were packed. A contingency of Germans had wandered over from Utah on a tour of the great Southwest or something. Mike didn't understand the language and couldn't find out for sure. They were there, though. That much he knew. Stiffing him every round. Bunch-a kids, just over 21. Only word they knew in English was "Becks."

He'd carded them when they first got there.

"Let me see your papers," he said.

He was trying to be funny but nobody laughed. Eddie overheard and thought it was a scream, but he'd been a big *Hogan's Heroes* fan as a kid.

Probably didn't get that in Dusseldorf. Nobody even heard of Bob Crane or Colonel Klink or the fact you're supposed to tip your server when traveling abroad. Least enough to cover the tax hit. Every round was costing them money. There were over two dozen of them, coming up and ordering beers in increments of six; $21 a pop. They must've gone to a bank and got a bunch of 20s and 1s.

"That'll be $21, sir."

Guy already had it on the bartop. A 20 and a one.

"Donka."

Him and Eddie were taking turns waiting on them—so that neither one took a disproportionate tax hit. Eddie'd came up a minute ago grumbling about how he'd just lost another 65 cents.

"I just lost another 65 cents," he said.

Mike was busy at the service bar making a cosmopolitan. He looked over at his partner and went, "Huh?"

"Sixty-five cents," Eddie explained. "The Krauts."

Mike started shaking the tumbler and with his free hand dumped ice from a 10-ounce martini glass he'd been chilling. He removed the top and used a strainer to pour the Pink Yuppie. That's what Mike called cosmopolitans; *Pink Yuppies*.

"Yeah? Sixty-five cents? What're you talkin' about?"

Eddie looked exasperated. He yanked a scrap of paper from his back pocket and showed it to Mike. There were mathematical calculations on it. Like some kind of secret formula that 65 cents somehow had significance in.

"Look," he went, pointing at the thing. "I figured it out. Every round those Krauts get costs us sixty-five cents! Right out-a our checks!"

Mike chuckled and shook his head, said, "Y'know, buddy . . . I think maybe you got too much time on your hands."

Eddie made a sound of disgust and hurried over to three older women sharing a bottle of merlot. One had a bar menu and was waving. Mike finished the server tickets and saw one of the Germans trying to get his attention. He edged around Donny the barback who was transferring two cases of Becks into the floor cooler. He'd been back and forth to the walk-in all night like a yo-yo. Five cases already, plus these two.

Donny had a conspiratorial look on his mug. "Heard this is costin' you guys 65 cents a round," he said. "What's *that* about?"

Eddie'd gotten to him.

Mike turned back.

"Listen, Donny. Why-n't you save yourself some trouble and grab one-a those kegger tubs from the liquor room. Line it with plastic and put about five cases-a Becks in it. Cover the thing with ice."

"Hey, good idea," said Donny, nodding his head. "Where ya want it?"

The German guy was waving frantically like his hand was on fire and only beer could put it out. Mike signaled that he was coming and told Donny, "Under the triple sink. Okay?"

"Sure thing, Mike."

He went over and the German guy pointed to his empty Becks bottle, then spread his fingers out and crooked the index from the other.

Mike smiled.

"It's called *six*," he said, losing patience. "You want six Becks."

"Yah. Becks."

The guy handed Mike his empty like a real smarty-pants. He threw it in the garbage can and headed for the cooler, trying to get control of his temper. He wanted to vault over the bar and teach that jerk how to say *ouch*. Sixty-five cents. A 20 and a one. He grabbed four beers and popped the caps and set them on top of the cooler, then went back for the others. Sixty-five cents. A 20 and a one. Mike popped the caps and wedged all six bottles in his fingers and brought them over to Adolf or whatever his name was.

"Twenty-one dollars, please."

The guy had the bills ready. Two of them.

"Keep it," he said, proud to be stiffing him.

Smarty-pants knew some English after all. Mike gave him a smile that must've looked rather menacing, even if you didn't know he was secretly plotting the overthrow of Bavaria. He stormed back to his register and punched the keys for six Becks. Twenty-one bucks. Sixty-five cents.

That's when he saw it.

There was a one and a *hundred*.

The guy must've mistaken the bills. Probably thought all American presidents looked alike. Andy Jackson. Ben Franklin. They were twin brothers in Berlin. Sixty-five cents. Mike looked up and the German guy had already moved away from the bar and was blabbing with his friends. A hundred bucks. Smarty-pants said to keep the change. Why not? He could make $80 bucks off the deal. They'd been stiffing him and Eddie all night.

Smarty-pants.

It served him right.

He gazed at ol' Ben and wondered what *he'd* do.

PARTY HARDY

Trini'd spoke with Jimbo from the day shift, front desk, a couple times. Felt him out. Guy was cool. Good boy but he was upwardly mobile. She could sense it. Invited him to a party Tom was having, showed up and was fine. Fit right in. Couple weeks later and Tom's friend Jack was coming into town. Needed a place to stay. There wasn't any room in Trini's studio. What were they gonna do?

Jimbo.

Trini walked up to him on a Wednesday and went, "Hey, Jim-baby."

"Yeah? Whassup, honey?"

"I need you to do me a favor."

Jim leaned back from the spine and looked at his new friend. He'd been to their party last weekend and liked everybody enough, but, on the other hand, he didn't really see any of them as going anywhere particularly fast. He wondered what kind of favor Trini had in mind.

"Uh-huh?"

"I got a friend comin' in town," she said. "Well, actually it's one-a Tom's homies. Needs a place to stay."

Homies.

Jim hated that term. That and "crib." He looked at people who said such things and wanted to vomit. *Let's go to my crib, homey.* Always sounded like the host had something creepy in mind. And, now, his new friend's boyfriend had a homie coming into town. Needed a place to stay. What'd *that* mean?

He went, "Yeah?"

"You got vacant rooms," she said, "don't ya?"

Jimbo could see where this was going. Vacant rooms. This idiot maid wanted him to hand her some keys. Because they were "friends." Because they'd partied together.

He said, "You gotta be kiddin'."

Trini just stood there.

She was serious.

"What, you got a turd in your pocket or somethin'? Ya got vacant rooms don't ya? I need somethin' for Tom's homie."

There it was again: *homie.*

He'd have given her the free room if she just hadn't said "homie" time after time, but she just kept saying "homie," like a moron, and it chapped his buttocks something fierce.

"No, I ain't givin' your homie-idiot a free room. What're you, nuts?"

Trini raised her left brow in a show of disbelief.

She went, "What?"

"You heard me," said Jim. "You tryin' to get me fired or somethin'?"

Trini sighed, closing her eyes like he was a dark-aged fool. Suddenly she got some gas, though, and felt a bubble going up to her heart.

"Gaghhh," she uttered.

Jim squished his brows together.

"Huh?"

"Aw, nothin'," she said, recuperating. "This whole thing, y'know? It's all, y'know . . . I dunno."

Some tourists came in through the automatic doors and they had bags in each of their hands. Jim looked at Trini and put his hands up as if to say, "Okay, yeah?"

She just stared at him a second and then seemed to focus.

"Listen, Opie, I seen your other side, boy. You can't play both ends. You got friends an' ya gotta take care of 'em. We took care-a you the other night.

You forget? Nah, I don't think so, Opie. Now it's time for payback. We need a favor. You gonna be cool or what?"

Jim wanted Trini to disappear, or at least explode. Make herself scarce. Whatever. He'd been there for 2 months. Liked the job enough, he supposed. Least enough not to want to lose it. Customers were coming. A businessman and his wife. The maid meanwhile standing there pressing him to steal. What to do, what to do.

He wanted to throttle her.

"Listen," he said, "I got customers."

"No, *you* listen," she said. "You take care-a your friends or your friends'll take care-a you. Comprende?"

Jim saw 40 yards of barbed wire road in front of him. The tourist duo stood in front and smiled, real quick, like they didn't really mean it. Just wanted to get their keys and split.

That's what he wanted to do: split.

"Welcome to *Freshwater Oasis Inn*, he said, instead.

"Yeah," said the guy. "We got a reservation."

SLICK RUDY COMES TO TOWN

Mike was working the bar alone on a brisk Monday evening. He liked working Mondays because a lot of conventions started up on Monday and, as a rule, even the regular customers tended to be more professional. Fridays and Saturdays would always be the best shifts, of course, but making rent on volume was a lot harder work. He'd take a Monday night's easy money 7 days a week.

The last bar gig he'd worked before coming to FOI was at Planet Hollywood. Big volume all the time. At the end, though, he detested it to the point where at night he'd have boring dreams about working. Nothing would happen in these dreams, mind you. He'd just be waiting on dullards and making stupid blender drinks and pink martinis and the like. The only thing that was dream-like about the experience was that the tips weren't real. He'd wake in the afternoon and feel like he'd just worked 8 hours for free.

Two weeks before leaving he was waiting on this barely legal twit. He'd approached her with the required, "Hi, there. Welcome to Planet Hollywood. What can I get for you?"

They were like polite robots at Planet Hollywood. Programmed and all.

She didn't even acknowledge his presence, but instead looked past him at the display of liquor bottles. The Galliano in particular seemed of interest to her, Mike recalled. He just stood there, though, waiting for the little starlet to utter her lines.

Finally, she decreed: "I want something strong . . . that doesn't taste like alcohol."

Without thinking, he suggested, "How's about my arm pits?"

She was not amused. After that, Mike knew it was time to leave. Gave his 2 weeks and from then on it's just another success story. Planet Hollywood became the desert sky, with infinitely more stars. He took Copper Hills and Mondays at FOI just fine.

"Hey, bartender," said a voice.

Mike looked over and a new guy'd just sat down. Kind of shifty-looking in the eyes. Had a 20 in his hand and was making great pains to ensure that Mike saw it. He went over.

"How're ya doin', buddy?"

"Yeah," said the guy. "Let me have a beer."

Hmmmmm. The guy's doin' **yeah.** *How's he doin'? He's doin'* **yeah.**
Yeah.

"What's yer flavor?"

The 20 was still fluttering in the breeze.

"Uh, make it a Lite."

The floor cooler was right there between them, so Mike leaned down and grabbed the guy's beer. Noticed the Lite was almost gone and turned around to discover Donny with a hand truck coming through the hatch. Four cases of Lite stacked on it. Best barback he'd ever had. Kind-a short, though.

"That's three bucks, pal."

Guy handed him a bill and he got to the register and punched the keys for *domestic beer.* Put the money on top of the cash drawer and saw it was a five. Looked over at the guy who was chewing on a toothpick and bobbing his head to some inner beat. Slick Rudy. The ol' bill switch-a-roo. Waving a 20 around and then palming it, paying with a smaller denomination.

Slick Rudy.

He made change for the five and brought the guy his two bucks, twisting around Donny who was filling the cooler with watery beer.

"There ya go," he said.

Slick Rudy: "Hey, I gave you a *twenty!*"

Mike leaned over the bar and got slightly in the man's face, showing him that Mike Scales was not to be toyed with.

"Tell ya what, friend. Leave your name and address . . . and if my bank's off tonight . . . I'll mail the difference to ya."

The guy worked his jaws but nothing came out.

Mike took a cocktail napkin and set it down in front of him. Grabbed a pen from behind Donny's ear and waved it.

"Name and address," he repeated, looking earnest.

The guy would have nothing of that.

"Hey," he blurted, "I wanna see a manager! You just ripped me off!"

Mike smiled. He held up a finger and then went back by his register and paged Heidi on the house phone. Couple minutes later she returned the call.

"Yeah, Heidi," he said, "I got this Bozo here did the palm job on me with a 20 and a five . . . y'know, and now he wants his change back."

"Did you tell him our policy?"

"Yeah, but he insists on talking to a manager."

"You sure it wasn't a 20?"

"Yep. This guy's a meatball."

She sighed.

"All right. I'll be there in a minute."

Mike went over to the guy and told him a manager'd be there shortly.

Slick Rudy grunted, "Yeah, whatever."

Mike could spot 'em a mile away. He'd worked with this bartender back at Planet Hollywood, real dingbat it turned out, and she'd actually fallen for that stunt once. Got all mad when the closing manager told her she'd have to make up the difference in her bank at the end of the night. Couldn't understand it. Girl just didn't pay enough attention to detail. Like this one time he was working with her, she'd been serving this homeless-looking woman at her end of the bar. Couple rounds. You can't refuse service to someone so long as they have money and behave themselves, but Mike had confronted the bartender anyway, her name was Maggie, and suggested that maybe if Maggie wasn't so attentive, y'know, the bag lady might take her wonderful business elsewhere.

"Yeah," Maggie hedged, "but what can ya do? She's a tourist."

Mike said, "What?"

"Yeah, payin' with traveler's checks."

He smirked.

"Traveler's checks? You gotta be kidding. Lemmie see 'em."

Maggie opened her register and took one out. It was a traveler's check all right, but made out to some woman named *Karen Whitestone* . . . and it was for *pounds*, not dollars. Twenty pounds. He turned it over and checked the signature. Chicken scratch. Laughable. No ID written down. Peered in Maggie's drawer and there was another just like it.

"So," he said, indicating the homeless woman who was presently slipping out the door, "that's Karen Whitestone, eh? You check ID on her?"

"Huh?"

Great googily-moogily. Rather unpleasant watching Maggie come up with the 40 bucks her bank was off that night. All petulant, yet weepy: "It's not fair!" she kept insisting. He wondered what Maggie was doing now. Probably joined the CIA or something. Wielded great power. Had a chauffeur, drove her to work in the morning. Made 200 large a year. Life was like that sometimes.

Unfair.

Heidi appeared at the service bar. Mike nodded toward the flim-flam man, just like he'd done years ago with m'lady Karen Whitestone. He could spot 'em a mile away. Had a look about 'em: shifty in the eyes.

WILL WORK FOR FOOD

Judy was back on the job after her brush with the banana peel and 3 weeks of workers' comp, but she was still hurting and had a brace around her lower back. Jorgé was pleased as punch because they'd had Nancy fill in for her and, well, Nancy could've 'filled in' for a house. That hair, that face . . . that can. He'd complained to Heidi about her as tactfully as possible, because, well, it just looked bad to dis someone merely because they had a weight problem, y'know, or they were ugly. It was like how some people didn't like him just because he was Hispanic. Jorgé figured anybody who thought like that was plain stupid, so he didn't want to be the same way . . . but, man, it was a pool deck and the cocktail waitress was required to wear shorts! Now, Judy was a fox, and having her prancing around the deck was a thing to behold. But, this Nancy from Iceland. Holy Toledo! The chick looked like she'd just shoplifted a beanbag chair and was hiding it in her butt! Scaring away all the customers!

So, after their first shift together he'd hunted Heidi down in the Oasis Lounge and asked if they could talk. The assistant general manager rolled her eyes, though, and cut him off almost immediately.

"I don't want to hear it, Jorgé," she said. *"It's just till Judy gets back; John's orders. If you got a problem with Nancy, talk to him."*

Well, that was that. On the bright side, though, when Frank got a load of her in that halter-top . . . man, he was running for the hills! Scared straight. At least something good'd come of it. And, well, he had to admit that Nancy turned out to be pretty cool once he got to know her. The whole thing sort of confirmed for him his own feelings about how it was unwise to judge people on looks alone. That you just had to give people a chance, y'know, and be cool. Actually, when he thought about it, Jorgé supposed that those 3 weeks with Nancy were really sort of a learning experience for him. That fat people, or ugly people, or, as in Nancy's case, fat *and* ugly people—well, they were really just regular folks under the skin.

So it was Tuesday just after noon when he came back from a beer run and Judy's familiar face was waiting for him in the service bar.

"God," he said to her, "am I glad to see *you!*"

"You too, Jorgé! How've you been?"

"Man, it's been horrible here without you! You should've seen the . . . well, never mind . . . so, how's your back? I thought you'd broken it! You okay now?"

"Yeah, it felt like I'd broken it. I can't believe I slipped on a banana peel! Who slips on a banana peel? It's such a cliché!"

Jorgé laughed.

"Yeah," he agreed. "No kidding. But, you're all right now?"

Judy stepped back so he could see the brace that went from the bottom of her halter-top to the waistband of her shorts.

"I gotta wear this for awhile till I build the strength back up in the muscles. Nice, don't ya think?"

Jorgé hedged. His mind stretched that thing around Nancy's gut till it got thin as a rubber band. The brace, that is.

"Well . . ."

Judy laughed.

"Yeah, I know," she said, but then got serious. "It still hurts like crazy when I stand, y'know, or move around. The workers' comp was finished, though, and I gotta pay the rent. I didn't really have a choice but to come back. It sucks, y'know?"

Jorgé's brow was all furrowed with concern. He was sort of in love with Judy but could never find the courage to ask her out. He was like that with girls he cared for. Real shy. Tongue-tied and stuff like that.

"Can you bend over? God, Judy. How're you gonna set the drinks down?"

"I dunno," she admitted. "Very carefully, I s'pose. Oh, well. What're ya gonna do? I gotta work."

"Uh huh," he said.

Nancy was back out on the floor in the Garden Vista and she had a deep, golden tan and a deuce almost immediately. She usually didn't get sat till about an hour went by, what with those hosts always messing with her. It'd been nice working these past 3 weeks with Jorgé on the pool deck. He was about the only nice guy here, except for maybe John the general manager. Everybody else was a jerk. She approached the two old ladies at her table by the restrooms and smiled.

"Welcome to Freshwater Oasis, ladies. Can I get you a drink to start with?"

"Yes, dear," said the one on the left. "I'd like a Rob Roy, please."

"Manhattan," chirped the other. "Don't skimp on the cherries."

"Excellent," Nancy said, writing their orders on the back of her check. "I'll come back with those in a minute and tell you about today's specials, okay?"

They both returned her smile and she nodded cheerfully and headed for the closest terminal. Nancy rang the drinks and then went over to the service bar and waited. That jerk Eddie was at the far end talking with another bartender whose back was to her. The redhead saw her, though, and came over pretty quick. God, she hated that guy. Biggest jerk in the whole world. Told her she had a *moose head!* No, she wouldn't say hi to save his life.

"Hey, Nance," he smiled, then leaned in closer like he wanted to have a heart-to-heart. "Listen, I'm sorry about the moose joke. I can be a real ass sometimes. I didn't mean anything, okay? Are we cool here?"

Nancy didn't even want to look him in the eyes less some evil part of his soul seep out and infect her. Instead she stared over his shoulder and damned if she didn't recognize the other bartender! She'd worked with him briefly in Phoenix! It was that Billy jerk, the little worm who'd gotten himself fired for stealing!

"Oh, my God" she gasped. "I don't believe it!"

Eddie got all confused and blurted, "What?"

John was making the rounds later before calling it a day and his last stop was always the pool deck where he'd have a smoke and kick back a while. He pushed through the glass doors and business was rather brisk for a Tuesday, but, then again, this was their busiest time of the year so he supposed it wasn't that odd after all. God, he'd been so frazzled lately with everything; he was losing his mind. One thing after another. Brain turning to soup.

The general manager made his way through the lounge chairs and found an empty table where he could relax under the umbrella. Lit up and stretched his stiff neck back and blew smoke into the spokes or whatever they called those metal things that held up umbrellas. He didn't really care. Just glad he'd made it through another day. Brought his head down slow and looked over and that's when he saw that Judy had returned to work. God, he'd forgotten that today was her first day back after that ridiculous banana peel business. What was that around her waist? Some kind of bandage. Yeah, it was one of those wrap things you see on the knees of 40-year-old joggers, but wider.

Judy was trying to set drinks on a table between two business types reclining on loungers. It looked weird. She wasn't bending her knees, that's what it was, like cocktail waitresses used to do at the old Playboy Clubs—not that he'd ever actually been to a Playboy Club. That was way before his time, but he'd seen a documentary about the clubs and the waitresses all did that bending-at-the-knee thing with the little bunny ears and tails and, my my my, it was nice, but this wasn't nearly as provocative. No, this was *painful* to watch. The girl could not bend over. It was her back. He watched as she finally managed to place the drinks and then limped off toward the bar, one hand screwed around to massage her spine. It was pathetic. He couldn't believe his eyes. This girl was still injured! What on earth was she doing at work?

John snuffed his cigarette in the ashtray and headed over toward the service bar area where Judy was slowly making her way down the steps. She was setting a check in the plastic holder when he came up behind her.

"Judy," he said, placing a hand lightly on her shoulder. "What are you doing here? You can hardly walk!"

She looked at him and seemed kind of dazed.

"Oh, hi, John," she said, gallantly attempting a smile. "Whadaya mean?"

"Judy, you should be home resting or somethin'. You can't be slinging drinks here! Good God—are ya kiddin'?"

Jorgé'd come up and was checking off her ticket.

"Yeah," he said, "that's what I been tellin' her all day. She's crazy, boss."

Judy closed her eyes for a second in frustration and took a deep breath and then let it out. As calmly as possible, she told her general manager, "I hafta work, John. I got bills to pay. What am I s'posed to do? Huh? You tell me."

There were tears welling in her pretty blue eyes.

Aw, man?

FOOT BLISTERS

It was Thursday night and Gabe had three blisters on his feet under the front desk. He'd been worrying about the gut that'd been mounding under his man-breasts, which were a problem in and of themselves, and walking to work seemed like a bit of exercise he could make use of.

Four miles.

That's how long it was, by foot or car. Problem was, though, today, he'd worn these fancy-pants shoes that weighed a lot and were like sticking his stumps in paint cans after mile no. 2. At that point, though, of course, it was a matter of principal that he complete the ordeal, less coming off as something less than a manly man—which was what he saw himself as—and, knuckling under, as it were, to a 2-mile cap on his ability. Well, no, wasn't gonna happen: he'd toughed it out.

But he was paying for it now.

On the phone, to Kathy Lawhorn: "Ayeeee!!! My poor little feetsies!!!!"

"Aw, you'll get over it, goofball."

"Aye yi yi!!!"

Kathy rolled her eyes.

"Listen, Gabe," she said, "I got work to do."

He sobered up.

"Okay," he went.

Click!

He was all alone. With his feet. His three blisters. All alone. Molly the night girl had called and told him she'd be a half hour late, and she was late from that. The fancy shoes. The blisters.

Looked mighty nice, though. The shoes.

The phone rang. He picked it up.

"Freshwater Oasis. This is the front desk; Gabe speaking."

He'd said that so many times in the last few years that it was like a blister on his throat. Felt pretty good, though. All in all. Beat the stuffing out of most anything else he could think of. Chartered accountancy. Private dickery. Tending bar.

Well, didn't mind the last so much. Did it for years. Losing his mind. God, he was losing his mind. Where was Molly?

"Yes," said a scratchy voice, kind of perturbed, "I'm in room 1510! There's a party next to me and I have to be up at 7:30 tomorrow morning!"

It was nearly 11:00. Gabe imagined the stars as they appeared out his picture window at home and tried to picture where that surly voice was needed so early in the morning. He'd worked the mid-shift so long. Never saw the sundown. Slept while people went to work in the morning. Exhaust from tailpipes. Morons honking their horns. Craziness. Just like this woman. She'd been honking her horn to get there just a while ago. He could sense it.

"I'm sorry, Mrs. Snotgrass," he said. "Where is the noise coming from? Next to you? On the right? Left?"

That was her name. Snotgrass. He'd looked it up on the computer while she was whining. Snotgrass. Sounded like some kind of varsity football field, everybody blowing their noses with no tissues. Right on the ground. Snotgrass. She was mad. Too much noise.

"Seems like it's *everywhere!*" she declared.

The blister under his right big-toe-whatever-you-call-it started smarting. Gabe didn't really care much suddenly about the noise complaint from Snotgrass. He was a pro, though, and forged ahead.

"Okay, Mrs. Snotgrass. I'm going to send someone up there and locate the disturbance. It'll just be a minute or two."

The woman suggested, "Let's be quick about it!"

Mrs. Snotgrass.

Click!

Gabe wondered why someone hadn't legally changed that name on some branch or another of their family tree. Snotgrass. Like, when was Snotgrass not ridiculous? In 1798? 1857? 1946? Was Snotgrass not Snotgrass at some point in time?

Man, Snotgrass was Snotgrass. Didn't matter when. Just hung up on him. After being snotty. Gabe set the phone back in its cradle and slipped his fancy shoe off and rubbed the jellyfish under his big toe. That's where the main blister was. He could feel it. What was he thinking walking to work that afternoon? Snotgrass. Where was Molly? He'd have to call someone to check out that noise complaint if she didn't show up in a minute. Maybe Kathy could spare a body. From housekeeping. Yeah, that's what he'd do. Call Kathy back.

Just then, though, his relief twirled in through the revolving doors and rushed across the slate. She was apologizing about her tardiness as she slipped behind the front desk and logged on to her terminal.

"It's all right," said Gabe, just wanting to split. "I got a noise complaint on the 15th floor. I'll check that out before I go home. You ready?"

"Yeah," she confirmed, nodding. "Sorry again about being late."

"No sweat," said Gabe, slipping the fancy-pants shoe back on and limping out toward the elevators. She'd worked there for a year and a half and Gabe couldn't remember her ever being late, or sick, for that matter. Molly was fine. He pressed the Up button and the door opened immediately. Got on and punched 15 and shot up into the shaft. Remembered he'd walked to work that day and didn't have his car. Hafta take a cab home. Hoped there was one. Not too many cabs at 11:30. What'd he been thinking? Four miles in Italian lowriders. Trying to flag down a cab in the middle of the night.

He'd checked the computer and there was nothing but vacancies around that Snotgrass woman. Except for the single across the hall where there was this even more ancient guest staying. Mrs. Paddlemaker, about 114 years old. *There's another good one,* Gabe mused: Paddlemaker. There must've been a convention in town that weekend.

International Sisterhood of Stupid Names.

Elevator came to rest on 15 and he got off and limped right toward the 10 unit. Could hear the music from there. Headbanger stuff. Sounded like Pantera. Huh? Couldn't be Mrs. Paddlemaker. Lots of voices. Someone having a big party. Young people. Laughing and hooting and so on. He knitted his brows and took the radio off his belt and called Molly down at the front desk.

"Molly, do ya copy?"

A second later: "Yeah, Gabe. Go ahead."

"I'm standing at the door of 1508. Could've sworn the computer showed vacancy. Check it for me, will ya?"

"Ten-four."

A second later: "Yeah, there's nobody in there. Place is vacant. There's a Snotgrass in 1510. Paddlemaker in 1511."

Someone rebel yelled from inside the eight unit.

Gabe went, "Ten-four."

He knocked.

No answer.

Pounded.

No answer.

Finally, he took his master key and slid it down the slot. Opened the door and poked his head in. About eight or nine people. In their 20s. Couple of the guys with long hair. Smelled like pot. Empty beer bottles everywhere. A Pantera CD playing in the BOSE.

"Excuse me, people!"

There was a guy seemed kind of familiar sitting on one of the wing chairs by the window. Girl in a black leather dress on his lap with her head buried in his neck. The dude looked up.

He laughed, "Can I help you?"

Then, the leather dress spoke.

"Huh?"

Gabe couldn't believe his eyes. He went, "Trini? Is that you?"

"Uh, Gabe," she slurred, all in a fog. "How're ya doin'? Wanna beer?"

DRY TRINI WITH A TWIST

Trini was real hung over. Just sitting there in the housekeeping office chewing on glass, big balls of cotton between her ears. She'd messed up and she knew it. Big time.

"I don't know what to say," she said.

Kathleen Lawhorn, as head of the housekeeping department, was there, of course, and she'd asked Heidi Bell to sit in as witness to the events that were about to unfold. As assistant general manager, Heidi had an interest in the proceedings, of course, and so it was on that Friday morning that Trini felt all small and sick as she faced these two. She was about to get fired, of course, and she knew it. But these two big shots just sat there shuffling papers as if a corporate merger were in the works.

Like, just get on with it.

Kathleen Lawhorn, or "Kat," as she was known familiarly in her department, was the first to open her all-important pie-hole.

"Trini, I've asked Miss Bell to sit in for this meeting. You know Heidi, don't you?"

Trini nodded and wished she were bent over cleaning a toilet so she could puke in it. God, she was still drunk. Great gobs of the night before were a mystery. She'd blacked out. Couldn't remember nothin'. Just a blur of that Gabe dork from the front desk suddenly appearing out of nowhere. Just a shape. Nose hairs. Sort of remembered the lobby and Mr. Nose Hairs pushing them through the revolving doors. Or, was that a dream? Someone got sick in the elevator. Was that last night?

God, she couldn't remember.

"I've spoken with Gabe from the front desk . . . and he described what went on last night."

Kat cleared her throat, then continued.

"This is very serious business here, Trini. I hope you're aware of that."

"Uh-huh."

That Heidi woman scribbled something in her notebook. Like she was a court reporter or somethin'. Like maybe she was gonna sketch a likeness of her, Trini wondered. What a bunch of bull. If they were gonna fire her, well, cut to the chase. Get it over with so she could go back home and crash.

"Like, am I gettin' fired or what? This is stupid."

Heidi started paying attention now. Kat leaned closer across the desk.

She said, "Excuse me? You think this is stupid here? I'll tell ya what's stupid, Trini. What's stupid is stealing keys to a room and partying there with all your little friends. That's what's stupid, Trini."

Trini made this *whatever* gesture with her hands and faded back in the chair. It was all her boyfriend's fault, that jerk. He was the one kept nagging at her to score a suite. All the time: *Do this for me, baby! C'mon! Do that!*

All the damn time.

The jerk.

"Yeah," she admitted. "You're right about that. There's nothin' I can do about it now, though, y'know. Nothin' I can do."

Trini wrapped herself in her own arms and stretched. As her back muscles flexed she felt the ribs adjust within her. They wanted to open up and spill their contents out on the floor. Like her soul was gazpacho. She felt like a bug to be stepped on. Felt like a bug. To be stepped on.

"I'm sorry, y'know. That's all I can say."

That Heidi woman looked at her watch while Kat made a pained face at Trini and sighed real loud. It was hot in there. No air to speak of. Stunk like disinfectant and old rag mops. Trini supposed she wouldn't really be missing any of that, of course, but she needed the bread. Needed to work.

"Well, you're sorry," Kat acknowledged. "Okay, it's just that—"

Heidi interrupted.

"Where'd you get the card key? Who at the front desk issued you this key?"

Trini glared at her. That smug pencil pusher. Wanted to slap her. Actually considered it a moment but that wouldn't look too hot on a job app, y'know, and she'd be having to send them out pretty soon, and so she just stayed there in her seat. Trini was getting fired, of course, and she knew that for a fact. But what they were really after was for her to trick on that Jimbo dude. The one that gave her the key. They wanted her to trick on ol' Jimbo.

"I whittled it from a bar of soap," Trini lied. "That what you wanna hear?"

Trini laughed at her little joke but the two of them weren't amused. That Heidi woman in fact started putting her pen and her notebook and all that garbage back in this big black shoulder bag she'd had by her feet on the floor. Like she'd heard enough and was gonna split. Go get her fangs sharpened or somethin'.

Like, so what?

Kat said, "Listen, Trini, I gotta be straight with you. You need to knock off this attitude right now. You're gonna be terminated immediately if you don't tell us who issued you that room key."

Terminated *immediately*? Wasn't that what this was all about? She was getting canned, right? Well, wait a minute . . . Trini began to see some light at the end of the tunnel. . .hmmm. Maybe she wasn't getting the boot. Maybe it was just that Jimbo guy they were all bunched up about.

"Yeah? And what if I tell you? You sayin' I get to keep my job?"

Heidi put her two cents in again: "You'll be suspended for 2 weeks. After that we'll reassess the situation and make a decision. Do you want to continue working here, Trini?"

Hey, maybe this was gonna work out after all!

"Sure, I do, Miss Bell. I love it here at FOI."

"So, who issued you the key card?"

Trini spilt the beans.

"It was Jimbo," she tricked.

And, of course, that was that. The meeting was over.

No more Trini.

SWIM-UP POO BAR

It was a lovely day. Frank and Jorgé the bartender were playing cribbage at the swim-up pool bar. Frank was kicking his butt. Jorgé'd told him a long time ago when Frank first offered to teach him the game, that, y'know, maybe he shouldn't be playing cards on the job? It just looked bad, y'know? But Frank reassured him: "What? Who you think's gonna come along and complain? God?"

Jorgé couldn't argue with that one. So he let Frank teach him how to play cribbage and now every day he was getting creamed because his attention was diverted with bartending. He'd been skunked once already and it wasn't even 2:00 in the afternoon yet. Frank was hung over, big time. Jorgé was probably lucky he was losing, but the ease with which Frank claimed victory each time kind of teed him off as well. Whatever. It wasn't Jorgé's fault he wasn't any good at cribbage. Frank had the big employee reviews coming up and that always made him a bit sour. Every Christmas, come rain or shine. Wasn't really the reviews, per se. John dealt with those. Frank just acted as good ol' Santy Claws or the Grinch depending on his general manager's recommendation. There wasn't much real joy in it for Frank. He was just a big money bag. The sound of carolers meant merely it was time for money to bleed out his wallet again, and that tattered bit of leather'd been incorporated into his hide to such an extent that its shrinkage caused great pain in his bowels.

Now Frank wasn't cheap, mind you. It's just that all he ever got was doodley-squat for Christmas, and, whoever said it was better to give than receive was a bald-faced liar. Sure, Christmas was nice and all, but try looking at 127 pairs of hands all stretched out in your face, a collective moan of what-have-you-done-for-me-latelys. Yeah, take a gander at that smash-'n-grab and then tell me how much *you* like the holidays.

"So, what're ya gonna do?" Frank grumbled, wondering when Jorgé was gonna make his move. "There's time limits on this game, y'know."

Jorgé slammed his cards on the bartop and went over to the service area where Nancy'd just planted three tickets. They'd reassigned her to the pool deck while Judy recovered from her back injury. He was missing that girl already. Sure, he still got to see her most days, but that was just in passing. John had let her work part time at the front desk with that Gabe guy, apparently they were short a clerk or something, which was cool, but he missed actually *working* with her. If you could call this work: playing cribbage every stupid day. God, Jorgé wished Frank'd slip on a banana peel or a pineapple wedge, have his can in a sling for about a month. That'd be cool. Then John could move his "office" out back by the dumpsters.

Yeah, that'd be a peach.

Frank: "Hey, what's yer problem?"

"Sorry," Jorgé huffed, snidely. "I work here, y'know. I got a damn job to do, Frank."

The owner of Freshwater Oasis Inn guffawed.

"Whatever," he said. "You're gonna lose just the same. Ain't nothin' you can do about it. Take yer time, amigo."

"I will," Jorgé promised. "And cool it with the Spanglish!"

Frank swiveled around on the submerged stool and soaked up the rays. He liked that Jorgé kid. Showed some *spunk*, and that was sorely missing with kids these days. Ahhhh. Christmas bonuses aside, the Southwest sure was beautiful in December. And, well, business really picked up as a result, and, okay . . .that's what paid the bonuses, after all. Man, the pool deck was crawling with tourists! There seemed to be a lot more kids than he remembered ever being there in years past. Couldn't stand kids for the most part. Place was crawling with them. Like cicadas. Sure, he liked his own kids, and, well, he liked his sisters' kids too. Actually, he enjoyed being an uncle even more than being a daddy. Yeah, a bunch more. A man could go home from his nieces and nephews, but try going home from your own kids. Get a moment's peace. Couldn't do that till they were grown up and away at college.

Which they were.

Frank was thinking about Junior at UNLV when a great scream reached out from across the deck and slapped him in the face.

"EWWWWW! SOMEONE WENT DO-DO IN THE POOL!!!"

Huh?

John was at the front desk talking with Gabe about the employee they'd just let go. The day guy, Jim, who'd been caught supplying vacant room keys for employees to party in. Gabe was of a mind that maybe they'd dealt with Jim a little too harshly in light of that Trini woman's track record, y'know, and how it was most likely her that instigated the whole thing, and, y'know, maybe Jim should've just been suspended or something? Well, that's what Gabe thought, at least, but John kept repeating how he didn't care if Trini indeed was responsible for Jim's "thievery," and, don't you know, that's just what it was! Thievery!

He kept saying that over and over.

"I'll not have thieves working the front desk here, Gabe. That's the bottom line."

Judy came out from the back room with a pile of printouts from the day before. They'd been checked by Sheri Eggmeyer that morning and were now headed for storage in a cabinet under the desk. Gabe went over to help.

"Hey," he said. "You're gonna hurt yourself! Let *me* get that!"

"No, no," she smiled. "I'm not an invalid, Gabe. No problem at all. But, y'know, thanks anyway."

John watched as she stowed the documents and was glad he'd been able to help the girl out. It wasn't her fault she slipped on that banana peel. A couple months working the desk, though, and she'd be back out on the floor and able to perform her regular server duties. Honest employees were at a premium in this business, and you took care of them whenever possible. They were not *disposable*. That's why John went into this business to begin with. He'd worked a bunch of jobs where he'd felt his input was not appreciated; like, if he disappeared the next day, well, who would really care? That's not how John pictured the way things should be managed. That's why he went the whole nine yards. People had bills to pay. The thieves? Well, who cares about criminals? They could make their own way through the forest.

Just then there was a great ruckus as Frank burst through doors leading from the pool deck. He was dripping wet and stood there with his arms flailing till he recognized John at the front desk. Looked like he'd been beaned on the head by a coconut.

"JOHN! GET OVER HERE!"
Oh, God. What now?

It was an hour later as the three of them stood alongside the vacated pool; Frank, John, and the building engineer, Bill Gardner. The former had a sorrowful expression on his face as he braced arms tightly around ribs and rocked back and forth on his heels. The latter had just scooted the last of the guests out from the pool area and locked the doors after them, and was now with his general manager and the owner and feeling somewhat out of place.

"Well," Bill proposed, nervously fidgeting with the stubble on his chin. "Thar she blow."

John looked sideways at him and made a face. They'd all been staring at the turd for some time now, and they all knew what it was, and it was just a question now of what to do about it. Bill Gardner was good about stating the obvious, and sometimes it rubbed John the wrong way. Sometimes John just wanted to fire Bill Gardner.

"You get those doors locked, Bill?"

"Uh-huh. Sure did, boss."

There was a moment of silence as they all went back to contemplating the great catastrophe that'd situated itself on the pool's deep end bottom. It was so tiny from this vantage point that John might've considered it inconsequential, really, and nothing to get all worked up about. Well, if it weren't for the laws pertaining to public health issues, and how, and he wasn't quite sure of this, but thought that you were supposed to drain a public pool if someone should perhaps release bodily fluids into it. But, it was so small! Was that really the law? Then, when you considered the draught the Southwest was in, and how costly it'd be to drain and then refill the pool? God, it all seemed so pointless!

"Damn," Frank murmured.

Just then Nancy came up behind them.

She apologized, "Excuse me, Mr. Fallin?"

John looked out from his reverie. He babbled, "Huh? Oh, Nance. What's up?"

Nancy had made up a sign to go on the doors. It was on the back of a beer box flap and read, "POOL CLOSED." She showed it to him.

"Is this okay for the doors? I mean, least till something better can be worked up?"

"Yeah, yeah. Thanks, Nance. That'll be fine."

Nancy smiled and went away in search of tape. Maybe Jorgé had some. John went back to staring into the pool and he lit a smoke and exhaled, hoping that when the smoke cleared the little kid's turd would be gone along with it.

The smoke dissipated.

"Good grief," worried John aloud. "Draining and refilling this pool's gonna cost a fortune. Y'know, what with the draught and all."

Frank didn't respond, so deep was he in his own reverie over the fact some little monster'd just crapped in his office. The man just stood there rocking on his heels and trying to imagine which one it was. He'd probably seen the little cretin actually do it. After all, he was looking off in that direction. Some little monster probably did it in his suit and then just pulled the leg out and let it drop. Real quick and devious. Then, he split. The little monster did his business and split!

Bill guffawed. "You kiddin'?" He was incredulous. "*Drain* the pool? That's the silliest thing I ever heared! Drain the pool? Hah! Ya just go in there an' grab it! Pour a gallon-a chemicals on the sucker! Drain it? Jeesh!"

Bill Gardner started stripping down to his boxers. John was willing to go with the flow and it looked like his building engineer had a good idea for once. Yes, go with the flow. Bill Gardner had a plan. Let Bill Gardner make the first move.

"What're ya doin', Bill?"

The world just sat around a while and stewed.

"Why, thas just a little ol' thing," Bill answered, hopping as he slipped his last gray sock off the ball of his right heel. "Pshaw! Drain the pool? We'll have this cleaned up in no time. Don' you worry 'bout it none, boss."

Bill dived in and headed for the bottom. John looked over at Frank and tried to gauge the expression on his face, which was turning from a rather stunned insane look to a more comprehensive stunned and insane look. It was just a bit more cognizant. A bit more cognizant, stunned and insane look. John just couldn't read it. Did that look mean it was okay to skip draining the pool? Or, well, not okay?

He could not tell.

"You okay, Frank?"

Frank seemed to come to his senses. Looked over at John.

"Whatever. I'm great."

Bill returned to the surface but he'd been unable to extract the package.

"Ooh, doggies!" he exclaimed. "Thas deeper down there-n it looks! Phew! I'll get it this time, though, you can count on it!"

Bill took a couple deep breaths and then a bigger one as he prepared to make a final trip to the abyss. Did a little acrobatic flip and his ass cracked the surface while he did an in-water dive to the bottom. Frank was watching and shook his head with wonder.

"What's with this moron? He a pearl diver or somethin'?"

John just wanted Bill to make the turd go away. Wanted to forget about the whole thing. The pool. Draining it. Refilling it. He thought that maybe changing the subject might help.

"Say, Frank, I been meanin' to ask ya. . ."

Frank looked over at him and squinted.

"Yeah?"

"That Riley jerk from the city. What'd you do to get him off our backs?"

Frank made a snorting sound.

"Aw, that was nothin'. The mayor's a golfin' buddy-a mine. Ya should-a just came to me in the first place. All's it took was one phone call."

Just then Bill Gardner burst through the water's surface. There was a small brown thing clutched in his fist. Though there'd not yet been any forensic analysis, smart money pegged it as a turd. Bill Gardner was suddenly its master and commander.

He squealed, "I got it!"

The owner and his general manager merely stared.

John, after awhile: "So, looks pretty good to me. No harm, no foul. Gallon-a chemicals. You don't really think we need to drain the pool now, do ya?"

Frank turned and looked at his general manager.

FRANK IN THE TANK

Frank repeated, "Drain the pool? Are you kiddin'? This ain't a pool, John! It's my damn office! Of course we're gonna drain it!"

John knew he was wrong, that draining the pool was not in fact the proper thing to do, but, still, Frank was God in this subworld. What Frank said was law. But, what a mind-boggling hassle! The pool'd be closed for days! He blinked real slow and contemplated the interior of his eyelids, and, when he looked back out on the world, Frank was already heading for the doors. The man barked a final order over his shoulder.

"Call me when the temp's 80 degrees."

And then he was gone.

Bill Gardner was at the side of the pool with the little turd in front of him on the deck. He looked deflated somehow.

Bill went, "Huh?"

"You heard the man," John answered. "Drain it."

John Fallin walked over to the swim-up bar where Jorgé and Nancy were talking in the service area. Both looked kind of rudderless, drifting as it were, not knowing what was happening within the context of their livelihoods. John didn't have any good news, that was for sure.

"Hey," he began, "how're ya all doin' here?"

Nancy said, "Fine."

Jorgé responded with the raising of his brow. "What's up?" he asked, already skeptical.

"We're gonna be shut down a couple days. I don't know what to tell you. I'm sorry. It's regulations, y'know. My hands are tied."

Nancy seemed to take it in stride, but Jorgé didn't say much of anything and rather disgustedly went about the business of shutting down the bar. After Nancy'd left, though, John came back and asked his bartender what the problem was. The guy was visibly upset, throwing boxes around and whatnot.

John: "Hey, it's just 2 days at most, Jorgé. What's the problem?"

Jorgé opened the drawer on his cash register and started counting his bank. He got halfway through his stack of 20s and seemed to arrive at some sort of decision in his brain. He dropped the bills and turned to face his general manager.

"Listen," he said, barely able to contain himself. "Regulations, my ass. It's not this being-shut-down business, though. Man, Lord knows I could use a couple days off. It's Frank! That's the problem!"

John screwed up his brows.

"Okay. What's wrong with Frank?"

Jorgé shook his head and tried to calm down, then continued.

"Every day, John! He's sittin' here all day! Gettin' hammered. Makes me play some stupid card game with him when I should be doin' my job, y'know, makin' some money! But all I do all day long is play stinkin' cribbage while he gets loaded and then the man stiffs me on the comp! I'm sick of it, John!"

"He does what?"

"Yeah, stiffs me. I says to him the first time, 'Hey, Frank—you need to sign this check so I can cash it out.' He goes, 'Hey, amigo, I don't sign for nothin' here! I own this joint! I don't ever wanna see no checks, amigo!' And so every day the guy ruins my business and I don't got nothin' to show for it! I'm sick of it, John! The guy's the stinkin' owner! Who'm I supposed to talk to about it? You? Hah! Well, I'll tell ya what, John. He calls me amigo one more time and I'm gonna clock the ol' bigot!"

There was a great sucking sound as the pool started draining. John wanted to slip into it and disappear. Didn't even care about the fact a turd had been in it a minute ago. No, John didn't care at all. He just wanted to disappear. Through the pipes.

AARDVARK TAKES A HOLIDAY

Eric was expecting a delivery from Tate Brothers but The Aardvark was a no-show. At just before noon he got worried and called in. Receptionist told him that Mack'd called off sick so another guy was doubling up on the routes and'd be a little late.

"Like, how late?" Eric inquired, annoyed.

"Just an hour or so."

"Whadaya mean an hour or so? He's already 2 hours or so."

"I'm sorry, Mr. Altman. He'll get there as soon as possible. Would you like me to see if I can reach him on the radio?"

Eric sighed.

"What would be the point of that? I need this stuff right now. I got prep cooks sitting around picking their noses."

"Well, I should hope not," quipped the smart ass. "Doesn't sound very sanitary."

Everyone's a comedian.

"Aw, whatever," Eric grunted, slamming the phone down.

It'd been a real rough day, so far. He'd found a letter on his desk first thing that morning from attorneys-at-law Grubstendt and Vickers, in regards to a lawsuit they were filing on behalf of one Dardina Traylor. A lawsuit claiming discrimination and wrongful termination. Huh? What a joke! Mike the bar manager stormed into his office some weeks ago screaming bloody murder about his sous chef. Apparently she'd been using bottles of $38 cabernet for marinades for 6 months, not writing it up on the spill sheet and causing liquor costs to go through the roof. He'd explained the process during training but she must not have been listening. Between this and the *dropped steaks incident,* Eric at that time was about at the end of the line with Dardina. Accidents will happen, of course, but you just can't teach someone common sense. So, anyway, he wrote her up and then she went over his head and complained to the general manager. That was the last straw. He canned the girl.

Big deal.

And now, The Aardvark was sick.

Poor guy. If it was a cold he'd probably not live to see another day, Eric hypothesized, picturing that obscenely long nose. Looked like an aardvark. He laughed despite the dreariness of it all, sitting there in his little cubbyhole office. He kept picturing himself in court having to deny that he was a racist. Just being accused of racism or discrimination was like already being guilty in everyone's eyes. The big, bad white man. He remembered giving Dardina the promotion to sous chef in the first place, how grateful she was and all, and he marveled at the double standard at play here. He wondered if these people who would sit in judgment of him planned on giving him any post-humanitarian of the year awards, y'know, for promoting a *black woman* back then in August or whenever it was. What a mess! Eric just wanted to go home, jump back under the covers, hit himself over the head with the clock radio, wake up a couple hours later, and rejoice that the day was over.

There were a lot of days like this, he reflected. Mornings where you stuck your nose out the front door and knew for sure that everything was gonna go wrong. A man just had to tough it out, though, and hope to hang his hat back up on the peg at night and still be intact. This was one of those days. He sat there in his office and relished a moment of peace before whatever was to come next.

Manuel stuck his mug in.

"Hey, Eric, Tate Brothers es here."

"Well, hallelujah!" he declared, springing instantly from the chair. "You da man, Manuel!"

"Que?"

"Nada," Eric laughed, moving past him toward the loading dock. The garage door was open when he got there and the driver was waiting with a handtruck full of boxes. "How're ya doin', Tate?"

The guy stared back at him with these yellow eye-whites, looked like he had scurvy or something. Eric wanted to offer him a lemon or maybe a red grapefruit. Something with vitamin C in it. An orange, perhaps.

"Another day, another dollar," the man philosophized.

How clever.

Eric liked The Aardvark better, though. Least he wore a belt around his waist. This guy's pants were hanging so low you'd have thought he was carrying a couple pork tenderloins in his back pockets. Those yellow eyes. Scurvy. Needed a lime or something.

"Yes, indeed," Eric agreed. "You got the whole order?"

The guy handed him a sheet. Eric looked it over and checked items off as he went through the boxes. Everything was there.

"Looks good to me," he said, cheering up for the first time that day.

"You the kitchen manager?" the guy asked.

Eric signed the invoice and handed it back.

"Yep."

The guy gave him a conspiratorial look, then indicated the open back door of his delivery truck with a thumb.

"I got some tenderloins just fell off. Willin' to part with 'em for cash. Give ya a real good deal, buddy. Half price, easy."

Eric stared into those yellow whites.

HALF POUND A BALONEY

Employees had begun to talk about Tony behind his back. Like, he was so skinny all of a sudden. Blotches on his face. Busboys and waiters sharing the same station would cover their personal glasses of Coke or whatever with doilies so he would not mistake them for his own and drink from them. Less they catch what he probably had.

AIDS.

It was a Thursday night and Tony got sat a six-top of senior citizen couples from Iowa, in town for a golf outing. These were just the types of people that Tony'd always been good at working. Though he did not golf himself, he most certainly liked drinking 12-packs and riding golf carts as much as the next guy. So it was that Tony approached the tourists with that same I-like-golf gusto and greeted them.

"Hey, folks! How're ya doin' tonight?"

Two of the wives looked up like they'd just seen a two-headed space alien from Lake Powell. One of the husbands was a big guy with a haircut that'd probably not been altered since he was a marine in '56. He cocked a brow as he beheld the skinny waiter and then made this exhaled sound of disgust.

He said, "Are *you* our waiter?"

"Yes, I am," answered Tony, not skipping a beat. "Welcome to the Freshwater Oasis Inn! My name is Tony and I'll be taking care of you tonight. I'll be explaining the menu shortly, and we have several delicious specials tonight, but can I get you folks something from the bar first?"

The crew cut was not impressed.

"Listen," he began, but then his wife grabbed him by the arm and made this *shooshing* sound. Of the three females, she'd been the one who'd a second ago not looked aghast. But he shrugged that off and insisted, "I wanna see the manager, okay? Go get me the manager."

Tony stood there and felt cold sweat squeezing out the pores of his eye sockets. His brain was in dry ice at the temples and all at once he felt sick to his stomach. A tapeworm slithered through it. Tony wanted to disappear. Be anywhere but here. Out on the golf course maybe, tooling along. Twisting the cap on a Big Mouth Mickey.

He gasped, "Excuse me?"

"You heard me," grunted the crew cut. "Get the manager!"

The wife: "Honey, please!"

"To hell with that!" said the guy, and then he turned back to Tony: "Get me the manager right now."

Tony held up his hands.

"Fine, fine. No problem."

Oh, God. Tony went looking for Heidi.

"We have a big problem," said Heidi to John the next day as he entered the office. He'd not even sat down and already John had a *big problem*. Well, tell me something new. He'd updated his resumé that afternoon and added his experience here at FOI. Wasn't really planning anything as yet, but he felt like this phase of his life'd pretty much run its course. Been played out, as it were.

"Oh, really?" he said, dropping his sunglasses on the desk. He sighed loudly and set his briefcase down on the chair, then opened it. In the best of all possible worlds, his briefcase would be full of Gummy Bears. . . but, instead, it held a bunch of written-out problems. Horror stories in neat little rows of letters and numbers and what-have-you. John was sick of it all. Sick to death.

"I think Tony has AIDS," his assistant general manager announced.

She just said it. Laid it out there on the line. Nothing more, nothing less. *Tony has AIDS.*

John's heart skipped a beat.

He blurted, "What?"

Heidi went on to explain about the night before and those people from Iowa. How she'd had to assign another server to their table because they didn't want Tony to be even near their food. About how she'd sat down with Tony at the end of the shift and asked straight-out why he'd lost so much weight, what was wrong with him, and how he calmly looked her straight in the eye afterwards and said he had a *tapeworm*. Heidi told John about how she'd rolled her eyes and almost started crying. She'd heard the tapeworm story before and wasn't buying it this time, and she'd said that to Tony but he insisted it was true.

"Heidi, I have a tapeworm! No kidding!"

John sighed and moved the briefcase onto his desk, then sat down and leaned back in his chair. He remembered Tony from Day #1. Felt sort of responsible for him, almost as if he were a part of the family. The FOI family. And now he was dying of a *tapeworm*.

"What are we gonna do, John? We can't have him waiting on customers, looking the way he does. He's *sick!* This tapeworm business is utter nonsense! What're we gonna do?"

John wished that Heidi every once in a while knew what they were gonna do. He started rubbing his jaw and closed his eyes for a moment. Poor Tony. God, what was *he* gonna do? There was the insurance. An HMO. Lousy, of course, but doctors at least. Medicine and so on. Prescriptions.

Oh, God.

"I don't know," he answered her, honestly. "A tapeworm. . . what, does he think we're stupid? I seen him too, Heidi. He looks awful."

"Yeah, no kidding," she said.

There was a full minute went by as they both brooded, considering the options. Which were few, if any. A very sad business. John knew it was impossible to catch AIDS off a waiter unless you were having sex with them or sharing a needle. But not everyone in the world was as enlightened, and, well, he couldn't blame his customers if their ignorance-based fears made them leery of being waited on by someone with AIDS.

Oh, God. Poor Tony.

Finally, Heidi offered: "We all got the same insurance, John. He's covered. We gotta find out what's actually wrong with him, though. I think he's got AIDS, obviously, y'know, but we gotta get it confirmed. Is there any way we can talk to the rep there and find out for sure? We can't do anything about this problem until we know the facts."

John just sat there and wondered what was the point.

SOME MAIDS CLEAN UP BETTER THAN OTHERS

All the Hispanic ladies in the housekeeping department were mad. Not merely because they'd been overlooked in Señora Lawhorn's search for Trini's replacement—in favor of a bilingual white woman named Wanda—even though the four workers had seniority to the tune of 15 years at FOI between them. No, it wasn't that. Nor was it the fact Lucy had been doing the mini-bar tasks on a part-time basis, 2 days a week for the past 3 years, and by all rights should've just moved into it full time when Trini was shown the door. No, it wasn't that. It would've made more sense, obviously, to give the job to someone who already knew it rather than hire some outsider and then have to train her.

Wanda. That was her name.

They called her *Wanda Blanco.*

Given the job instead of Lucy who'd worked her butt off for years and deserved a promotion. Deserved, at least, a little respect.

Some newcomer; an Anglo.

No, it wasn't the racial discrimination that had them all up in arms. They'd been dealing with Senõra Lawhorn's prejudice for some time now. It was the fact this Wanda Blanco was stealing their tips off the nightstands every morning when she entered guestrooms to check the mini-bars. Not *all* their tips, mind you. No. That would've been too obvious. What a maid usually could expect from a room—like, if people'd been there a weekend, and the maid would be anticipating anywhere from $6–10—well, that tip on the nightstand would turn out to be in the range of $2–4. So, Wanda Blanco was ripping off half their gratuities every day—and that's what they were all mad about.

They met in the laundry room at shift change one Saturday afternoon and discussed what they were going to do about the situation. All the ladies had families to support. Why, Guadeloupe had four kids and a husband out of work! This was really hurting them all! Maria'd done some calculations and had the figure at around $50–60 a week this Wanda Blanco was stealing from her alone, and then you times that by four, and—something had to be done!

It was decided that Lucy had the best English amongst them and would be the one to voice their suspicions to Señora Lawhorn. Tell the manager what they thought was going on with this new mini-bar maid. Tell Señora Lawhorn that Wanda Blanco was stealing all their hard-earned money. This woman was not only ripping them off, but she was also lording over them like the big boss. She'd been there 2 weeks is all, and she was suddenly the big boss! Saying she did not have to do this, she did not have to do that. Telling *them* what to do.

And stealing their tips!

Lucy was near tears as she sat in the housekeeping office across from Señora Lawhorn. Her English wasn't very good to begin with, but, when she was nervous . . .

After much stumbling, Lucy blurted: "She steal our tips!"

"What're you talking about? Who steals your tips?"

"Wanda Blanco!"

Now the tears came. Kat watched her a sec and realized she was referring to the new girl, Wanda Kovad. Stealing their tips? What was she talking about? Why didn't these people make more of an attempt to learn the language of the country they now called home? It was insulting, that's what it was. They just moved in and expected everybody else to accommodate them. Like, this nonsense where they whined about how public schools should have Spanish-speaking instructors. Her tax dollars paying for it. The whole thing was ludicrous.

Excuse me?

"Are you referring to Miss Kovad? The new girl? Wanda? You're accusing Wanda Kovad of stealing your tips? Do you have any proof of this, Lucy?"

"Mucho dinero!"

Kat rolled her eyes.

Monday morning rolled around and Bill Gardner was in the maintenance office and he was still half asleep. Bill's cousin Bill'd thrown a pig roast the day before, and, *whew, way too many brewskis*. Bill Gardner busted another foil pouch of coffee and set it to brewing there on the counter. The room'd been maxed out over the last 6 years, whenever there wasn't any pressing business, like, stuff they needed to do on the premises. Bill'd went to great pains installing every refurbished guestroom convenience there was for him and his men. And, so it was that used pipes'd been lain and there was a used shower and a full used kitchen and this and that used kaboodle. Nice place to kick back and relax. The maintenance office. Place was almost posh, was what it was.

The radio: "Bill? Come in, Bill. This is Kat. Do you copy?"

"Oh, boy. Here we go," he moaned.

Bill moseyed over to the big table and sat back down where his paper was spread out, the Sports section, opened wide to some gibberish about rich so and so he didn't care about much . . . and never would. These "celebrities," least that's what the press called 'em, were so far from where Bill and his kin were toiling, that Bill actually read the sports page each day with relish like some towner would a police log. *Voyeurism*, he believed that's what it was called. Ho, ho, ho. Looking to get a laugh over some dolt he knew secondhand who'd fell upon some great woebegone misfortune. Some dolt who'd brought it upon himself. Some dolt that should-a had nothing to lose to begin with.

And, now he'd lost it.

Ho, ho, ho.

"Bill? Do you read me? Come in, Bill. Over."

He picked the thing up.

"Yeah, Kat. This is Bill. Read ya loud'n clear. Over."

"Hey, Bill. What's yer 20? Over."

There was a sophisticated lingo when you talked on the radio at FOI or any other establishment. A lingo that everyone played along with despite how ridiculous it really was. Rules held over from when everybody was a kid playing with walkie-talkies. Stupid rules, of course, that were deemed so when anybody really thought about them who was not steeped in them. Anybody who wasn't trying to make their job seem more important than it truly was. Anybody looking in from the outside.

"I read ya loud an' clear. Whadaya want? Over."

There was a pause as a horse fly landed on Kat's shoulder and bit her. The pain was akin to a small tack being driven into her collarbone. Her finger had just depressed the Send button, though, so her exclamation carried out over the airwaves.

"Ahhhhh!"

Bill waited down the hall from room 2011 and was wedged inside the dumb waiter closet. God, it was hot. Real hot. Like a million degrees. He felt like a complete idiot. A hundred and sixty-eight pounds of gristle left on a room service plate. Like this was the closet he should be in. A big dummy. Sweating. God, it was unreal. He kept stepping out every couple minutes because he was so hot. Stepping out and getting a breath. Kat'd told him not to do that, but, he'd begun to think: *This is stupid. What do they take me for?*

He was out taking a break one time, though, when that Wanda Kovad woman came strolling off the elevator to check the mini-bars. He had to think, quick. What would James Bond do? Well, James Bond was a Limy. He improvised and made like there was some business he was doing in that dumb-waiter room. Bill was hoping that she didn't know that it was in fact a service door, so, on a wing and a prayer, he stared back into it and blustered, "Donny, snake that drain out . . . right now! Yeah, that's right! That's right!"

He'd stolen almost the entire script from his Cousin Bill on their last trip to Vegas—everything but the name. At any rate, the maid accepted his presence as righteous and went about her business. Bill slipped back into the dumb-waiter closet and commenced to sweating again. This whole thing was stupid. Christ, he couldn't even see out! How'd he have even seen that Wanda woman if he'd not been outside like he was told not to be? What was the point of him standing there inside the closet? He couldn't see nothin'. Kat Lawhorn, head of the housekeeping department, had enlisted him in this half-assed sting. That broad didn't know nothin' about stings, though. Not one stinkin' thing.

"Kat! Come in! This is Bill! Over!"

"I hear ya, Bill. What's the status? Over."

"The eagle has flown! Over!"

Wanda was inside the 11 unit. She went straight for the bedroom and saw the $20 on the nightstand.

"Ooh, mama!" she exclaimed.

Wanda liked 20-dollar bills. She reached into the side pocket of her apron and extracted a wad of currency. At first she grabbed a 10 and traded it for the 20, then walked a few feet toward the mini-bar and thought better of it. She returned to the nightstand and exchanged a five and a one for the 10, took the one back, and then she was halfway to the mini-bar again before she reconsidered and went back and traded four ones in for the five. Only then did the mini-bar maid tend to the mini-bar.

"Stupid mini-bar," she muttered.

Wanda walked out of there after a while and closed the door behind her. She was just heading for the elevator, though, when that Kathleen woman stepped out of the 8 unit and confronted her.

"Wanda," she said, "I need to speak with you for a moment."

Wanda went, "Huh?"

She couldn't see it, but the Andy Jackson in her pocket had secret coded markings on it. Bill Gardner emerged from the dumb waiter closet and looked like he was about to faint. He'd sweated out half the alcohol he'd consumed the day before at his Cousin Bill's pig roast. Could've used a brewski, that's for sure. They just weren't ever there when he needed 'em.

"Thanks, Bill," Kat said. "Could you open the 11 unit, please?"

Now it was Wanda Blanco's turn to sweat.

FRANK EYES EVERYONE OVER

John sat in his own office at his own desk but he was in the guest spot now. It was time for the yearly employee reviews, and John was the no. 1 employee, but Frank the owner by rights got the Captain's chair. It was really kind of silly. They went through this every December 22. Frank would first look at the numbers accounting had prepared, analyze them against their projections from the year before, and then he would assess John's performance and dole out the bonus check like he was Santa Claus. But Frank really didn't know all that much about the nuts and bolts of running a hotel, so when he faked his way through the printouts and whatnot, nodding here and there, John wanted to laugh. All Frank cared about was the bottom line. Profit or loss. Which was it?

Frank was pleased. Business had been very good—in fact, up 12% from the previous year. Frank had not said boo to anybody other than Lex Lilly, his business manager, but he was mulling over the possibility of expanding with another property in Tuscon. It was still the desert there, God knows, and visitors needed fresh water as much as the next guy. John seemed the perfect candidate to run it all. Frank would call it:

FRESHWATER OASIS INN II

Freshwater Oasis *Into!* He envisioned the entire southwest dotted with Roman numerals, though none would be as perfect as the second. Frank dropped the last bit of accountant gibberish on the desk and smiled at his general manager.

"Up 12%, huh?"

John nodded with confirmation: "Yep."

Frank lit a match and got his cigar going and then leaned back in John's swivel chair and smoked. This whole thing was really kind of silly. Frank didn't know beans about these figures and always had Lex go through them first and tell him what the real important stuff was. She even wrote the bonus checks. Whatever. He would just show up and hand 'em out and pretend he was on top of everything. Like St. Nick coming down the chimney. Merry Christmas! Being successful in business demanded a great deal of task delegation. And you had to *know* people. That's what it was all about. Frank was good at hiring key staff and then letting them do all the sweating. He squinted at John now through a cloud of Cuban smoke and wondered if his general manager knew how little he actually knew about the hotel business.

Three hundred and sixty-four days out of the year Frank's briefcase sat in a corner of his closet and collected dust, but today it was full of checks. He snatched it off the floor, hit the tabs, and opened the brown waste of cowhide. John's envelope was right on top. He'd added ten grand above Lilly's calculated figure as per their contract, and he could not wait to see his general manager's reaction. John Fallin had worked hard all year and earned it. Frank took the envelope and set it in front of him. The poor guy looked like his hair was *fallin'* out.

"You goin' bald?"

John laughed.

"I dunno," he admitted. "Am I?"

"Your hairline," Frank pointed out with the cigar. "I don't remember it bein' like that 6 years ago. Great googily-moogily. It recedes any more'n it'll be on someone else's head."

John laughed some and opened the envelope. He *had* noticed the fact he was growing bald. Every time he combed his hair in the morning there was less of it. Tried not to dwell on it, but, of course, Frank will be frank. He considered the check and it was substantially more than the percentage he was due according to their contract. Exactly $10,000 more than he was expecting.

"Thanks, Frank," he said. "I mean it. Thanks."

Frank held up a hand.

"Don't say another word. You earned it, buddy. Get yourself some Rogaine."

Frank reached back into the briefcase and extracted a stack of envelopes for the staff to be handed out at the New Year's party. The management team had debated previously as to what to give the workers in terms of bonuses, and he'd been told that several options had been on the floor. One idea was to take everyone out for dinner and cocktails at a ritzy local place. Another was a river-rafting trip where they'd all get on a bus and go somewhere and blah, blah, blah. There were a couple more ideas but they all got pretty costly when you factored in the numbers . . . like, when 87 employees all brought their spouses or dates. It'd been that Gabe smart ass from the front desk, though, who'd come up with the best idea when he shouted:

"Show me the money!"

Smart ass, but he was right. So they decided to skip those other grandiose plans and opted to spread the wealth through bonus checks. Money was money. Buying someone a teddy bear didn't mean squat when they couldn't afford air conditioning. Just give them cash. Amounts varied depending on the individual's length of service, but even the newest hire got at least 50 bucks. And free drinks. The entire staff would get together on the second of January for a party in the Oasis Lounge. Business was dead following the New Year, so closing the lounge off one night wasn't any big deal. Frank liked that idea a lot better than having to concoct some lame excuse as to why he couldn't go rowing down the stinkin' Columbia River. Like telling John that he'd slipped a disc or somethin'.

"I dunno, Frank. That river-rafting trip idea . . . seemed like it was right up your alley."

"Yeah, I know," Frank said, flicking his ash in the wastebasket. "But the people have spoken. What can I do?"

John took the envelopes and went over to the file cabinets. He stuck them in the top one that he had a key for and locked it. It was Saturday, just before noon, and they still had to go through the review process for all the managers who did not have any contractual agreements with FOI. They were all eligible for bonuses, but John had no authority to get into Frank's checkbook and needed to okay any amount beforehand. John was the one who conducted employee reviews with the staff and management, and he already had sat down with all of the parties last week, but Frank liked to play Santa Claus with his managers. So, he would conduct his own little reviews and basically regurgitate John's assessment before he handed out the checks. And now was the time allotted for John to feed him his lines.

It was silly.

John knew that, but Frank will be Frank.

It was Sunday morning and Gabe'd just got the memo that Frank would be conducting year-end reviews for management. They would take place on Friday, "in his office." The memo had gone on to say that managers should "dress appropriately." It was 20 minutes later and Gabe was still highly amused. *Dress appropriately.* He loved that.

He saw Heidi bustling across the lobby, and there weren't any guests around, so he shouted, "Yo! Heidi Ho!"

Heidi stopped in her tracks and looked mortified for a second till she realized they were virtually alone in the lobby. Just some mop in the corner with a man attached to it. She shook the thoughts of murder from her head and went over to Gabe.

"Y'know," she said, leaning on the marble, "one of these days your mouth's gonna be the end of you."

Gabe slid the memo across to her.

"Hey, ya seen this? It's from *Frank.*"

Heidi picked up the slip of paper and read it, her brows furrowing as the words sunk in.

Aghast, finally, she quoted from the text: *"Dress appropriately?"*

Gabe broke down into hysterics. Frank's office was the swim-up pool bar! Appropriate dress was a swimming suit! They'd be getting reviewed sitting on one of those stools in water up to their, well . . . he could not stop laughing at the thought of it! Heidi Bell and Kathleen Lawhorn in their swimming suits, getting reviewed by that Frank moron! It was perfect!

"No way," Heidi declared, and then she looked at the front desk manager who was having a seizure or something. "I'm glad *you* think this is funny. It's, it's . . . God, it's unreal! Sexual discrimination! I've never heard of anything like this! It's bad enough we hafta go through this process with John, jumping through hoops, but then we gotta do a striptease for the owner! I'm not gonna stand for it!"

Gabe was still doubled over laughing as she stormed off in search of Kathleen Lawhorn, like *that* was gonna do any good.

Kat was already reading the memo in her office and had a stunned look on her face when the assistant general manager burst in.

Heidi was steaming. She hissed, "I cannot *believe* this!"

Neither could Kat.

"Does this mean, like, uh . . . we're supposed to wear swimsuits?"

"Yeah, you got it! That's what it says, sister!"

Heidi still had Gabe's copy of the memo in her hand. She crumpled it up now and dropped it in the wastebasket at the side of the housekeeping manager's desk, then folded her arms across her chest and dared any man in the world to look at her sideways. She would murder them twice. No, three times.

Kat declared: "I'm not wearing any swimsuit to this ridiculous review. You talk with John about this?"

"John's out of town for a couple days. On 'business,' he said. Real mysterious. Just left me a note."

"What?"

"Yeah, he's gone. Didn't say nothin' to me about any business trip. I don't get it."

Kat reread the memo and shook her head. This was absurd. She'd already gotten a horrible review from John last week, and now the owner wanted her half-naked in the swimming pool while he hassled her some more. There was no way in the world she was gonna play along with this garbage. No way. Not in this lifetime.

"What're ya gonna wear?"

Heidi was in a navy blue skirt with matching jacket, a cream-colored silk blouse, and conservative brown heels.

"You're lookin' at it," she answered.

It was Friday morning and John'd gotten back from Tucson late the night before. He was yawning and drinking coffee in the office with Frank who was all dressed up for the "manager reviews" he'd be conducting later. The first bit of ventriloquism was scheduled for 9:00 AM with Gabe DeFlores, the lucky devil. Frank was sharp as a tack, though, pouring over some notes he'd taken last week while John wasted an hour and a half telling him what to say. It was an exercise in silliness. Basically he was just gonna parrot what John'd already told them during his review, and then he was gonna hand out the checks like he was Santa Claus. The man was actually wearing a pair of half-glasses that John knew for a fact were nonprescription. What was the point?

"So, what'd ya think-a Tucson?"

John shrugged his shoulders. Frank's empire. He was still undecided. They'd talked at great length after last week's *bull* session and John had advised Frank that he was pretty much through with FOI after the New Year. Told him about how burned out he was and all. About how his job had become just so much babysitting and the pressure was driving him nuts. Frank had been stunned to say the least, and, though he'd wanted to keep this Tucson thing under his hat for a while, he'd felt at the time that it might be a good idea to bring his general manager up to snuff. So he'd told John about the expansion plans and what it could mean to his future in this business if he were to become FOI's "regional manager." As if that were something John aspired to or was even remotely interested in; Frank boasted that he would suddenly be in charge of not one but *two* hotels! And so it was that he suggested John take a couple days off and scout some locations that he and Lex were already considering in Tucson. Stay at a nice joint with a pool maybe and just try to get a feel for the region. Kick back, y'know, and relax on FOI's dime.

Now, John had said nothing of this to Frank, but in all honesty, he doubted his own abilities at running a second hotel when his first was presently in such a state of chaos. There wasn't enough of him to go around. How could he leave Heidi in charge of this operation—and just go gallivanting off to open another? The very idea was absurd! He'd not alluded any of these self-doubts to Frank last week, of course, and merely agreed to take him up on his offer of a couple days paid vacation. Sure, he'd driven around town a bit and checked out the sights, and liked the place in general, Tucson, but mostly he'd just kicked back around the pool and smoked. He drank a bit too and things seemed brighter after a couple days, but now he was back at FOI and felt like bricks were sitting again on his chest. So, what'd he think-a Tucson?

"I dunno," John admitted. "Both sites had their own merits. It's doable, certainly, but this Roman numeral thing makes me wanna hurl."

Frank took his fake glasses off and laughed.

"But it's *Freshwater Oasis In-to*. Get it?"

John said, "Yeah, I get it."

It was just before 9:00 AM and parts of the management team had assembled and were congregating around the lobby waiting for the fun to begin. Gabe had seen Frank come in earlier and told Heidi that John was there too but they were having a meeting or something. So Heidi told Kat and they were both present at the front desk hoping to have a word with John . . . y'know, tell him how they felt about this review-in-a-swimsuit deal, and how they were mad as hell and I'm not going to take it anymore! It was sexual discrimination! They were both in business attire and had no intention of stripping down for Frank or God or the President of the United States of America.

Gabe, on the other hand, had just changed clothes and was sporting blue trunks, a Hawaiian shirt with cockatoos on it, and a pair of bright yellow aqua socks with black piping. He was stowing his regular duds in a cabinet under the desk when Bill Gardner emerged from the elevator wearing similar trunks (but in black), a matching black wife-beater shirt, and green floppers. Tony and Mike weren't in attendance yet, but their reviews weren't scheduled till later. Both, though, had assured Heidi they'd be attired in proper business suits. It was just these two idiots who'd knuckled under to Frank's improper request.

Heidi was disgusted with Gabe.

"Well," she said, "I hope you're proud of yourself."

Just then John emerged from the office chuckling and shut the door behind him. Maybe Frank was inside applying suntan lotion to his nose or something. Heidi was disgusted with John too. Allowing something like this to take place and then skipping town so he didn't have to deal with it. Unprofessional is what it was.

"Oh, you're back," she said. "Nice trip?"

John looked up and saw her standing there with Kat.

"Hey, ladies," he said, smiling as he came over. "Yeah, was in Tucson. Beautiful place. Real nice. I miss anything while I was gone? Lawsuits? Somebody hang themselves in the honeymoon suite?"

Heidi just stared at him with her eyes smoldering. John looked over at Kat and she was glaring at him the same way. Something was up. He addressed Heidi again.

"Is there a problem here?"

"Yeah, there's a problem," she blurted. "This review business in the swim-up pool bar! I will not allow myself to be degraded, and neither will Kathleen! There will be no swimsuits—you can tell Frank that! If he's got a problem with it, well, so be it!"

John squinted.

"Whoa. What are you talking about?"

Heidi kind of sputtered.

Kat filled in for her: "We're not wearing thongs for our employee reviews with Frank!" She indicated Gabe with her thumb. "Maybe this bozo thinks it's fine and dandy, but *we* don't."

Gabe'd just finished shuffling some papers he had in a file folder and had come over and leaned down a ways on the marble. He responded to the insult by making a face at the housekeeping woman, and then started laughing. John noticed he was wearing beach clothes or something. Had an orange bird on his shirt. By this time Bill Gardner had flopped across the tiles and positioned himself across the desk from Gabe. He too was wearing a swimsuit. Everybody was losing their minds. *Everybody.*

Bill went, "Mornin', folks. Life's a beach."

"You people are all nuts," John declared. "I don't have the slightest idea what you're talking about. Who is conducting employee reviews in the pool? Frank? You're out of your mind."

Heidi babbled, "But what about the memo?"

"I wrote the memo," John said. "There wasn't anything about a pool in it. Who said anything about having to wear a swimsuit? Interviews are takin' place right back there. In the stinkin' office. You guys crazy or somethin'?"

There was silence a couple secs.

Gabe broke it: "So, we're *not* having the reviews, uh, in the, uh, swim-up pool bar?"

"No, you idiot!"

Heidi and Kat started laughing. The door opened and Frank peeked his head out.

"Hey, DeFlores!" he shouted. "Is DeFlores out there?"

John looked at his front desk manager and joined the ladies in laughter. Gabe just stood there in his Hawaiian shirt with the birds on it.

He groaned, "Oh, God. . . ."

There was no way out. He grabbed his file folder and started heading for the office where Frank's big head was holding the door open.

"DeFlores! Is that you? Jeez, ya could-a maybe put some pants on or somethin'! What's wrong with you? Get in here, DeFlores!"

"Yes, Mr. Stratten."

Bill Gardner waited for the door to shut behind Gabe, then hightailed it back to the elevator and split. He could still hear everybody laughing on the second floor.

"Close call," he muttered.

JINGLE HELL

It was Christmas day and everyone who had the great misfortune to work that shift was well aware of their lowly status at FOI. See, 'cause all the big wigs (i.e., managers, employees with seniority, etc.) were sitting at home opening presents and sipping eggnog with brandy in it and blah blah whatnot and what-have-you, and they were prob'ly roasting chestnuts and listening to Bing Como singing in the background and all that jazz. Y'know, enjoying the holiday, but they sure as jingle bells weren't standing at the front desk waiting for whats-hisname to sign it on the register. No, it weren't no holiday for Dwayne Pinnick.

Dwayne was new to the front desk, so he got the duty, and he'd got it the day before too. That was Christmas Eve. Pffft. Dwayne was not enthused about FOI so far. Not by a long shot.

"Sir, will you be needing an extra key card or just the one?"

The guy just stared at him. Finally he blurted, "How many people do I look like?"

"Excuse me?"

"How many keys do you think I need for my room? I'm here by myself. It's Christmas. You see anybody here standing with me? Tell ya what, buddy, let me have *nine key cards* for my room."

Dwayne didn't want to play this game.

"Very well," he said, issuing the jerk a single key card in a little manila sleeve with the FOI logo on it. "Your room's on the third floor. Take a right after you get off the elevator, sir, and . . . enjoy your stay at FOI."

The guy laughed real quick and it snorted out his nose.

He said, "It better be worth the seven-fifty."

They stood there in time a moment. It might have been Christmas, or it might have been the stinkin' 4th of July, but, at least for Dwayne, y'know, since he started this gig a week ago, well, all his days ended in a big Y. Every bless'd one of 'em.

"Merry Christmas," he wished.

The guy scooped his duffel bag off the floor and slung it over a shoulder. "You too," he said, and split.

Dwayne Pinnick watched him head toward the elevators and imagined the guy's face when he opened the door to room 3003. That's the room that Heidi had left instructions for him to assign this rude, miserable little man. Dwayne'd never seen it himself, of course, but he'd heard plenty about it from that maintenance man with the stutter. Milt was his name. The janitor, that is. Poor guy'd drawn holiday duty too, Dwayne supposed because he'd done something terribly wrong, or, well, maybe just because-a the stutter. Who knows? At any rate, Milt had gone to great pains yesterday describing that hideous room on the third floor . . . about how it was a flaw in the original design of the hotel, see, because it looked out over the garage roof where the generators were, and n-n-nobody could get a decent night's sleep in that haunted room . . . for all the constant whirring and blah blah! Big units, right outside the window! Kept people from sleeping!

So they just used it for housekeeping storage all year long.

Yawn.

But the maintenance guy with the stutter explained to him about how the evil assistant general manager made poor Milt clean all that junk out of room 3003, y'know, so they could rent it out to Mister Duffel Bag on Christmas day. For seven dollars and fifty cents. Seems he was one of the three or four jerks who'd called FOI to task on that printing error, y'know, the one they sent to all the people on their mailing list? Yeah. The one saying how FOI would rent them a room for $7.50 a night . . . when what they really meant to say was that they'd rent them a room for $75 a night. Hah! What a bunch of morons! And so this joker called 'em on it and there he was by the generators, most likely unpacking that miserable little duffel bag by now and wishing he'd brought along some earplugs.

Serves him right.

God, Dwayne hated this job already. What a waste of time. That Gabe guy'd made it sound so wonderful during the interview process, y'know, what with big chances for promotion and the bit about the health insurance after 3 months. What he didn't take into consideration, though, was just how impossible it'd be for Dwayne to even make it 90 days. Dwayne wanted to quit right now. He walked out from behind the desk and stretched his legs a while; the place was dead, y'know, it bein' the holiday and all. He sauntered across the lobby floor and got a pop from the bartender in the Oasis Lounge, this new girl who looked like she was about ready to shoot herself or something. There was just one guy at the bar and he looked like he might want to join her. *Jingle Bells* was playing on the stereo.

Merry Christmas!

Dwayne thanked the lady and went back out through the lobby with his pop, sipping syrupy bubbles through a couple thin, green straws. *Laughing through the snow, on a one-horse open sleigh. Blah blah blah blah blah, blah blah blah blah blah.*

Ha ha ha!

Whatever. He walked around the desk and took his position in front of the terminal. Assume the position! Five more hours till relief came. Seemed like a year from now. They were makin' him work New Year's Eve as well. Then the next day too. That'd be a peach. Killing time, and vice versa. He was doodling on the back of an office supplies requisition form, though, about 10 minutes later, when all of a sudden the elevator came jingle-jangling to a stop and out popped Mister Duffel Bag all ticked off about something.

Prob'ly the room.

So the guy stormed across the lobby floor and there he was now in front of Dwayne.

"I'm *not* staying in that room!" he snapped. "It *sucks!* You're gonna issue me a new room right now, buddy! D'ya unnerstand?"

It was Christmas. Christmas day. Dwayne did not want to play this game.

CONCLUSION

John had gone home to shower and change after work, but was now back strolling through the nearly empty lobby. There was just a middle-age guy checking in with the new guy, Dwayne, who was on duty for the year-end employee appreciation party. Gabe had introduced them before his impromptu scouting trip to Tucson, and, later, after double-checking the man's references, he'd given his front desk manager the go-ahead to hire him. For at least the time being, there would be no more hiring without John's approval. At least till he had a handle on things.

And now, here he was.

The guy looked up from the terminal where he'd been punching in some numbers. John hadn't noticed before, but his eyes were slightly crossed.

"Good evening, Mr. Fallin," he said, sort of smiling.

"Hey, Dwayne," John replied. "How are ya?"

"Great," the guy answered, a little too enthusiastically. And then: "Enjoy yourself at the party!"

John smiled and nodded.

"Thanks," he said, then continued walking out toward the pool area. They'd decided to hold the holiday shindig on the pool deck because of a last-minute booking. Seems there'd been a snafu at the Bennett Arms where two parties had been booked for the same night. Their general manager had called just the other day and asked if John could help him out. John was glad to hear that general managers of other properties had such things as *snafus.* For a long time he'd suspected that dealing with mix-ups and calamities was just something that he did, y'know, as skipper of the Freshwater Oasis Inn.

But, alas, there were other unfortunates in the world. John was so sick of this three-ring circus that he feared if he blinked hard enough he'd not feel the urge to open his eyes again till Social Security kicked in. His "scouting" trip to Tucson. Good grief! It was nothing more than philosophical suds out by the pool. He'd taken a gander at the sites, of course, but that only took about 2 hours and was accomplished before even registering at the hotel. The rest of the time was spent getting a tan and thinking, *should I stay or should I go?*

Not should *I stay here* or *go to Tucson,* mind you, as John was way beyond that line of thinking . . . but the real issue here was whether or not he even wanted to work at FOI anymore. Everything was such a mess. Everything! And now Frank wanted him to open up yet another can of worms? Should I stay or should I go?

He still didn't know.

John arrived at the glass double doors and the party was rolling. He planned on coming to some sort of resolution tonight in that regard. Needed to talk to Frank and come clean with his reservations about the inn. There'd been so many mistakes made. John was not without blame; he knew that. Fish stinks from the head. John was the head. Frank was oblivious for the most part but still a good guy in his heart, so John had no intention of misleading the man. There'd been profits, sure, but that wasn't everything. Things could be better—more profitable, more professional. There was a house cleaning in order. John simply could not see it any other way. Black and white. Heads would have to roll.

Without order, there is chaos.

Order would have to be restored.

He stood there a minute and looked out at the people. The only faces he didn't know were those of the caterers they'd hired for the party. Lots of faces. It'd been a fleeting 6 years since he'd come to work for FOI. Lots could happen in that short space of time, and lots did. He remembered staffing the joint months before it even opened and remembered feeling pretty cocksure about his choices to lead the myriad departments at the inn. Remembered feeling pretty solid, y'know, about his assistant general manager and his housekeeping manager and blah, blah, blah . . . Bill Gardner! Man, this whole thing was an accident waiting to happen! Did he want to stick around and watch?

"Hey, Johnny-boy," said a voice behind him, with an accompanying prod in his back. "Stick 'em up."

John turned and it was Gabe. He remembered the other day when that goofball showed up for his employee review wearing nothing more than a swimming suit and some ridiculous shirt with birds on it. Good grief. He started laughing.

"Hey, Gabe," he said, then pointed at the man's elegant black suit. "Go figure. One day you're getting reviewed in a swimsuit . . . an' next day you're at the pool party in a $3,000 tux. You must be some kind-a renaissance man."

"Ha, ha, ha. Well, aren't you the comedian. I suppose I'll be hearing about that unfortunate misunderstanding for months."

"Yes," John assured him, "you will. . . . By the way, is that Dwayne guy cross-eyed?"

"What?"

"Cross-eyed. I just passed the front desk. The new guy looks kind-a weird."

"Well, I don't know," Gabe admitted. "I never noticed anything. Maybe he was staring at his nose. I seen it before: people getting all fixated on their noses. Maybe that's what it was. The man's in love with his nose."

Not likely. John opened the door and held it while Gabe went through, then followed him in to the party. How'd he miss those eyes?

Frank saw John make his appearance on the pool deck with that Hawaiian-shirt-wearin' meatball, Gabe DeFlores, and he was *late*. That did not bode well in terms of him making the right decision about staying with FOI; looked like he'd already made it, and it was the *wrong* one. A man don't come late to the employee appreciation party when he's the stinkin' general manager. Like maybe somebody'd made John a better offer. Probably those busybodies at the Bennett Arms. Sheri the Egg Lady'd said something to Lex about John talkin' on the phone with the general manager there. Maybe that's what it was.

"Damn," he muttered.

His girlfriend was sitting next to him and went, "Huh?"

Olivia Lacy, 25, just out of cosmetology school. They'd been dating for about a year now and Frank was pretty much sick of her. Maybe it was a generation thing, y'know, and he simply didn't understand half of what she was talking about—but, nah, she was just plain stupid. Poor Olive. He'd bought her a real nice Camero about 8 months back. Cherry red. And all he'd told her was, *"Listen, hon, all's ya gotta do . . . is every time ya fill the tank up at the gas station, just have Charlie check the oil."*

Charlie was his mechanic at the Sun station. So 2 weeks ago he gets a call on the cell and it's Olive all frantic and weepy because the stupid car don't work. He tells her to calm down and has the thing towed over to Charlie's, and, lo and behold, the engine's all froze because the bimbo'd never put even one drop of oil in it! That's all he'd asked her to do was have Charlie check the oil! That's all she had-ta do was put oil in the damn thing, but she didn't! And now the car was totaled!

He had yelled at her just recently on the way home from the Sun station where the Camero was lying in state: *"But I told you to have Charlie check the oil every time you filled up! You gotta be kiddin'!"*

"But I never got it filled all the way, Frankie! I was always just gettin' five or ten bucks' worth! I'm sorry!"

Then she started bawling again.

She was a very pretty girl, but . . . she just . . . did . . . not . . . think. That's about the time he changed her nickname from "Olive" to: *Oblivia Spacy*. Oh, well. In a hundred years it wouldn't matter. So they were at the year-end party and he muttered *damn* and she went *huh* and he turned to look at her.

"Speak again, sweet lips?"

"I didn't hear what ya said, Frankie."

"It was nothin', Oblivia. I was just talkin' to myself."

"Did you hear anything new?"

Frank stared at her. "Listen," he said, "I'm gonna go get another scotch. You want somethin' from the bar?"

"I wanna dance!"

John was at the bar that was really just a long folding table with paper on it and an impromptu service area setup on top. They had well liquor, red and white wine, pop, juices, and two kegs of Budweiser—one lite, one regular. John had just secured himself a plastic cup with regular in it and was sticking a 20-dollar bill in the bartender's tip jar. People in the service industry tended to party a little harder than, say, chartered accountants, so John wanted to ensure that he was looked out for in the immediate future. It got to be a jungle there around free booze when folks like him were involved.

He shouted over the din, "I'd like for you to think of me tonight as the King of Significance."

The guy saw the 20 and smiled.

"No problem, Your Highness! Thanks! No problem at all."

John smiled and was just backing out of the throng when Frank tapped him on the shoulder.

"Yo, John! Get me a scotch/rocks while you're in there!"

The bartender was already waiting on somebody else but saw John's raised hand and nodded. A minute later King John was handing Frank his scotch.

"Thanks, buddy. We need to talk."

"Yeah, we do at that."

Tony didn't feel so hot. He'd been taking his medicine but not enough to do any real good insofar as that tapeworm was concerned. He'd just been taking enough medicine to feel sick all the time. He'd been pretty vigilant the last 3 days or so, but ya had to do it for 2 weeks straight or it was ineffective, and now tonight he was drinking gin and tonics and it said right there on the bottle that you weren't supposed to do that. So, whatever good the medicine was doing was probably negated by the gin and tonics, and so he just kept getting skinnier and skinnier and everybody thought he was dying!

What he really needed to do was quit drinking so much. He sat there at a table by himself and looked around at everybody having fun. The deck was packed and couples had started dancing to this pseudo ska band that one of the hostesses' boyfriend played bass in. The band members were Caucasian but the drummer and lead singer had rebellious dreadlocks. La de da. Big deal. All the tables were full except the one he was sitting at. Tony wanted to stand up and scream:

"I DON'T HAVE AIDS!!!"

Whatever. They could think what they wanted. It did sort of bother him, though, that all these people had jumped to the conclusion that he had AIDS because he was gay. Well, he was *not* gay. So all of these people thought he was a homosexual. Wasn't that just dandy? Tony looked over the deck and imagined everyone thinking he was gay. Tony didn't give a hoot what somebody did in the privacy of their bedrooms, but it rankled him when they sat back and judged *him* because of the way *he* looked. Or maybe they thought his mannerisms were effeminate. Who's to say what goes on in people's minds? Maybe he should be real unprofessional and start dating a fellow employee like that Ed guy who'd been seeing Kelly the cocktail waitress. There he was right now, over by the bar, alone, his red hair glowing like some kind of landing beacon for promiscuous thieves. That relationship worked out real well, didn't it? And then that Jorgé bartender dancing like a fool with the other cocktail waitress; Judy, wasn't that her name? Yeah, the one that slipped on a banana peel and almost broke her back? Slipped on a banana peel? Ex-squeeze me? Well, she looked all right now. A complete recovery: THANK GOD!

Oh my, she was nearly tap-dancing. With moves like that, Tony thought, Judy should've been able to avoid that banana peel. It was a mystery wrapped up an enigma. It was a blah blah blah blah blah. That Jorgé bartender gets 500 bucks cash from Frank for his Christmas bonus? He'd heard the moron boasting earlier at the bar. What did *Tony* get? A check for a lousy grand? He was management, for Pete's sake! Jorgé gets $500 *and* the girl! Tony just sat there with his tapeworm and shrunk ever smaller and more insignificant. He needed a fresh gin and tonic. This one was all ice and four dead lime wedges.

Just then this woman appeared out of nowhere. Looked kind of familiar. She was wearing one of those skirts with shorts inside. Kind of cheap, but she shook down all right in it. Waltzed right over and stood there.

"Hey, Tony. How's it goin'?"

"Great," he lied, looking sort of perplexed. "How're you?"

"Nancy," she offered, answering his next as-yet-unformatted question. "I had my hair cut."

He peered closer.

"Oh, my God! I don't *believe* it!"

Nancy laughed.

"Looks different, huh?"

"You ain't kiddin', Nance! Wow!"

"Mind if I sit down?"

"By all means!"

"I'm getting old," John confessed. "These kids today . . . the tattoos, the way they dance . . . rap music. I just don't get it anymore."

"This ain't rap. It's reggae, isn't it?"

"No, I mean on the radio. MTV. I feel like one of those old farts in the newsreels talking about how the Beatles are spawn of the devil. Y'know? The music just doesn't make sense. Ever try to hum along with Enema or whatever his name is? That little blond kid? Won all the awards? Rap? It's not music, Frank. How do they even dance to it?"

Frank shook his head in agreement, though the only enema he'd ever experienced was at the business end of a rubber hose.

"I hear ya, buddy. But it's only a matter of time before the little woman spots me over here . . . and then drags my lame butt out there on the dance floor. Talk about your enemas. Jeez. Prob'ly fall in the damn pool. Make a fool of myself. So, what I'm sayin' here is we gotta make this quick. What're we gonna do, John? You in or out?"

They had commandeered a couple chairs and were sitting over by the south-end stairwell. It gave them a perfect angle on the party yet still offered a little privacy. John took a deep breath and let it out slowly. Frank removed a couple Cuban cigars from the breast pocket of his suit and offered one to what he hoped was still his general manager. John took the smoke and leaned in to Frank's lighter. After a while they were both puffing along on the clickety-clack track to throat cancer.

"I dunno, Frank. I been thinkin' a lot about things. We got some serious problems here at the inn that really aren't reflected in profit-and-loss statements."

Frank smirked. There were no serious problems at the inn when year-end statements showed big profits, least in his mind. He dismissed the issue in its entirety and thought instead about his general manager showing up late to his own employee appreciation party. It was rude, plain and simple. No two buts about it.

"By the way," he said, "I was wonderin' . . . why you showed up over an hour late for the start of this party. Seems kind of insulting to all these folks been workin' so hard for you all year. Know what I mean?"

John screwed his brows up and blew a plume of smoke into the night.

"What, are you kiddin'? I was still workin' when the party started. Long day, Frank. I had to go home and shower, y'know, change clothes."

"Oh."

John took a sip off his beer and set it down on the concrete between his feet.

"I stepped on gum today, Frank. Purple gum. Out in the parking lot. Can you believe it?"

"You're kiddin'!"

"Nope. Anyway, I like the Tucson idea. Like it a lot. I like the idea of running two hotels. I like the idea of leaving things in Heidi's capable hands when I put the new pieces together in Tucson. I like the idea of sleeping peacefully every night while I'm overseeing this new development, knowing that Kat Lawhorn and Bill Gardner are on duty. Frank, I like all those ideas."

"Well, then . . . what's the problem?"

John chuckled.

"I'll tell ya what the problem is, Frank. The problem is that Heidi's hands aren't capable, and Bill and Kat couldn't play hopscotch together without tripping over each other's purple gum. That's the problem, Frank."

Now it was Frank's turn to knit brows.

"What're you talkin' about? You hired 'em. They been here since day one. Suddenly they ain't no good? This is nuts, John."

John rolled his eyes. Frank could not possibly understand the things he dealt with on a daily basis. Bad management decisions being made by his department heads. Decisions that affected other departments. Everything was interrelated. Situations where John had to intervene and correct things because the managers were just too dense . . . too ethically corrupt . . . too shortsighted to see the bigger picture. It was all about teamwork and people being on the same page, yet the management team he'd assembled so long ago had fragmented to the point where nobody knew what anybody else was doing anymore, and it was all John could do to hold things together. He was nothing more than a Band-Aid, or a babysitter. Frank could not possibly understand this, but he spent the next 45 minutes spelling it all out. Keeping it simple, to the point, and, when he was finally done with his recitation, John picked the slightly warm cup of beer back up and drained it.

"So," he concluded, "when I think about opening up a new hotel and whatnot, spreading myself even thinner, letting the patients run the asylum as it were . . . well, Frank, I feel like I'm gonna have a brain meltdown."

John crushed the empty plastic cup in his hand and tossed it in the soil of a potted cactus. The thing looked like something off the set of an old *Star Trek* episode. A giant organic shoetree that was threatening to bust out of its now too-small container and go on some sort of plant rampage. Skewer everything on the pool deck that didn't move fast enough, like John and his five-toed team of sloths.

He sighed.

Frank had listened patiently for the better part of the last hour, and he'd heard quite enough. He looked out over the pool deck at 143 souls that depended on him for their livelihoods, good people, and he knew in his heart that whatever failings they had were correctable. In all his years on this planet, if there was one thing Frank knew it was that nobody was perfect. Except for Barbara Streisand.

Frank spoke.

"Lighten up, ya dork. People are people. I listened to everything ya said, John, and it's the biggest load-a bull I ever did hear. If these managers that *you* hired and *you* trained . . . well, if they're incompetents . . . it's because *you* are incompetent. And I don't think that you are incompetent, John. Don't get me wrong. You do a fine job here at the inn. I couldn't ask for a better general manager. But I get all chafed when I hear someone moaning about how his underlings ain't got no ethics. You're the boss, John. You write the rules. You're the one's supposed to establish how high the bar is, and if you ain't done the groundwork . . . well, whose fault is that? What's the program here, John? Is there some big program here that your management team ain't following? If there is, buddy, well by all means fire 'em! Let's get rid of 'em all, John! Right now! Say the word!"

John sat there a full minute. His cigar had gone out. In his own way, Frank could sometimes be pretty profound. It was like watching a gorilla cut diamonds. The man was right, though. There wasn't any program. John expected everyone to behave according to some invisible code, and then he got disappointed when they came up short. What did he expect? Good grief. *John* was the problem.

Eventually John cleared his throat.

"This dork needs another beer. Whadaya say, partner?"

"Now you're talkin'."

Bill Gardner was in his Sunday-go-to-meetin' clothes. Never did understand how they could've invented such a thing as ties. Like wearin' a noose or somethin'. What's the point? Didn't make no sense to him. Like a lot of things, ties seemed like some kind-a torture device women came up with to get back at men for mistreating them. Or they bought 'em ties for Christmas and birthdays so they could drag 'em off to the theater when romantic comedies were playin'. Like the ones with that British guy, Hugh something or other. The moron that was shacked up with that beautiful Hurley girl with the sexy accent? Well, good ol' Hugh had the same accent but it wasn't sexy on him. Anyway, didn't he get caught with his pants down by the police? Yep, he sure did. Ha, ha. The guy must-a been crazy! Prob'ly 'cause he was named *Hugh*. Everybody sayin' to him, *Hey, you!* Who names their kid Hugh? Crazy people. Every movie he was ever in was terrible, naturally, whadaya expect, but the women just ate that syrupy nonsense up like it was grits. Only thing worse than romantic comedies was goin' to see one in a tie.

Bill chuckled to himself despite the fact he could hardly swallow because-a that rope around his neck. Had it draped over a nail in his closet for 10 years at least. Maybe it'd shrunk? Yeah, it was prob'ly too small. He hooked an index finger between the collar and his neck and pulled real hard, yeah-baby, give daddy some room. Uh-huh, that's a little better. He'd found himself a spot on the left end of that table where the booze was. Every time the beer-tender weren't busy he'd order another brewski. He'd take the new cup and set it in the old cup and by now the stack was so high it looked like he was drinkin' an accordion. Why not? It was free, wasn't it?

In this life, a man had-ta just take what was due him. You snooze, you lose. Plain and simple. His Cousin Bill was supposed to be his guest for this shindig but somethin'd come up. Well, *come out*, more accurately. Ha, ha. At the last minute Cousin Bill's wife went into labor and he had to take her on over to the hospital. It was her fifth kid, though, and Cousin Bill said he figured it'd drop out pretty fast . . . so maybe he'd be able to get on over here before the first keg run dry. Damn well better if he expected to get his foot in the door with the big cheese on those security bars for the ground-floor units. Bill didn't have a clue why they was suddenly all hot about security and what-have-you, but they was, and twice already they'd had guys in Polo shirts out giving estimates for the work. Polo shirts! No reason in the world why Cousin Bill couldn't bid on the job. He's already showed 'em what kind-a work he was capable of—what with that pretty gazebo he'd build for 'em out by the parkin' lot. That security bar job'd be a big one, that was for sure. Yeah, Cousin Bill'd better hightail on out here and corner that Yankee.

You snooze, you lose.

"Hey, beer-tender! Gimmie another reg'lar!"

So, Bill was waiting for his umpteenth brewski when he heard a great retching sound. He turned to his right and all the spiffy people were moving away from some skinny dude in a suit. Oh, yeah, it was that waiter, Tony—the one with that terminal AIDS disease that gay guys got. Great googily-moogily, but he was retchin' up a storm! Some fat girl propping him up like he was nothin' but a bag of bones. Sure had a lotta beans in him for bein' such a little man. Bill'd never seen so much puke in his life . . . and, and . . . there was somethin' else!

Looked like spaghetti, but *nasty!*

Bill blurted, "What in God's name is *that?*"

When Gabe observed Frank and John coming toward the bar, he saw it as his big opportunity to redeem himself. He felt like such an idiot! Everyone'd been laughing at him all week, even the maids pushing carts full of toilet paper through the lobby, snickering in Spanish, ever since that stupid bathing suit incident. Even Bill Gardner, that yahoo! Laughing at him! Bill Gardner! Yahoo! Wearing a swimsuit of his own but he'd slinked away, hadn't he? That *yahoo!*

The tux had cost $4,500, but it was worth it. Gabe felt like James Bond as he glided past arms and asses and elbows and eventually found himself a spot by the end of the table. It was the suit. Oceans of bodies just seemed to part for him. People made room. He stood there for a minute and tried to remember what it was that Frank drank. Bourbon? Scotch? It was brown, he knew that much. John drank brown stuff too but it was beer. That was easy. He'd snap his fingers and the tux would order one draft, a scotch/rocks, and a bourbon/rocks. About the time Frank and John came up they'd be ready and waiting for them. He'd drink whatever it was that Frank didn't. He'd wind up smelling like a rose.

"Oh, bartender? Over here?"

Just then there was a voice at his biceps.

"Escuse! Escuse, señor!"

Gabe looked down.

"What?" he asked, annoyed. "What is it, little man?"

The guy had a mop. He was gesticulating with it like he wanted to mop Gabe's feet or something. *Ick.* Those were $300 shoes! Gabe stepped aside to give the guy a wide birth, but the deck was slippery and he almost fell on his can. He looked down then and was horrified to note that he was standing in a puddle of vomit! A *huge* puddle of vomit. And, it wasn't just vomit, there was something *slithering* in it!

A gigantic *worm!*

"Aw, man," he groaned.

Frank went, "What on earth are you doin' there, DeFlores?"

Gabe looked up from the puddle and thought he was going to cry. The band was on a break. Complete silence. Everybody was staring at him with these amazed grins on their faces. It wasn't any magical tuxedo that parted the Red Sea; it was vomit! *Worm* vomit! His mouth started working but no sound came out. He didn't know what to do. He thought back to high school when he'd had a chorus role in the stage version of *South Pacific*. He started singing:

"Ain't nothin' like a dame . . ."

Nancy assisted Tony back from the bar area and had him reclining on a lounger. She was taking his shoes off very carefully so as not to get any intestinal bits on her hands. A crowd had formed around them but Tony didn't seem to mind. She'd never witnessed anything like that before. Not in her whole life! Poor Tony was all pasty and sweating but he looked somehow relieved.

He clenched both fists over his head and exulted: "GREAT GOD ALMIGHTY! I'M CURED!

Glossary of Key Words

Accountability: Hospitality managers are personally accountable for the ethical quality of their decisions as well as those of their subordinates.

Act utilitarianism: Every time we act we ought to calculate and determine which among all the options open to us would promote the greatest net utility for all.

Alcohol abuse: When drinking alcoholic beverages causes problems.

Alcohol dependence/alcoholism: Addiction to alcohol. An inability to abstain from drinking alcoholic beverages even though to do so causes problems.

Analysis: A systematic way of thinking about something to reach a decision.

Arrogance: Where we behave as though we think we are better than others.

Attitudinal: Ethics is attitudinal. An attitude is an inclination to make certain choices in particular circumstances.

Behavioral objectives: Where we state what the trainees will be able to do upon completion of the training.

Biases: Personal beliefs that influence one's decisions in an often prejudicial manner.

Burnout: A state of emotional exhaustion caused by the stress of one's work or responsibilities.

Categorical imperative: There is only one law of morality and it is that we should act in ways that we would want our acts to become laws for everyone else's behavior.

Chain of command: Graphically depicted in organizational charts, who reports to whom.

Civics: The study of how to be good citizens.

Civility: The determination to behave in ways that are a positive influence on society as a whole.

Coaching: A supervising technique that encourages and rewards adequate (meet the standards) performance and discourages and corrects inadequate performance. We monitor the performance of the employees on the job and offer praise and/or give immediate corrective feedback to ensure that employees maintain the standards achieved in the original training.

Collusion: A secret agreement between buyer and seller.

Commitment to excellence: Hospitality managers pursue excellence in performing their duties and are willing to put more into their job than they can get out of it.

Concern and respect for others: Hospitality managers are concerned, respectful, compassionate, and kind. They are sensitive to the personal concerns of their colleagues and live the "Golden Rule." They respect the rights and interests of all those who have a stake in their decisions.

Consequences: The possible results of a decision.

Contingency plan: We employ whatever actions we have predetermined to be appropriate when a situation arises. If *this* happens, then we will do *that*.

Controls: Means by which managers attempt to direct, regulate, and restrain the actions of people in order to achieve desired goals

Cost control: The process whereby managers attempt to regulate costs and guard against excessive costs.

Counseling: We meet with individual employees to help them seek solutions to their problems that are interfering with their ability to maintain the standards they achieved in the original training.

Courtesy: We use good manners in all our social encounters.

Critical control points: Places in the production process where control measures can be implemented to avoid loss or waste.

Cultural relativism: Ethics are not universal. Whatever a society agrees is correct is deemed correct for that society.

Delegation: The process of assigning responsibility and authority to employees in order to accomplish an objective.

Demographics: Descriptive statistics that classify populations by age, sex, income, etc.

Denial: When alcohol (or any other addictive substance or activity) abusers will not recognize their drinking as problematic.

Deontological: Theories that facilitate understanding and moral decision making that are focused on the acts themselves (the means are more important than the ends).

Discrimination: A bias in the treatment of a person or group.

Diversity: Variations within a group in terms of culture, education, language, ages, genders, race, religion, etc.

Divine command theory: See **Supernaturalism.**

Emotivism: A variation of subjectivism where it is believed that moral judgments are not testable facts, so what we like is neither good nor bad, simply what we like.

Empathy: Because we all have the same feelings, we are capable of understanding how other people feel in particular situations.

Ethics: The moral rules of conduct we decide to live by.

Ethics code: A list of moral rules that members of particular groups or professions agree to follow.

Ethics program: The ongoing activities and training designed to promote ethical awareness and the reinforcement of expected ethical behavior.

Etiquette: The combination of attitude, behavior, and grooming that meets the conventional standards required for acceptance in polite society.

Evaluation: Determining whether the training actually solved the problem it was designed to solve.

External locus of control: The belief that we do not have control over our lives.

Fair Labor Standards Act: Law that provides for minimum wages, maximum hours, overtime pay, and child labor protection.

Fairness: Hospitality managers are fair and equitable in all dealings; they do not abuse power arbitrarily nor take undue advantage of another's mistakes or difficulties. They treat all individuals with equality, with tolerance for and acceptance of diversity and with an open mind.

Formal training: A structured form of training following a predetermined plan of instruction.

Golden Rule: Do unto others as you would have others do unto you.

Honesty: Hospitality managers are honest and truthful. They do not mislead or deceive others by misrepresentations.

Humiliation: Where we are publicly shamed or embarrassed.

Humility: To be humble, which is characterized by thinking and behaving without excessive pride and/or arrogance.

Integrity: Hospitality managers demonstrate the courage of their convictions by doing what they know is right even when there is pressure to do otherwise.

Internal locus of control: The belief that we have control over our lives.

Intuitionism: There are self-evident objective truths within us that any mature person can know.

Leadership: Hospitality managers are conscious of the responsibility and opportunities of their position of leadership. They realize that the best way to instill ethical principles and ethical awareness in their organizations is by example. They walk their talk!

Lesson plan: A document that consists of subject matter for the training topic, all the learning activities and materials, and the trainer directions and script for presenting the instruction.

Loyalty: Hospitality managers demonstrate loyalty to their companies in devotion to duty and loyalty to colleagues by friendship in adversity. They avoid conflicts of interest; do not use or disclose confidential information; and should they accept other employment, they respect the proprietary information of their former employer.

Marketing: Involves selecting whom we wish to serve, determining what they would like, and then how, when, and where they would like it.

Meta-ethics: The study of ethics that asks how we determine what our moral principles are.

Needs assessment: The first step in any design project where we determine the specific training needs.

Normative ethics: The study of ethics that asks what principles ought we live by.

OSHA: The Occupational Safety and Health Administration; a government regulatory agency charged with monitoring safety in the workplace.

People skills: The combination of communication skills, social skills, and empathy, that when working together enable us to be positively effective with our employees.

Philanthropy: Sharing some of our money and talents for the benefit of needy people.

Point-of-Sale System (POS):   A network of cashier and server terminals that typically handles food and beverage orders, transmission of orders to the kitchen and bar, guest-check settlement, timekeeping, and interactive charge posting to guest folios.

Pride: Taking undeserved or deserved credit while failing to acknowledge help and gifts that made the achievement possible.

Proactive: To think in advance how we will handle situations that could arise in the future—avoiding problems.

Profession: An occupation that requires specialized knowledge and skills and is generally looked on with respect by most people.

Promotion: Communicating information between seller and potential buyer to influence attitudes and behavior.

Property Management System (PMS):   Comprehensive computer software program that performs both back- and front-office functions as well as supports a variety of other functions such as housekeeping, sales, catering, energy management, and call accounting.

Psychomotor: A type of muscular activity required to execute and achieve a particular result.

Reasonable care: The duty to take sufficient reasonable care to eliminate or minimize unsafe conditions so that guests or employees do not become victims of injuries, accidents, criminals acts, or fire trauma.

Reciprocity norm: The learned expectation that we should return help to those who have helped us.

Reputation and morale: Hospitality managers seek to protect and build the company's reputation and the morale of its employees by engaging in conduct that builds respect and by taking whatever actions are necessary to correct or prevent inappropriate conduct of others.

RFP: Request for proposals.

Rule utilitarianism: Every time we act we obey the set of rules that, taken together, promote the greatest utility for all. We only have to calculate consequences when two rules are in conflict.

Sales: The exchange of a product for an agreed-upon amount of money from a seller to a buyer.

Shared ethical values: A communal sense of right and wrong.

Social contact theory: Good or right is solely determined by the rules we need to make and follow in order for us to live together peacefully.

Social drinker: To drink alcoholic beverages moderately and only on social occasions.

Social responsibility norm: We should help those who need our help, even if costs outweigh the benefits.

Spotters/secret shoppers: People who have been hired by the facility to evaluate the service while acting as customers.

Stakeholders: The individuals who may be affected by a decision.

Stereotype: A generalized belief about a group of people.

Subjectivism: Right and good is whatever we enjoy doing.

Supernaturalism: Good or right is what God wills us to do.

Supervision: The ongoing training where we make sure that the standards reached in training are maintained on the job.

Target market: The people we have selected to serve.

Task analysis: Where we break down a task into all of the minute steps it takes to complete the task.

Teleological: Theories that facilitate understanding and moral decision making that are focused on the outcomes of acts (the ends justify the means).

Time management: Prioritizing our activities and using time effectively to minimize deadline anxiety, procrastination, and job fatigue.

Training plan: Includes a list of all the training topics and a schedule of when, where, and by whom they will be presented.

Trustworthiness: Hospitality managers are trustworthy and candid in supplying information and in correcting misapprehensions of fact. They do not create justifications for escaping their promises and commitments.

Utilitarianism: Good or right actions are those that result in happiness.

Virtue: Character traits that result in habitual good behavior.

Virtue theory: Where we identify, define, and justify character traits that result in habitual good behavior.

Work ethic: The sense that work is necessary and good for us, and it manifests itself in good work habits such as timeliness and being on task while on the clock.

Appendix A

Principles and Standards of Ethical Supply Management Conduct

with Accompanying Guidelines

PRINCIPLES AND STANDARDS OF ETHICAL SUPPLY MANAGEMENT CONDUCT

> LOYALTY TO YOUR ORGANIZATION
> JUSTICE TO THOSE WITH WHOM YOU DEAL
> FAITH IN YOUR PROFESSION

From these principles are derived the ISM standards of supply management conduct. (Global)

1. Avoid the intent and appearance of unethical or compromising practice in relationships, actions, and communications.
2. Demonstrate loyalty to the employer by diligently following the lawful instructions of the employer, using reasonable care and granted authority.
3. Avoid any personal business or professional activity that would create a conflict between personal interests and the interests of the employer.

4. Avoid soliciting or accepting money, loans, credits, or preferential discounts, and the acceptance of gifts, entertainment, favors, or services from present or potential suppliers that might influence, or appear to influence, supply management decisions.

5. Handle confidential or proprietary information with due care and proper consideration of ethical and legal ramifications and governmental regulations.

6. Promote positive supplier relationships through courtesy and impartiality.

7. Avoid improper reciprocal agreements.

8. Know and obey the letter and spirit of laws applicable to supply management.

9. Encourage support for small, disadvantaged, and minority-owned businesses.

10. Acquire and maintain professional competence.

11. Conduct supply management activities in accordance with national and international laws, customs, and practices, your organization's policies, and these ethical principles and standards of conduct.

12. Enhance the stature of the supply management profession.

Approved January 2002

GUIDELINES

Preamble

A distinguishing characteristic of a profession is the ability to combine ethical standards with the performance of technical skills. In fact, "professional" is described in *Webster's New Collegiate Dictionary* as "characterized by or conforming to the technical or ethical standards of a profession." *Webster's* goes on to describe "ethic" as "a theory or system of moral values, the principles of conduct governing an individual or group." In order to achieve stature as a profession, those in supply management must establish and subscribe to a set of ethical standards to guide individual and group decisions and actions.

These *Principles and Standards of Ethical Supply Management Conduct* with Accompanying Guidelines are established to encourage adherence to an uncompromising level of integrity. They are designed to heighten awareness and acceptance of appropriate conduct. They are not intended to supplant an organization's policies pertaining to ethical practice. These *Principles and Standards of Ethical Supply Management Conduct with Accompanying Guidelines* are intended to be a model for consideration. Further, they are recommended as guidelines to all those who influence the supply management process, including supply management professionals, engineers, quality control personnel, sales representatives, and senior management.

An element of a recognized profession is a set of principles and standards. The goal of this booklet is to convey the principles and standards which the supply management profession considers just, fitting, and correct. It is the responsibility of each supply management professional to strive to achieve acceptance of and adherence to these principles and standards. Supply management organizations are encouraged to have an ethics policy and reporting process in place that is clearly and consistently communicated to employees, including those outside the supply organization, and suppliers.

Although no set of principles and standards can be all-inclusive, these were established to cover major domestic and international supply management issues. Sensitivity to and consideration of other cultures including the laws, customs, and practices of other nations must be acknowledged.

Information contained in this booklet is intended to provide insight for handling difficult day-to-day issues. Standards and guidelines cannot take the place of good judgment. When in doubt, consult with management, professional colleagues . . . and of course your conscience.

Each section contains:

- A Statement of the Standard
- Commentary
- Guidelines

1. Perceived Impropriety

Avoid the intent and appearance of unethical or compromising conduct in relationships, actions, and communications.

The consequences of a perceived impropriety can be the same as consequences of an actual impropriety. Therefore, it is essential that any activity or involvement between supply management professionals and active or potential suppliers which in any way diminishes, or even appears to diminish, open and fair treatment of suppliers is strictly avoided. Those who do not understand the circumstances will judge based on appearances. Supply management professionals must consider this and act accordingly.

The following are recommended guidelines in dealing with perception:

- Situations may occur in which, through unanticipated circumstances, a business relationship transpires with a personal friend. The perception (as well as the potential) of a conflict of interest should be discussed with management, and a reassignment of procurement responsibility should be considered.
- Business meeting locations should be carefully chosen. Environments other than the office may be perceived as inappropriate by the business community or by co-workers.
- Displays of personal preference may give an impression of impropriety and should be avoided. Conversation that delves excessively into personal affairs should be avoided.

- Positive action should be taken by management to alleviate suspicion of impropriety.

2. Responsibilities to the Employer

Demonstrate loyalty to the employer by diligently following the lawful instructions of the employer, using reasonable care and granted authority.

It is the duty of the supply management professional to ensure that actions taken as an agent for the employer will serve the interests of the employer to the exclusion of personal gain. This requires application of sound judgment and consideration of both the legal and ethical implications of our actions.

The following are recommended guidelines for satisfying responsibilities to our employers:

- Understand the agency authority granted, and apply the legal and ethical requirements embodied in the agency relationship with the employer.
- Obtain the maximum value for monies expended as agents for the employer.
- Avoid activities which would compromise, or create the perception of compromising, the best interests of the employer.
- Avoid using the employer's purchasing power to make purchases for specific individuals' non-business use. If employer-sponsored personal purchasing programs exist, the supply management professional should make certain that the arrangements are fair to suppliers, employees, and the employer.
- Maintain up-to-date knowledge of applicable laws, purchasing and supply management techniques, and management responsibilities.

3. Conflict of Interest

Avoid any personal business or professional activity that would create a conflict between personal interests and the interests of the employer.

Supply management professionals must not use their positions in any way to induce another person to provide any benefit to themselves, or persons with whom they have family, business, personal, or financial relationships. Even though a conflict may not technically exist, supply management professionals must avoid the appearance of such a conflict. Whenever a potential conflict of interest arises, the supply management professional should notify the appropriate person for guidance or resolution.

The following are recommended guidelines to avoid conflicts of interest:

Conduct to be Avoided

- Engaging in outside business, or employment by an outside organization, which may encroach upon the supply professional's primary responsibility of loyalty to the goals of the employer.

- Engaging in improper personal business with, or employment by, an organization which competes with, or is a supplier to, the employer. Examples include but are not limited to:
- Owning or leasing any property with knowledge that the employer has an active or potential interest therein.
- Lending money to, or borrowing money from, any customer or supplier.
- Using the organization's name (unless authorized) to lend weight or prestige to sponsorship of a political party or cause, or endorsing the product or service of another organization.

Personal Investment.   Ownership of stock in a supplier of goods or services, competitor, or customer should be reported to the employer for review and guidance to avoid the potential for impropriety. Interests by members of the professional's immediate family are considered to be of the same significance as direct ownership.

Outside Activities.   Supply management professionals must not use their position with their employer when participating in outside educational, professional, political, philanthropic, social, or recreational activities, which might be detrimental to their employer's business or reputation.

Conflict of Interest Statements.   Supply management professionals are encouraged to disclose any potential conflict of interest, and to advocate that their employer obtain conflict of interest statements from all employees upon employment, and annually thereafter.

Self-Evaluation Procedure.   Supply management professionals are encouraged to perform an annual self-evaluation of their outside interests which may have the potential of being contrary to the best interests of their organization or the profession.

4. Issues of Influence

Avoid soliciting or accepting money, loans, credits, or preferential discounts, and the acceptance of gifts, entertainment, favors, or services from present or potential suppliers that might influence, or appear to influence, supply management decisions.

Those in a position to influence the supply process must be dedicated to the best interests of their employer. It is essential, for all in a position to influence a purchasing decision, to avoid any activity which may diminish, or even appear to diminish, the objectivity of the decisionmaking process.

In some circumstances, items which could be considered an issue of influence may be a bona fide business activity. In such cases, extreme care should be taken to evaluate the intent and the perception of acceptance of such an offer to ensure:

- It is legal.
- It is in the best interests of the employer.
- It will not influence the purchasing decision.
- It will not be perceived by peers or others to be unethical.

Sources of influence include:

- Management Policies
- Gifts, Gratuities, and Entertainment
- Product Samples
- Business Meals
- Personal Relationships
- International Practices
- Political Considerations
- Advertising
- Market Power
- Specifications and Standards

The following are recommended guidelines when dealing with issues of influence:

Management Policies. Supply management professionals should encourage and recommend the development and implementation of management policies that reduce or eliminate inappropriate influences on the supply process.

Gifts, Gratuities, and Entertainment. Gifts, gratuities, and entertainment include material goods, services, or activities offered with the intent of, or providing the potential for, influencing a buying decision. As such, these may be offered to a supply professional or to other persons involved in the supply process (or members of their immediate families). They may be offered in various forms.

- Extreme caution must be used in evaluating the acceptance of gifts, gratuities, or entertainment, even if of nominal value, and the frequency of such actions (the collective impact) to ensure that one is abiding by the letter and the spirit of these guidelines.
- Soliciting gifts, gratuities, or entertainment in any form for yourself or your employer is unacceptable.
- Avoid accepting monies, credits, and prejudicial discounts.
- Establish nominal value in organization policy to address supplier offerings of nominal value as a gesture of goodwill, or for public relations purposes.

- Refuse gifts exceeding nominal value, and return them with a polite explanation, or if perishable, either return the gifts or donate them to a local charity in the name of the supplier.
- Seek direction of management if concerned that a business relationship may be impaired by refusal of a gift, gratuity, or entertainment.

Product Samples.   Product test samples may be offered by suppliers. If test samples exceed nominal value, supply management should consider issuing a document to cover the transaction. This document should clarify the responsibility for the cost of the samples and should address any obligation for sharing test results with the supplier.

Business Meals.   Occasionally, during the course of business, it may be appropriate to conduct business during meals.

- Such meals shall be for a specific business purpose.
- Frequent meals with the same supplier should be avoided.
- The supply management professional should be in a position to pay for meals as frequently as the supplier. Supply management professionals are encouraged to budget for this business activity.

Personal Relationships.   Personal relationships are an inherent aspect of supply management. Supply management professionals interact extensively with suppliers' representatives. Individuals in many other functional areas in both the buying and supplying organizations also interact extensively with each other. The development of personal relationships from such interactions is both expected and desirable as it leads to relationships based on understanding and trust. It must also be recognized that the purchasing decision must not be influenced by anything other than what is in the best interest of the organization, and that personal relationships that develop beyond what is necessary to ensure understanding and trust may be inappropriate. It is important, therefore, for supply management professionals to closely monitor the nature of relationships with suppliers' representatives to ensure that personal friendships do not develop that would result in decisions not in the organization's best interest.

International Practices.   There may be great cultural variation with respect to the appropriateness of business gifts, meals, entertainment, and the nature of personal relationships. In some cultures, business gifts, meals, and entertainment are normal and expected, as are close personal relationships. In other cultures, business is transacted at arm's length, and business gifts, meals, and entertainment, as well as close personal relationships, are viewed as inappropriate when making supply management decisions. It is important, therefore, for supply management professionals to understand such variation and establish policies and procedures to deal effectively with suppliers from different cultures to ensure making supply management decisions that are in the best interest of the organization. This requires that suppliers be informed of the organization's policies with respect to business gifts, meals, entertainment, and the nature of personal relationships. It also requires that supply management professionals act courteously to suppliers' representatives who may inadvertently act in ways contrary to the organization's policies.

Political Considerations.   All organizations are subject to internal and external forces and pressures. Internal forces and pressures result from an organization's culture. External forces and pressures consist of economic conditions, laws, regulations, public opinion, special interest groups, and political entities. The negative influence of internal and external forces and pressures on supply management can be minimized when the organization adopts practices based on ethical principles and standards.

Advertising.   Care should be exercised when accepting promotional items or participating in activities that tend to promote one supplier over another, or could be perceived as preferential supplier advertising by the supply management professional.

Market Power.   Supply management professionals must be aware of their organization's position (e.g., economic size, power, etc.) in the marketplace and ensure this position is used within the scope of ethical behavior by the supply management professional and the organization.

Specifications and Standards.   Supply management professionals must ensure that specifications and standards are objectively written in a manner that encourages competition when appropriate, excludes unnecessary restrictive requirements, and appropriately defines quality.

5. Confidential and Proprietary Information

Handle confidential or proprietary information with due care and proper consideration of ethical and legal ramifications and governmental regulations.

Proprietary and confidential information requires protection. Such information may or may not be upheld by patent, copyright, or non-disclosure agreement. Proprietary and confidential information should be released to other parties (internal and external) only on a need-to-know basis. It is the responsibility of the individual sharing confidential or proprietary information to ensure that the recipient understands his or her obligation to protect such information.

Examples of information which may be considered confidential or proprietary include:

- Pricing
- Bid or quotation information

- Cost sheets
- Formulas and/or process information
- Design information
- Organizational plans, goals, and strategies
- Profit information
- Asset information
- Wage and salary scales
- Personal information about employees, officers, and directors
- Supply sources or supplier information
- Computer software programs

Recommended guidelines for dealing with confidential or proprietary information:

- Each organization should develop and communicate a policy covering proprietary and confidential information.
- Proprietary and confidential information must be identified as such when communicated, whether disclosed electronically, in writing, or orally.
- Use of confidentiality agreements that clarify the parameters for use of information and responsibilities inherent in its use is recommended.
- The supply professional and others within the organization are cautioned not to accept confidential or proprietary information unless they have the need for such information.
- When dealing with any information, whether or not confidential or proprietary, care should be exercised in determining the effects of its use.

6. Supplier Relationships

Promote positive supplier relationships through courtesy and impartiality.

Supply management professionals should promote mutually acceptable business relationships with suppliers and customers. By affording all business contacts the same courtesy and impartiality in all phases of business transactions, professionals will enhance the reputation and good standing of their employer, the supply management profession, and themselves.

Fairness and impartiality should be extended to all legitimate business concerns. While it may be desirable to build long-term relationships with selected suppliers, such relationships should not deter the potential of establishing similar working relationships with other suppliers.

The following are recommended guidelines for maintaining positive supplier relationships:

- Establish parameters for bidding, rebidding, and/or negotiations prior to the issuance of a request for quotation or similar document to ensure a fair, consistent, and unbiased process.

- Maintain confidentiality regarding proprietary information as well as suppliers' prices and terms, unless otherwise required by government regulation.
- Achieve a prompt and fair resolution of problems.
- Avoid unreasonable demands.
- Ensure prompt and open communications.
- Exercise professional, cooperative, and objective behavior in business relationships and avoid partiality, or the appearance of partiality, in business dealings.

7. Reciprocity

Avoid improper reciprocal agreements.

If supply management professionals or their organizations give preference to suppliers because they are also customers, or when the organization influences a supplier to be a customer, the professional or the organization is engaging in a practice known as reciprocity. Agreements involving a specific commitment to buy in exchange for a specific commitment to sell also constitute reciprocity. These purchasing actions are illegal if they tend to restrict competition or trade or if they are coerced, since such acts may be construed as "restraint of trade" in violation of Sections 1 and 2 of the Sherman Act.

Supply management professionals and their organizations must be able to recognize reciprocity and its ethical and legal implications.

Reciprocity is both a legal and an ethical issue that may result in legal sanctions against the organization, its management, and/or its supply management personnel.

The following are recommended guidelines in dealing with reciprocity:

- Dealing with a supplier that is also a customer may not constitute a problem if, in fact, the supplier is the best source.
- Supply management strategy must include a positive effort to oppose any corporate or organizational commitment to, or pursuit of, any form of improper reciprocity.
- Supply management professionals should become sufficiently knowledgeable of the provisions in antitrust laws to recognize a potential legal problem and to know when to seek legal counsel.
- If a supply management professional believes the potential for improper reciprocity exists, or is being encouraged by marketing, sales, or management to engage in reciprocity, legal counsel should be sought.
- Lists of suppliers should not be provided to sales or marketing for their use in pursuing improper reciprocal agreements.
- Supply management professionals must be especially careful when dealing with suppliers that are customers when making sourcing decisions.

8. Applicable Laws

Know and obey the letter and spirit of laws applicable to supply management.

Supply management professionals should obtain and maintain an understanding of the legal concepts that govern their activities as agents of their employers, and of the various laws that govern the purchase and sale of goods and services. These include laws and regulations at the international, national, state, and local levels.

Some of the laws and regulations that supply management professionals should be aware of include:

- Agency law
- Contract and commercial laws, including the Uniform Commercial Code (UCC) and the Uniform Computer Information Transactions Act (UCITA)
- Electronic commerce laws, including the Uniform Electronic Transactions Act (UETA) and the federal Electronic Signatures in Global and National Commerce Act (E-Sign)
- Antitrust laws, including the Sherman Act, the Clayton Act, and the Robinson-Patman Act
- The Federal Trade Commission Act
- Government procurement regulations, including the Federal Acquisition Regulations (FARs) and the Defense Acquisition Regulations (DARs)
- Patent, copyright, trade secret, and trademark laws
- Environmental laws, including Environmental Protection Agency (EPA) laws
- Employment laws, including Equal Employment Opportunity Commission (EEOC) laws
- Worker health and safety laws, including Occupational Safety and Health Administration (OSHA) laws
- Foreign Corrupt Practices Act
- Import/export compliance laws
- United Nations Convention on Contracts for the International Sale of Goods (CISG)
- Similar laws in other countries

The following are recommended guidelines for understanding and complying with applicable laws:

- Supply management professionals should pursue training in the legal aspects of supply management to understand the laws that govern their conduct and to know when to seek legal counsel.
- Interpretation of the laws should be left to legal counsel. It is often beneficial to involve legal counsel early in analysis and planning in order

to identify and avoid potential legal pitfalls, rather than to only involve legal counsel after problems arise.

- Supply management professionals involved in governmental procurement must understand and apply laws that are specific to their particular governmental body.

9. Small, Disadvantaged, and Minority-Owned Businesses

Encourage support for small, disadvantaged, and minority-owned businesses.

All business concerns, large or small, majority- or minority-owned, should be afforded an equal opportunity to compete. Most government entities and many businesses have developed specific guidelines and procedures to enforce policies designed to support and stimulate the growth of small businesses and those owned by minorities or other disadvantaged groups.

The following are recommended guidelines for support of small businesses and those owned by minorities and other disadvantaged groups:

- Adhere to all applicable laws and regulations.
- Work to ensure development and implementation of a program within the supply professional's organization, as appropriate.
- Actively strive to attain organizational and/or governmental goals regarding purchases.
- Participate in organizations whose purpose is to stimulate growth of these entities.
- Actively identify small, disadvantaged, and minority-owned businesses as potential suppliers.
- Encourage employees to support supplier development of small businesses, minority-owned businesses, and those owned by other disadvantaged groups.

10. Professional Competence

Acquire and maintain professional competence.

Professional competence is expected of supply management professionals by their employers, their supply management peers, others in their organizations, suppliers, and by society at large.

A distinguishing characteristic of a profession is the ability to combine ethical standards with the performance of technical skills. Because of the impact that the conduct of supply management professionals has on the stature of the profession, it is important for all those in the profession to consider what is meant by professional competence and how it is perceived by others.

Professional competence can be defined in many ways. Most definitions include the concept of mastery of a body of knowledge, continued efforts to increase one's ability and knowledge of the profession, communication skills, the willingness to share knowledge with others, and conformance to the highest standards of ethical behavior.

Professional competence is also assessed by others, based on dress, conduct in business settings, and how the professional presents himself or herself.

The following are recommended guidelines for achieving a high level of professional competence:

- Ensure a basic understanding of all the requirements to be recognized as a competent supply management professional.
- Monitor trends, and the development of new knowledge, in the profession.
- Conduct a self-assessment of talents and skills.
- Establish a self-development program designed to meet the needs of immediate and future employment.
- Seek out mentors and role models.
- Serve as a mentor.
- Earn, and maintain, the C.P.M., A.P.P., or other related credentials.
- Become actively involved in a professional association.

11. National and International Supply Management Conduct

Conduct supply management in accordance with national and international laws, customs, and practices, your organization's policies, and these ethical principles and standards of conduct.

Legal systems vary throughout the world, as do business customs and practices. Supply professionals therefore must be knowledgeable about these variations, and potential conflicts inherent in them, when doing business across borders.

The following are recommended guidelines:

- Be especially sensitive to customs and cultural differences with respect to social and business behavior and issues of influence.
- Recognize that suppliers may not be familiar with laws, customs, and practices of various countries, or with the supply professional's organization's policies. Consequently, it is important to ensure that appropriate information is effectively communicated to them.
- When confronted with issues such as facilitating type payments (e.g., payments made to expedite "routine government action"), which may be permissible in certain circumstances, be guided by organization policy and by the Foreign Corrupt Practices Act or other applicable laws.
- Recognize that national laws may not apply in other countries. For example, outside the United States, ISM's "Reciprocity" and "Small, Disadvantaged, and Minority-Owned Businesses" Standards and Guidelines may not apply.

- Utilize organization management, legal counsel, and other available resources for guidance whenever there is uncertainty as to actions to take.
- Ensure that suppliers comply with appropriate employment and environmental standards.
- Become aware of standards, statements, and information such as the Ethical Trade Initiative and ISO 14000.

12. Responsibilities to the Profession

Enhance the stature of the supply management profession.

The stature of the profession is enhanced through ethical actions and behavior of supply management professionals. When combined in professional groups or associations, such actions and behavior become highly visible and enhance the stature of the profession. This has a direct impact on the profession, the professional's organization, peers, and suppliers.

The following are recommended guidelines dealing with enhancing the stature of the profession:

- Support professional development and interchange of ideas through membership in professional and service organizations.
- Actively seek and support change in ethical standards and practice when appropriate (e.g., changes in the environment or technology).
- Supply professionals are obligated to support only those actions and activities that uphold the highest ethical standards of the profession.
- Support the ethical principles and standards of the organization(s) with which the individual professional is affiliated.
- Encourage, support, and participate in ongoing ethical training and review within business and professional organizations.

ACKNOWLEDGMENTS

In 1986, the Purchasing Management Association of Arizona, after two years of development, published its "Guidelines for Ethical Procurement Practices."

When the NAPM Ethical Standards Committee began deliberations for creation of the *Principles and Standards of Purchasing Practice*, the Arizona association kindly gave permission for us to use its Guidelines as the model. For this, ISM is grateful.

ISM—P.O.Box 22160 Tempe, AZ 85285-2160
480-752-6276/800-888-6276
Fax: 480-752-7890

Appendix B

American Society of Association Executives Standards of Conduct

As a member of the American Society of Association Executives, I pledge myself to:

1. Maintain the highest standards of personal conduct.
2. Actively promote and encourage the highest level of ethics within the industry or profession my association represents.
3. Maintain loyalty to the association that employs me, and pursue its objectives in ways that are consistent with the public interest.
4. Recognize and discharge my responsibility and that of my association to uphold all laws and regulations relating to my association's policies and activities.
5. Strive for excellence in all aspects of management of my association.
6. Use only legal and ethical means in all association activities.
7. Serve all members of my association impartially, provide no special privilege to any individual member, and accept no personal compensation from a member, except with full disclosure and with the knowledge and consent of my association's governing board.
8. Maintain the confidentiality of privileged information entrusted or known to me by virtue of my office.
9. Refuse to engage in or countenance activities for personal gain at the expense of my association or its industry or profession.
10. Refuse to engage in or countenance discrimination on the basis of race, sex, age, religion, national origin, sexual orientation, or disability.

11. Always communicate association internal and external statements in a truthful and accurate manner by ensuring that there is integrity in the data and information used by my association.

12. Cooperate in every reasonable and proper way with other association executives, and work with them in the advancement of the profession of association management.

13. Use every opportunity to improve public understanding of the role of associations.

This Code of Standards of Conduct for members of the American Society of Association Executives has been adopted to promote and maintain the highest standards of association service and personal conduct among its members. Adherence to these standards is expected from members of the society, and serves to assure public confidence in the integrity and service of association executives.

NARRATIVE DESCRIPTION OF CODE PROVISIONS

1. *Maintain the highest standards of personal conduct.* As with an elected official, an association executive's personal conduct is held up to public scrutiny due to the dual obligation to serve both the association's members' interests as well as the public's interests. This fiduciary standard requires the association executive to be a leading citizen of the community. Maintenance of this code requires extraordinary moral turpitude on the part of the association executive.

2. *Actively promote and encourage the highest level of ethics within the industry or profession my association represents.* Association executives fulfill an important leadership role within the industry or profession they represent and within society at large. In this role, they have the opportunity and the obligation to enhance the ethical awareness of their members both actively through the promulgation of ethical concepts at every appropriate opportunity, and implicitly, by example.

3. *Maintain loyalty to the association that employs me, and pursue its objectives in ways that are consistent with the public interest.* An association executive has a primary and fundamental responsibility to loyally serve the interests of the association and the members of the association. At the same time, however, the executive has a responsibility not to promote activities contrary to the public good. Where an association executive believes that the direction of the association is in conflict with the public interest, there is a responsibility to notify the members of this opinion; and, should the conflict become irreconcilable, the executive has a responsibility to maintain individual integrity and act to protect the public interest.

4. *Recognize and discharge my responsibility and that of my association to uphold all laws and regulations relating to my association's policies and activities.* An association executive has a responsibility to be familiar with the basic principles of law and regulation that affect the association. As a leader of the association, there is a responsibility to help members understand the legal

framework within which they operate in the association, and to make sure that all policies of the association are formulated, and all activities are conducted within this framework.

5. *Strive for excellence in all aspects of the management of my association.* Association executives have a responsibility to keep current with the best thinking in the field of association management and to apply their best management ability in all of the affairs of the association.

6. *Use only legal and ethical means in all association activities.* Misbehavior or inappropriate activity on the part of an association executive reflects badly on the association profession as a whole and can damage the credibility of all associations and their members. This is particularly important and sensitive when an association is attempting to influence legislative, regulatory, or judicial bodies. Association executives have a responsibility to understand the boundaries of appropriate behavior in efforts to influence these bodies and should stay within these parameters and take steps to ensure that members stay with them.

7. *Serve all members of my association impartially, provide no special privilege to any individual member, and accept no personal compensation from a member, except with full disclosure and with the knowledge and consent of my association's governing board.* By virtue of position, association executives may find themselves in a position to grant special favors to members, vendors, and others. Association executives have a responsibility to make the best possible management decisions in the interest of the association without regard to personal or other interests. Therefore, executives should take special care to avoid either the fact or the appearance of a personal interest in decision making. Association executives have a responsibility to represent the interests of all members impartially and should avoid incurring an obligation to a single individual or some fraction of the membership.

8. *Maintain the confidentiality of privileged information entrusted or known to me by virtue of my office.* Association executives frequently have access to privileged information. When members call on the association for advice or counsel in dealing with problems or opportunities; when the association conducts special surveys; when the association executive engages in personal conversations with officers, directors, or members; the information gained should be held in confidence. If association executives find themselves the unwilling recipients of information that they feel they cannot in good conscience hold in trust, they should remove themselves from the source of that information.

9. *Refuse to engage in or countenance activities for personal gain at the expense of my association or its industry or profession.* A wide variety of activities are suggested by this proscription. Moonlighting without the permission of the association—particularly in areas where it could be perceived that the secondary employment is in conflict with the interest of the primary employer, i.e., the association—would be one example of an unethical mode of behavior prohibited by this section. Soliciting or accepting special favors from suppliers to the

industry while representing an employing association should be measured in the context of proprietary and best interests of the association.

10. *Refuse to engage in or countenance discrimination on the basis of race, sex, age, religion, national origin, sexual orientation, or disability.*

11. *Always communicate association internal and external statements in a truthful and accurate manner by ensuring that there is integrity in the data and information used by my association.* The essence of effective communication is credibility. The association executive has a responsibility to maintain credible lines of communication both within the association and between the association and its publics. All communications should represent honest, unimpeachable statements of fact, and opinions should be clearly demarcated.

12. *Cooperate in every reasonable and proper way with other association executives, and work with them in the advancement of the profession of association management.* Theodore Roosevelt said, "Every man owes a part of his time and his money to the profession which supports his way of life." Association executives have an ethical responsibility to work cooperatively with other association executives both in the interest of the profession itself and in the interest of establishing a model of cooperative behavior for society at large. Association executives who do not actively take part in the affairs of their own professional association are in a weakened posture to influence their own members to participate in their associations.

13. *Use every opportunity to improve public understanding of the role of associations.* The role of associations in our society is little known or understood. Yet, the contributions associations make, and the impact they have, are extremely significant. All too often, the public only learns of an association's activities in some negative way. The positive story of the contributions made to improve the fabric of American life needs to be told more effectively. Association executives should be ambassadors to the general public and work to improve its understanding of the constructive role played by associations and association executives.

American Society of Association Executives
The ASAE Building
1575 I St. N.W.
Washington, DC 20005-1103
Phone: (888) 950-2723, (202) 371-0940 (in Washington, DC)
Fax: (202) 371-8315

Appendix C

Marriott Corporate Policy 1, Ethical Conduct, Marriott Hotel & Resorts

Marriott International, Inc. (the "Company") will conduct its business in accordance with uncompromising **ethical** standards. Adherence to such standards should never be traded in favor of financial or other business objectives. High **ethical** standards are necessary to maintain both competitive advantage and the pride and confidence of our associates, and to provide quality products and services to customers and clients.

The Company expects every associate to adhere to high **ethical** standards and to promote **ethical** behavior. Associates should avoid seeking loopholes, shortcuts or technicalities, and should reject the notion that unethical behavior is acceptable because "everyone is doing it." Every action should be judged by considering whether it is legal, fair to all concerned, and would withstand the scrutiny of outsiders. Associates whose behavior is found to violate **ethical** standards will be subject to disciplinary action including, where appropriate, termination.

In order for the Company to conduct its business in accordance with high **ethical** standards, every **Marriott** associate will:

1. **Obey all relevant laws,** including those that apply to alcoholic beverages, anti-trust, campaign finance, civil rights, copyright protection, environmental protection, foreign corrupt practices, securities and taxes. While the Company does not expect its associates to be experts in legal matters, it holds each associate responsible for being familiar with the laws governing his or her areas of responsibility. Associates should seek advice from the Law Department whenever they have a question concerning the application of the law. From time to time, the Law Department will prepare a "Business Conduct Guide" and circulate it to appropriate management.

2. **Treat all associates fairly, with dignity, and with respect.** All associates are entitled to a work environment free of verbal, physical and sexual harassment. The Company is committed to the principles and procedures set forth in its "Guarantee of Fair Treatment." The Company is also committed to providing equal employment opportunity for minorities, women, veterans and disabled persons. The Company believes promotion of work force diversity is an important objective in its own right, is a source of competitive advantage, and is a requirement of Equal Employment Opportunity laws.

3. **Report financial condition and results of operations fairly and honestly.** The Company's books and records will be kept in accordance with generally accepted accounting principles, and with established finance and accounting policies. Accrual and reserve entries, and the capitalization of costs will be used only for legitimate business purposes. All associates will cooperate fully with internal and outside auditors during their examinations of the Company's books, records and operations.

4. **Deal honestly and fairly with clients, customers, suppliers and financial partners.** The long term success of the Company depends upon establishing mutually beneficial relationships. While the law requires that we obey the letter of all written contracts and agreements, we will also try to uphold the spirit of all business arrangements.

5. **Avoid conflict of interest.** Associates should avoid actual or potential conflict of interest situations. Consequently, an associate having any interest, direct or indirect (other than an interest of 5% or less in a publicly-held company), in any supplier, customer, competitor or franchisee of the Company, should make prompt disclosure to the Company and obtain approval from the appropriate authority to continue the relationship. Management associates should not offer their skills or services to competitors, or engage in outside businesses which compete with or sell goods or services to the Company. Employing immediate family members in direct supervisory-subordinate relationships should be avoided.

6. **Avoid the improper giving and receiving of gifts.** The exchange of gifts with customers and suppliers is a normal and acceptable business practice. However, giving or receiving gifts of significant value could compromise the objectivity of an associate as well as create the appearance of a possible impropriety. Accordingly, gifts given or received by an associate in excess of $50 (retail value) must be disclosed to the associate's supervisor, and on the annual CP-1 Questionnaire. The supervisor will determine whether the gift should be accepted, turned over to the Company, or returned. Gifts of perishable items (e.g., flowers and fruit baskets) or commemorative items (e.g., plaques and framed photographs) are not subject to this $50 limit. They should, however, have little or no intrinsic or resale value. Business entertainment should be lawful and appropriate, and within acceptable boundaries of good taste and business purpose.

7. **Safeguard the Company's assets.** Personal use of supplies, equipment or premises belonging to the Company or its clients is prohibited, unless prior

permission is received from a supervisor and adequate compensation is arranged. Every associate is responsible for safeguarding Company assets under the associate's control.

8. **Separate personal political activities from the Company's business.** The Company encourages individual participation by associates in the political process. This includes service on governmental bodies and participation in partisan political activities. However, such activities should not be carried on in a way which interferes with the associate's job responsibilities. Associates should not make political contributions using Company funds, or take public positions on behalf of the Company without first obtaining approval from the Company's General Counsel. The Company engages in political activity through the **Marriott** International Political Action Committee (MARPAC). Management associates are encouraged to contribute to MARPAC but should not be coerced, intimidated, rewarded or pressured to do so.

9. **Report observed violations of standards.** The integrity of the organization is diminished whenever these standards are violated. The Company expects associates to report violations, of which associates have knowledge, to their supervisors.

10. **Associates can, under the "Guarantee of Fair Treatment," report ethical violations to their immediate supervisor, Human Resources Representative, the Law Department or Internal Audit. The Company will honor all requests for confidentiality.**

11. **Every business unit and administrative department will establish procedures for associates to report ethical violations on a confidential basis.**

12. **On an annual basis, Internal Audit will obtain certifications (CP-1 Questionnaire) from a broad range of management associates.**

Appendix D

Some Messages to the Executives of Ramada Inns

From the Chairman of the Board, Marion W. Isbell, during the 1960s and early 1970s

MONEY IS MADE FROM IDEAS

Hard thinking, figuring, developing new ideas and new methods, and a quiet, unassuming attitude, are characteristics that will put you ahead. Let others boast of your accomplishments. State facts and opinions meekly and rely on proof of facts to bolster your position. This is what pushes one to the top. Never act over-aggressive in an effort to build your own personal image.

PULLING TOGETHER

When a decision is made at the top, everyone must pull together to make that decision work. After a decision is made, we become as one horse and a horse can only go one way at a time; but two jackasses (tied together at one company) can pull in opposite directions, but they don't go anywhere unless they decide to go the same direction.

GOOD RULES TO FOLLOW FOR SUCCESS IN BUSINESS

1. The welfare of the company must come first.
2. Cooperation and teamwork will produce better results. Fighting, jealousy, bickering, lying, misstating facts to prove you are right will destroy you and can cost the company greatly.

3. Personal ambitions, animosities, and the belief that you must always be right can cost you your future—with any company. *No one can be right all the time.*

4. MATURITY—A person has not reached maturity until he is big enough to admit it when he is wrong.

5. HONESTY—My adult life has been dedicated to the proposition that honesty of purpose, word, and promise are absolute essentials in business relations and are the easiest and quickest ways to success. Sometimes the short-term cost has been great, but always the long-term reward has been greater.

6. *No one likes a bragger or a loudmouth*
   a. Another great help to success is never to brag, as to say, "I told you so."
   b. Don't try to outshout another person. Wait and calmly state your case.
   c. Never give the other person the idea that you think you are smarter than he is.
   d. Always compliment the other person on his good points and play down your own.
   e. Remember that disillusionment is one of the first steps to wisdom.
   f. Jumping to conclusions, making hasty, uninformed decisions without proper and timely consideration, is one of the quickest ways to wreck a company.

7. *No one wants to do business with a sharpy*—Never attempt to take advantage of another person in lease, contract, purchase, sale, or agreement because of some tricky wording that works against the other person without his knowledge. You and the company will get a sharpy reputation and others will be afraid to do any business with you. Also, remember there is always the possibility of the other person's being a better sharpy than you.

A good way not to antagonize the other person and let him help to make the right decision is to state that you have some reservations about your stated position and then put as a question facts that you can substantiate and let the other person argue that your earlier opinion was right because of the positive nature of the facts that you presented negatively. If you know you are right, let the other person argue your case; then you will come to a speedy meeting of minds without malice or jealousy.

CREATIVE THINKING ON YOUR OWN TIME

It is always difficult to do creative thinking during office hours, with the pressure and interruption that a job requires. A person who tries to have a busy social life in the evenings and on weekends also will not find time for creative thinking. It is not reasonable for an executive working just office hours, or coming in late and leaving early and taking long lunch hours, to advance in the company or to receive remuneration equal to that of the person who, by extra effort, develops new ideas and ways for the company to increase its profits. Remember, we are all supposed to have been created equal in the sense that every person has the same 24 hours per day to live. The question is where do you want to go—how many of these 24 hours do you play? How many do you sleep? And, most important, how many hours do you work? It's the working of more hours that makes us more and more *unequal* as the years roll by.

A simple example of creative thinking was the country mother and housewife with the wood cooking stove and fireplace who trained her two sons and husband to bring an armload of wood back to the house every time they visited the outhouse, situated back of the woodpile. In this way, no one ever had to make a special trip just to get wood for the fire.

OPPORTUNITY IS EVERYWHERE BUT IT IS UP TO YOU TO RECOGNIZE IT

Several executives who have left this company during the last six years would now have been millionaires, but they left for highly touted empty promises. Which reminds me of the young farmer who sold his farm down south because he thought there was no future in cotton farming with the new competition from man-made fibers. He roamed the country, going from job to job; and when he was old and poor he returned to have a last look at the old home place, only to discover that the person who bought this farm was now a millionaire cattle raiser. Was this cattle raiser lucky? Maybe, but if so, luck came to a very hardworking, creative-thinking, deserving man.

DON'T BE ONE OF THE MAJORITY

One of the most used activities of the mouth, besides eating, is the habit of the majority of people—using it to run down their friends, their neighbors, their relatives, and mostly their fellow workers. If you can't break the habit entirely, taper off by running down only your friends; but never, never run down a fellow executive of the company for which you work. And remember, the best way to eliminate an enemy is to make of him a friend. Also, you make your own life happier.

Remember, we here at Ramada can only have one president at a time. The same is so for the office of President of the United States, for that matter. But this does not keep tens of thousands of other men from aspiring to the job for themselves or for their sons. They won't all make it to the president's chair, to be sure, but consider what they may have accomplished for themselves and their families out of the extra effort put forth in their climb to higher and higher goals even though they didn't make it to the very top. I hope each of you will agree that this is a good creed for you to follow on *your* way up.

—Marion W. Isbell

INTEGRITY

Why and how *integrity* makes for a more serene and happy life:

Integrity means having a conscience and, more important, listening to it and following it. No one but you can force yourself to live up to the best in you.

Integrity means not saying to others what they want to hear unless it is the absolute truth.

Integrity means having the courage of your convictions and stating them loudly and clearly.

Integrity means not giving one opinion to one person and an opposite one to another person.

Integrity means having the gumption to speak out against what you think is wrong as well as to agree with what is right. A friend who expects you to lie for him is no friend.

If you always think and act with *integrity* you will always have that great feeling of confidence, warmth, and relaxation—and never that feeling of fear. A person with *integrity* never jumps or worries when the boss walks in; instead he has that inner feeling of confidence, knowing that he is doing his best at all times.

Integrity is the hallmark of self-respect. Your fellowman not having integrity may not condemn you to your face for lack of integrity, but nonetheless, he won't trust you or respect you or consider you a true friend.

Integrity gives a person the strength to welcome challenge, the feeling of confidence, the strength to make proper decisions because you have no reason to distrust yourself.

Integrity makes one shock-resistant. You have the built-in confidence a clear conscience gives.

Integrity is total honesty—not even a postage stamp used at someone else's expense.

Integrity gives a person the extra energy and clarity of thought that make ultimate progress and achievement inevitable.

No person who has *integrity* has anything to fear from life.

There are many other benefits from *integrity*—friendship, trust, admiration, respect, promotion, and the fact that most people seem to recognize *integrity* instinctively and are irresistibly attracted to it.

—Marion W. Isbell

A PUBLIC STATEMENT TO ALL TAXPAYERS

Hundreds of thousands of people work just long enough to become eligible for unemployment benefits. Other hundreds of thousands are on relief because they will not take jobs below what they consider to be below their dignity or their highest skill. All this while hundreds of thousands of jobs as household workers, yard workers, and farm laborors go unfilled.

What is better for the country or the nonworking man, for that matter, than that all should learn to work. Learn to love work. Learn to enjoy the greatest God-given pleasure in the world—the pride and joy of personal achievement or accomplishment! One of the best incentives to work is the fear of hunger.

Most nonworkers would eventually learn to love work. Many of us humans eventually don't really want to work for work's sake. We first learn to work because we want the things in life that money will buy. But what of the poor fellow who can get a check from the government each week not working? He doesn't know—he may be able to reach the top through any source of endeavor if he once applies himself. It is like saying, "You can't tell a book by its cover."

All of which brings me down to the statement I wished to make in the first line of this statement. Let's get a dollar's worth for every dollar we spend in government.

I say 80 million workers and their families will vote for a president who says, "Not one dollar for an able bodied man who refuses to work when offered a job."

Supplemental aid? Yes, up to a decent poor-man standard of living. Aid for dependent children, the blind, the crippled, the sick, and the aged if they don't have sufficient assets of their own. Even aid for doctors and hospitals for the genuinely sick. But not one dollar for the lazy loafer who would rather have twenty-five dollars per day for not working than get fifty dollars per day for working. We need a system of incentives to get the unwilling worker to become a willing worker.

I think if an accurate survey were made, you would find that out of 180 million Americans, 90 percent of the crimes of robbery, burglary, and such are being committed by the nonworking people consisting of only 2 to 3 percent of the total population.

—Marion W. Isbell, June 1, 1970

Index